The
Illustrator
and the Book
in England
from
1790 to 1914

The Illustrator and the Book in England from 1790 to 1914

Gordon N. Ray

The Pierpont Morgan Library

Oxford University Press

Formal Bibliographical Descriptions by
THOMAS V. LANGE

Photography by
CHARLES V. PASSELA

Oxford University Press, Ely House, London W.1

LONDON OXFORD GLASGOW NEW YORK
TORONTO MELBOURNE WELLINGTON CAPE TOWN
IBADAN NAIROBI DAR ES SALAAM LUSAKA ADDIS ABABA
KUALA LUMPUR SINGAPORE JAKARTA HONG KONG TOKYO
DELHI BOMBAY CALCUTTA MADRAS KARACHI

ISBN 0-19-519883-2

PRINTED IN THE UNITED STATES OF AMERICA

LIBRARY OF CONGRESS CATALOGUE CARD NUMBER 76-10042

Table of Contents

Preface

IN the last few years The Pierpont Morgan Library has presented through a number of exhibitions and publications aspects of the history and art of the printed book. To create in this way a "musée du livre" seemed to us entirely appropriate for an institution which is as much a museum as a research library, and which, although it includes all of the arts, places a special emphasis on art and literature, on drawing—or illustration—and printing.

In 1973 we began the celebration of our fiftieth year as a public institution by a notable exhibition and publication entitled the *Art of the Printed Book*. These were prepared by Joseph Blumenthal, one of the most distinguished printers of our time. We have also had an exhibition devoted to ancient classical texts and their transmission through the Middle Ages and the Renaissance in magnificent examples of calligraphy and printing, and other exhibitions concerning late medieval illumination, early printing in France and in Italy, sixteenth-century bindings, modern British bindings, and American bindings. But looking back over recent years, and ahead to the autumn of 1976, we find as well a series of studies about the book and drawings or watercolors in England, primarily from the late eighteenth century through the nineteenth century. In these exhibitions and books we are trying to establish for a wider public the English achievement in draftsmanship and design. We have not depended on our own fine collections; we have, instead, endeavored to present private collections in which the materials are extraordinarily rich but not generally known.

And so the Morgan Library has had exhibitions and published volumes on the Blake collection of Mrs. Landon K. Thorne, drawings and watercolors from the collection of Mr. and Mrs. Paul Mellon, and illustrated children's books in the collection of Miss Elisabeth Ball. In September, 1976, the Library will present the William Morris collection of Mr. John M. Crawford, Jr., in a book and an exhibition concerning Morris and the book arts.

The present volume depends almost entirely on the collection of Dr. Gordon N. Ray and is central to our survey of the English graphic achievement. It is the first comprehensive and detailed study of English book illustration between 1790 and 1914. It attempts in essay and illustration and by full bibliographical descriptions to give a comprehensive view of that time when England's illustrated books were as fine as any in the world. The roll call of artists includes almost everyone of importance working in the nineteenth century, and a large number of these artists made book illustration their principal occupation. One of our aims has been to make certain that these artist-illustrators receive proper recognition for their remarkable accomplishments.

Knowing that it is often difficult for scholars to reconstruct the development of even the most important private collections of books and of art, we have also begun to ask contemporary collectors to tell their own stories. In the present volume Dr. Ray writes of the principles he has followed and the opportunities he has had for building this part of his very large library. He also suggests what other collectors, private or public, may be able to do in forming collections of comparable materials. As he wrote a dozen years ago in two essays in *The Book Collector* concerning his library, the interest of his story for fellow-collectors lies in seeing what has been done "by a private individual of relatively restricted resources through steady buying, chiefly in bookstores, to a much smaller extent from catalogues, and only in a minor way at auction." Dr. Ray gives us at the same time a chance to share some of the pleasures of the chase itself.

This book is published just eighteen years after the beginning of Dr. Ray's own "musée du livre." Although he began his collecting when a small boy—of postage stamps first of all, but he quickly turned to books—it is only in the past twenty-one years that he has had any "substantial sums to spend for books." No more than part of those resources went for English and French illustrated books: he has continued to add to his library a considerable number of books and manuscripts in English and French literature of the same period.

It is with great pride and gratitude that we present these books, manuscripts, drawings, and engravings from Dr. Ray's library, and his commentary on the books and their illustrators. No one is better qualified to write on English books and English literature of this period. For thirty-five years everyone who has read about nineteenth-century culture has been indebted to Dr. Ray's books and essays. We at the Morgan Library are especially in his debt for taking so much time to prepare this volume, as well as constantly serving the Library in his position as Vice-President of its Board of

Trustees. Dr. Ray intends that most of the books described will remain in the Library on deposit.

This volume is the first to be published by the Morgan Library in conjunction with the Oxford University Press. It has been planned and to a considerable extent designed at the Library, but, as is true of all of our recent publications, its typographical distinction could not have been achieved without the close collaboration of Mr. Roderick D. Stinehour. In this case, the layout of the book was extremely complicated, but its difficulties have been surmounted with ease by The Stinehour Press, and the hundreds of illustrations beautifully reproduced by The Meriden Gravure Company. We are most grateful to them, and to those close friends who have provided books or drawings for this publication: Mrs. Donald F. Hyde, Mr. H. Bradley Martin, Mr. Paul Mellon, Dr. Morris H. Saffron, Mr. Robert H. Taylor, and Miss Julia P. Wightman; we are as well indebted to the Columbia University Libraries, the University of Pennsylvania Library, and The Metropolitan Museum of Art.

CHARLES RYSKAMP
Director

Introduction for Collectors

I

THIS BOOK began as a catalogue for an exhibition at The Pierpont Morgan Library in March and April of 1976, but it has ended by being a good deal more comprehensive than that exhibition. There being no earlier study devoted to a full consideration of English book illustration between 1790 and 1914, it seemed unenterprising to limit the works described and commented upon to those for the display of which space was available. Instead an attempt has been made to set forth the subject in the sort of detail that would allow its ramifications and relationships to be explored with thoroughness and permit major illustrators to be presented in depth without slighting lesser figures.

The 125 years chosen were a period during which England held its own in book illustration with any country in the world. Despite the appearance of occasional fine books in earlier years (exampled in the section of "Forerunners" below), not until the 1790s did English illustration begin to compete on equal terms with illustration on the Continent of Europe. For the next century and a quarter the demand for illustration never faltered, nor did the succession of artists who supplied it. The dominant means of reproduction changed from copper engraving first to aquatint, lithography, and steel engraving, then to wood engraving, and finally to photomechanical processes mitigated by a renewed emphasis on individual craftsmanship. Different modes of illustration succeeded one another. Romantic preoccupation with what Blake called "the visionary or imaginative" on the one hand and what Ruskin characterized as "the landscape feeling" on the other gave way to the emphasis on comedy and melodrama that marked the second quarter of the century. This yielded in turn to the realism touched by emotion of the Sixties School and arrived at last at the exuberant scene of the end of the century which saw the subtle and daring conceptions of sophisticated artist-craftsmen coexisting with a broader appeal to the general imagination by notable popular artists in line and color. That great watershed the First World War ended this "golden age of illustration," as it is sometimes called, and when illustrators returned to their task in 1919, they did so with diminished confidence and for a less engaged audience.

The variety and profusion of the nineteenth century has defeated most authors of comprehensive works on the history of book illustration. In *Fine Books* A. W. Pollard tells how he began with "a confident determination to cover the whole ground, from the beginnings of printing and printed book-illustration down to our own day," only to find himself concluding, "with obvious marks of compression and fatigue, about 1780."[1] In the same way, author after author, breathless and exhausted, has in effect dropped out of the race towards the end of the eighteenth century. Those who have pushed on, even David Bland in his *History of Book Illustration*, have limited their consideration to a small number of salient books, in order to avoid a nineteenth-century chapter that would dwarf all the rest.

The problem of the would-be surveyor is intensified by the existence of a small library of books and articles on the various aspects of English book illustration during the period. He cannot plead lack of information, yet he cannot hope to deal adequately with all illustrators who on the basis of this information seem to demand attention. A choice from among these studies is offered in the Bibliography, but a word should be said here about the books which have proved most helpful. There has been one previous attempt to cover most of the period under consideration. This is Philip James's *English Book Illustration, 1800–1900*, a small monograph of 1947 based on a drastically restricted exhibition that James had organized in the wartime London of 1943. It is a pioneering work of real value. Martin Hardie's *English Coloured Books* of 1906, though superseded with respect to detailed information by later writers, is still the most humane and delightful account of its subject. Forrest Reid's classic *Illustrators of the Sixties* of 1928 deals with the wood engravings of the third quarter of the century with a sympathetic and informed appreciation unlikely ever to be equalled. Basil Gray's *The English Print* of 1937, though not primarily concerned with books, remains the most discriminating survey of original graphic art during the period. Percy Muir's *Victorian Illustrated Books* of 1971 preserves for posterity the extensive knowledge and trenchant judgments of a great bookseller concerning his favorite era. Ruari McLean's *Victorian Book Design* of 1963 and its expanded version *Victorian Book Design and Colour Printing* of 1972 triumphantly returned to public appreciation the achievements of Victorian

1. (London, 1912), p. vii.

book craftsmen in areas outside imaginative literature. If Thomas Balston is not added to this honor roll, it is only because he did not attempt a consecutive account of the turn-of-the-century illustration which he knew so thoroughly; even so his scattered writings on the field have been invaluable.

The title chosen for this book is a conscious echo of the landmark exhibit at the Museum of Fine Arts in Boston during 1961 recorded in *The Artist and the Book, 1860–1960, in Western Europe and the United States*. Seen in the perspective of the history of painting, book illustration is usually regarded as a "minor art," which labors under the constraint of representing a set subject and relies typically on craftsmen to reproduce the artist's conception. One purpose of *The Artist and the Book* was to show how during the century under review artists freed themselves from this double burden, by denying the obligation of representation on the one hand and by working through original graphics on the other. In his introduction Philip Hofer told of the decision in general to omit "reproductive illustrations," because of the "loss of irreplaceable artistic values" that they entail, though some examples of this kind of work were allowed where craftsmen were responsible for the reproductions. With regard to process prints the exclusion was even more severe. "The layman may be content with photomechanical prints. The connoisseur never is except for reference purposes." Thus conceived, *The Artist and the Book* was a dazzling demonstration of the thesis "that during the last century *the book has, in fact, become a major vehicle of artistic expression*."[2]

This survey has a different perspective. Though for fifty-five years the period it covers coincides with that of *The Artist and the Book*, only thirteen of the books described also appear in that work.[3] Its point of departure comes from a sentence in Blake's defense of graphic art against painting: "he who draws best must be the best Artist."[4] Its emphasis is on the primacy of the image, by whatever means it is presented. We may be grateful that Blake's illustrations to *The Book of Job* (8), Cruikshank's to *Oliver Twist* (116), and Martin's to *Paradise Lost* (69) are from the hand of the artist who conceived them, without therefore underestimating Turner's designs

2. *The Artist and the Book* (Boston, 1961), pp. 7–8.

3. Lear's *Nonsense Songs* (95), *Dalziel's Arabian Nights* (151), *Dalziel's Bible Gallery* (158), *Historical and Legendary Ballads and Songs* (163), *Goblin Market* (165), *The Parables of Our Lord* (170), *London* (207), Virgil's *Eclogues* (222), Chaucer's *Works* (258), *La charrue d'érable* (269), Nicholson's *Twelve Portraits* (294), *Le Morte Darthur* (314), and *Salomé* (315).

4. See p. 7 below.

for *Liber Studiorum* (10), Millais's for *The Parables of Our Lord* (170), or Doré's for *London* (207), where the hand of a craftsman has intervened. Indeed, even the line block and the three-color process had their aesthetic, a mastery of which distinguishes work like Beardsley's illustrations for *Salomé* (315), Edmund J. Sullivan's for *Sartor Resartus* (310), and Arthur Rackham's for *Peter Pan in Kensington Gardens* (329) from the routine efforts of their day.

Once reproductive illustrations are admitted, it becomes possible to show in book form many of the significant English painters at work between 1790 and 1914. Blake, Rowlandson, Turner, Cotman, Martin, Boys, Roberts, Maclise, Lear, Millais, and Nicholson are well represented; Fuseli, Wilkie, Constable, Girtin, Palmer, Mulready, Rossetti, Holman Hunt, Leighton, Whistler, and Burne-Jones make their impression; even Bonington, Dadd, and F. M. Brown are not entirely omitted. But this Tate Gallery in little is only the beginning of the story, for the contribution of professional illustrators is still more significant than that of artists who were primarily painters. Most remarkable is the work of artists who made illustration the principal occupation of their lives, notably Stothard, Bewick, Cruikshank, Phiz, Leech, Doyle, Owen Jones, Humphreys, Hughes, Foster, Houghton, Walker, Pinwell, Keene, du Maurier, Crane, Caldecott, Kate Greenaway, Lucien Pissarro, Thomson, W. Heath Robinson, May, Sullivan, Beardsley, Beerbohm, Jessie M. King, and Rackham. Hardly less salient are the artists who were professional illustrators for substantial segments of their careers, notably Sandys, Ricketts, Strang, Housman, Craig, Robert Anning Bell, and W. Graham Robertson. It is only just that these artist-illustrators should now be receiving the sort of attention that in the past has been largely reserved for painters: that their best books should be reproduced in inexpensive facsimiles,[5] that exhibitions should set forth their careers in detail, and that monographs should be devoted to them.

This revival of interest in illustrated books, deriving directly from the images they contain rather than from the relation of these images to painting, is part of a larger phenomenon of our age, a concern for the past simply because it is the past. There is now an all-encompassing delight in authentic objects from earlier days which bear witness to the conditions that produced them and thereby call to mind bygone

5. The most recent examples are Millais's *The Parables of Our Lord* (170), Doré's *London* (207), and Beardsley's *The Rape of the Lock* (316).

ways of life. Such an extension of the appeal of art—its democratization, if one wishes —is surely a welcome development, but as far as illustrated books are concerned, it is not without its dangers. To an increasing extent English books of the nineteenth century are being plundered for their illustrations. Not long before his death I asked Major J. R. Abbey what sort of books he would collect if he were starting his career anew. His answer was books with engravings on steel. This was excellent advice in 1969. It is less so today, for the "breakers" have pursued these volumes with such determination that copies in collector's condition have become very hard to find. To visit a print shop today, indeed, is to discover that most of its stock is made up of illustrations from books, not only steel engravings, hardly dry from the colorist, but copper engravings, aquatints, lithographs, etchings, wood engravings, and even photomechanical process plates. At a leading emporium in London, for example, the larger colored lithographs from Roberts's *Holy Land* (88) are now priced in three figures, while a page from Doré's *London* (207) commands a fiver. With such incentives to destruction collectors who preserve fine copies of English illustrated books are doing posterity a service.

In this survey only two categories have been excluded among the illustrations of the period: books illustrated with photographs and periodicals. With regard to the first, the exclusion has been absolute, not from any sense that photography is a "foe-to-graphic-art" (a common enough Victorian position), but rather in the conviction that the criteria for judging photographically illustrated books are radically different from those for judging other kinds of illustrated books. Moreover, such an omission can be allowed without qualms of conscience. Nineteenth-century books illustrated with photographs are now fully appreciated, and indeed they will soon be comprehensively reviewed in *The Truthful Lens*, a book recording an exhibition at the Grolier Club during 1975. A few exceptions have been permitted to the rule excluding periodicals, where the accomplishment of an illustrator could not be adequately represented without such material, but for the most part it was possible at least to suggest this aspect of the work of the time through contemporary collections of periodical illustrations in book form. Otherwise, it seemed that arbitrarily limiting the survey by excluding certain types of publications (as being albums or portfolios, for example, rather than true books) would fail to do justice to the diversity and abundance of the field. It should also be noted that this is a survey of the illustrated book in England,

Drawing by Henry Stacy Marks from the Smallfield Album

not of the English illustrated book. This distinction made it possible to include such notable work as Bartolozzi's for *Imitations . . . of Holbein* (19), Doré's for *London* (207), and Camille Pissarro's for *La charrue d'érable* (269).

I should mention finally that the sole criterion for selecting a book has been the interest of its illustrations. Hence the presence or absence of the great printers of the period is largely a matter of accident. Bensley and Bulmer are well represented because their stately quartos and folios are often splendidly illustrated. William Pickering and the Chiswick Press, on the other hand, are present only through Henry Shaw's *Dresses and Decorations of the Middle Ages* (102) and *Decorative Arts of the Middle Ages* (234). His *Compleat Angler* of 1836 may be a handsomer book, but its illustrations are commonplace. Among the ventures in fine printing at the end of the century the Vale and Eragny Presses receive substantial attention because they emphasized illustration, while the Doves and Ashendene Presses are omitted because they excluded or subordinated it. The space accorded William Morris and the Kelmscott Press is modest because he was more concerned with decoration than illustration. There is one minor exception to this total concentration on illustration. The achievement of four illustrators—Beardsley, Housman, Ricketts, and Rossetti—would have been incompletely recorded without notice of their binding designs, selections from which have accordingly been included.

To the books themselves relevant drawings, engraver's proofs, and autograph letters and manuscripts have been added. Indeed, about a third of the entries in the catalogue concern this sort of material, which because of its uniqueness has often been chosen for reproduction in preference to illustrations from books. Where the examples described belong to groups of related items, the extent of these assemblages has been noted for the information of future students. Catalogue entries for such supplementary material are not numbered, however, because this book is for collectors, including of course both private individuals and institutional librarians, and in theory every numbered entry should be collectible. I say "in theory" advisedly, since Blake's *Jerusalem* (4), for example, is not likely to appear on the market, nor does a Kelmscott Chaucer on vellum (258) often present itself. Most of the books described can still be found, however, and many of them with some ease.

Book collectors find particular satisfaction in lists of outstanding works in a given field. They are part of the collecting game, a way of adding enjoyment to the hunt, yet they also offer guidance for the neophyte and set standards against which the veteran can measure his success. Hence I have provided a list of one hundred outstanding illustrated books published in England between 1790 and 1914 (see Appendix). In addition to the formal descriptions and commentary of the Catalogue, a plate is devoted to each of these books in a concluding section. By leafing through these plates, which are arranged in chronological order except that books illustrated by the same artist are grouped together, the reader may experience in brief compass the sequence of styles through which English book illustration passed during the 125 years under review.

In arriving at my final selections I secured comments from twenty knowledgeable scholars, collectors, and book dealers on a preliminary list of seventy-five titles. I began with the lower number to leave room for the additions I knew I would want to make on the basis of the advice thus obtained. My expectations were not disappointed. The replies I received made me acquainted with a number of significant books concerning which I had known nothing and brought me to a juster appreciation of some that I had undervalued. Not only were twenty-five further titles readily forthcoming, certainly with no reduction in overall quality, but I also found reason for changing ten of my original selections.

It might be thought that this province of the world of books would be a quiet preserve in which each collector cultivates his garden, benignly approving the efforts of his neighbors. This is not altogether the case. The various schools of nineteenth-century English illustration still command intense loyalty. Indeed, as far as one or two of my respondents were concerned, I sensed that the presence on the same list of books they admired and books they disliked was a distasteful anomaly, even if the latter were the best of their kind.

Such partisanship has its roots in history. One kind of illustration did not displace another without a struggle. By those accustomed to copper engraving, both lithography and steel engraving were at first regarded as cheap and unsatisfactory substitutes. Chromolithography, which appears today to have begun so brilliantly with the imposing books of the 1840s and 1850s, also had its disparagers. Behind Ruskin's often quoted admonition, "Let no lithographic work come into the house,"[6] may lie the increasing use of chromolithography during the years following the Exhibition of 1851. Certainly the commercial exploitation of the process soon made "chromo" a term of abuse among persons of taste, serving as a symbol for what Laurence Housman was to describe in writing of the Great Exhibition as the English public's "sincere craving for what was elaborately and barbarously bad in art."[7] The revival of etching during the latter half of the century was in part the reply of fearful illustrators to the encroachments of photography. And when photomechanical reproduction established itself as the usual mode of illustration in the 1890s, the artist-craftsmen of the time saw their work as an assertion of the values of an older tradition against degraded machine-made objects.

As with processes, so it was with styles. This parallel history of conflict is too long even to summarize, but as a typical example, consider the fortunes of the Sixties School of illustrators in the 1890s. Though many practitioners continued to work in the Sixties style, it was also being sharply challenged. Whistler insisted that a "picture should have its own merit, and not depend on dramatic, or legendary, or local interest,"[8] and Walter Crane upheld the claims of "decorative treatment" as opposed to "pictorial statement," maintaining that the page was "a space to be made beautiful in design."[9] Thus the way was prepared for Beardsley and Art Nouveau. Yet this development coincided with a rearguard action by Joseph Pennell and Gleeson White asserting the superiority of Sixties illustrators over Cruikshank and his contemporaries. These critics, writing more for amateurs than for artists, seem to have been particularly moved by the neglect of Sixties books by collectors. Pennell in 1895 asserted that the "greatest bulk" of the designs of Cruikshank, Phiz, Doyle, and Leech was "simply rubbish,"[10] and Gleeson White two years later presented a more detailed indictment along the same lines.[11] This somewhat artificial controversy has

6. See below, p. 51.
7. *Arthur Boyd Houghton* (London, 1896), p. 11.
8. *The Gentle Art of Making Enemies* (London, 1890), p. 127. Quoting this statement in *Illustrators of the Sixties* (London, 1928), Forrest Reid replied: "if a picture be not devoid of any intellectual, spiritual and emotional content, its subject *must* contribute to the appeal it makes" (p. 5).
9. *Of the Decorative Illustration of Books Old and New* (London, 1896), pp. v, 6.
10. Quoted by J. R. Harvey, *Victorian Novelists and Their Illustrators* (London, 1970), p. 161.
11. *English Illustration, the 'Sixties'* (London, 1897), pp. 18–19, 138–139.

continued down to the present. Even the usually equable Forrest Reid noted with some asperity in 1928 that books of the sixties were "given over to mice and damp, while Cruikshanks and Rowlandsons are treasured under lock and key."[12] With today's renewed interest in Cruikshank and his contemporaries—particularly as inheritors of the great tradition of English caricature established by Hogarth, Gillray, and Rowlandson—this mock battle is at least being fought on more nearly equal terms.[13]

That the ground they cover is still hotly contested makes it all the more interesting to ask the question: on the basis of my one hundred outstanding books, who are the great illustrators of the period? Blake, Turner, Rowlandson, Lear, Ricketts, and Beardsley are represented by three books apiece. Indeed, Turner is represented by four if *River Scenery* (12), the illustration of which he shared with Girtin, is included. Yet even this generous recognition does not take account of *The Pastorals of Virgil* (7) in the case of Blake or of *The Southern Coast* (11) in the case of Turner. Millais with two books and part of a third comes next. Yet *The Small House at Allington* (169), which contains the best of his designs for Trollope's Barsetshire novels, had to be omitted. Bewick, Cruikshank, Martin, Boys, Leech, Foster, Hughes, and Sullivan have two books apiece. Cruikshank might well have been given a third, perhaps *Sketches by "Boz"* (114–115) or one of the volumes in which he collected his own designs. Arthur Hughes offered a particular problem. In my preliminary list of seventy-five books he was represented by *Enoch Arden* (174) and *Sing Song* (179). After considering objections to these choices, I shifted to *Tom Brown's School Days* (176) and *At the Back of the North Wind* (177), but even so I had to omit both of Maurice Sendak's selections: *Dealings with the Fairies* (175) and *The Princess and the Goblin* (178).[14] It should be noted finally that Palmer has one book to himself and figures in another, while Houghton shares in three, and Holman Hunt, Sandys, Whistler, and Lawless share in two. If I had bowed to general opinion, Houghton's *Home Thoughts and Home Scenes* (200) would also have been one of the hundred.

12. *Illustrators of the Sixties*, p. 75.

13. See Harvey, pp. 160–162.

14. The other "favorite titles" proposed by this artist, who brilliantly continues the Victorian tradition of fantastic illustration, were George Cruikshank's *Comic Alphabet*, Ruskin's *The King of the Golden River* (142) illustrated by Doyle, Doré's *Histoire de la sainte Russie*, and Wilde's *A House of Pomegranates* illustrated by Ricketts and Shannon.

This recapitulation should have the effect of reminding the reader that a list of outstanding books is only one approach among several to determining the best illustrators of a period. Judged by this test, the career illustrator, who makes his impression through many books over dozens of years, is bound to suffer. Cruikshank is the chief example among the artists already mentioned, but others should also be noted. Phiz figures solely through *The Pickwick Papers* (125) because he went on repeating himself, though at a high level, throughout his career. Yet *Martin Chuzzlewit* (128) or *Dombey and Son* might well have been included. Doyle's *In Fairyland* (146) was a mandatory choice, yet I was severely censured for omitting not only *The King of the Golden River* (142), a favorite with several of my respondents, but also *The Foreign Tour of Brown, Jones, and Robinson* (143) and *The Newcomes* (144). The claims of du Maurier's designs for *Esmond* (196) and *Trilby* (199) are obvious. And even if most of Rackham's best work came after my chronological boundary, should I not have added *A Midsummer Night's Dream* (330) to *Peter Pan in Kensington Gardens* (329)?

Another sort of inevitable injustice occurs in books where the mode of reproduction can be almost as important as the artist who used it. Aquatint engraving is the principal example. Twelve titles out of one hundred is an adequate proportion for the field, yet there are many other books with aquatint engravings at much the same level of achievement as in the volumes selected. Among those proposed by my respondents were Ackermann's *History of the University of Cambridge*, Alken's *National Sports of Great Britain*, Thomas and William Daniell's *Oriental Scenery*, Jenkins's *Naval Achievements of Great Britain*; Loutherbourg's *Romantic and Picturesque Scenery of England and Wales*, Malton's *Picturesque and Descriptive View of the City of Dublin*, and Nash's *The Royal Pavilion at Brighton*. For some amateurs at least the books of the sixties present the same problem. Take the Dalziel Brothers' fine quartet of "English Idylls" as an example. *A Round of Days* (153) appears in my list of one hundred titles because it was the first of the four. *Wayside Posies* (154), Jean Ingelow's *Poems* (155), and *North Coast* (156) are hardly inferior to it. Other areas where the mode of reproduction makes a particular appeal are color printing and chromolithography.

Finally, I should note several isolated titles which were high on the list of "also-rans." *Stanfield's Coast Scenery* (67) might have been included as an example of steel engraving at its best. Admirers of Ruskin urged that a place should be made for him, but the illustrations even of *Examples Illustrative of the Stones of Venice* (31A) seemed to me too miscellaneous to warrant the book's selection. It was argued that Allingham's *The Music Master* (147), exhaustively described by Forrest Reid as the starting point of the Sixties School, should command a place. I thought it was sufficiently recognized by reproducing an engraver's proof of its one outstanding illustration, Rossetti's "The Maids of Elfen-Mere." For several years Gustave Doré was virtually an Englishman by adoption, and there was never any doubt in my mind about choosing his *London* (207), though one respondent demanded Doré's exclusion on the principle "Once a Frenchman, always a Frenchman!" But should not this masterpiece of inspired reporting have been supplemented by his illustrations to an English work of imaginative literature: *Paradise Lost*, *The Idylls of the King*, or, best of all, *The Rime of the Ancient Mariner*? I should add that Morten's *Gulliver's Travels* (209) was at last omitted, after having figured on my initial list of seventy-five, because I came to feel that his illustrations to the voyages to Lilliput and Brobdingnag derived too markedly from Doré's for Rabelais's *Oeuvres* of 1854 and Balzac's *Contes drolatiques* of 1855. Among the books of the turn of the century for which room could not be found, I particularly regret W. Heath Robinson's illustrations for *Poems of Edgar Allan Poe* (304), Sime's for *The Sword of Welleran* (323), New's for *The Compleat Angler* (324), and Nielsen's for *East of the Sun and West of the Moon* (333).

Fortunately it was possible to include in the Catalogue, often with reproductions, many of the titles finally omitted from my list of one hundred. Without this safety valve it would have been much more difficult to arrive at the final selections. However much certain omissions may be regretted, the list at least testifies convincingly to the remarkable quality of book illustration in England between 1790 and 1914. Indeed, one of my respondents, who has specialized in earlier periods, confessed that it made him think he had been "hanging around the wrong centuries."

III

I can best conclude this introduction with a brief account of how the books in the ensuing Catalogue, or at any rate the ninety-five percent of them that are from my collection, were brought together. Though I intend to be simply personal and historical, my narrative should offer some useful illustrations of general principles, since sound book-collecting tactics are much the same, no matter what the area chosen. The noncollecting reader will find my story more comprehensible if he first grasps the fact that there is a point of no return in the career of a collector, after which it is no longer a question of whether or not he collects, but merely of what he collects. I passed this point thirty years ago.

My concentration on English illustrated books began in 1958. Looking back on this chapter in my collecting life, I see how fortunate was my timing. Two things are needed to keep a collector interested in a chosen specialty: he must be continuously absorbed in the field and the material must be there to collect. During the past two decades nineteenth-century English art has been studied in detail as never before, and nineteenth-century English book illustration has been a principal beneficiary of the resulting increase of knowledge. It was an exciting experience to sense again and again the importance of unknown or forgotten artists and books only to have this insight confirmed when scholarship began to chart the areas to which they belong. With regard to my second condition, until about 1970 English illustrated books, except in a few categories, were largely unwanted. Not only could one find what one sought, one could often wait for the exceptional copy. When major collections were offered for sale, like those of J. N. Hart and Tom Balston, they could sometimes be had for modest sums. It occurred to me every fall, as I reviewed the harvest of summer collecting trips abroad, how little I had paid for English illustrated books as compared with French illustrated books of comparable merit. This gap, alas, is rapidly closing.

Until 1958 the emphasis in my collecting had been on first editions of English and French literature, chiefly of the nineteenth century, but I had learned some lessons that I could carry over into my new field. Like Michael Sadleir I was persuaded that "*condition* is three-quarters of the battle for any fine collection of any epoch."[15] I knew the necessity of keeping in touch with all major sources of supply. It was not enough to maintain a familiarity with the stocks of New York antiquarian dealers, to bid judiciously at auction sales, and to act quickly with regard to bookdealers' catalogues; one should also have ties with those dealers elsewhere in the United States and abroad who were likely to have the kind of material desired. I was alert to the special interest of exceptional copies: books made attractive by their associations, their bindings, and their added contents. I was aware how a collection of books could be enhanced if supplemented with related material such as autograph letters and manuscripts, engraver's proofs, and drawings. Finally, when I was well embarked on my new field, a

15. *XIX Century Fiction: A Bibliographical Record*, 2 volumes (London, 1951), I, vi.

special strategy suggested itself. Since I had started virtually from scratch, I should be on the lookout for chances of buying collections. In an area so extensive it was impracticable to rely entirely on the sort of title-by-title collecting on which one would ideally like to depend.

Here I may offer in evidence an article in the *Book Collector* of 1964 which describes the progress of my collection to that date. After telling of its earlier focus on nineteenth-century English and French literature, I related how I had come to extend its scope to fine bindings and illustrated books. The French wing of my collection, I wrote, had "made me aware of a certain drabness in the English tradition, particularly as it applied to 19th-century books." Having had it impressed upon me that the book could be an attractive physical object as well as a literary treasure, I decided "to attempt in a small way and for the 19th century only, but with attention to England as well as to France, a 'musée du livre' such as the great collections of René Descamps-Scrive and Henri Beraldi provided until their dispersal in 1925 and 1934–35 respectively. The hundreds of unique items assembled by these collectors would not come my way, nor could I hope that my copies for the most part would approach theirs in quality. Yet for 19th-century France comparable coverage at least might be achieved, while for 19th-century England, where except for two or three hotly pursued specialties there was virtually no competition, something a good deal more ambitious might be attempted."

Most of the ensuing account of my attempt to achieve this "museum of the book" was devoted to my collection of fine bindings, but I did relate how my literary interests had already led me to the etched illustrations of Cruikshank, Leech, and Phiz; how my pursuit of "the black-and-white illustrations of the Romantic period" had brought considerable success with Turner and Blake; and how I had exercised unaccustomed restraint in buying volumes illustrated with colored aquatints because they "represented a territory already ardently cultivated with a scale of prices fully reflecting the demand." Indeed, I noted as an anomaly, which "might interest future historians of taste," the fact that my comprehensive collection of books illustrated with engravings after Turner, most of them on large paper and bound in contemporary morocco, had been "bought between 1961 and 1963 at about the cost of a good copy of *The Microcosm of London*."[16]

16. "A 19th-Century Collection: A Museum of the Book," *Book Collector*, XIII (Summer, 1964), 175, 182, 183.

(68) "South Front of Mansion House & Conservatory," from *Views of Sezincot House*; etching by John Martin, aquatint by F. C. Lewis

As was to be expected, the process of writing about my collection gave me a clearer idea of where I wanted to go with it. Over the next few years I bought some of the big aquatint books I had previously avoided, including *The Microcosm of London* (33) in 1969, and, more important, Daniell's *Voyage Round Great Britain* (41) in 1968. I moved into a field then almost entirely neglected, the volumes illustrated with lithographs and later chromolithographs of the middle third of the century. My most significant acquisition here, Roberts's *Holy Land* (88) in the twenty original canvas portfolios, was acquired in 1965. I was also active in seeking out missing titles in other areas. Haden's *Etudes à l'eau-forte* (219) came in 1964, Blake's *Book of Job* (8) and Constable's *English Scenery* (71) in 1967. These were piecemeal additions, however, and my hope of achieving a "museum" of the nineteenth-century English illustrated book would have remained remote if a signal opportunity had not presented itself.

At their sale of December 21, 1964, Sotheby's offered a collection formed by J. N. Hart of 426 proofs of wood engravings of English artists of the third quarter of the nineteenth century. Knowing that Hart together with Harold Hartley had supplied "nearly all the illustrations" in Forrest Reid's *Illustrators of the Sixties* (p. v) and that Reid had thanked Hart for reading his manuscript, I was immediately interested. My cabled bid for the collection, sight unseen, was successful, and it arrived in time to supply much of the material for an exhibit at the Grolier Club entitled "Illustrated Books of the 1860s," arranged by A. Hyatt Mayor, which was shown from February through April of 1965. Thus stimulated, I also purchased the bulk of Hart's collection of Sixties books when it was sold at Sotheby's later in the year.

Hart was a man of substantial means who had sought out not only engraver's proofs but copies of books remarkable for their bindings or associations. His standard of condition was high. Then late in life he had added Forrest Reid's collection to his own. Reid was an impecunious man of letters, but, as he observes in his chapter on collecting in *Illustrators of the Sixties* (p. 7), he was lucky enough to be buying at a time when his specialty was a "hunting-ground open to all" and there were few volumes that had "acquired a sale-room value." Moreover, his knowledge was unmatched, and he was untiring in his pursuit. Though his books were for the most part in less than pristine condition, his success with the rarities of his specialty was remarkable. Since I had myself been collecting Sixties books for some time, my acquisition of the Hart-Reid collection left me with many duplicates, a selection from which I gave to the Princeton University Library to supplement the collection of Victorian bindings and illustrated books presented by my friend Robert F. Metzdorf. Even so, the Hart-Reid purchase added several hundred volumes to my collection, and indeed left me with few significant lacunae in books with wood-engraved illustrations of the period 1855–1880.

By the beginning of 1970 I was reasonably content with my collection of English illustrated books before 1890, though I still had a substantial list of desiderata. I should probably have left the next quarter century uncovered, except for favorite artists like Beardsley and Edmund J. Sullivan, had an irresistible stroke of fortune not swept me into the field. On July 17, 1968, Christie's had offered selections from the library of Thomas Balston (1883–1967) for sale in their rooms. Balston was a publisher of distinction and a discriminating patron of the arts, particularly of original wood engraving. He was also an unremitting collector, who made his various collections the basis for authoritative books and articles. If he had a particular area of concentration, it was English book illustration during the late nineteenth and early twentieth centuries. The materials sold by Christie's were chiefly from the literary side of his library, though most of his private press books were also included. During my annual visit to England in the summer of 1970 I saw in the basement of my principal London dealer a large collection of English illustrated books. They were arranged on low shelves, extending nearly the length of the room, over which boards had been laid to make a large working table. Expressing my surprise at their presence, since the dealer's interest lay in other areas, I learned that they were the remainder of Tom Balston's collection, bought *en bloc* after they had been deemed unsuitable for disposal at auction. My time was short, but I looked hastily at a few volumes under one side of the table and made an offer for the collection. Only after my friend had accepted it did I realize that I had bought as many volumes again on the shelves supporting the other side. This was a propitious beginning, and as parcels from London arrived throughout the following fall (they were sent a few at a time to suit the convenience of the packer), I came to understand what a treasure had come my way. Balston knew English book illustration from 1885 to 1930 as no one else of his day had known it, and this was his choice from the field, minus of course the books which had been sold at Christie's. As I repaired my previous neglect of this period, I discovered the full extent of my good fortune. Apart from the publications of private presses and books illustrated by the three-color process, I found that I already possessed most of the volumes which I would otherwise have had to search out title by title. I should also mention two later additions from Tom Balston's collection. Among his enthusiasms was John Martin, concerning whom he was the ranking authority, and in 1974 I acquired his copies of Martin's *Sezincot House* (68) and the part issue of *Illustrations of the Bible* (70). One of the plates in the former, a magnificent folio of colored aquatints so rare as to be virtually unknown, is reproduced facing page xxvi.

During the past five years I have had two principal objectives: to bring in the titles required to make my coverage of the years 1890 to 1914 reasonably comprehensive and to supplement my collection of books with drawings, proofs, and autograph letters. The gradual dispersal of a fine collection of private press books by a New York dealer has helped me towards the former aim, but I have made little progress with books illustrated by the three-color process. Tom Balston had few, and my own enthusiasm for them has been readily contained, particularly at the prevailing level of prices. Since the current vogue of drawings for illustrations is of recent origin, I had good luck for several years with my second objective. Here too where possible I employed the strategy of buying collections.

From early years the illustrator whom I found most congenial has been Edmund J. Sullivan. When I began to look for unique material related to book illustration, it was natural that I should seek drawings from his hand. A chance mention of my interest to a small London dealer in the summer of 1970 brought an overwhelming response. The death of the artist's daughter, Lillian Eileen Sullivan, had resulted in the dispersal of most of Sullivan's sketchbooks and finished drawings at a virtually unadvertised house sale where the dealer was represented. I bought nearly everything he had, and during the next two years I acquired further drawings and sketchbooks from other book and art dealers and in the auction rooms. The resulting assemblage must go a good way towards reconstituting what was in Lillian Sullivan's possession. Included are twenty-two sketchbooks, 474 drawings (most of them finished), many lithographs and proofs of process illustrations, much manuscript material, and a number of books which Sullivan had annotated and decorated. There are sketchbooks or important groups of finished drawings (in some cases both) for his illustrations to Borrow's *Lavengro*, Carlyle's *The French Revolution* and *Sartor Resartus*, Chesterton's *The Wisdom of Father Brown*, FitzGerald's *The Rubaiyat of Omar Khayyam*, Fouqué's *Sintram and His Companions*, Goldsmith's *A Citizen of the World* and *The Vicar of Wakefield*, Hughes's *Tom Brown's School Days*, George Outram's *Legal and Other Lyrics*, Tennyson's *A Dream of Fair Women* and *Maud*, and Sullivan's own *The Kaiser's Garland* and *Line*. More desirable still, however, are the drawings of his later years for *Don Quixote*, *King Lear*, and Stevenson's *Dr. Jekyll and Mr. Hyde* and *Weir of Hermiston*, which were never published. If I have treated Sullivan with particular fullness in the Catalogue, even extending the entries concerning him beyond my chronological limit, the reader will understand why.

It would be wearisome to do more than list the other substantial groups of drawings and prints that have come my way. They include one early acquisition, 449 colored caricatures by James Gillray, 185 of them from the collection of H. Minto Wilson, purchased in 1964–1965; and a number of others added during more recent years: forty-six drawings by Sir John Gilbert for the title pages of *The Illustrated London News* in 1970, fifty-one drawings by Randolph Caldecott and two early sketchbooks of Charles Keene in 1972, some four hundred drawings and proofs of Phiz in 1973, and a substantial selection from Kerrison Preston's collection of the sketchbooks, drawings, and manuscripts of W. Graham Robertson in 1974. One such acquisition I should describe rather than list, however, since drawings, proofs, and photographs from it figure at several points in the Catalogue. This is an album kept by the painter Frederick Smallfield and his wife from the 1860s to the 1880s. The gifts from artists in their circle that it contains are sometimes slight but never perfunctory, inspired as they were by a desire to please discriminating and well-liked friends. Among those represented are H. H. Armstead, Philip Hermogenes Calderon, John Austen Fitzgerald, J. A. Hodgson, Charles Keene, M. J. Lawless, H. Walter Lonsdale, Henry Stacy Marks, Matthew Morgan, and Telemaso Signorini—a visitor from Italy who enjoyed the Smallfields' hospitality. Typical is the drawing by Marks on page xviii, a spirited protest against the invasion by photography of the portrait painter's province during the 1860s.

*   *   *

Drawing of King Lear by Edmund J. Sullivan

Drawing for an unidentified boys' story by Randolph Caldecott

Drawing of episodes in a contested election by Randolph Caldecott

In conclusion I take pleasure in acknowledging the obligations I have incurred in the preparation of this book. The scholars, collectors, and book dealers who commented on my preliminary list of seventy-five outstanding illustrated books published in England between 1790 and 1914 were Robin de Beaumont, Michael Brand, Colin Franklin, William E. Fredeman, Philip Hofer, E. D. H. Johnson, Kenneth A. Lohf, H. D. Lyon, Allan Life, David Magee, Ruari McLean, Percy Muir, Charles Ryskamp, Maurice Sendak, Allen Staley, Alan G. Thomas, Arthur E. Vershbow, Robert R. Wark, Carl R. Woodring, and Jacob Zeitlin. Parts of my text were read by Messrs. Franklin, Life, Lohf, McLean, Muir, and Woodring. Mr. Ryskamp not only read the whole of the text but also through advice and action resolved many problems concerning both exhibition and book. To all these gentlemen I offer my thanks.

My chief debt, however, is to Thomas V. Lange, Assistant Curator of Printed Books at the Morgan Library, who provided the formal bibliographical descriptions of the Catalogue—a formidable task carried out with high professional skill—and supervised the installation of the exhibition at the Library. I should also express my gratitude to the other staff members who worked on the project, notably Charles Passela, Supervisor of Photography, whose expertise never faltered through what must have come to seem an interminable assignment, and Mrs. Patricia Reyes, Associate Conservator.

GORDON N. RAY

December, 1975

Self-portrait by Charles Keene

The Catalogue

NOTE ON
BIBLIOGRAPHICAL DESCRIPTIONS

Each entry describes the specific copy examined, which is from Mr. Ray's collection unless otherwise stated, with mention of anomalies such as misbound text, missing plates, and hitherto unnoted states of illustrations. Bindings may vary on other copies. Page size is measured to the nearest ⅛th of an inch, with height preceding width. Titles are transcribed literally but not typographically, punctuation being added where necessary. Printers are recorded where their slugs appear. If imprints list multiple booksellers or printers, only the first or principal appears in the description. In the collations, initial and final blank leaves are not counted. In most instances the illustrations have been counted and the medium identified. The word 'tinted' means litho- or block-tint, and 'colored' means hand-colored. Wood engravings are differentiated from woodcuts. For their assistance in the preparation of these bibliographical entries, I would like to thank Gerald Gottlieb, Paul Needham, Evelyn Semler, Susan Vosk, and especially Eve Marie Utne.

THOMAS V. LANGE

Forerunners

Despite the notable work of Francis Barlow, William Faithorne, and Wenceslaus Hollar, the most striking precursor before 1700 of the romantic and postromantic illustrated book in England is the 1688 edition of *Paradise Lost*. The eighteenth century before 1790 offers a much wider choice. Pine's Horace marks a high point of Augustan taste. Bickham's *Musical Entertainer* and Bentley's *Designs for Gray's Poems* are distinctively English adaptations of the French rococo style that then dominated Europe, while the Baskerville *Orlando Furioso* showed that a French masterpiece could be produced in England. An authentic native tradition is seen in the process of formation in Hayman's *Don Quixote*, Stubbs's *Anatomy of the Horse*, and Hogarth's "Works." The last assemblage epitomizes as well the English achievement in prints, which during the latter part of the century outshone that in books. It is to be regretted that James Gillray cannot be represented by a similar contemporary and authorized collection.

John Baptist Medina (1659–1710) and others

JOHN MILTON

Paradise Lost. A poem in twelve books . . . The fourth edition, adorn'd with sculptures. London, Miles Flesher for Jacob Tonson, 1688. [4], 343 (i.e., 345), [6] p. Illus: Engraved front. port. and 12 engraved plates, 8 of which are after B. de Medina. Printer: Miles Flesher. Page size 14 × 9½ inches. Half calf. Wing M2147; Pforzheimer 720.

The unsigned plates for Books I and II give this volume its importance, linking the early masters of the print with Blake and Fuseli. Without them this would be merely one more handsome but conventional baroque book. Suzanne Boorsch ("The 1688 *Paradise Lost* and Dr. Aldrich," *Metropolitan Museum Journal*, VI [1972], 133–150) has shown that the plates for Books II and XII, and in all probability for Book I as well, derive from engravings after old masters in the collection of Dr. Henry Aldrich.

Engraving after an unidentified early master for *Paradise Lost*, 1688, Book I

John Pine (1690–1756)

QUINTUS HORATIUS FLACCUS

Opera. London, John Pine, 1733–37. 2 v. I: [30], 264, [1] p. II: [22], 191, [13] p. Illus: Engraved throughout, with plates, ports., vignettes, and initials by John Pine. Page size: 8¼ × 5¼ inches. Morocco by Matthews. Rothschild 1546, 2nd issue.

Pine's complete command of his craft makes this the most elegant of English eighteenth-century books in which text and illustrations alike are entirely engraved.

George Bickham (d. 1758) and others

GEORGE BICKHAM, JR.

The Musical Entertainer, engraved by George Bickham junr . . . London, Charles Corbett [1737–1739]. 2 v. in 1. I: [2], 100 l. II: [2], 100 l. Illus: Engraved throughout with head- and tailpieces, vignettes, and other decorations by Bickham. Page size: 15⅝ × 9⅝ inches. Contemp. calf.

Bickham's designs for this dazzling book, which is also entirely engraved, constitute a conspectus of the images offered by English and continental artists of the period including Hogarth (see II, 64), but it is the eight plates after Gravelot which stand out. As Hanns Hammelmann has shown, Gravelot contributed to more than fifty books during his fifteen years in London.

Hubert Gravelot,
engraving for Bickham's
Musical Entertainer

Richard Bentley (1708–1782)

THOMAS GRAY

Designs by Mr. R. Bentley, for Six Poems by Mr. T. Gray. London, for R. Dodsley, 1753. [8] p., 35, [1] l., printed on rectos only. Illus: 6 engraved plates, 13 engraved vignettes, and 6 engraved initials by Müller and Grignon. Page size: 15 × 10¾ inches. Contemp. mottled calf. Rothschild 1061.

Another fine rococo book, this time with occasional neo-Gothic intrusions. This is a copy of the first issue, in which the half title reads "Designs, &c."

Richard Bentley, *Designs . . . for Six Poems by Mr. T. Gray*

Francis Hayman, early state and finished engraving for *Don Quixote*

Francis Hayman (1708–1776)

MIGUEL DE CERVANTES

The History and Adventures of the Renowned Don Quixote. Translated from the Spanish of Miguel de Cervantes Saavedra. To which is prefixed some account of the author's life. By T. Smollett, M.D. Illustrated with twenty-eight new copperplates designed by Hayman, and engraved by the best artists . . . London, for A. Millar . . . , 1755. 2 v. I: [4], xxviii, 403 p. II: viii, 466, [1] p. Illus: Engraved front. and 27 plates after Hayman. This copy is extra-illustrated with one duplicate plate and 14 early states of the plates, and 152 plates after Vanderbank, Coypel, Hogarth, and others. Page size: 9 × 11 ⅜ inches. Red morocco by J. Mackenzie.

Hayman was the most proficient English illustrator of his time, and this is his best book. The copy described is a unique one, containing fourteen early states of Hayman's plates as well as the large series after Coypel of 1724, the series after Vanderbank of 1737, and the reductions of the Coypel series published in 1746. Preliminary etchings for mid-eighteenth-century French books are rare; those for English books of the same period are virtually unfindable. This unique set was bound by J. Mackenzie in the 1830s, probably for Henry B. H. Beaufoy, F.R.S.

George Stubbs, *The Anatomy of the Horse*

George Stubbs (1724–1806)

GEORGE STUBBS

The Anatomy of the Horse. Including a particular description of the bones, cartilages, muscles, fascias, ligaments, nerves, arteries, veins, and glands. In eighteen tables, all done from nature. London, by J. Purser for the author, 1799. [4], 47 p. Illus: 24 etched plates by Stubbs. Page size: 17¼ × 22 inches. Half leather.

This book is a landmark in the history both of anatomy and of art. Stubbs's statement in his preface that "all the figures . . . are drawn from nature, for which purpose I dissected a great number of horses" may have given offence, but it is precisely because his book was intended for farriers and horse dealers as well as painters, sculptors, and designers that it made its mark. The fine exactness and austere truth of his engravings give them a timeless beauty.

Various Artists

LUDOVICO ARIOSTO

Orlando Furioso. Birmingham, G. Baskerville for P. Molini, 1773. 4 v. I: [32], lviii, 362 p. II: [1], 450 p. III: [1], 446 p. IV:[1], 446 p. Illus: Engraved front. in v. I, and 46 engraved plates after Cipriani (14), Moreau le jeune (11), Eisen (8), Cochin fils (6), Charles Monnet (6), and Greuze (1). Printer: J. Baskerville. Page size: 9½ × 5¾ inches. Contemp. red morocco. Cohen, p. 95–97; Gaskell 48.

Though printed by Baskerville, this luxurious book is altogether in the prevailing French mode. No doubt because of its English origin, it has never enjoyed quite the reputation that its employment of the best French artists and engravers would otherwise have guaranteed it.

William Hogarth (1697–1764)

WILLIAM HOGARTH

[**Works**. After 1775.] 3 v. Illus: 85 engraved plates by Hogarth. Page size: 18×24¾ inches. Original boards with decorated leather labels.

Though not regularly published, this collection of Hogarth's engravings approaches book form closely enough to warrant its inclusion. Hogarth sold bound sets of his prints as early as 1736, and his widow continued this practice after his death. These three volumes contain all the prints for sale in 1765 at her shop, the Golden Head in Leicester Fields, except "Before" and "After," as well as five others, the latest of which is dated 1775. The large plates are bound as issued, the small are mounted on leaves of the same size. In 1783 Mrs. Hogarth announced, with expert confirmation, that her husband's plates had not been retouched since his death. (Paulson, *Hogarth's Graphic Works*, I, 68–71.)

Leather label for Hogarth's "Works"

William Blake (1757–1827)

To begin a survey of this kind with Blake is bold yet exhilarating: bold, because what follows may seem an anticlimax; exhilarating, because no great artist has ever been more completely committed to illustration. His statement of the case for original graphic art is well known: "he who thinks he can Engrave, or Paint either, without being a Master of drawing, is a Fool. Painting is drawing on Canvas, & Engraving is drawing on Copper, & nothing Else. Drawing is Execution, & nothing Else, & he who draws best must be the best Artist." ("Public Address," *Poetry and Prose of William Blake*, ed. Keynes, London, 1932, p. 822.)

Until late in his life Blake earned his living as a reproductive engraver. During his first three de-cades, indeed, there was no reason to think of him as anything more than a skilful artisan laboring within the familiar conventions of his craft. Since his early work is relatively unimportant, his career as an engraver of the designs of others can be appropriately represented by Gay's *Fables* and Stedman's *Narrative* of the 1790s, in both of which he substantially altered the designs from which he worked. These books are supplemented elsewhere by his engravings after Flaxman in *The Iliad* (21) and *Compositions from . . . Hesiod* (22).

Blake's first significant original work was the *Songs of Innocence* of 1789, in which both text and illustrations are etched in relief and colored by hand. This little volume set the pattern for his splendid series of Illuminated Books. He had completed nine more titles by 1795, while *Milton* (1801–1808) and *Jerusalem* (1804–1820) were major accomplishments of his later years. It is sad to think that such things are no longer for the private collector.

Blake's other outstanding volumes choose themselves: *Night Thoughts*, *The Grave*, *Thornton's Virgil*, and *The Book of Job*. Each in a different way is a high point of the illustrated book in England. His fragmentary *Illustrations to Dante*, first published in 1838, should also be mentioned. These seven engravings, which are not inferior to those for *The Book of Job*, were all that he had completed at the time of his death.

REFERENCES   Bentley and Nurmi; Easson and Essick; Keynes, *Blake Studies*; Keynes, *Thornton's Virgil*; Keynes, *William Blake's Engravings*; Ryskamp; Wright.

1   JOHN GAY

Fables . . . with a life of the author and embellished with seventy plates. London, for John Stockdale, 1793. 2 v. in 1. I: Engraved t.p., xi, 225 p. II: Engraved t.p., vii, 187, [1] p. Illus: Engraved titles and 71 engraved plates by various artists, including 12 plates by William Blake. Page size: 10½×6½ inches. Contemp. calf. Bentley and Nurmi 371A.

Blake's twelve engravings follow designs in earlier editions of the *Fables*, but they are freely adapted.

(2) John Gabriel Stedman, *Narrative of a Five Years' Expedition . . .*

(1) John Gay, *Fables*, "The Philosopher and the Shepherd"

2   JOHN STEDMAN

Narrative of a Five Years' Expedition, against the Revolted Negroes of Surinam . . . illustrated with 80 elegant engravings from drawings made by the author . . . London, for J. Johnson and J. Edwards, 1796. 2 v. I: Engraved t.p., xviii, 407 [i.e., 417], [7] p. II: Engraved t.p., iv, 404, [7] p. Illus: Front. in v. I, engraved titles, and 81 engraved plates, including 13 signed by and 3 attributed to William Blake. Inserted in this copy are an engraved port. of Lewis, Duke of Brunswick, and a watercolor drawing by John Stedman. Page size: 10⅜ ×8¼ inches. Contemp. half calf. Bentley and Nurmi 408A.

Blake's sixteen engravings are ranked by Keynes among his "most interesting and important book illustrations" (Ryskamp, p. 10). This copy is inscribed: "John G. Stedman to Lieut. Colonel Ferrier &c."

❧ John Gabriel Stedman, watercolor drawing, 10½ ×7⅝ inches, mounted opposite the frontispiece of Volume I of the copy described above.

John Gabriel Stedman, watercolor drawing of a scene in Surinam

It would appear that Stedman's drawings for his *Narrative* have not survived. This sketch of a scene in Surinam has the pencil notation "Stedman's drawing" on the reverse. Though not without charm, it is very much the work of an amateur artist. Keynes's surmise that Blake modified Stedman's drawings "to a greater or less extent in his engraved versions" (Ryskamp, p. 9) would seem to be established. If further confirmation of Stedman's modest ability as a draftsman is needed, it is supplied by a crabbed print of Lewis, Duke of Brunswick, drawn and engraved by him in 1784, which is also bound in this volume. See Keynes, *Blake Studies*, p. 100.

3 EDWARD YOUNG

The Complaint, and the Consolation, or, Night Thoughts . . . London, by R. Noble for R. Edwards, 1797. viii, [1], 95, [2] p. Illus: 43 engravings by William Blake surrounding the letterpress text. Printer: R. Noble. Page size: 16¼ × 13 inches. Half morocco. Bentley and Nurmi 422.

Blake made 537 drawings in watercolor around pages of the first edition of Young's poem, inlaid in album sheets measuring 21 by 16 inches. He chose forty-three of these for engraving in what was intended to be a first installment of illustrations to the *Night Thoughts*. Perhaps baffled by the novelty of Blake's interpretations, the public was not receptive, and the book remains a remarkable fragment. Here is the offered "Explanation" of the frontispiece to Night the Third: "A female figure, who appears from the crescent beneath her feet to have surmounted the trials of this world, is admitted to an eternity of glory: eternity is represented by its usual emblem—a serpent with its extremities united." Copies of *Night Thoughts* are occasionally found with contemporary coloring. See Plate v.

4 WILLIAM BLAKE

Jerusalem. The emanation of the giant Albion. [London], Printed by W. Blake, 1804[–1820]. 100 relief etched plates, here printed in black, uncolored. Inserted are proof impressions of plates 28, 45, and 56. Page size: 14⅝ × 10½ inches. Red morocco by Bedford. Keynes and Wolf copy F.

Pierpont Morgan Library

Jerusalem is the longest and most important of Blake's experiments in illuminated poetry. Like the others, it is entirely his creation. Not only was he responsible for both text and illustrations, which make a seamless web, but he also printed and distributed the volume. The advance of Blake studies in recent years has made *Jerusalem* far more accessible than in the past. Indeed, David Erdman, who notes that the upper panel of Blake's page 33 (Keynes 37) depicts the Giant Albion's "sensation of dying in the arms of the 'Slain Lamb of God,'" while the lower shows Jerusalem witnessing the scene, "though the red-winged spectre still darkens communication," is able to trace in convincing detail the ramification of Blake's symbolism (*The Illuminated Blake*, Garden City, 1974, p. 312). See Plate VI.

5 WILLIAM HAYLEY

Ballads . . . founded on anecdotes relating to animals with prints, designed and engraved by William Blake. Chichester, J. Seagrave for Richard Phillips, 1805. [5], 212, [1] p. Illus: Engraved front. and 4 plates by William Blake. Printer: J. Seagrave. Page size: 6¼ × 3⅞ inches. Contemp. half vellum. Bentley and Nurmi 374.

This little volume for "young Readers" may serve to represent several that Blake illustrated during the years when Hayley was his patron. His engravings are adaptations and reductions of those in the rare part issue of 1802.

6 ROBERT BLAIR

The Grave, a poem . . . illustrated by twelve etchings executed from original designs. London, by T. Bensley for R. H. Cromek . . . , 1808. Added etched t.p., xiv, 36, [4] p. Illus: Etched port. of W. Blake by Schiavonetti, added etched t.p., and 11 plates by Schiavonetti after Blake. Printer: T. Bensley. Page size: 13½ × 10⅞ inches. Half calf. Bentley and Nurmi 350B.

R. H. Cromek, the proprietor of this venture, was evidently uneasy about the public's response to Blake's drawings. He employed Schiavonetti to engrave them, though Blake had expected to do the

(5) William Hayley, *Ballads*, frontispiece

work himself. And he turned to Fuseli, as a representative of "elegant and classical taste," for a conciliatory preface. After noting how Blake had domesticated the hereafter in this "moral series," Fuseli praised his designs in what can only be called equivocal language. They "sometimes excite our wonder, and not seldom our fears, when we see him play on the very verge of legitimate invention; but wildness so picturesque in itself, so often redeemed by taste, simplicity, and elegance, what child of fancy, what artist would wish to discharge?" (p. xiv). The knowledge that with these cautious preparations *The Grave* became by far the most popular of Blake's works among his contemporaries is a poor exchange for not having his own engravings of these superb designs.

The Soul exploring the recesses of the Grave

(6) Robert Blair, *The Grave*

6A ROBERT BLAIR

The Grave, a poem . . . illustrated by twelve etchings from original designs. To which is added a life of the author. London, by T. Bensley for R. Ackermann . . . 1813. Added etched t.p., [2], liv, 42 p. Illus: Etched port. of W. Blake by Schiavonetti, added etched t.p., and 11 plates by Schiavonetti after Blake. Printer: T. Bensley. Page size: 14 × 11½ inches. Quarter calf. Bentley and Nurmi 350C.

This reprint of *The Grave* by Ackermann, then the leading publisher of illustrated books, attests to its continued vogue.

6B JOSE JOAQUIN DE MORA

Meditaciones Poeticas . . . Londres, R. Ackermann . . . , 1826. Added etched t.p., iii [i.e., iv], 31 p. Illus: Etched port. of W. Blake by Schiavonetti, added etched t.p., and 11 plates by Schiavonetti after Blake. Printer: Carlos Wood. Page size: 13 × 10 inches. Contemp. half calf. Bentley and Nurmi 393.

Ackermann devised his second reprint for sale in Central and South America. The author declares in his preface that his verses are to be regarded solely as illustrations of the prints of the celebrated artist "Guillermo Black."

7 ROBERT THORNTON

The Pastorals of Virgil, with a course of English reading, adapted for schools . . . illustrated by 230 engravings . . . Third edition . . . London, published by F. C. & J. Rivingtons . . . 1821. Collates as in Bentley and Nurmi. Printer: J. M'Gowan. Page size: 6¾ × 4 inches. Contemp. calf. Bentley and Nurmi 411.

Through the intervention of his friend John Linnell, Blake was employed by Dr. Robert John Thornton, to whom we owe *The Temple of Flora* (39), to provide some further embellishments for his scrubby but abundantly illustrated school text. The poem chosen for Blake's attention was Ambrose Phillips's imitation of Virgil's first eclogue. Blake carried out this commission by making his first and only wood engravings. It appears from early proofs that, except for the initial plate, he cut them in groups of four on large blocks. They were so printed, but since the blocks proved too big for Thornton's page, the individual engravings had first to be separated and cut down. That Thornton had no sense of *lèse majesté* in making these adjustments is seen in a note appended to the first cut: "The Illustrations of this English Pastoral are by the famous BLAKE, the illustrator of *Young's* Night Thoughts, and *Blair's* Grave; who designed and engraved them himself. This is mentioned, as they display less of art than genius, and are much admired by some eminent painters." (I, opposite p. 13.) Despite their undignified debut, these little engravings had a potent influence on those with eyes to see. The world to which they offer admission became that of Samuel Palmer's etchings (215, 220, 222) and Edward Calvert's woodcuts (249).

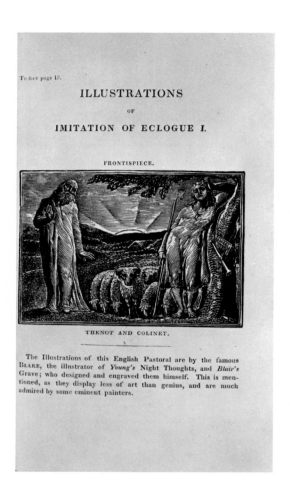

(7) Robert Thornton, *The Pastorals of Virgil*

8 WILLIAM BLAKE

Illustrations of the Book of Job . . . London, William Blake, 1825. Illus: Engraved title and 21 plates by William Blake. Proof impressions on drawing paper. Page size: 16 × 10½ inches. Purple morocco. Bentley and Nurmi 339.

Blake had long been fascinated by Job's story. The best of his early engravings is "Job and his friends" of 1786 or 1787. In the years that followed he returned again and again in his drawings to this book of the Bible. During the second decade of the century he made a set of watercolors on the subject for Thomas Butts. A second set for John Linnell, begun in 1821, led to a commission from his friend and fellow artist for engravings of the story. For *The Book of Job* Blake evolved a page design which is the reverse of that for the *Night Thoughts*, with the main drawing in the center and calligraphic texts, suitably decorated, surrounding it. The mod-

est size of the central panels does not prevent them from ranking with the supreme masterpieces of graphic art. *The Book of Job* was published in an edition of 315 copies at ten guineas for India proof impressions and five guineas for ordinary impressions. There was a further issue of 100 copies in 1874. (Bentley and Nurmi, pp. 94–95.) See Plate VII.

&❧ Pen and ink and watercolor drawing of "When the morning Stars sang together," from the complete Butts set of 21. Image size: 11 × 7¼ inches.
Pierpont Morgan Library

This drawing comes from the first and finest of the sets of designs by Blake for *The Book of Job*, that which he made for Thomas Butts. Unlike other designs in the set, there is little difference between the drawing for "When the morning Stars sang together" and the engraving Blake made from it. See Frontispiece.

J. M. W. Turner (1775–1851)

Turner made nearly nine hundred drawings for engravings on copper or steel. His earliest artistic training was in the workshop of the mezzotint engraver John Raphael Smith. He demonstrated his command of the medium in his etchings and mezzotints for the *Liber Studiorum*. The close supervision he exercised over his engravers is attested by the hundreds of trial proofs recorded by W. G. Rawlinson in his catalogue of *Turner's Engraved Work*. Thus Rawlinson does not exaggerate when he writes that "probably no painter before him so well understood the methods, the capabilities, and the limitations of engraving" (I, ix). Turner's personal mark is as firmly impressed on his engraved illustrations, indeed, as is Dürer's on the woodcuts done from his designs.

Turner's work as an illustrator falls into two divisions, the larger engravings on copper of his middle years and the smaller engravings (chiefly vignettes) on steel of his later life. Both are of very high quality. There are many volumes other than those described below which would warrant inclusion if space were available: among books with engravings on copper, Hakewill's *Picturesque Tour of Italy*, 1820; Whitaker's *History of Richmondshire*, 2 volumes, 1823; and Scott's *Provincial Antiquities and Picturesque Scenery of Scotland*, 2 volumes, 1826; among books with engravings on steel, Byron's *Life and Works*, 1832–1834; Scott's *Poetical Works*, 1834, and *Prose Works*, 1834–1836; and *Finden's Landscape Illustrations of the Bible*, 2 volumes, 1836.

Turner's principal works were typically issued in several forms. Purchasers of his *Southern Coast*, for example, could choose among engravings printed on Royal Quarto, as proofs on Imperial Quarto, and, "for the accommodation of the Curious," as India-paper proofs on Imperial Quarto. For his later books, portfolios of the illustrations without accompanying text were also available.

Since our concern is with Turner as an illustrator, his engravings are recorded as they appear in books. Collectors of prints may prefer the portfolios, where impressions of the plates are sometimes superior.

The word "picturesque," which often appears in the titles of Turner's books, is a key to his conception of illustration. Though his drawings were usually of identifiable places, he treated his subjects with great freedom, suppressing details that did not suit the vision that had formed in his imagination and adding others, yet never falsifying the broad features of his scene. If the resulting engravings leave something to be desired with regard to topographical exactness, this consideration hardly interferes with the viewer's enjoyment of them as poetical creations. The touches provided because Turner was persuaded that "the public wanted sparkle" (Rawlinson, I, xxxii) are another matter. One can bear with equanimity the "lights" that he so freely added in the process of engraving, but not the preposterous doll-like figures that sometimes crowd his foregrounds. But these are small blemishes in one of the supreme *oeuvres* of landscape illustration.

REFERENCES Finberg, *Liber Studiorum*; Finberg, *Southern Coast*; Muir, *Victorian Illustrated Books*; Ochner; Rawlinson; Ruskin, *Modern Painters*.

9

The Copper-Plate Magazine, or elegant cabinet of picturesque prints, consisting of sublime and interesting views in Great Britain and Ireland, beautifully engraved by the most eminent artists from the paintings and drawings of the first masters. London, for J. Walker, engraver, & H. D. Symonds, [1794–1798]. 5 v. I–IV: Engraved t.p., [1] l., 50 l. letterpress text, [1] l. V: Engraved t.p., [1] l., 50 l. letterpress text, [2] l. Illus: Engraved titles and 250 engraved plates after Corbould, Girtin, Repton, Walker, and others, including 14 plates after Turner. Page size: 8½ × 10½ inches. Contemp. red morocco.

This series, subsequently renamed *The Itinerant*, contains the earliest engravings after Turner. His fifteen drawings, for which he was paid £2 each, were made at the scenes depicted. Their mechanical reproduction contrasts sharply with what Turner was later to elicit from engravers working under his direct control.

10 J. M. W. TURNER

Liber Studiorum. London, J. M. W. Turner, [1807–1819]. Illus: Etched and mezzotint front. and 70 plates after Turner. Bound in is the wrapper for part 8, initialled by Turner. Page size: 11 × 16⅜ inches. Red morocco.

Turner undertook this "book of studies" for landscape pictures, his first important series of engravings, both to extend his reputation in a way impossible through painting alone and to meet the proposal of the painter William Frederick Wells that he give a work to the public which would do him justice should inferior reproductions later be made of his designs. Wells's implicit reference was to Earlom's *Liber Veritatis*, after the drawings of Claude Lorrain, two volumes of which had appeared in 1777, and the title of *Liber Studiorum* was accordingly chosen for Turner's undertaking.

When the part issue began in 1807, Turner intended that the work should extend to a frontispiece and 100 plates, but he discontinued publication after the seventy-first appeared in 1819, though plates for twenty further subjects were carried to various stages of completion. The series was well received, but by 1819 Turner had left behind him the classical severity of the period in which he did most of his drawings for the *Liber Studiorum* (67 of those for the 71 published plates date from 1806 to 1810), and the lighter and happier mood of his engravings for *The Southern Coast* and his mezzotints on steel of *The Rivers of England* had become more congenial to him than the somber tone of his earlier "arrangements in brown." Turner executed the foundation etchings for the *Liber Studiorum* himself, and in eleven instances he also carried out the mezzotinting: Frontispiece (in part), Junction of the Severn and the Wye, Inverary Pier, Crypt of Kirkstall Abbey, Calm, Mer de Glace, Entrance

of Calais Harbour, Berry Pomeroy Castle, The Source of the Arveron in the Valley of Chamouni, Aesacus and Hesperie, and Interior of a Church.

Though critics continue to dispute whether the *Liber Studiorum* should be praised chiefly for its fidelity to nature, its exemplification of the principles of composition, or its exhibition of "the associative imagination developed in the most profuse and marvellous modes" (Ruskin, *Modern Painters*, II, section II, paragraph 20), all agree that it is among the masterpieces of mezzotinting. Finberg estimated that between 170 and 200 sets of the published plates were printed. Unbroken series have become very hard to find. See Plate XIII.

11

Picturesque Views on the Southern Coast of England, from drawings made principally by J. M. W. Turner, R.A. and engraved by W. B. Cooke, George Cooke, and other eminent engravers. London, by John and Arthur Arch . . . , 1826. 2 v. in 1. [8] l., [158] p. Illus: 48 engraved plates and 32 engraved vignettes after Clennell, Collins, Prout, and others, including 39 engraved plates and 1 vignette after Turner. All plates are India-paper proofs initialled by Turner. Printer: W. Nicol, Shakespeare Press. Page size: 14½ × 10⅜ inches. Contemp. purple morocco by Hering.

This book, forty of the engravings in which are after Turner, appeared in parts between 1814 and 1826. It thus ran in double harness with William Daniell's *Voyage Round Great Britain* (41), and the two works between them helped to awaken the British to the glories of their coastline. *The Southern Coast* ranks immediately after the *Liber Studiorum* and *Picturesque Views in England and Wales* among books illustrated by Turner with engravings on copper. Described is an Imperial Quarto copy with plates on India paper, described by Finberg as "excessively rare."

12

River Scenery, by Turner and Girtin, with descriptions by Mrs. Hofland. Engraved by eminent engravers, from drawings by J. M. W. Turner, R.A. and the late Thomas Girtin. London, W. B. Cooke, 1827. Engraved t.p., 22 p. Illus: Etched and mezzotint front. and 19 plates, 4 after Girtin and 16 after Turner. All plates are India-paper proofs. Printer: W. Wilson. Page size 14⅜ × 10½ inches. Green morocco.

Though the contents page lists only eighteen plates, there are actually twenty, four after Girtin and

Drawn by J.M.W.Turner.R.A

Engraved by W.B.Cooke

ILFRACOMBE,
NORTH DEVON.

London, Published by John Murray, Albemarle Street, July 1814.

(11) *Picturesque Views on the Southern Coast of England*

sixteen after Turner. They were issued in parts between 1823 and 1827, and Turner's "Shields, on the River Tyne" and "Newcastle-on-Tyne" of the former year mark a date in the history of illustration for they constitute the first significant use of steel plates for engraving. Turner's rendering of light on clouds and water puts these scenes among his finest prints, while Girtin's darker engravings have a gloomy majesty. See Plate x.

13 SAMUEL ROGERS

Italy, a poem. By Samuel Rogers. London, for T. Cadell, 1830. vii, 284 p. + 1 p. ads. Illus: 55 engraved vignettes after Turner, Stothard, and others. Printer: T. Davison. Page size: 8⅛ × 5½ inches. Orig. boards.

Turner had at first been skeptical about the use of steel for engraving, though he did allow its employment in *The Rivers of England*. Rawlinson relates (I, xl) that when Sir Thomas Lawrence "expressed to him his surprise that he still employed copper, . . . Turner retorted that 'He did not choose to be a basket engraver.' On being asked to explain his meaning, he replied: 'When I got off the coach at Hastings the other day, a woman came up with a basket of your *Mrs. Peel* [a well-known Lawrence portrait] and wanted to sell me one for sixpence.' " Turner was later converted to steel, at least for his smaller plates, and certainly *Italy* brought him a much wider audience than his earlier work had attracted. Among his new admirers was the thirteen-year-old John Ruskin who relates in *Praeterita* (chapter 4) how the vignettes in the book "determined the main tenor of my life." Turner's illustrations for the companion volume of Rogers's *Poems* of 1834 are if anything superior to those for *Italy*. In both books his delicate and graceful vignettes, which are miracles of fine detail, seem fairly to float upon the page. See Plate xiv.

13A SAMUEL ROGERS

Italy, a poem. By Samuel Rogers. London, Edward Moxon, 1838. viii, 274 p. + 2 p. ads. Illus: 25 engraved plates after Turner, 21 engraved plates after Stothard, 9 engraved plates after other artists, and 6 misc. engraved vignettes. All plates are India-paper proofs. Printer: Bradbury & Evans. Page size: 11⅝ × 8⅝ inches. Contemp. red morocco.

The engravings after Turner for Rogers's *Italy* and *Poems* are seen at their best in the handsome quarto edition of 1838, where the illustrations in the text were replaced with unsold sets of proofs. It will be noticed that the steels were very large; hence the absence of plate marks in the octavo editions.

14

Picturesque Views in England and Wales, from drawings by J. M. W. Turner, esq. R.A. With descriptive and historic illustrations by H. E. Lloyd. London, for the proprietor by Moon, Boys, and Graves, 1832 [II: For the proprietor by Longman, Orme, Brown, Green, and Longmans, 1838.] 2 v. I: 3 l., 60 l. letterpress text. II: 2 l., 36 l. letterpress text. Illus: 96 engraved plates, all after Turner. All plates are India-paper proofs. Printer: J. Haddon. Page size: 14⅜ × 10½ inches. Contemp. red morocco by J. Mackenzie.

This is the most grandiose of Turner's illustrated books, and like the *Liber Studiorum* it remained incomplete. Originally intended to include 120 engravings, its appearance in parts between 1827 and 1838 brought the total only to ninety-six. Nearly every aspect of Britain outside of London is displayed in its pages: both natural panoramas of seacoast, rivers, lakes, hills, and valleys, and man-made scenes of cathedrals, castles, country houses, colleges, and towns. "Dudley," with its ruined castle and monastery seen in the moonlight on a hill above the flaring iron-forges of the nineteenth-century town, might have served as frontispiece to Carlyle's nearly contemporary *Past and Present*. Rawlinson did not exaggerate when he called the book "the most brilliant and finished piece of landscape engraving which up to that time had ever been produced" (I, xlviii). See Plate xv.

⊷ Nine progressive India-paper proofs for an unpublished vignette of Lowestoffe Lighthouse. Sheet size: 6⅜ × 4¾ inches.

Rawlinson conjectures (I, 171) that this plate and those associated with it may have been intended as vignette frontispieces for *England and Wales*. Turner's virtual collaboration with his engravers is demonstrated in the many changes he called for between the preliminary etching and the finished state. Three of the proofs (3, 5, and 7) have been touched by him. In addition to his written instructions, he used white chalk to indicate lightening, pencil to indicate darkening, and picked out the

Preliminary etching and touched progress
proofs for an unpublished vignette
of Lowestoffe Lighthouse

"lights" with a penknife. The series was once in
the collection of Sir Frank Short, himself an etcher
of distinction, who re-engraved Turner's *Liber
Studiorum* mezzotints in facsimile, adding his version of drawings intended for the series but not
executed.

15 SAMUEL ROGERS

Poems. London, for T. Cadell and E. Moxon, 1834. viii, 295, [1] p + 2 l. ads. Illus: 1 engraved plate and 32 engraved vignettes after Turner, 35 engraved vignettes after Stothard, and 4 other engraved vignettes. Printer: Bradbury & Evans. Page size: 8⅛×5¼ inches. Orig. boards.

The companion volume to *Italy* above.

15A SAMUEL ROGERS

Poems. London, Edward Moxon, 1838. viii, 266 p. Illus: 35 engraved plates after Turner, 23 engraved plates and 12 engraved vignettes after Stothard, and 3 other engravings. All plates are India-paper proofs. Page size: 11⅝×8⅝ inches. Contemp. morocco.

16 LEITCH RITCHIE

Wanderings by the Loire . . . with twenty-one engravings from drawings by J. M. W. Turner, esq. R.A. London, for the proprietor by Longman, Rees, Orme, Brown, Green, and Longman . . . , 1833. [8], 256 p. Illus: Added engraved t.p. and 20 engraved plates after Turner. Printer: J. Moyes. Page size: 9¼×6 inches. Publisher's green morocco by F. Westley.

Wanderings by the Seine . . . with twenty engravings from drawings by J. M. W. Turner, esq. R.A. London, for the proprietor by Longman, Rees, Orme, Brown, Green, and Longman . . . , 1834. [8], 256 p. Illus: Added engraved t.p. and 19 engraved plates after Turner. All plates are India-paper proofs before titles.

Printer: J. Moyes. Page size: 9¼×6 inches. Publisher's green morocco by F. Westley.

Wanderings by the Seine, from Rouen to the source . . . With twenty engravings from drawings by J. M. W. Turner, esq. R.A. . . . London, for the proprietor by Longman, Rees, Orme, Brown, Green, and Longman . . . , 1835. [6], 258 p. Illus: Added engraved t.p. and 19 plates after Turner. All plates are India-paper proofs before titles. Printer: J. Moyes. Page size: 9¼× 6 inches. Publisher's green morocco by F. Westley.

These three volumes are usually called *Turner's Annual Tours*, after the wording on their engraved title pages. The plates were reissued in 1837 as *The Rivers of France*. Shifting temporarily from vignettes to full-page plates, Turner achieved his best landscapes on steel in this series.

17 THOMAS CAMPBELL

The Poetical Works . . . London, Edward Moxon, 1837. ix, [2], 306 p., + 2 p. ads. Illus: 20 engraved vignettes after Turner. Printer: Bradbury & Evans. Page size: 7¾×5¼ inches. Green morocco.

The vignettes for this elegant book were Turner's last important illustrations. They are in no way inferior to those for Rogers's two volumes. Since Turner has been criticized for his use of figures, it is only fair to show his success with the ghostly "Death-Boat of Heligoland."

(17) Thomas Campbell, *Poetical Works*, "The Death-Boat of Heligoland"

Engraving on Copper

By 1790 line engraving on copper had been the rule for book illustration during nearly three centuries. For several decades thereafter it continued to be the commonest process, though the aquatint plates of the time made the illustrations even to such imposing works as Boydell's Shakespeare (9 volumes, 1802) and Milton (3 volumes, 1794–1797) seem heavy and mechanical in comparison. After 1830, copper engraving lost ground rapidly to engraving and etching on steel, lithography, and above all wood engraving. During its last decades of dominance, it provided the embellishment of many attractive books, chiefly volumes of views where J. M. W. Turner set the standard, or literary works. It was also employed in volumes of facsimiles, an art which reached a high level both in black and white under the direction of the antiquarian W. Y. Ottley and in color with *Imitations of Holbein* and Savage's *Hints on Decorative Printing* (99) as the chief monuments.

REFERENCES Balston, *Signature*; Bentley; Bray; Coxhead; Gray; Ormond and Turpin.

Thomas Stothard (1755–1834)

Though Stothard was elected to the Royal Academy as a painter in 1794, he owes his continuing reputation largely to his illustrations. His Victorian biographer, Mrs. Bray, claims "TEN THOUSAND DESIGNS" for him (p. 188). No doubt this figure is an exaggeration, but his drawings interpreting poetry, drama, and fiction must nonetheless total several thousand. Among his larger illustrations those for *The Pilgrim's Progress* and *Robinson Crusoe* are perhaps the most accomplished, but even these do not have the appeal of the vignettes which he drew for Rogers's poems. His illustrations for *The Pleasures of Memory* (54) are among the best wood engravings of the early years of the nineteenth century, while those on steel for *Italy* (13) and *Poems* (15) would be more appreciated if they were not overshadowed by Turner's

(18) Daniel Defoe, *Robinson Crusoe*

designs. Of Stothard's professional expertness there can be no doubt, but he was also the very type of the amenable artist, content always to give the publishers what they wanted. The rejections that such a stance implies are unwittingly suggested by the complacent Mrs. Bray when she refers in passing to Blake as "That amiable, eccentric, and greatly gifted artist, who produced so many works indicative of high order of genius, and sometimes no less of an unsound mind" (p. 20).

18 DANIEL DEFOE

The Life and Surprizing Adventures of Robinson Crusoe, of York, mariner . . . London, for John Stockdale, 1790. 2 v. I: [21], 389 p. II: v, 456, [14] p. Illus: Engraved titles, fronts., and 13 plates after Stothard, and 1 engraved port. Page size: 9⅛ × 5¾ inches. Contemp. red morocco.

Stothard took more pains with these two substantial volumes than he did with his routine assignments in *The Novelist's Magazine*, and the result

(20) Johann Caspar Lavater, *Essays on Physiognomy*, "The Witch of Endor"

was the first well-illustrated edition of Defoe's classic story. The effectiveness with which he could depict a striking episode is shown in his representation of Crusoe "exceedingly surprised with the print of a man's naked foot on the shore" (I, 194). Confusion, astonishment, and incipient terror are conveyed by Crusoe's attitude, while the dog's indifference underlines one's sense of his master's concern, and the menace pervading the scene is heightened by its lowering backdrop.

Francesco Bartolozzi (1725–1815)

19

Imitations of Original Drawings by Hans Holbein, in the collection of His Majesty, for the portraits of illustrious persons of the court of Henry VIII. With biographical tracts. Published by John Chamberlaine, Keeper of the King's drawings and F.S.A. London, printed by W. Bulmer and co., 1792[–1800]. 2 v. Col-lates as in Abbey. Page size: 21 3/8 × 16 1/2 inches. Contemp. red morocco. Abbey, *Life*, 205.

Bartolozzi was not an original artist, but he was a master of stipple engraving, particularly as used for color printing. He did all but four of the plates for Bulmer's noble folios, which were published in parts between 1792 and 1800. Holbein's portraits of the leading figures at the court of Henry VIII, preserved in the royal collection, were "drawn with chalk, upon paper stained of a flesh colour, and scarce shaded at all." In a copy like this, where the plates are proofs before letters mounted on thick paper with two black wash borders (a state not described by Abbey in *Life in England*, pp. 142–144), Bartolozzi's engravings render the originals with remarkable fidelity. This magnificent work is surely the finest early example of English color printing. The reduced reissue of 1812, reprinted in 1828, gives no idea of the book's quality. See Plate I.

Henry Fuseli (1741–1825)

20 JOHANN CASPAR LAVATER

Essays on Physiognomy, designed to promote the knowledge and the love of mankind . . . illustrated by more than eight hundred engravings, accurately copied; and some duplicates added from originals. Executed by, or under the inspection of, Thomas Holloway. Translated from the French by Henry Hunter . . . London, for John Murray . . . 1792. 3 v. in 5. I: [22], 281 [i.e., 285] p. II: ix, 285 p. III: [6], 240–444 p. IV: ix, 252 p. V: [6], 253–437, [11] p. Illus: 174 engraved plates and numerous engraved vignettes, mostly by T. Holloway, including 3 plates by Blake; this copy lacks 1 plate. Page size: 13⅛ × 10¾ inches. Contemp. blue morocco. Bentley and Nurmi 390.

As Lord Clark has recently noted, Fuseli's ambition was "to render the most dramatic episodes of Shakespeare in the pictorial language of Michaelangelo," the Michelangelo, that is, of *The Last Judgement* (*The Romantic Rebellion*, New York, 1973, p. 61). The best realization of this aim among Fuseli's illustrations is to be found, not in the Boydell Shakespeare, but in Lavater's *Essays on Physiognomy*. Lavater remarks of his friend and fellow countryman: "Spectres, Demons, and madmen; fantoms, exterminating angels; murders and acts of violence—such are his favourite objects" (II, 288). The exhibits he provides in demonstration include terror and malignity (as seen in the countenances of Brutus and Satan), madness ("a real scene in the Hospital of St. Spirito at Rome"), the supernatural (the Spirit of Samuel, the Witch of Endor, and Saul), and murder (Count Bracciaferro with his slain mistress). Fuseli's drawings are rendered with unusual distinction in the engravings of T. Holloway and in one instance Gillray (II, 280–296).

John Flaxman (1755–1826)

With the exception of those for Hesiod, the narrative designs of this notable sculptor all date from his sojourn in Rome in 1792–1793. Flaxman's choice of great classics for the subjects of his illustrations and his spare but elegant style—chiefly inspired, it would seem, by Greek vase painting—made an irresistible appeal to the taste of the age. Certainly he achieved his aim of encouraging "the immense flood of Grecian light & glory which is coming on Europe" (quoted by Bentley, p. 8).

Circumstances dictated that his drawings for Homer, Dante, and Aeschylus should first be engraved by Thomas Piroli in Rome, and that those for the *Iliad* and the *Odyssey* should first be published there, but his outlines were widely copied and continually reprinted. It seems appropriate to represent him in this survey by the first London editions of the two series of drawings in the engraving of which Blake had a hand.

21

The Iliad of Homer engraved from the compositions of John Flaxman R.A. sculptor. London, for Longman, Hurst, Rees, & Orme . . . 1805. Illus: Engraved t.p. and 39 engraved plates: 34 by Piroli, 2 by Parker, and 3 by Blake. Page size: 10⅞ × 16¾ inches. Calf. Bentley and Nurmi 368A.

Flaxman relies on his designs to tell Homer's story, contenting himself with a brief caption and a line or two of verse for each plate. As might be expected from a sculptor, attention in his scenes is focussed wholly on his figures. Only the barest hint of background is allowed, and props are reduced to an occasional chair or divan. This edition adds five drawings to the thirty-four of that published at Rome in 1793. Three of these were engraved by Blake. See Plate XII.

22

The Theogony, Works & Days, & The Days of Hesiod, engraved from the compositions of John Flaxman R.A., sculptor. London, [Longman, Hurst, Rees, Orme, & Brown, 1817.] Illus: Engraved t.p. and 37 engraved plates by Blake after Flaxman. Page size: 10¾ × 16½ inches. Contemp. red morocco by J. Wright. Bentley and Nurmi 367A.

Flaxman's last series of designs was not completed until long after his return to England. He was consequently able to entrust the engraving of these thirty-seven designs entirely to his friend Blake.

Thomas H. Shepherd (fl. 1825–1840)

23 JAMES ELMES

Metropolitan Improvements; or London in the Nineteenth Century: displayed in a series of engravings of the new buildings, improvements, etc. by the most eminent artists, from original drawings, taken from the objects themselves expressly for this work, by Mr.

Thos. H. Shepherd . . . with historical, topographical, and critical illustrations by James Elmes . . . London, Jones & co., 1827. [2], vi, 172, ii, [2] p. Illus: Engraved t.p. and 79 engraved plates after Shepherd. Printer: J. Haddon. Page size: 10⅝×8¼ inches. Contemp. half morocco by Simier.

London and Its Environs in the Nineteenth Century, illustrated by a series of views from original drawings by Thomas H. Shepherd. With historical, topographical and critical notices. Series the first, comprising the earlier edifices, antiquities, etc. London, Jones & co., 1829. Engraved t.p., 160, iii p. Illus: Engraved front., engraved t.p., and 79 engraved plates after Shepherd. Page size: 10⅝×8¼ inches. Contemp. half morocco by Simier.

These two volumes offer an encyclopaedic survey of London buildings at the end of the third decade of the nineteenth century. Their title pages are somewhat misleading. *Metropolitan Improvements* was printed in parts between 1827 and 1829, and the ensuing volume, though described as "Series the First," appeared in parts between 1829 and 1831. It was logical that Shepherd should begin with *Metropolitan Improvements*, since the novelty of his enterprise lay in the record that volume provides of the buildings erected during George the Fourth's regency and reign, yet the second volume has its timeliness as well, since it shows the street life of London about 1830, even if the buildings in the background date from earlier periods. Along with Rowlandson's *Microcosm* (33), Boys's *Original Views of London as It Is* (87), and Doré's *London* (207), this is one of the notable illustrated books devoted to the metropolis in the nineteenth century. See Plate XXX.

24   WILLIAM YOUNG OTTLEY

A Collection of One Hundred and Twenty-Nine Fac-Similes of Scarce and Curious Prints, by the Early Masters of the Italian, German, and Flemish Schools; illustrative of the history of engraving . . . with introductory remarks and a catalogue of the plates by William Young Ottley, F.A.S., member of the Society of Arts and Sciences at Utrecht. London, for the proprietor . . . , 1828. [4], xxxvi, xxv p. Illus: Added engraved t.p. and 129 engraved plates. Also included is an extra set of the nielli printed in silver. Printer: J. M. M'Creery. Page size: 14½ × 10½ inches. Contemp. calf.

The increasing vogue of engraved illustrations after 1790 was accompanied by a revival of interest in early prints. Volumes of impressions from the surviving plates of sixteenth- and seventeenth-century etchers and engravers were published, and histories of the print began to appear illustrated with facsimiles of works of the early masters. Perhaps the most accomplished of the latter is this book, one of several by Ottley, which was offered in two forms: with 100 plates at twelve guineas and with 129 plates and the nielli (or "Niellos," as Ottley calls them) finished in silver at fifteen guineas. Good as the reproductions of the nielli are, however, perhaps the most convincing plate is "Solomon's Idolatry" by the Master "M.Z.," which has sometimes been accepted as authentic when separated from the volume.

William Henry Bartlett (1809–1854) and others

25   JOHN BRITTON

Picturesque Antiquities of the English Cities. Illustrated by a series of engravings of antient buildings, street scenery, etc. . . . London, Longman, Rees, Orme, Brown, and Green . . . 1830. xii, 88 p. Illus: Wood-engraved title and 23 vignettes, mostly after W. H. Bartlett; 60 engraved plates, mostly after Bartlett. Printer: C. Whittingham. Page size: 12⅝×9½ inches. Green morocco by J. Mackenzie.

The antiquary and topographer John Britton (1771–1857) was the begetter of scores of volumes illustrative of older English architecture. Though he described this volume as "the most losing speculation" he ever embarked upon, its engravings, many of which are after the ubiquitous W. H. Bartlett, are perhaps the most interesting of those in any of his works, if only because for once private as well as monumental buildings get their share of attention.

Edward William Cooke (1811–1880) and others

26   GEORGE COOKE

Views in London and Its Vicinity. Complete in forty-eight plates, engraved in copper, by George Cooke, from drawings by Callcott, R.A., Stanfield, A.R.A., Prout, Roberts, Stark, Harding, Cotman, Havell, etc., etc., after the original sketches made on the spot by Edward W. Cooke. London, Longman and co. . . . [1826–1834]. 3 l., 7 p. Illus: 49 engraved plates by Cooke. Page size: 10½×7⅛ inches. Contemp. half morocco.

PRISON SHIP.
At Deptford

(26) George Cooke, *Views in London and Its Vicinity*, illustration by Samuel Prout

This book appeared in twelve parts between 1826 and 1834. George Cooke engraved the plates after drawings by his son Edward and his friends among the topographical and marine artists of the day including Callcott, Prout, and Stanfield. The most personal and homogeneous of smaller books of engravings devoted to scenes in and around London, it has the Thames as its particular focus. George Cooke combined great talent as a reproductive engraver with a sharp eye for opportune or unusual subjects: the new London bridge under construction, a diving bell in use after the Thames tunnel was breached in 1827, or a prison ship such as that from which Magwitch escapes in *Great Expectations*.

Daniel Maclise (1806–1870)

The Victorian revival of the last thirty years has to some degree restored Maclise's reputation as an artist, and the same interest in character and story that today makes his historical paintings appealing is to be found in his illustrations. Indeed, early recognition came to him in part from the brilliant "Gallery of Illustrious Literary Characters" which he began as "Alfred Croquis" in *Fraser's Magazine* during 1830, three years after he came to London from Cork. He continued to make drawings for illustrations during the rest of his career. Though only his *Irish Melodies* now seems a notable accomplishment, this book might have been approached in interest by *The Story of the Norman Conquest* of 1866, if he had been luckier in his engraver.

&• Pen drawing of "R. Montgomery, the author of 'Satan'" from *Fraser's Magazine*, "Gallery of illustrious literary characters." Image size: 6⅛×3¼ inches.

The verses accompanying Maclise's design in *Fraser's Magazine* suggest that the fool looking over the mirror and touching Montgomery's pen is the famous clown Gomery, who was supposed to be the poet's father.

27 FRANCIS SYLVESTER MAHONEY

The Reliques of Father Prout . . . collected and arranged by Oliver Yorke; esq., illustrated by Alfred Croquis . . . London, James Fraser, 1836. 2 v. I: Added etched t.p., xv, [1], 324 p. II: Added etched t.p., [4], 323 p. Illus: Etched titles, 3 etched plates, and 13 etched vignettes by Maclise. Bound in is a set of proofs before letters. Printer: Robson, Levey, & Franklyn. Page size: 6⅝×4¼ inches. Red morocco by Riviere.

The learned and facetious Mahoney wrote the papers making up these volumes for *Fraser's Magazine*, to which he was a prominent contributor under the name of "Father Prout," and it was fitting that "Alfred Croquis" should illustrate his fellow countryman's book. In this copy, possibly intended for presentation to Mahoney himself, there is a *suite* of the engravings on thick paper.

&• Pen and ink drawing of an imaginary coat of arms. Signed and dated by the artist. Sheet size: 7¾×5¼ inches. Inserted in v. I of *The Reliques of Father Prout*.

An imaginary coat of arms with a border of fantastic figures, no doubt drawn by Maclise for inclusion in this special copy.

28 CHARLES DICKENS

The Chimes: a goblin story of some bells that rang an old year out and a new year in . . . London, Chapman and Hall, 1845. Added etched t.p., [6], 175 p. Illus: Etched front. and added etched t.p. after Maclise, and 11 wood-engraved vignettes after J. Leech, R. Doyle, and C. Stanfield. Printer: Bradbury & Evans. Page size: 6½×4⅛ inches. Publisher's red cloth.

The frontispiece and engraved title page constitute Maclise's most elaborate composition in the fairy and goblin vein.

Daniel Maclise, pen drawing of an imaginary coat of arms

29 THOMAS MOORE

Moore's Irish Melodies. Illustrated by D. Maclise, R.A. London, for Longman, Brown, Green, and Longmans, 1846. Added t.p., iv, 280, + 4 p. ads. Illus: Added t.p., front., and 218 p. of text with borders and designs after Maclise, by the omnigraphic process. Page size: 10¼×7⅜ inches. Contemp. half morocco.

Maclise labored hard to make this book a worthy tribute to Tom Moore, whom he loved and revered, inventing decorative borders for every page in addition to his abundant illustrations, and even doing some of the preliminary etching himself ("D. Maclise, R.A. del. et aquafˢ" [sic], p. 1). The gratified poet wrote of the volume's "national character," an "Irish pencil" having "lent its aid to an Irish pen" (p. iv). Yet the book is totally unpolitical. It is a landmark, instead, in the history of style.

By his treatment of illustration and text as a unit and by his infinite elaboration of detail, Maclise not only introduced to England the effects achieved by the German illustrators of the 1830s and early 1840s, but also anticipated the French Art Nouveau volumes that began with Grasset's *Quatre Fils Aymon* of 1883. See Plate L.

30 ALFRED, LORD TENNYSON

The Princess: A medley by Alfred Tennyson, D.C.L., Poet Laureate. With twenty-six illustrations engraved on wood by Dalziel, Green, Thomas, and E. Williams, from drawings by Daniel Maclise, R.A. London, Edward Moxon, 1860. [5], 188 p. Illus: 26 wood-engraved vignettes after Maclise. Printer: Bradbury & Evans. Page size: 8½ × 6 inches. Publisher's red cloth.

Maclise's drawings for this book were as fully developed as those for *Irish Melodies*, but wood engraving did not suit his style as well as line engraving, either here or in the Moxon Tennyson (148).

John Ruskin (1819–1900)

31 JOHN RUSKIN

The Stones of Venice . . . the foundations . . . [II: The sea-stories . . . ; III: The fall . . .] with illustrations drawn by the author . . . London, Smith, Elder, and co., 1851–53. 3 v. I: xv, [1], 413 p. II: vi, [1], 394 p. III: [4], 362 p. Illus: 53 engraved, lithograph, and mezzotint plates, and numerous woodcuts in the text, all after Ruskin. Printer: Spottiswoodes and Shaw. Page size: 9¾ × 6¾ inches. Publisher's brown morocco by Westleys and Co.

Ruskin not only provided the drawings for his books but also closely supervised their reproduction. His aim was exposition, not visual delight, and the resulting illustrations leave much to be desired from the aesthetic point of view. To render "the character of the architecture" dealt with in *The Stones of Venice*, he not only "used any kind of engraving which seemed suited to the subjects—line and mezzotint, on steel, with mixed lithographs and woodcuts," but also provided in "a detached work" the unreduceable plates of larger illustrations (pp. x-xi). The result is an impressive book, if not a harmonious one, particularly when seen in one of the rare copies which George Smith had bound in morocco, using the same stamps as for the volumes in cloth. This copy is inscribed: "From G. Smith Esqre to Mrs Ruskin."

31A JOHN RUSKIN

[**Examples etc. Illustrative of the Stones of Venice.** London, 1851.] [2], 6 p. Illus: 16 etched, engraved, lithograph, and mezzotint plates after Ruskin. Page size: 21½ × 14¾ inches. Contemp. half calf. Abbey, *Travel*, 174.

This is the "detached work" referred to above. Ruskin notes in his preface that he would have preferred to employ Lupton's mezzotints throughout, but the limited number of his subscribers allowed him to provide only four such plates, most of the rest being tinted lithographs by Boys. He "used the help of the daguerreotype without scruple" in completing the mezzotints, willingly sacrificing "details in the shadowed parts" to achieve a "bold Rembrandtism."

⚬ Pencil and watercolor drawing of Gothic capitals for *The Stones of Venice*. Inscribed by the artist. Sheet size: 8 × 5¼ inches.

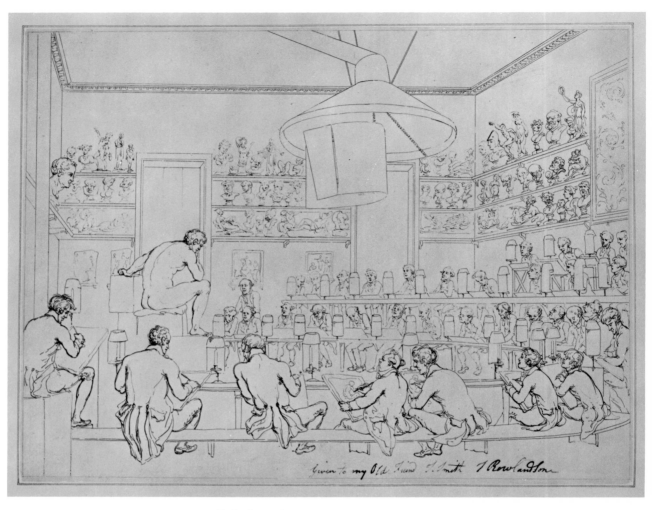

Etched proof of "The 'Life Class' at the Royal Academy" for *The Microcosm of London*

Thomas Rowlandson (1756–1827)

Rowlandson's thousands of watercolor drawings have given him a prominent place in the history of English painting, just as his hundreds of single prints have given him a prominent place in the history of English caricature. Our concern is with the illustrations which he did for books. He was equally at home realizing in line the characters of a classic novel, giving the animation of human activity to an architectural sketch by Pugin, or devising a grim or rowdy episode for Combe's jingling rhymes. Throughout his large *oeuvre* as an illustrator, his inventiveness and vitality are as remarkable as his draftmanship.

In his youth Rowlandson embarked on a career as a landscape painter, but his appetite for high living and his unequalled readiness in dashing off sketches soon diverted him from this ambition. The most familiar anecdote concerning him tells of his holding up his pencils after a disastrous night of gambling with the remark: "I've played the fool, but here is my resource." Thus his irregular pattern of life was established, and many of the resulting drawings were for illustrations. In addition to the volumes listed below, particular mention should be made of his hilarious commentary on Boswell's *Journal of a Tour to the Hebrides* called *Picturesque Beauties of Boswell* (20 etchings, 1786), though here he was working from the drawings of Samuel Collings; his two celebrations of anti-Gallican patriotism, *Hungarian and Highland Broadsword Exercise* (24 aquatints, 1799) and *The Loyal Volunteers of London and Environs* (87 aquatints, 1798–1799); and the smaller plates of *Miseries of Human Life* (50 aquatints, 1808). It used to be the custom to deplore Rowlandson's "fatal facility" in the minor branches of art, but one may doubt if the paintings we have lost would have given pleasure as acute and widespread as the many and varied smaller designs we have gained.

REFERENCES Abbey, *Life in England*; Abbey, *Scenery*; Grego; Hardie; Prideaux; Riely; Tooley; Wark; Wolf.

32 HENRY FIELDING

The History of Tom Jones, a foundling . . . Edinburgh, by and for J. Sibbald, 1791. 3 v. I: xix, 280 p. II: xi, 350 p. III: vii, 316 p. Illus: 12 etched plates by Rowlandson. Page size: 8 × 4¾ inches. Contemp. half calf.

Rowlandson's free and easy way of life and robust nature made him a congenial illustrator of the English novelists of the age. *The Vicar of Wakefield* was once cited as his best book in this line because of its lack of "coarseness," but *Tom Jones* is a far more typical effort. He also turned his hand to *Joseph Andrews*, *Humphry Clinker*, *Peregrine Pickle*, *Roderick Random*, and *A Sentimental Journey*.

33

The Microcosm of London. [London, 1808–1810.] 3 v. Collates as in Abbey; plates 5, 6, 7, 9 in the first state. Printer: T. Bensley. Page size: 10¾ × 13 inches. Contemp. half calf. Abbey, *Scenery*, 212.

Ackermann's record of "London in Miniature" is primarily devoted to the city's notable buildings as depicted by Pugin, but it is Rowlandson's artfully disposed figures, often shown by the score and sometimes by the hundred, that bring Pugin's spa-cious exteriors and interiors to life. No graphic artist has surpassed Rowlandson in presenting the patterned activity of day-to-day communal existence. See Plate XVI.

Etched proof touched with graphite of a rejected version of "The 'Life Class' at the Royal Academy," in *The Microcosm of London*, v. I, pl. 1. Signed and inscribed by the artist: "Given to my Old Friend T. Smith." Sheet size: 7⅞ × 10¼ inches.

34 WILLIAM COMBE

The Tour of Doctor Syntax, in Search of the Picturesque; a poem . . . London, R. Ackermann, 1812. Collates as in Tooley. Printer: Diggens. Page size: 9⅜ × 6⅛ inches. Brown morocco by Bradstreet. Tooley 427, first issue.

The Second Tour of Doctor Syntax, in Search of Consolation; a poem. Volume second . . . London, R. Ackermann, 1820. Collates as in Abbey. Printer: Diggens. Page size: 9⅝ × 6¼ inches. Brown morocco by Bradstreet; original wrappers and ads bound in, lacking wrappers to part 6. Abbey, *Life*, 272; plate 22 in the first state.

The Third Tour of Doctor Syntax, in Search of a Wife; a poem. London, R. Ackermann, [1820–1821.] Collates as in Abbey. Printer: Diggens. Page size: 9¾ × 6¼ inches. Brown morocco by Bradstreet. Abbey, *Life*, 267.

Pierpont Morgan Library

The misadventures of this elderly pedant gave Rowlandson ample scope for the comic designs of which he was a master, and the three books which deal with Syntax were his greatest success as an illustrator. Yet it has to be granted that Combe's narrative grows tedious long before the end of the third volume. Unlike Mr. Pickwick, who begins by enduring similar tribulations, Syntax had in him no capacity for development. In effect his experiences remain variations on a single joke. See Plate XVII.

Drawings and proofs for the three *Tours of Doctor Syntax*: 6 colored proof etchings, 8 published drawings, 16 unpublished drawings, and 2 doubtful drawings. Sizes vary.

Pierpont Morgan Library

35 WILLIAM COMBE

The English Dance of Death, from the designs of Thomas Rowlandson, with metrical illustrations by the author of "Doctor Syntax" . . . London, R. Ackermann,

The Serjeant's tongue will cease to brawl
In every Court of yonder Hall.

Drawing for "The law overthrown" in *The English Dance of Death*

1815–16. 2 v. Collates as in Abbey. Printer: J. Diggens. Page size: 9⅞×6 inches. Half red morocco. Abbey, *Life*, 263.

The Dance of Life, a poem . . . illustrated with coloured engravings by Thomas Rowlandson . . . London, R. Ackermann, 1817. Collates as in Abbey. Printer: J. Diggens. Page size: 9⅞×6 inches. Half red morocco. Abbey, *Life*, 264.

Rowlandson's *Dance of Death*, the only series on the subject since Holbein's to rival that master, is the perfect complement to his *Microcosm of London*, for here the artist is concerned for the most part not with crowds, but with scenes of violent action or intense emotion drawn from private life. Far from seeming repetitious, the figure of King Death provides a sardonic presence which adds immensely

to the scenes he stage manages. His absence from *The Dance of Life* makes the plates for that volume seem insipid in comparison. See Plate XVIII.

☙ Pen and ink, graphite, and watercolor drawing of "The law overthrown" in *The English Dance of Death*, II, 210. Sheet size: 5¼×8⅞ inches.
  Dr. Morris Saffron

The vigor and animation of this preliminary drawing, illustrative of the couplet "The Serjeant's tongue will cease to brawl / In every court of yonder Hall," are not entirely caught in Rowlandson's etching. Death, who has contrived the Serjeant's fatal accident, remains quite unmoved by the writ with which he is threatened.

Aquatint Engraving

Though colored aquatint engraving flourished in England for no more than half a century, the books adorned by this process remain among the most attractive in the history of illustration. The general employment of aquatint coincided with the great age of English watercolor painting, which it was ideally suited to render with ease and exactness. If the greatest painters of the time did not make drawings for aquatinting, artists of secondary rank found the process a congenial way of bringing their work to the attention of the public, often under the aegis of the publisher Rudolf Ackermann. The subjects they covered ranged from domestic architecture and scenery to satirical or farcical representations of the human comedy. But foreign lands were also extensively displayed, as were the sport and costume of the day. In other books aquatint was used to demonstrate the principles of some practical art, like landscape gardening, or to record a fragment of contemporary history, like the appearance of a new railway line. In this small library of books a fresh and sunlit England remains unspoiled to delight the modern eye.

REFERENCES Abbey, *Life in England*; Abbey, *Scenery*; Abbey, *Travel*; Grigson and Buchanan; Hardie; Klingender, ed. Elton; Prideaux; Schwerdt; Thomas; Tooley; Van Devanter.

Joseph Farington (1747–1821)

36 WILLIAM COMBE

An History of the River Thames [second title: An history of the principal rivers of Great Britain] . . . London, for John and Josiah Boydell, 1794–96. 2 v. I: xiv, [4], 312 p. II: [8], 294 p. Illus: Etched front. in v. I, 2 engraved maps, and 76 colored aquatint plates after Farington. Printer: W. Bulmer & co. Page size: 16½ ×12½ inches. Contemp. red morocco. Abbey, *Scenery*, 432, first printing.

One of the earliest of the great aquatint topographical works, this book has as its assets the lovely and varied scenery along the Thames, Farington's stately drawings, and Bulmer's noble printing. It is by far the most attractive of Alderman Boydell's folio publications. See Plate II.

Thomas Girtin (1775–1802)

37

[**A Selection of Twenty of the Most Picturesque Views in Paris, and Its Environs,** drawn and etched . . . by the late Thomas Girtin; being the only etchings of that celebrated artist: and aquatinted in exact imitation of the original drawings . . . London, M. A. & John Girtin, 1803]. 8 plates [of 20], all labelled "Subscribers print": nos. 2, 5, 9, 14, 17, 18, 19, 20. Various sizes; sheet size of illustrated print: 9⅞ × 17⅜ inches. Unbound. Abbey, *Travel*, I, 87–90.

Together with Rowlandson, Girtin was the most considerable artist whose designs were rendered in aquatint. Girtin etched the plates for this rare series between June 16 and October 4, 1802. After his death on November 9, they were aquatinted by F. C. Lewis and others. (Abbey, *Travel*, I, 87–90.) The "View of the Pont St. Michel taken from the Pont Neuf" is one of the most dramatic of the series. See Plate IX. There are four mezzotints after Girtin in *River Scenery* (12).

Humphrey Repton (1752–1818)

38 HUMPHREY REPTON

Observations on the Theory and Practice of Landscape Gardening. Including some remarks on Grecian and Gothic architecture, collected from various manuscripts . . . the whole tending to establish fixed principles in the required arts. London, for J. Taylor, 1803. Collates as in Abbey. Page size: 14× 11½ inches. Orig. printed boards. Abbey, *Scenery*, 390.

The overlays in Repton's books on landscape gardening, by means of which he showed selected prospects before and after he had turned his hand to them, have caused collectors to treasure his engravings as curiosities, but they are remarkable as well for the excellence of his draftsmanship. See

Plate XI. The *Red Books*, from which Repton records (p. 7) that he drew illustrations for this and other volumes, will soon be published in facsimile. They contain painted overlays, just as in his printed books.

Victor Reinagle, Robert John Thornton, and other artists

39 ROBERT JOHN THORNTON

New illustration of the sexual system of Carolus von Linnaeus: comprehending an elucidation of the several parts of the fruitification; a prize dissertation on the sexes of plants; a full explanation of the classes, and orders, of the sexual system; and **The Temple of Flora,** or the garden of nature, being picturesque botanical, coloured plates, of selected plants, illustrative of the same, with descriptions . . . London, for the publisher, T. Bensley, 1807. Collates as in Grigson and Buchanan. Page size: $21\frac{7}{8} \times 17\frac{5}{8}$ inches. Contemp. morocco.
  Pierpont Morgan Library

This sumptuous volume, the most celebrated of English flower books, is the concluding section of Dr. Thornton's *New Illustration of the Sexual System of Linnaeus,* a pretentious botanical compilation which began to appear in 1797. Thornton's aim was to "enlist the fine Arts" in the service of "the Science of Botany." He even created a Linnaean Gallery, paralleling Boydell's Shakespeare Gallery, from the paintings in which he selected those to be engraved for *The Temple of Flora.* His grandiose schemes met with failure, but his memory is kept green by the exotic melodrama of the aquatints in his book, each of which was planned in detail by him. After contemplating "The Night Blowing Cereus," even W. S. Gilbert's notion of falling in love with a poppy or a lily no longer seems outside the range of possibility. In this engraving "the flower" is after Victor Reinagle, "the moonlight" after Abraham Pether. See Plate VIII. Another engraving, "Roses," is aquatinted from a drawing by Thornton himself. A much inferior quarto edition of *The Temple of Flora* appeared in 1812.

Augustus Pugin (1762-1832) and others

40 WILLIAM COMBE

A History of the University of Oxford, its colleges, halls, and public buildings . . . London, R. Acker-

mann, 1814. 2 v. Collates as in Abbey: all plates present in colored and uncolored India-paper impressions. All plates in the first state. Not mentioned in Abbey: Pl. 5 is dated December, 1813, in the uncolored, and March 1, 1814, in the colored version; pl. 50 is dated June 1, 1814, in the uncolored, and May 1, 1814, in the colored version. Page size: $15\frac{3}{4} \times 12\frac{1}{2}$ inches. Contemp. red morocco. Abbey, *Scenery,* 279.

Though the India-paper impressions that accompany the colored plates in the fifty large-paper copies of this book are attractive enough, a comparison of the two shows how much the appeal of aquatint depends on the expertise of the bands of colorists, usually children, maintained by Ackermann and other publishers. See Plate XX.

William Daniell (1769-1837)

41 RICHARD AYTON

A Voyage Round Great Britain, undertaken in the summer of the year 1813, and commencing from the Land's-End, Cornwall, by Richard Ayton. With a series of views, illustrative of the character and prominent features of the coast, drawn and engraved by William Daniell, A.R.A. London, for Longman, Hurst, Rees, Orme, and Brown, 1814-25. 8 v. Collates as in Abbey. Page size: $14\frac{3}{4} \times 10\frac{3}{4}$ inches. Brown morocco by Simier. Abbey, *Scenery,* 16.

This is at once the most ambitious and the most successful of English books illustrated with aquatints. Though Daniell spent twelve years in its preparation, the work is remarkably harmonious. However rugged the scenes presented, they nearly always appear in their benign aspect, with some suggestion of useful human activity to be observed in even the wildest prospects. No doubt Daniell, who drew from life, chose agreeable days for his sketching, but it may be surmised that the book also reflects a consciously imposed point of view, manifested as well in his palette of subdued blues, greens, and greys. In sets like this with the plates mounted on cards (said to be 25 in number), *A Voyage Round Great Britain* is among the most luxurious of all illustrated books, virtually a small art museum. See Plate XIX. Ayton's text for the first two volumes is remarkably entertaining. He and Daniell afterwards came to a parting of the ways, perhaps because Ayton's interest in such subjects as miners and Sunday excursion workmen introduced an element of social realism to the book which clashed with Daniell's conception of it.

(43) John Buonarotti Papworth,
Hints on Ornamental Gardening

C. Wild and others

42 W. H. PYNE

The History of the Royal Residences of Windsor Castle, St. James Palace, Carleton House, Kensington Palace, Hampton Court, Buckingham House, and Frogmore. By W. H. Pyne, illustrated by one hundred highly finished and coloured engravings, facsimiles of original drawings by the most eminent artists . . . London, for A. Dry, 1819. 3 v. Collates as in *Abbey.* Inlaid in v. I is a 16-p. list of paintings and persons mentioned. Laid in is the original prospectus for the book. Page size: 13⅛ × 10⅝ inches. Contemp. green morocco. Abbey, *Scenery,* 396.

Both exteriors and interiors are shown, as in *The Microcosm of London,* but here it is the latter that predominate. The extraordinary richness of color in these plates contrasts sharply with the quiet tones used by Daniell in his *Voyage Round Great Britain.* See Plate XXI.

John Buonarotti Papworth (1775–1847)

43 JOHN BUONAROTTI PAPWORTH

Hints on Ornamental Gardening: consisting of a series of designs for garden buildings, useful and decorative gates, fences, railings, etc., accompanied by observations on the principles and theory of rural improvement, interspersed with occasional remarks on rural architecture . . . London, R. Ackermann, 1823. Collates as in Abbey. Page size: 10½ × 6⅞ inches. Half calf. Abbey, *Life,* 46.

To the folios of the Regency succeeded the smaller aquatint books of the 1820s. Among the pleasantest of these is Papworth's presentation of the structures by which a garden may be adorned in accordance with "the *principles* of Pictorial Art."

Robert Cruikshank (1789–1856)

44 RICHARD WESTMACOTT

The English Spy: an original work, characteristic, satirical, and humorous. Comprising scenes and sketches in every rank of society, being portraits of the illustrious, eminent, eccentric, and notorious. Drawn from the life by Bernard Blackmantle. The illustrations designed by Robert Cruikshank. London, Sherwood, Jones, and co., 1825–26. 2 v. Collates as in Abbey. Printer: Thomas Davison. Page size: 9½ × 6. Contemp. blue diced russia. Abbey, *Life,* 325.

During the 1820s the raffish life of English pleasure-seekers was the subject of a number of books illustrated with aquatints. This is the liveliest and most authentic of the lot, thanks in part to the animated drawings of George Cruikshank's brother. See Plate XXVI.

Thomas Talbot Bury (1811–1877)

45 THOMAS BURY

Coloured Views on the Liverpool and Manchester Railway, with plates of the coaches, machines, etc. from drawings made on the spot by Mr. T. T. Bury. With descriptive particulars, serving as a guide to travellers on the railway. London, Ackermann & co., 1833. [1], 8 p. Illus: 13 colored aquatint plates after T. T. Bury, 2 folding colored aquatint plates after I. Shaw, and 1 unsigned folding colored aquatint plate. Printer: Frederick Shoberl. Page size: 13½ × 11 inches. Contemp. half calf. Tooley 121.

This book was first published with six plates in 1831. It proved popular, and other editions fol-

(47) Engraved title page by Henry Alken for Robert Smith Surtees's *Jorrocks's Jaunts and Jollities*

lowed, of which this is the most complete. This classic record of the beginnings of the railway age was also one of the last significant books illustrated with aquatints. Lithography was already sweeping the field for pictorial records of this kind. See Plate XXXIV.

Henry Alken (1781–1851)

Alken was the premier sporting illustrator of his time. He worked in colored aquatint in a style akin to that of Rowlandson and the early George Cruikshank, passing from broad caricature in his early books to a more sober recording of the passing scene in his later. Four entries stand out in his long bibliography. His most ambitious book is the folio *National Sports of Great Britain* of 1821, but the three sporting classics, "Nimrod's" *Life of a Sportsman* and *Memoirs of the Late John Mytton, Esq.*, and Surtees's *Jorrocks's Jaunts and Jollities*, are a good deal more savory. For these works Alken continued to employ aquatint long after most other illustrators had abandoned the process. Alken's books used to figure in the library of every sporting gentleman, but as this social type disappears, they are finding their way into the hands of the collector of illustrated books and the social historian.

46 C. J. APPERLEY

The Life of a Sportsman. By Nimrod: with thirty-six coloured illustrations, by Henry Alken. London, R. Ackermann, 1842. Collates as in Tooley. Printer: Wright & co. Page size: 9½×6 inches. Publisher's green cloth. Tooley 65, first issue.

In this "half-true, half-fictitious" story "Nimrod" traces the career of the younger son of a country gentleman through rat-catching "to the rabbit and the badger, progressing, gradually, to the higher sports of the field," and finishing as a fox-hunter, horseman, and coachman "of the first class." His hero is even tempted by, but eventually overcomes, "the dangerous seductions of the race-course," thus fulfilling his creator's aim of imparting "a moral tone" to his narrative. These varied experiences gave Alken the subjects for his fullest panorama of English sporting life. See Plate XLII.

47 ROBERT SMITH SURTEES

Jorrocks's Jaunts and Jollities; being the hunting, shooting, racing, driving, sailing, eating, eccentric and extravagant exploits of that renowned sporting citizen, Mr. John Jorrocks . . . with fifteen coloured illustrations by Henry Alken. Second edition. London, R. Ackermann, 1843. Collates as in Tooley. Printer: W. Spiers. Page size: 8¼×5½ inches. Publisher's green cloth. Tooley 471.

This book attracted little notice when it appeared in 1838 with illustrations by Phiz (126), but Alken's aquatints quickly made it a sporting favorite. Though he catches admirably the color and the flow of Surtees's narrative, he left it to Leech to realize the possibilities of Mr. Jorrocks as a character (137).

48 C. J. APPERLEY

Memoirs of the Life of the Late John Mytton, esq. . . . with notices of his hunting, shooting, driving, racing, eccentric and extravagant exploits. By Nimrod. With numerous illustrations by H. Alken and T. J. Rawlins. Third edition, with a brief memoir of Nimrod, by the author of "Handley Cross". London, R. Ackermann, 1851. Collates as in Tooley. Printer: G. Barclay. Page size: 9½×6 inches. Publisher's green cloth. Abbey, *Life*, 385 (second edition); Tooley 68.

"Nimrod" forwent his aspirations towards "moral tone" in this lively account of a rugged, hard-living, devil-may-care country squire, greatly to the improvement of his narrative. Alken provided only twelve plates when the book first appeared in 1835. There are eighteen in this edition, which has the added distinction of a life of "Nimrod" by Surtees.

Thomas Bewick (1753–1828)

How Bewick extended the possibilities of wood engraving is well known. "Chief among his innovations," writes Philip James (*English Book Illustration, 1800–1900*, p. 18), "was a new conception of the black and white picture. He did not think of it as a white space on which black outlines and solids made a linear design printed in relief. . . . Instead he began with a black void out of which the subject appears in a varying range of grey tones with pure white for the lightest parts." Bewick's use of end-grained blocks was widely imitated both in England and on the Continent. Among his apprentices were some of the most distinguished engravers of the first half of the nineteenth century. When later artists like Gordon Craig and William Nicholson revived the tradition of creative work on wood, they turned to Bewick's example in freeing themselves from the trammels of reproductive engraving.

Bewick himself gave little thought to his role in the history of wood engraving. Instead he used his craft to carry out his practical purposes as a teacher and moralist. Yet in addition to the illustrations required by his text, he allowed himself in his tail-pieces, or "tale-pieces" as he was known to call them, to present scenes from the English countryside which have the effect of personal digressions. For most of his admirers these evocative vignettes, in which Bewick's powers of observation have full play, are the best part of his work. This was true of Charlotte Brontë, for example, who in the first chapter of *Jane Eyre* shows her heroine as a child poring over Bewick's *History of British Birds*, caring little for the letterpress, but finding a story in every vignette, "mysterious often to my undeveloped understanding and imperfect feelings, yet ever profoundly interesting":

I cannot tell what sentiment haunted the quiet solitary churchyard, with its inscribed headstone; its gate, its two trees, its low horizon, girdled by a broken wall, and its newly-risen crescent, attesting the hour of eventide.

The two ships becalmed on a torpid sea, I believed to be marine phantoms.

The fiend pinning down the thief's pack behind him, I passed over quickly: it was an object of terror.

REFERENCES   Bewick; Gray; James; Stone; Weekly.

A General History of Quadrupeds. The figures engraved on wood by T. Bewick. Newcastle upon Tyne, by and for Hodgson, R. Beilby, & T. Bewick . . . 1790. viii, 456 p. Illus: 303 wood-engraved vignettes of quadrupeds, tailpieces, etc., by Bewick. Page size: 8⅞ × 5⅝ inches. Orig. boards, uncut. Roscoe 1b, variant A.

Desiring to instruct his readers in an agreeable way, Bewick faithfully depicted each quadruped in proper sequence. Exotic animals like the lion and the hippopotamus, which he took from books, may be unconvincing, but he never fails with the dogs, sheep, and cats, which he drew from life. As the book progresses, the formal ornaments which serve as tailpieces to the sections give way to the glimpses of country life in which Bewick strikes his distinctive note.

50 OLIVER GOLDSMITH AND THOMAS PARNELL

Poems by Goldsmith and Parnell. London, by W. Bulmer & co., 1795. xx, 76 p. Illus: 2 wood-engraved t.p. vignettes, 5 wood-engraved plates, and 6 wood-engraved vignettes by T. and J. Bewick. Page size: 11¼ × 8⅞ inches. Contemp. green morocco.

Thanks to Bulmer, this is by far the handsomest of contemporary volumes containing Bewick's work, but the engravings themselves hardly reach the level of excellence attained by some of those in the *History of British Birds*. See Plate III.

History of British Birds. The figures engraved on wood by T. Bewick. Vol. I. Containing the history and description of land birds. Newcastle, by Sol. Hodgson for Beilby & Bewick . . . 1797. xxx, [1], 335, [1] p. Illus: 208 wood-engraved vignettes of birds, tailpieces, etc., by Bewick. Page size: 9 × 5½ inches. Contemp. green morocco. Roscoe 14b, variant B.

History of British Birds. The figures engraved on wood by T. Bewick. Vol. II. Containing the history and description of water birds. London, by Edward Walker for T. Bewick . . . 1804. xx, 400, 50, [1], 49, [1], + 1 p. ads. Illus: 237 wood-engraved vignettes of birds, tailpieces, etc., by Bewick. Printer: E. Walker. Page size: 9 × 5½ inches. Contemp. green morocco. Bound in are: **A Supplement to the History of British Birds** . . . parts I & II . . . Newcastle, by Edward Walker for T. Bewick, 1821. Illus: 77 wood-engraved vignettes of birds, tailpieces, etc., by Bewick. Roscoe 17c, variant B; 25b; 27b.

As he continued his effort "to render a delightful portion of Natural History more interesting and generally known" (II, iv), Bewick put to good use the lessons he had learned from the *Quadrupeds*. He limited himself to British birds, which he could observe at first hand, and the scenes of English life, previously confined to tailpieces, became more numerous and elaborate, more varied and poetic. The *History of British Birds* is consequently his masterpiece with respect both to craftsmanship and creative imagination. See Plate IV.

(49) Thomas Bewick, *A General History of Quadrupeds*

51A Thomas Bewick

Figures of British Land Birds, engraved on wood by T. Bewick. To which are added a few foreign birds, with their vulgar and scientific names. Vol. I. [all published] Newcastle upon Tyne, by S. Hodgson for R. Beilby and T. Bewick, 1800. 2, 132, [1] l., printed on rectos only. Illus: 250 wood-engraved vignettes of birds, tailpieces, etc., by Bewick. Page size: 9⅝ × 5⅞ inches. Modern boards, uncut. Roscoe 16, variant A.

This volume, "thrown off" for friends "desirous of possessing good impressions of the British Birds, unaccompanied with the descriptive part," testifies to a growing appreciation of the artistic value of Bewick's engravings.

52 Various authors

Select Fables: with cuts, designed and engraved by Thomas and John Bewick, and others, previous to the year 1784: together with a memoir; and a descriptive catalogue of the works of Messrs. Bewick. London, Emerson Charnley . . . 1820. [1], xl, 323 p. Illus: Wood-engraved front. and 336 wood-engraved vignettes, most by the Bewicks. Printer: S. Hodgson. Page size: 8⅞ × 5⅝ inches. Contemp. diced russia.

Bewick deplored this well-produced volume, which to his mind could only serve "to feed the whimsies of bibliomanists," but he tolerated its publication. Though some of the engravings hardly rise above the chapbook level (a number of them are copies), the book is useful as a record of his work before he achieved his mature style.

53 Various authors

The Fables of Aesop, and Others, with designs on wood, by Thomas Bewick. The second edition . . . Newcastle, E. Walker for T. Bewick and son . . . 1823. xxiv, 376 p. Illus: 323 vignettes, head- and tailpieces, etc., by Bewick. Printer: E. Walker. Page size: 8½ × 5 inches. Contemp. calf by R. Riviere. Roscoe 46b, this copy with both the cancellans and the cancellandum.

Bewick intended these fables to inspire virtue in "the Youth of the British Isles." He used his headpieces to depict the incident in each tale that pointed its moral. The resulting glut of narrative sometimes makes the design as heavy as the frame that surrounds it. The tailpieces have no such weight to bear, and in them Bewick's free-ranging observation can be as rewarding as in his *History of British Birds.*

Wood Engraving between Bewick and the Dalziel Brothers

Bewick and his pupils, among them Luke Clennell, William Harvey, John Jackson, Robert Johnson, Ebenezer Landells, and Charlton Nesbit, dominated the craft of wood engraving during the first third of the nineteenth century. Thanks to their example, English craftsmen developed a technical skill unmatched on the Continent. By the 1830s wood engraving had become a highly organized trade, compared by Reynolds Stone to "the *Formschneider* activity of the sixteenth century on an enormous scale" (*Wood Engravings of Thomas Bewick,* p. 21). The production of wood-engraved books multiplied, with an inevitable decline in discrimination, and wood engravings for *Punch, The Illustrated London News,* and other illustrated periodicals founded in the 1840s were sometimes hastily and carelessly done. Yet it is going too far to dismiss this period, so far as wood engraving is concerned, as "the dark age of illustration," as does Philip James (p. 32), or to ignore it entirely, as do other historians. These years saw the appearance of a number of fine books, which are enjoyable in themselves, not merely interesting as precursors of the revival of the sixties.

references James; Life; Linton; Stone.

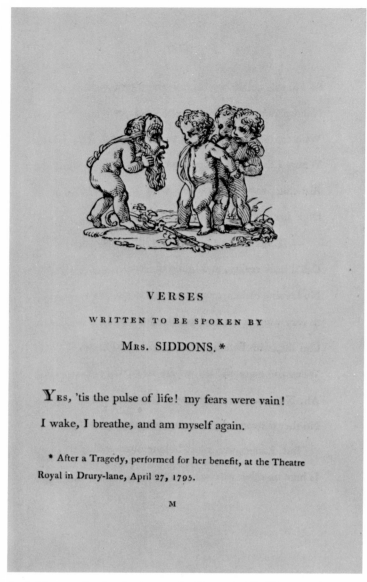

(54) Thomas Stothard, vignette for Rogers's *The Pleasures of Memory*

Thomas Stothard (1755–1834)

54 SAMUEL ROGERS

The Pleasures of Memory, with other poems . . . a new edition, with engravings on wood by Mr. L. Clennell, from drawings by T. Stothard, esq. R.A. London, for T. Cadell and W. Davies, 1810. [8], 167, [1] p. Illus: 34 wood-engraved vignettes by Clennell after Stothard. Printer: T. Bensley. Page size: 6¼ × 3⅞ inches. Contemp. calf.

Luke Clennell, the most gifted of Bewick's pupils, had a lightness of touch that made him particularly adept at reproducing Stothard's delicate and graceful drawings. Rogers's *Poems* of 1812 is an extended version of this volume with many added engravings by Clennell.

William Harvey (1796–1866) and James Northcote (1746–1831)

55 JAMES NORTHCOTE

One Hundred Fables, Original and Selected, by James Northcote, R.A. etc., etc. Embellished with two hundred and eighty engravings on wood. London, George Lawford, 1828. 2 l., iii, 272 p. Illus: Engraved front., 183 wood-engraved vignettes and 100 wood-engraved initials after W. Harvey and Northcote. Printer: J. Johnson. Page size: 10 × 6¼ inches, large paper. Publisher's purple cloth.

56 JAMES NORTHCOTE

Fables, Original and Selected. By the late James Northcote, R.A. **Second Series.** Illustrated by two hundred and eighty engravings on wood. London, John Murray, 1833. lx, 248 p. Illus: 177 wood-engraved vignettes and 101 wood-engraved initials after W. Harvey and Northcote. Printer: C. Whittingham. Page size: 10 × 6¼ inches, large paper. Publisher's purple cloth.

In his preface to *One Hundred Fables* Northcote states that "although the original inventions and designs for the prints at the head of each Fable are my own, yet they have been most excellently drawn on wood" by Harvey, who was solely responsible for the initial letters and tailpieces. Even at its best, as in this book and in *The Tower Menagerie* of 1829, Harvey's work hardly matches Bewick's, but the two volumes of *Fables* make a handsome set, particularly on large paper. In a letter written not long before his death, which is reproduced in facsimile by the gratified publisher, Bewick called *One Hundred Fables* "a brilliant Book." "Little did I think while I was sitting whistling at my work bench," he added, "that wood-engraving would be brought so conspicuously forward, and that I should have pupils to take the lead, in that branch of the art, in the great Metropolis." See Plate XXIX.

Thomas Landseer (1795–1880)

57 ROBERT BURNS

An Address to the Deil, by Robert Burns; with explanatory notes. Illustrated by numerous engravings on wood after designs by Thomas Landseer. London, William Kidd, 1830. [1], added wood-engraved t.p., 23, [1] p. Illus: Added wood-engraved t.p., front.,

6 plates, and 2 wood-engraved vignettes, all after Landseer. Printer: C. Whittingham. Page size: $7\frac{1}{8} \times 4\frac{3}{4}$ inches. Contemp. half morocco; original wrappers bound in.

This little book is a British counterpart to the albums of lithographed *diableries* which appeared across the channel at the same period. The engraved title page is a strikingly original design, and the succeeding illustrations include several fine scenes of a devil-beset Scotland.

Jean Gigoux (1809–1894)

58 ALAIN RENÉ LE SAGE

The Adventures of Gil Blas of Santillane translated from the French of Le Sage by T. Smollett, M.D. and illustrated by Jean Gigoux. London, J. J. Dubouchet . . . 1836. 2 v. I: 486 p. II: 478 p. Illus: 459 wood-engraved vignettes and 135 wood-engraved initials after Gigoux. Printer: R. Willoughby. Page size: $9\frac{3}{4} \times 6\frac{1}{8}$ inches. Publisher's green cloth.

Beginning in 1835 with the Paris edition of this book, so notable for the liveliness and abundance of its illustrations, there was a remarkable flowering of French books with wood engravings. A number of these were quickly republished in London with English texts. In addition to *Gil Blas*, there were *Don Quixote*, 3 volumes (1837), and *Manon Lescaut* (1841), both illustrated by Tony Johannot; La Fontaine's *Fables* (1842), illustrated by Grandville; and *Paul and Virginia* (1839), a somewhat curtailed version of the celebrated Curmer *Paul et Virginie* of 1838, illustrated by many artists. If the English themselves could offer nothing to match these volumes until *The Book of British Ballads*, they could at least take consolation in the omnipresence of English engravers in the lists of illustrations.

John Constable (1776–1837) and others

59 THOMAS GRAY

Elegy Written in a Country Church-Yard. London, John Van Voorst, 1839. vi, [2] p., 32 l. + 6 p. ads., text printed on rectos only. Illus: Wood-engraved t.p. vignette and 32 wood-engraved vignettes after Cattermole, Constable, C. Landseer, W. Mulready, T. Stothard, W. Westall, and others. Printer: S. Bentley. Page size: $7\frac{7}{8} \times 5\frac{1}{4}$ inches. Publisher's brown cloth.

When this book appeared in 1834, the editor presented it as the first attempt to embellish Gray's poem with wood engravings, which had "in some

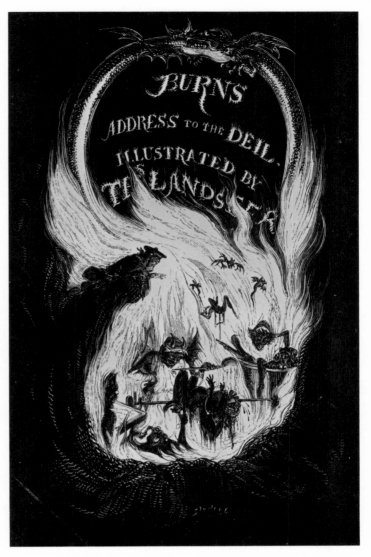

(57) Thomas Landseer, illustration for Burns's *Address to the Deil*

measure" superseded "the use of Copper and Steel" (p. v). The title page cut of Stoke-Poges church, after Constable's drawing, was added in this edition. There are two other engravings after Constable.

George Cattermole (1800–1868) and Phiz

60 CHARLES DICKENS

Master Humphrey's Clock . . . with illustrations by George Cattermole and Hablot Browne. London, Chapman & Hall, 1840–41. 3 v. I: [2], 306 p. II: vi, 306 p. III: vi, 426 p. Illus: Wood-engraved fronts., 168 wood-engraved vignettes, and 24 wood-engraved initials after Cattermole and Phiz. Printer: Bradbury

(60) George Cattermole, illustration for Dickens's *The Old Curiosity Shop*, Little Nell, her father, and Quilp

& Evans. Page size: 10 × 6⅝ inches. Publisher's purple cloth.

This odd mélange which includes *The Old Curiosity Shop*, *Barnaby Rudge*, and an elaborate surrounding apparatus, is the pinnacle of Dickensian Gothic. Appropriately enough, it is illustrated with wood engravings in the text rather than full-page etchings, as in Dickens's earlier novels. Phiz, who is in excellent form, predominates, but there are also fifteen engravings after George Cattermole, whose wonderful clutter of antiquarian or architectural detail is well suited to Dickens's chosen subjects.

Richard Dadd (1819–1887), Henry James Townsend (1810–1890), and others

61 SAMUEL CARTER HALL, EDITOR

The Book of British Ballads [II: Second series] . . . London, Jeremiah How, 1842–44. I: [4], vi, 233, [1] p. II: viii, 235–440, [2] p. Illus: 339 wood-engraved vignettes after E. Corbould, "A. Croquill," R. Dadd, J. Franklin, W. P. Frith, J. Gilbert, W. B. Scott, T. Sibson, J. Tenniel, H. J. Townsend, and others; many pages with wood-engraved borders and initials. Printer: I: Vizetelly brothers. II: A. Spottiswoode. Page size: 10 × 7⅛ inches. Publisher's red morocco.

Though Lane's *Arabian Nights*, 3 volumes (1839), is larger in scope, this is the most ambitious English book with wood engravings during the period under survey. Samuel Carter Hall claims in his preface to have provided "examples of the genius of the more accomplished Artists of Great Britain," thereby challenging "the embellished volumes of Germany and France." ("The supremacy of our English engravers, in this class of Art," he continues, "has long been established.") On the whole his claim was justified. The unusual layout of the page, which left the illustrators with long vertical panels to fill, proved stimulating rather than discouraging, and the designs of Hall's staff artists, E. Corbould, J. Franklin, and John Gilbert, are always workmanlike in their embodiment of the popular Victorian conception of the Middle Ages. The great successes of the book, however, are two excursions into the supernatural: Richard Dadd's "Robin Goodfellow," his one attempt at book illustration, and H. J. Townsend's "Glenfinlas." See Plate XLIII.

61A SAMUEL CARTER HALL, EDITOR

The Book of British Ballads . . . London, Jeremiah How, 1842. V. I. only; [all published in this form?] [4], vi, 233, [1] l., printed on India paper, on one side only. Illus: 182 wood-engraved vignettes after E. Corbould, "A. Croquill," R. Dadd, J. Franklin, W. P. Frith, J. Gilbert, W. B. Scott, T. Sibson, J. Tenniel, J. H. Townsend, and others; many pages with wood-engraved borders and initials. Printer: Vizetelly brothers. Page size: 10⅛ × 7⅝ inches. Green morocco.

This is a rarity of Victorian bookmaking, an India-paper copy printed on one side of the page only. Small editions of the outstanding French illustrated books of the period were issued on *papier de Chine* as a matter of course, and collectors now regard them as treasures. That an English publisher in this instance followed the French example is further testimony to the importance attached to *The Book of British Ballads*.

William Mulready (1786–1863)

62 OLIVER GOLDSMITH

The Vicar of Wakefield . . . with thirty-two illustrations, by William Mulready, R.A. London, John Van Voorst, 1843. xv, 306 p. + 6 p. ads. Illus: 32 wood-engraved vignettes after Mulready. Printer: S. & J. Bentley, Wilson, and Fley. Page size: 8¼ × 5⅞ inches. Publisher's brown cloth.

By choosing the leading genre painter of the day to illustrate Goldsmith's popular classic, the publisher hoped to appeal not merely "to the eye" but also "to the understanding" through his artist's emphasis on "character and construction." And indeed, Mulready, in his thirty-two compact drawings, one at the head of each chapter, not only depicts Dr. Primrose and the other personages of the story, even those with walk-on roles, with a sure and individualizing touch, but also arranges his scenes with as much care as if they were destined to be rendered in oil. As interpretations of fictional narrative, his illustrations sustain comparison with those of Millais, du Maurier, and Walker for the novels of the 1860s. See Plate XLIX.

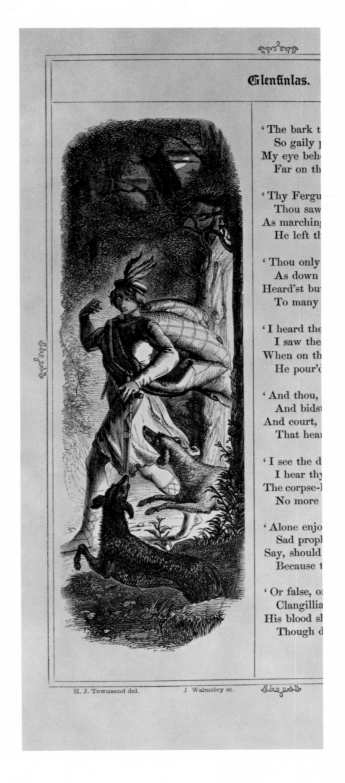

(61) H. J. Townsend, illustration for "Glenfinlas" in *The Book of British Ballads*

(67) William Clarkson Stanfield, illustration for *Stanfield's Coast Scenery*

Books with Steel Engravings

The heyday of engraving on steel was the second quarter of the nineteenth century. Thomas Lupton introduced the technique in 1822 with a mezzotint which yielded 15,000 impressions, many times the number that could be taken from a copperplate. As noted above, it was adopted the following year for mezzotints after Girtin and Turner in *River Scenery* (12). Though steel is much more difficult to engrave than copper, the commercial possibilities it held out soon made it the usual choice of publishers of large editions. The immense vogue between the late 1820s and the early 1840s of annuals like *The Keepsake* and topographical volumes like those illustrated by W. H. Bartlett would have been inconceivable without this new process. Moreover, the use of steel offered certain advantages to the artist. Constable and Martin employed it for mezzotints, and Turner found that the finer lines resulting from its hardness made possible a delicacy and lightness ideally suited to vignettes. Until a few years ago it was assumed that books with steel engravings would always be abundantly available because of the quantities in which they had been printed. Collectors are now discovering that the attrition of time and the depredations of the "breakers" have in fact made acceptable copies hard to find. One can only hope that their belated interest will encourage someone to write the authoritative work on steel engraving which is warranted by its great if transitory popularity and the many fine books to which it gave rise.

REFERENCES Beck; Gray.

63

The Keepsake for 1828 . . . London, for the proprietor by Hurst, Chance, & co. . . . 1827. Engraved t.p., x [1], 312 p. Illus: Engraved front. after Lawrence, engraved t.p. after Corbould, 1 colored engraved plate after Stothard, 16 engraved plates after H. Corbould, J. Martin, R. Smirke, T. Stothard, J. M. W. Turner, J. W. Wright, and others, and 2 wood-engraved vignettes after Corbould. Printer: Thomas Davison. Page size: 7¾×4¼ inches. Red morocco by Riviere.

There were many series of "annuals," that is to say gift books for the Christmas trade, in the late 1820s and the 1830s. Among their titles are *The Christian Keepsake*, *The Forget-Me-Not*, *Gems of Beauty*, and *The Landscape Annual*. In his article "A Word Upon the Annuals" (*Fraser's Magazine*, December, 1837) Thackeray describes their usual makeup. There is "a large weak plate" of a woman who "pats a greyhound, or weeps into a flower-pot, or delivers a letter to a bandy-legged page." Opposite is a song, perhaps entitled "The Forsaken One of Florence," by L.E.L. or Miss Mitford or Lady Blessington, "about water-lilly, chilly, stilly, shivering beside a streamlet, plighted, blighted, love-benighted, falsehood sharper than a gimlet, lost affection, recollection, cut connexion, tears in torrents, true-love token, spoken, broken, sighing, dying, girl of Florence." *The Keepsake* was the best of these series. Its literary contents cannot be defended, but it was handsomely produced, and its steel engravings, at least when they are after drawings by Martin or Turner, can be attractive.

63A

The Keepsake for 1828 . . . London, for the proprietor by Hurst, Chance & co. . . . 1827. Collates as above. Illus: as above; the uncolored plates are India-paper proofs. Page size: 8¾×5⅞ inches, large paper. Publisher's calf.

A copy of the large-paper issue of the same book with the plates on India paper. Among the illustrations is Martin's design for an eastern tale called "The New Deev Alfakir."

(63A) John Martin, illustration for "The New Deev Alfakir," *The Keepsake for 1828*

64

Finden's Gallery of the Graces. A series of portrait illustrations of British poets. From paintings designed expressly for this work by the most eminent British artists. London, David Bogue, [1832–1834]. [6, 74] p. Illus: 36 colored engraved plates after E. Landseer, D. McClise, E. T. Parris, J. W. Wright, and others. Printer: Bradbury and Evans. Page size: 9¼×6⅜ inches. Publisher's green morocco.

This sequel to *Le Byron des Dames* first appeared in parts between 1832 and 1834. Most of the poetry is of the sort mocked by Thackeray, but the delicately colored engravings have great period charm.

William Henry Bartlett (1809–1854)

65 WILLIAM BEATTIE

Switzerland. Illustrated in a series of views taken expressly for this work by W. H. Bartlett, esq. by William Beattie . . . London, George Virtue, 1836. 2 v. I: Added engr. t.p., iv, [2], 188 p. II: Added engr. t.p.,

(66) William Henry Bartlett, illustration for William Beattie's *The Ports . . . of Great Britain*

[4], 152 p. Illus: Added engraved titles and 106 engraved plates after W. H. Bartlett, and 1 folding lithographic map. Printer: R. Clay. Page size: 10⅝ × 8½ inches. Contemp. black blind-stamped morocco by Gaskill of Philadelphia.

The indefatigable Bartlett was the chief producer of volumes of steel-engraved views. For many years he ranged through two continents making or collecting drawings, and since his level of competence hardly varies, the interest of a given title depends largely on the country with which it deals. If his *American Scenery* and *Canadian Scenery* are currently in most demand, it is because plates from these volumes provide the breakers with their readiest market. Collectors not seeking representations of familiar scenes will probably find the grandeur of his Swiss subjects most appealing.

66 WILLIAM BEATTIE

The Ports, Harbours, Watering-Places, and Scenery of Great Britain. Illustrated by views taken on the spot, by W. H. Bartlett; with descriptions by William Beattie . . . London, George Virtue, 1842. 2 v. I: Added engr. t.p., [3], 190 p. II: Added engr. t.p., [3], 155 p. Illus: Engraved fronts., added engraved titles, 122 engraved plates and 1 wood engraving after Bartlett. In this copy the engraved front. for v. I is bound in v. II; an engraved dedication plate to Queen Victoria is inserted as the front. of v. I. Printer: J. Rickerby. Page size: 10½ × 7⅞ inches. Publisher's green morocco.

That even Bartlett could have his moments, chiefly when he deserted foreign lands for native scenes, is witnessed by these volumes. The plates may seem coldly literal when compared with those for Turner's *Southern Coast*, but they rise above the steady mediocrity of most of Bartlett's work. In the gold-stamped morocco binding supplied by the publishers, this is perhaps the handsomest of steel-engraved books of the 1840s.

William Clarkson Stanfield (1793–1867)

67

Stanfield's Coast Scenery. A series of views in the British Channel, from original drawings taken expressly for the work . . . London, by Smith, Elder, and co., 1836. Added engr. t.p., viii, 128 p. Illus: Engraved front., added engraved t.p. and 38 engraved plates after C. Stanfield. Printer: Stewart and co. Page size: 14 × 10½ inches. Publisher's purple morocco.

The prizes among books with steel plates are those in which the engravers had drawings of real merit to reproduce. Turner's work is *hors concours*, but books illustrated by Harding, Prout, and Stanfield also fall into this category. Most spirited of all are Stanfield's marine drawings, and this book can be very attractive on large paper in the publisher's gold-stamped morocco binding.

(67) Publisher's gold-stamped morocco binding

John Martin (1789–1854)

The spirit in which Martin worked is suggested by a passage in his catalogue for the large oil painting "The Fall of Nineveh," which he exhibited in lonely magnificence in 1827: "The mighty cities of Nineveh and Babylon have long since passed away. The accounts of their greatness and splendour may have been exaggerated. But, where strict truth is not essential, the mind is content to find delight in the contemplation of the grand and the marvellous. Into the solemn visions of antiquity we look without demanding the clear daylight of truth. Seen through the mist of ages, the *great* becomes *gigantic*, the *wonderful* swells into the *sublime*." (Quoted by Balston, *John Martin*, p. 107.) This grandiose vision led Martin to the pursuit of what Charles Lamb called the "material sublime." An engineer as well as an artist, he calculated his effects with care. In a pamphlet about "Belshazzar's Feast," a painting five by eight feet, Martin points under the heading "Scale of preparation" to "a figure six feet high, by which the length of the Halls is found to be one mile" (Balston, p. 261). In his mezzotints he turned to Milton and the Bible for vast scenes of the triumphs and disasters worked by supernatural intervention which he could similarly display in small compass. The multiplication of impressions made possible by the use of steel plates caused his illustrations to be widely circulated, and for fifty years they held sway over the literary imagination, both in England and in France. After a long period of neglect, they are now finding new admirers.

REFERENCES   Balston, *John Martin*; Balston, *Library*; Klingender, ed. Elton; Seznec; Todd.

68

[**Views of Sezincot House.** 1818?]. Illus: 10 colored aquatint plates by Martin. Page size: $20\frac{5}{8} \times 14\frac{1}{4}$ inches. Contemp. red velvet.

This early book is so rare as to be virtually unknown, yet it is one of the masterpieces of aquatinting. In 1817 Sir Charles Cockerell, a nabob with a taste for Hindu architecture, employed Martin to depict Sezincot House in the Cotswolds. This still-surviving mansion in the ancient Indian style had just been completed by his architect brother Samuel Pepys Cockerell, working from drawings by Thomas Daniell. Its resemblance to the Regent's Brighton pavilion, deriving from coincidence rather than imitation, was first pointed out by Humphrey Repton. The ten plates etched by Martin and aquatinted by F. C. Lewis show not only the main buildings but also the grounds with their cave and pool, adorned by the "Temple of Suryah" and "Fountain of Maha Dao." *Sezincot House* was issued privately in a very small edition. In its binding of contemporary red velvet, this must be the most splendid of surviving copies. It bears the bookplate of George, Duke of Cambridge, who became Commander-in-Chief. Since he was born in 1819, he must have had it from an earlier recipient. See above, opposite page xxvi.

69   JOHN MILTON

The **Paradise Lost** of Milton with illustrations, designed and engraved by John Martin . . . London, Septimus Prowett, 1825–27. 12 parts, here bound as two vols. I: [5], 228 p. II: [4], 218 p. Illus: 24 mezzotint plates by Martin. Bound in are the original wrappers. Printer: T. White. Page size: $14\frac{7}{8} \times 10\frac{7}{8}$ inches. Half morocco.

This book was one of the great publishing enterprises of the age. It appeared in eight different formats, four with the large plates (8 by 11 inches) and four with the small (6 by 8 inches). Martin executed the forty-eight mezzotints himself. The apocalyptic romanticism of his conceptions had many sources: the monumental buildings of London, the engravings of Piranesi, the many recently published volumes of eastern views, even incandescent gas, coalpit accidents, and Brunel's new Thames Tunnel. The resulting illustrations may be heterogeneous, but they are also unforgettable. When Berlioz visited London in 1851, he attended the annual service of charity schoolchildren at St. Paul's, where he heard a chorus of 6,500 voices. That night he dreamed of Martin's "Satan Presiding at the Infernal Council." "J'entends sans cesse rouler dans ma tête cette clameur harmonieuse, *All people that on earth do dwell*, et je voyais tourbilloner l'église Saint Paul; je me retrouvais dans son intérieur; il était, par une bizarre transformation, changé en pandaemonium: *c'était la mise en scène du célèbre tableau de Martin.* Au lieu de l'archévêque dans sa chaire, j'avais Satan sur son trône; au lieu de milliers de fidèles et d'enfants groupés autour de lui, des peuples de démons et de damnés dardaient du sein des ténèbres visibles leurs regards enflammés, et l'amphithéâtre de fer sur lequel ces millions étaient assis vibrait tout entier d'une manière terrible, en repandant d'affreuses harmonies." (Quoted by Seznec, p. 34.) See Plate XXVII.

69A JOHN MILTON

The **Paradise Lost** of Milton with illustrations, designed and engraved by John Martin . . . London, Septimus Prowett, 1827. 2 v. I: [3], 228 p. II: [4], 218 p. Illus: 24 mezzotint plates by Martin. Printer: T. White. Page size: 10½ × 7⅛ inches. Contemp. blue morocco by Charles Murton.

The octavo edition of *Paradise Lost* is also a handsome book, but the mezzotints suffer greatly from reduction.

&❧ Graphite drawing with scratched highlights, a version of "The Expulsion from Paradise" in *Paradise Lost.* Sheet size: 5¾ × 7⅝ inches.

Charles A. Ryskamp

70

[**Illustrations of the Bible.** 1831–35.] 10 parts, here bound as 1 v. Illus: 20 mezzotint plates by Martin, each with 1 l. letterpress text. Page size: 18⅛ × 13¾ inches. Contemp. cloth over boards.

Martin served both as printer and publisher for his Old Testament illustrations. The mezzotints were superbly produced, but all expense was spared with regard to the accompanying text which consisted of a series of single sheets, inches smaller than the illustrations, with titles and part numbers written initially by the artist himself. From the beginning, sales were unsatisfactory, and they dwindled to hardly more than a score of copies as the part issue straggled to its conclusion. Hence Martin never proceeded to the New Testament, and posterity was deprived of his version of The Revelation of St. John the Divine. Yet the Bible mezzotints are in no way inferior to those for *Paradise Lost*. Except for the absence of aerial views, the landscape of Martin's imagination has not changed. Again there are lush valleys with stupendous mountains in the background as the setting for the opening domestic episodes and colossal cities as the setting for the crowded later scenes in which the destiny of a nation is traced. The cloth cover of this copy, lettered in gold "The Book of Martyn," suggests that it may have belonged to the artist himself. See Plate XXVIII.

70A

Illustrations of the Bible. Designed and engraved by John Martin. London, Charles Tilt, 1838. [4, 20] l., text printed on one side only. Illus: 20 mezzotint plates by John Martin. Page size: 17 × 11⅝ inches. Publisher's green cloth.

Disheartened by the failure of his venture, Martin sold his remaining Bible prints as well as the plates themselves to Charles Tilt. This publisher issued a proper book containing them in 1838, noting in his preface that "the circulation of this Series of Plates was, from circumstances, confined almost entirely among MR. MARTIN's friends." In book form the mezzotints achieved the success that they should have commanded from the first. Early copies, like this one, often have fine impressions, since Tilt exhausted the stock of prints he had obtained from Martin before putting his plates to use.

John Constable (1776–1837)

Constable's first biographer, C. R. Leslie, used Coleridge's words, "a secret confided to the public and very faithfully kept," to describe the reception accorded Constable's *English Scenery*. The neglect with which the painter was treated by his contemporaries has yielded to ever-increasing acclaim. Yet his one book has never achieved the standing it deserves, perhaps because of the apathy with which mezzotint has been regarded since the eighteenth century. There are signs, however, that its hour may finally have come.

Constable employed the young engraver David Lucas (1802–1881) to make these mezzotints on steel in 1829. Though a longer sequence was at one time planned, he finally fixed on five numbers of four plates each with frontispiece and vignette added. The series sold poorly, both in the part issue (1830–1832), which was protracted by Constable's indecision and Lucas's dilatoriness, and in book form. Indeed, when Leslie published the first edition of his *Life of Constable*, he was able to buy 180 sets of the mezzotints for inclusion in its pages. Lucas subsequently executed twenty-six further mezzotints after Constable, in most of which he had the painter's guidance.

Though Constable did not himself work on the plates of *English Scenery*, his collaboration with Lucas was very close, and he hoped that the book would bring him the wide recognition that the *Liber Studiorum* had secured for Turner. His particular aim was to initiate the public into "The Phenomena of Chiar'oscuro," as observable in "the delightful Home Scenery of England," so presented as to show "the day, the hour, the sunshine, and the shade." Certainly no prints better display the effects of light upon clouds, fields, trees, and water under different atmospheric conditions than Lucas's firmly organized yet ethereal mezzotints. Though they lack the appeal of color,

they otherwise exemplify just the aspects of Constable's art that made him the leading precursor of impressionism.

REFERENCES Gray; Shirley.

71 JOHN CONSTABLE

Various Subjects of Landscape, Characteristic of English Scenery, principally intended to display the phenomena of the chiar'oscuro of nature: from pictures painted by John Constable, R.A. Engraved by David Lucas. London, by Mr. Constable, 1833. [4] l. Illus: Mezzotint front. and 21 mezzotint plates after Constable. Page size: 10⅞ × 16⅝ inches. Contemp. half morocco. Inserted is an a.l.s. dated West Walk, October 30, 1833, from Constable to Mr. Hardisty. 3 p., with address. 8vo.

An exceptional copy given to Mrs. Hardisty by Constable in gratitude for "all her kind notice" of his "dear little Girls." It is inscribed: "Rosa Hardisty, The Gift of John Constable RA—Hampstead October 1833," and he has annotated thirteen of its plates: Spring ("A Mill in a Common"), Autumnal Sun Set ("Peasants returning homeward"), Noon ("West End fields Hampstead"), Yarmouth, Norfolk ("Morning Breeze"), Summer Morning ("Harwich Harbour in the distance"), A Heath ("Hampstead Sand Pit"), A Seabeach ("Brighton a heavy surf"), Mill Stream ("River Stour near Flatford Mill"), Old Sarum ("Evening—'Here we have no abiding City' "), A Summerland ("Rainy Day"), A Mill ("Dedham Essex"), Weymouth Bay, Dorsetshire ("Tempestuous afternoon"), Hadleigh Castle near the Nore ("Morning"). In an accompanying letter to Mr. Hardisty of October 30, 1833, presenting the book, Constable writes: "I have this morning carefully looked over a copy of my Work—and with my little retouchings here and there—I believe it

(72) C. R. Leslie, *Memoirs of the Life of John Constable*

would not be in my power to find a better one. . . . My book is esteemed by my professional friends—more perhaps than by the world—which I indeed anticipated—but why should artists—and others in their publications—climb downwards—and be so ready to follow—instead of lead, the taste of the publick." See Plate xxxv.

72 C. R. Leslie

Memoirs of the Life of John Constable, Esq. R.A., composed chiefly of his letters . . . London, James Carpenter, 1843. [3], 152 p. Illus: Mezzotint front. after Leslie, and 22 mezzotint plates after Constable. Printer: C. Whittingham. Page size: $14\frac{3}{8} \times 10\frac{1}{2}$ inches. Publisher's quarter morocco.

As already noted, the twenty-two plates of *English Scenery* supply the illustrations for Leslie's biography. Since he used the stock that remained at Constable's death, there is little difference in quality between the prints in this book and those

issued in 1833. Indeed, they may even be in earlier states, since Constable preferred to provide his friends with copies embodying his "little retouchings here and there." This copy has the pencilled note "Abram Constable Esq—selected by C R Leslie." Abram Constable, the painter's brother, has also signed it in three places.

73 John Constable

English Landscape Scenery: a series of forty mezzotint engravings on steel, by David Lucas. From pictures painted by John Constable, R.A. London, Henry Bohn, 1855. [8] p. Illus: 40 mezzotint plates after Constable. Page size: $16\frac{5}{8} \times 11\frac{1}{2}$ inches. Publisher's half morocco.

This volume contains the twenty-two mezzotints on steel of *English Scenery* and eighteen others. Though Lucas's plates were worn and considerably reworked by the time they were used for this book, Andrew Shirley's reference (p. 156) to "Bohn's degraded republication" is too severe.

John Constable 47

(76) John Sell Cotman, *Liber Studiorum*

Etching in the Early Decades of the Nineteenth Century

During the first half of the nineteenth century etching was widely employed in books, at first on copper but after 1825 increasingly on steel. Regarded almost exclusively as a convenient means of reproducing drawings for illustrations, initially of landscapes and buildings but latterly of scenes in novels, it became the principal technique of such comic illustrators as Cruikshank, Thackeray, Leech, and Phiz. Their contributions to magazines, however, were often engraved on wood by professional craftsmen.

REFERENCES Clark; Gray; Kitson; Life; Popham; Rienaecker; Sparrow.

Thomas Gainsborough (1727–1788)

74

A Collection of Prints, Illustrative of English Scenery; from the drawings and sketches of Gainsborough: in the various collections of the Right Honourable Baroness Lucas; Viscount Palmerston; George Hibbert, esq., Dr. Monro, and several other gentlemen. Engraved and published by W. F. Wells and J. Laporte [1802–1805]. 2 l. Illus: 71 soft-ground etched plates, some with wash, some with scraped highlights. Printer: Watts and Bridgewater. Page size: 12 ¼ × 15 ⅝ inches. Three-quarters calf. Abbey, *Life*, 203 (1819 reissue).

These seventy-one soft-ground etchings were published by Wells and LaPorte, who etched the plates, between March 1, 1802, and January 1, 1805: thirty-one prints in 1802, twenty-eight in 1803, nine in 1804, and three in 1805. It seems reasonable to assign the book to 1805. In this copy twenty-eight of the plates are tinted by hand in one or more colors. The etchings are usually seen in Boydell's reissue of 1819, which has sixty plates.

John Sell Cotman (1782–1842)

75   DAWSON TURNER

Architectural Antiquities of Normandy by John Sell Cotman; accompanied by historical and descriptive notices by Dawson Turner esq., F.R. and A.S. . . . London, for John and Arthur Arch . . . 1822. 2 v. in 1. I: viii, [6], 58 p. II: [4], 59–125 p. Illus: 1 etched vignette, 96 etched plates by Cotman, 1 wood-engraved vignette. Printer: Sloman. Page size: 19⅛ × 13⅜ inches. Half red morocco.

Dawson Turner's "notices" are not without significance as an early inquiry into French Gothic architecture, but the glory of the book is Cotman's 100 etchings, in which he transcends by far the role of antiquarian recorder his patron had assigned to him. He knows how to give artistic interest even to studies of architectural detail, and when he has before him a subject like the "West Front of Rouen Cathedral," which cost him "more than twenty weeks' hard labour," or the various Norman castles, the result is superb. See Plate XXII.

76

Liber Studiorum; a series of sketches and studies, by John Sell Cotman . . . London, Henry G. Bohn, 1838. 2 l. Illus: 48 etched and soft-ground etched plates by Cotman. Page size: 19 × 13½ inches. Three-quarters green morocco.

These soft-ground etchings were executed for the most part between 1805 and 1814, but they were not published until Bohn included them in his five-part collection of Cotman's etchings in 1838. A separate issue of the *Liber Studiorum* on small paper was published at the same time. Done entirely for Cotman's own pleasure, they have a charm that is lacking in many of his more elaborate and finished plates for *Architectural Antiquities of Normandy*.

Augustus Welby Pugin (1812–1852)

77   AUGUSTUS WELBY PUGIN

Contrasts: or, a parallel between the noble edifices of the fourteenth and fifteenth centuries, and similar buildings of the present day; shewing the present decay of taste: accompanied by appropriate text. By A. Welby Pugin, architect. London, for the author, 1836. Added etched t.p., iv, 50 p. + 2 p. ads. Illus: Etched front., added etched t.p., and 13 etched plates by Pugin. Printer: James Moyes. Page size: 11⅞ × 9¼ inches. Contemp. green cloth.

Pugin's aim in this entertaining book is to show "the wretched state of architecture at the present day" when contrasted with that of the fourteenth and fifteenth centuries. He writes with verve and wit, but his etchings are his most mordant strokes. Designed to arouse rather than to inform his readers, they constitute one of the most effective uses of illustrations for polemical purposes in England during the nineteenth century. See Plate XXXVII.

77A   AUGUSTUS WELBY PUGIN

Contrasts: or, a parallel between the noble edifices of the Middle Ages, and corresponding buildings of the present day; shewing the present decay of taste. Accompanied by appropriate text. By A. Welby Pugin, architect. London, Charles Dolman, 1841. Added lithographic t.p., v, 104 p. Illus: Lithographic front., added lithographic t.p., 16 lithographic plates, 1 woodcut plate and 2 woodcut vignettes by Pugin. Printer: Richards. Page size: 11⅛ × 8½ inches. Publisher's green cloth.

In this edition of *Contrasts* Pugin moderated his Catholic bias, greatly extended his text, and added five illustrations. One of these, his contrast between a Catholic town in 1440 and in 1840, is particularly telling. The later illustrations were reproduced lithographically, a point that does not seem to have been noted previously, and they are inferior to those in the edition of 1836.

Thomas Sibson

78

Illustrations of Master Humphrey's Clock, in seventy plates, designed and etched on steel. By Thomas Sibson. The Old Curiosity Shop – Barnaby Rudge. London, Robert Tyas, 1842. 8 p. Illus: Woodcut t.p. vignette, etched front., and 71 etched plates by Sibson. Page size: 10⅛ × 6⅝ inches. Red morocco.

When first published (60), *The Old Curiosity Shop* and *Barnaby Rudge* were illustrated with wood engravings rather than with etchings, as had previously been the rule in Dickens's novels. Sibson filled the resulting gap with a series of unauthorized etchings on steel. We are thus enabled to see what a clever contemporary illustrator not under Dickens's supervision could make of his novels. One notices particularly how well Sibson used his freedom, not merely in his choice and interpretation of characters and scenes, but also in the *croquis* with which he adorns some of his plates.

The most notable example is a page of Dick Swiveller's doodlings on an envelope bearing the recently issued "penny black" postage stamp. Sibson was a favorite with the Pre-Raphaelites. Writing of his "able and remarkable etchings," W. M. Rossetti noted: "There was a series of these, very familiar to my Brother and myself towards 1842, illustrating Dickens's *Old Curiosity Shop* and *Barnaby Rudge*: at a later date my copy of this series was so much admired by Burne-Jones that I presented it to him." (*Rossetti Papers, 1862–1870*, London, 1903, p. 157.)

(77) Augustus Welby Pugin, *Contrasts*

(78) Thomas Sibson, etching for Dickens's *The Old Curiosity Shop*

The First Half Century of Lithography

The early history of lithography in England was marked by a promising head start, three decades of dawdling, and twenty-five years of solid achievement. This achievement, unfortunately, has been a long time gaining recognition. Dazzled by admittedly more spectacular accomplishments across the channel, where a score of notable artists headed by Daumier, Delacroix, and Géricault turned their hands to lithography, and bemused by Ruskin's often quoted admonition to students that they should "let no lithographic work come into the house if you can help it, nor even look at any" (*Elements of Drawing*, p. 340), amateurs for many years disdained English books illustrated with lithographs. Only with the appearance between 1952 and 1956 of Major Abbey's three great catalogues, in which lithography was accorded equal standing with aquatint, were collectors alerted to the possibilities of the field. In recent years, lithography has become if anything almost too popular, given the dwindling availability of the books in which it was employed.

After Aloys Senefelder invented lithography in 1798, he sought to extend its use throughout Europe. He entrusted its English promotion to an associate named Philipp André, who in April, 1803, issued the first part of *Specimens of Poly-autography, Consisting of Impressions taken from Original Drawings made Purposely for this work*. Though six parts of six prints each were planned, only two were published. The artists included Thomas Barker of Bath, Barry, Fuseli, Stothard, and West. It has become a work of great rarity, even in the reissue of 1806.

Despite its fragmentary state, André's venture was the most impressive early lithographic album published anywhere, but there was little in the way of a sequel in England. What is usually seen as the supreme advantage of the process, the almost unlimited number of satisfactory impressions that can be taken from a lithographic stone, made it appear cheap and unworthy to artists accustomed to the small editions obtained from copperplates. Not until 1819, when Senefelder's pupil Charles Hullmandel established his lithographic printing shop in London, did lithography come into wide use. One of his early publications was that masterpiece of French lithography, the so-called "*série Anglaise*" (*Various Subjects Drawn from Life on Stone*, 12 lithographs, 1821) of Théodore Géricault. In general, however, the medium was used for drawing manuals, routine volumes of views, and reproductions of sketches by aristocratic ladies. It is not surprising, then, that in his textbook, *The Art of Drawing on Stone* of 1824, Hullmandel should have complained that in England lithography was "despised and abused by artists of talent." He hoped that these artists would eventually follow the lead of their French colleagues. With the prejudice against lithography as a "democratic process" thus overcome, the superior classes, who currently viewed lithographs "with as much concern as they would hieroglyphics," might at last show the interest in them displayed by the French. (Man, p. xxv.)

During the 1830s this change gradually came about. The gentlemanly John Doyle ("H.B.") used it for the 917 political caricatures with which he amused the upper classes between 1829 and 1851. Count D'Orsay made more than 100 lithographic profile portraits of social, political, and literary celebrities. Though Constable and Turner never employed lithography, it became customary for portfolios of sketches by lesser artists like Haghe, Harding, Lewis, Nash, Prout, and Stanfield. With the disappearance of aquatint, indeed, lithography, in black and white, tinted, or colored by hand, was confirmed as the standard medium for the illustration of large books, a status it retained until it was superseded in turn by chromolithog-

(79) John Thomas Smith, *Antiquities of Westminster*, lithograph   (79) John Thomas Smith, *Antiquities of Westminster*, engr

raphy in the 1850s. During this period the notable English lithographic works—the books of Bourne, Boys, Lear, Prout (in *Flanders and Germany*), Roberts, and Simpson—made their appearance.

REFERENCES Abbey, *Life in England*; Abbey, *Scenery*; Abbey, *Travel*; Curtis, *Bonington*; Groschwitz; Hardie; Hogarth, *Artist as Reporter*; Klingender, ed. Elton; Man, *Artists' Lithographs*; Man, *Prints*; Pennell, *Lithography*; Roundell; Ruskin, *Elements of Drawing*; Twyman.

79 JOHN THOMAS SMITH

Antiquities of Westminster . . . containing two hundred and forty-six engravings of topographical objects, of which one hundred and twenty-two no longer remain. By John Thomas Smith . . . London, for J. T. Smith . . . 1807. [6], xv, [1], 276 p. Illus: 5 woodengraved vignettes, 37 etched, engraved, and aquatint plates (14 colored), 1 lithographic plate, all by or after Smith. Printer: T. Bensley. Page size: 13⅞ × 11½ inches. Original boards. Abbey, *Scenery*, 211.

The first issue of this book has its place in history because it contains at page 48 what is said to be the earliest English lithographic book illustration. The subject is the Painted Chamber of the Palace of Westminster in 1800. The lithograph is offered as "a specimen of a new mode of producing prints," which could be expected to "furnish many more impressions, without retouching, than a common plate." Despite the cooperation of Philipp André, the publisher of *Specimens of Polyautography*, the experiment was a failure. It took "almost as much time to finish up a drawing on stone as it would have to engraven it on copper," and the stone itself was spoiled after 300 impressions. (Pp. 48–50.) An engraving on copper had to be substituted. This copy contains both lithograph and engraving. It may be mentioned that *Antiquities of Westminster*, a book plagued by misfortunes, was not completed until 1809, when *Sixty-two Additional Plates to Smith's Antiquities* appeared.

Thomas Barker (1769–1847)

80

Forty lithographic impressions from drawings by Thomas Barker, selected from his **Studies of Rustic Figures** after nature. Bath, published by subscription, 1813. [5] p. Illus: 40 lithographic plates by Barker. Printer: Wood & co. Page size: 16½ × 13. Publisher's green cloth.

Issued in an edition of "no more than Two Hundred Copies," this is the most substantial English album of lithographic "incunables." Barker's method was to sketch members of the poorer classes, usually children or old men, "from the life at various times as the objects presented themselves," and afterwards to make facsimiles of these drawings on stone. In his preface he announced another collection, which in fact was published the following year as *Thirty-two Lithographic Impressions from Pen Drawings of Landscape Scenery*.

81

Castles of Alnwick, & Warkworth, &c. from sketches by C. F. Duchess of Northumberland. [London?], 1823. [4], 36 l. Illus: Lithographic t.p., 29 lithographic plates (1 colored), 9 lithographic vignettes (1 tinted), and 7 wood-engraved initials. All but the colored plate are printed on India paper. Printer: W. Nicol. Page size: 11⅛ × 8½ inches. Contemp. (publisher's?) quarter morocco.

This volume, which is saved from being what we would today call a "vanity" publication chiefly by J. D. Harding's participation as lithographer, may stand as a particularly handsome example of the sort of work which came Hullmandel's way before lithography gained general acceptance by professional artists in England. This copy is inscribed: "Given by Her Grace the Duchess of Northumberland to Earl Talbot at Alnwick Castle 9th October 1832."

Richard Parkes Bonington (1802–1828)

82

[**Scotch Sketches** drawn on stone by the late R. P. Bonington. London. Published by Colnaghi Son et [sic] Co. No 11, Pall-Mall East. 1829.] Thirteen lithographs on India paper dated 1828. Atherton Curtis, *Bonington*, 31–43.

Bonington was the great early English master of lithography, but during his short life he worked almost entirely for French publications. Hence it is not appropriate to show his so-called "*petite Normandie*"—the *Restes et fragmens d'architecture du moyen age* of 1824—or the segments of Baron Taylor's *Voyages pittoresques et romantiques dans l'ancienne france—La Normandie*, 2 volumes (1820–1825), and *Franche Comté* (1825)—in which his best-known lithographs appear. All that can be offered are India proofs of the thirteen plates of Colnaghi's English reissue of his contributions to F.-A. Pernot's *Vues pittoresques de l'Ecosse* (1826) as they figure in a magnificent *oeuvre* of Bonington established in a folio album by his friend J. Carpenter. These lithographs ostensibly follow the drawings of

(80) Thomas Barker, *Studies of Rustic Figures*

Pernot, but Atherton Curtis believes that in the landscape plates Bonington worked with considerable freedom, while the figure plates depicting "A Duel between Frank and Rashleigh" in *The Bride of Lammermoor* and "The Escape from Argyle Castle" in *A Legend of Montrose* are entirely his own.

A word should be added about Carpenter's remarkable collection of prints by and after Bonington. He was the publisher of the young artist's chief contemporary memorial, *Subjects from the Works of the Late R. P. Bonington Drawn on Stone by J. D. Harding*, the twenty-two plates of which are represented in the album by proofs on India paper. Also present are "*la petite Normandie*" on yellow paper and five other lithographs by Bonington as well as early states of "Bologna," his one completed etching. But the most remarkable testimony to Carpenter's piety is afforded by fine impressions of forty-two contemporary prints after Bonington, in addition to Harding's *Subjects*, some of which are described as "unique." The album has the bookplate of Napoleon III, and a note on

the final page suggests that it was acquired from Carpenter in 1849 when the Emperor was still "S.A.I. le Prince Napoléon."

Samuel Prout (1784–1852)

83

Facsimiles of Sketches Made in Flanders and Germany and drawn on stone by Samuel Prout . . . [London], C. Hullmandel's Lithography, [1833]. Lithographic t.p., and dedication l., 2 l. letterpress. Illus: 50 lithographic plates by Prout. Printer: Hullmandel. Page size: 21 7/8 × 14 5/8 inches. Contemp. purple cloth.

Prout was a pioneer lithographer who employed the process as early as 1817, when most of his fellow artists were ignorant or contemptuous of it. His friend and disciple Ruskin specifically exempted Prout from his dismissal of lithography in *The Elements of Drawing*, noting that "all his published lithographic sketches are of the greatest value, wholly unrivalled in power of composition, and in love and feeling of architectural subjects" (p. 339). Joseph Pennell had reservations about

THE ESCAPE FROM ARGYLE-CASTLE

(82) Richard Parkes Bonington, *Scotch Sketches*

some of Prout's volumes of lithographs, but even he endorsed what Ruskin called the "grand subjects" of *Flanders and Germany*. Unfortunately these lithographs are now assiduously sought after as single prints, and complete copies of the book have virtually disappeared. The volume is inscribed: "R: Elizabeth Prout the gift of her affectionate father S. Prout June 21st 1833," and the impressions of the lithographs, many of them on grey paper, are particularly fine. See Plate XXXVI.

John Frederick Lewis (1805–1876)

84

Lewis's Sketches of Spain & Spanish Character made during his tour in that country in the years 1833–4. Drawn on stone from the original sketches entirely by himself. London, F. Moon . . . [1836]. 2 l. Illus: Colored lithographic t.p. vignette and 25 colored lithographic plates by Lewis. 2 l. of text lacking in this copy. Printer: C. Hullmandel. Page size: 21¾ × 17¾ inches. Original portfolio. Tooley 302.

The occasional large-scale scenes in "Spanish" Lewis's portfolio are remarkably varied: a mosque in Cordova, the Rock of Gibraltar, a plaza in Seville, and the river Tajo near Ronda. As a rule, however, the artist has narrowed his attention to the people he saw around him, peasants, smugglers, monks, and rustic beauties, following their daily rounds or watching a bullfight, drinking in a posada, or dancing on a terrace. In examining copies with the lithographs colored by hand, one has the sense of becoming for the time being the privileged observer of a simple, unhurried, cheerful world. Like Prout's *Flanders and Germany*, this work of Lewis's escaped Ruskin's ban against lithographs in *The Elements of Drawing*, where it is described as "very valuable" (p. 340).

John Cooke Bourne (b. 1814)

85 JOHN BRITTON

Drawings of the London and Birmingham Railway, by John C. Bourne, with an historical and descriptive account, by John Britton . . . London, J. C. Bourne . . . 1839. 26 p. Illus: Tinted lithographic t.p. and 30 tinted lithographic plates by Bourne, 1 wood-engraved vignette after Bourne, 1 engraved map. Printer: Moyes and Barclay. Page size: 21¼ × 14⅝ inches. Publisher's (?) morocco. Abbey, *Life*, 398 (different printer).

This copy is inscribed "To Mariano Montealegre As a memento of esteem and regard from his sincere friend Mrs. Robert Stephenson—November 1839." Robert Stephenson (1803–1859), the husband of the donor and the son of George Stephenson, was Engineer-in-Chief of the London and Birmingham Railway, completed between 1833 and 1838 at a cost of £6 million. Bourne's drawings, made during the later phase of its construction, "represent, not only some of the most striking scenery upon the line, but the peculiar manual and mechanical operations connected with the execution of the principal works. Amongst them the process of tunnelling, the formation of embankments and cuttings, the gear and machinery used in sinking shafts, and the subterraneous works of the stationary engine-house at Camden Town, are at once remarkable and interesting." (P. 13.) Stephenson's expedients for dealing with the problems presented by the terrain yielded Bourne some striking drawings. Most difficult and expensive of all was the Kilsby Tunnel, where eighteen working shafts were needed to cope with "the great quantities of water and quicksand." Illustrations XXX and XXXI show scenes under a working shaft, where the opaqueness of the humid atmosphere is strikingly presented, and under one of the great ventilating shafts. (P. 23.) See Plate XXXIX.

86

The History and Description of the Great Western Railway, including . . . numerous views of its principal viaducts, bridges, tunnels, stations . . . from drawings taken expressly for this work, and executed in lithography, by John C. Bourne . . . London, David Bogue, 1846. [2], iv, [1], 58, [57]–75 p. Illus: Added tinted lithographic t.p., 33 lithographic plates, some tinted, 5 lithographic vignettes, 3 colored lithographic charts and maps. Page size: 21 × 16½ inches. Three-quarters calf. Abbey, *Life*, 399.

The London and Birmingham Railway had been a high-pressure commercial venture, connecting one trading metropolis with another, which left in its wake the devastation so memorably described in chapter 6 of *Dombey and Son*. The London and Bristol line was altogether more genteel, both in its purpose and its setting. The task assigned to Isambard Kingdom Brunel was to build a broad-gauge, high-speed railway that would carry chiefly first-class passengers through some of the loveliest scenery in England. Hence Bourne paid less attention in his drawings to the line's engineering features than to its surroundings, which remained picturesque despite the intrusion of "progress." To a modern eye, indeed, he makes even the terminals seem attractive, and a panorama such as that from above the Box Tunnel, a few miles on the London side of Bath, is breathtaking. Though *The Great Western Railway* was in no way inferior to its predecessor, the timing of its appearance was unlucky. The "Railway Mania" of 1845 had induced in the British public a certain skepticism about the glories of steam transportation.

Thomas Shotter Boys (1803–1874)

87   CHARLES OLLIER

Original Views of London as It Is. Drawn from nature expressly for this work and lithographed by Thomas Shotter Boys . . . With historical and descriptive notices of the views by Charles Ollier. London, Thomas Boys, 1842. Letterpress t.p., lithographic dedication, each plate with 1 l. letterpress text, printed on rectos only. Illus: 26 colored lithographic plates by Boys. Page size: 22½ × 18 inches. Publisher's portfolio. Abbey, *Scenery*, 239.
  Paul Mellon

Boys learned lithography in Paris, and his early prints appeared in several French publications including Taylor's *Voyages pittoresques*. During his brief period of prosperity after returning to England in 1837, however, he produced two of the great English illustrated books, this volume and *Picturesque Architecture in Paris, . . . etc.* (225). *London as It Is* became an immediate success, particularly in its colored form, and he is said to have tinted thirty copies himself. Boys is now recognized as a significant painter, and the importance of *Picturesque Architecture* grows more apparent every year. Hence it no longer seems adequate to call him "the Rowlandson of Victorian London," as used to be the fashion, yet his vivid realization of the thronging metropolis in the early 1840s, which made his contemporaries admit that familiar city scenes could be as "picturesque" as mountains or lakes, has lost none of its appeal. A facsimile edition of *London as It Is* was published by Charles Traylen in 1954–1955. See Plate XLI.

David Roberts (1796–1864)

88   GEORGE CROLY

The Holy Land, Syria, Idumea, Egypt & Nubia. From drawings made on the spot by David Roberts, R.A. with historical descriptions, by the Revd. George Croly, L.L.D. Lithographed by Louis Haghe. London, F. G. Moon, 1842[-45]. Collates as in Abbey; this copy is in 20 original parts, with the plates "colored and mounted as originals, in portfolio." Page size: 24¼ × 17¼ inches. Orig. portfolios. Abbey, *Travel*, II, 385.

For this work, which was completed by *Egypt and Nubia* (21 parts, 1846–1849), Roberts's drawings of 1838 and 1839 were lithographed by Louis Haghe. His prints are the same size as Roberts's originals, which are almost equally divided between large plates like "Jerusalem, from the Mount of Olives" and smaller plates like "Jaffa." In telling of the importance to his own artistic development of Roberts's drawings, Ruskin describes them as "the first studies ever made conscientiously by an English painter, not to exhibit his own skill, or make capital out of his subjects, but to give true portraiture of scenes of historical and religious interest" (*Praeterita*, volume II, chapter 2). With the advent of photography Roberts's fidelity of detail became less useful, but the aesthetic value of *The Holy Land* was not diminished. The work may fairly be compared, indeed, with Daniell's *A Voyage Round Great Britain* (41), in that just as Daniell's volumes are the most ambitious and impressive of English books illustrated with aquatints, so Roberts's are the most ambitious and impressive of English books illustrated with lithographs. See Plate XLIV.

William Simpson (1823–1889)

89

The Seat of War in the East, by William Simpson . . . First [Second] series. London, Paul & Dominic Colnaghi . . . 1855–56. Collates as in Abbey; this copy lacks the lithographic dedication leaf, the letterpress text, plates 18, 46, 50, 51, and keys for plate 20 and the Second series. Printer: Day & son. Page size: 21¾ × 14⅛ inches. Publisher's brown cloth. Abbey, *Travels*, 237.

If W. H. Russell established the profession of "special correspondent" by his dispatches to the

VIEW FROM ABOVE THE TUNNEL. BOX.

(86) John C. Bourne, *The Great Western Railway*

Times from the Crimea, Simpson at the same time created the profession of pictorial journalist. His drawings from "the seat of war" reached the public in lithographed form not long after Russell's words. Though he offered a faithful picture of the violence and misery of the Crimean campaign, he did so with due decorum. Battle scenes are prominent, but they are usually viewed as part of a distant panorama in which the eye is relieved by the beauty of headlands or coastline. An example is provided by "The Charge of the Light Brigade." (Simpson made this drawing in the Crimea on October 25, 1854; it was published in London on March 1, 1855.) See Plate LIV. When he dealt in detail with the army's activities, he tended to present moments of relative calm: incidents of camp life or meetings of officers, rather than hand-to-hand combat. Typical of these smaller scenes is "One of the Wards of the Hospital at Scutari," where Florence Nightingale is to be seen at center left. Though Simpson was a superb reporter, he remained an artist as well, and the lithographs made from his drawings, particularly in their hand-colored form, are among the great achievements of Victorian illustration.

(89) William Simpson, *The Seat of War in the East*

Edward Lear (1812–1888)

Though Lear was a landscape painter by profession, his accomplishments were as varied as his personality was idiosyncratic. Late in life he reproached himself for writing "such volumes of stuff," but each of his books—whether he was dealing with birds, or scenery, or nonsense—is made valuable by his individual touch. One of his endearing traits was an inexhaustible capacity for being wrong about himself. Though proud of *A Book of Nonsense*, he sold the copyright after the third edition for £125, only to see it reach nineteen further editions during his lifetime. He looked to his oil paintings for his reputation as an artist, but it turned out to be his watercolors, largely disregarded by his contemporaries, that have caught posterity's attention. We may be sure that this "mad old Englishman," as he came to call himself, would have regarded the proposition that every scrap of his work, whether written or graphic, would be eagerly collected nearly ninety years after his death as a stroke of hyperbolic nonsense beyond even his reach.

REFERENCES   Field, *Edward Lear*; Hofer; Noakes.

90   EDWARD LEAR

Illustrations of the Family of Psittacidae, or Parrots: the greater part of them species hitherto unfigured, containing forty-two lithographic plates, drawn from life, and on stone, by Edward Lear, A.L.S. London, E. Lear, 1832. 3 l. Illus: 42 colored lithographic plates by Lear. Printer: C. Hullmandel. Page size: 21 1/4 × 14 3/8 inches.
   H. Bradley Martin

Lear was only eighteen when he began this book, for which he was his own publisher, yet he was already an experienced ornithological draftsman. Though he ended the venture after part 12 of an intended 14, he was well satisfied with his achievement. In a letter written many years later he noted that the volume "had interest as the first book of its kind drawn on stone in England of so large a size, & as one which led to all Mr. Gould's improvements" (quoted by Field, pp. 114–116). These claims are modest indeed for the chief ornithological work of an artist whom Sacheverell Sitwell has called "perhaps the best of all bird painters" (*Fine Bird Books*, p. 25). The *Parrots* is a rare book, since Lear had the stones destroyed to protect his 175 subscribers. See Plate XXXI.

91

Views in Rome and Its Environs: drawn from nature and on stone by Edward Lear. [London], T. M'Lean, 1841. Collates as in Abbey. Printer: C. Hullmandel. Page size: 21 1/2 × 14 1/2 inches. Publisher's quarter green cloth. Abbey, *Travels*, 183; Field, p. 118.

Beginning in 1837 Lear spent several winters in Italy. *Views of Rome* records his first impressions of the land that was to become a second home to him. In these panoramic lithographs he is more concerned with the dramatic scenery around Rome than with the Holy City itself. Their freshness and ample size combine to make them his most successful topographical prints, though one misses the engaging personal commentary that he provides in his later volumes of scenery. See Plate XXXII.

92   EDWARD LEAR

A Book of Nonsense. By Derry Down Derry . . . [London], Thomas M'Lean, 1846. 2 v. Lithographic t.p. and 67 lithographic plates with litho. text by Lear. Plates as listed by Field: I: Title, 63, 5, 10, 43, 16, 54, 1, 19, 68, 23, 64, 22, 12, 28, 66, 7, 56, 6, 31, 59, 52, "There was an old man of Calcutta," 29, 21, 32, 41, 48, 11, 4, 26, 30, 25, 14. II: "There was an old lady whose folly," 39, 65, 46, 67, 13, 38, 15, 40, 61, 17, 36, "There was a young lady whose nose," 53, 27, 18, 44, 57, 47, 8, 42, 24, 37, 58, 34, 45, 50, 62, 69, 9, 35, 55, 2, 70. The 3 named plates, according to Field, first appeared in the second edition. Page size: 5 1/2 × 8 1/8 inches. Red cloth, orig. covers bound in. Field, p. 125–136.

Lear describes the origin of this book, which gave the limerick general currency, in his preface to *More Nonsense*: "Long years ago, in days when much of my time was passed in a Country House [Knowsley Hall, the seat of the Earl of Derby], where children and mirth abounded, the lines beginning 'There was an old man of Tobago,' were suggested to me by a valued friend, as a form of verse lending itself to limitless variety for Rhymes & Pictures; and thenceforth the greater part of the original drawings and verses for the first 'Book of Nonsense' were struck off with a pen" (p. viii). There are various versions of the verses which Lear took as his model. That cited by his biographer (Noakes, p. 45) runs:

> There was a sick man of Tobago
> Liv'd long on rice-gruel and sago;
> But at last, to his bliss,
> The physician said this—
> "To a roast leg of mutton you may go."

Since *A Book of Nonsense* appeared two months before *Excursions in Italy*, Lear's caution lest he prejudice the reception of his more conventional volume may have led him to sign it "Derry Down Derry." Most copies of the first edition of *A Book of Nonsense* seem to have been read to pieces. Even those that survive are usually in deplorable condition. This has escaped unscathed except for some light coloring in volume II. See Plate XXXIII.

92A EDWARD LEAR

A Book of Nonsense. By Derry Down Derry . . . [London, Thomas M'Lean, 1856?] Lithographic t.p. and 72 lithographic plates with litho. text by Lear. This copy is apparently a variant copy for presentation of the second edition. Plates as listed by Field: Title, 58, 23, 5, 56, 22, 18, 15, 20, 59, 37, 68, 34, 12, 19, 10, 9, 14, 55, 54, 8, 52, 48, 41, 24, 62, 4, 6, 2, 28, 63, 66, 21, 7, 16, 32, 1, 25, "There was an old man of Calcutta," 67, 64, 35, "There was a young lady whose nose," 33, 11, 44, "There was an old person of Buda," 46, 39, 13, 43, 50, 27, 30, 3, 40, 51, 29, 45, 49, 31, 61, 69, 47, 60, 42, 26, 57, 65, "There was an old lady of Prague," 53, 38, 70. According to Field, plates 9, 52, 33, and 70 appeared only in the first edition; plates 10, 2, 46, 69, and 60 have second edition readings. "There was an old man of Calcutta" and "There was a young lady whose nose" first appeared in the second edition; "There was an old person of Buda" and "There was an old lady of Prague" first appeared as plates 42 and 90 of the third edition. Page size: $5\frac{3}{8} \times 7\frac{3}{4}$ inches. Orig. wrappers,

rebacked. Wrappers appear to be a variant: no imprint or price appears, and the word "To" with a blank space follows the title. Field, p. 125–136.

Lear made new lithographic stones for this second edition, which may well be rarer than the first. The third edition, with forty-five new limericks, appeared in 1861. Though 1,000 copies were printed, it too is virtually unfindable.

93 EDWARD LEAR

Illustrated Excursions in Italy. By Edward Lear. London, Thomas M'Lean, 1846 2 v. in 1. I: xii, 144 p. II: [11], 45, [1] p. + 2 p. ads. Illus: Wood-engraved t.p. vignettes and 53 word-engraved vignettes after Lear, 55 tinted lithographic plates by Lear, 2 lithographic maps, 4 p. music. Printer: S. & J. Bentley, Wilson & Fley. Page size: $14\frac{5}{8} \times 10\frac{5}{8}$ inches. Brown morocco. Abbey, *Travels*, 172 (v. I only); Field, p. 121–124.

In these two volumes Lear carried his explorations of central Italy further afield, to the little-known Abruzzi provinces in the first and to the "States of the Church" in the second. As in *Views in Rome* his interest is in "romantic" and picturesque panoramas, which he presents in abundance, both through his lithographs and through the wood-engraved vignettes made from his drawings. Though he finds it necessary to apologize in volume I for the accompanying narrative, taken from journals kept during his "rambles" (I, vii), the wholly factual text of volume II is in fact a sad letdown. It was perhaps Lear's awareness of this truth that led him, when he returned to books of scenery later in his career, to present his lithographs as illustrations to various volumes of *Journals of a Landscape Painter*.

94 EDWARD LEAR

Journals of a Landscape Painter in Albania, &c. By Edward Lear. London, Richard Bentley, 1851. [3], 428 p. Illus: Lithographic map, 20 lithographic tinted plates by Lear. Printer: Schulze & co. Page size: $10 \times 6\frac{1}{4}$ inches. Publisher's blue cloth. Abbey, *Travels*, 45; Field, p. 148.

Lear visited Albania, Turkey in Europe, and Greece in the fall of 1848 and the spring of 1849. His diary and hundreds of drawings provided him with a variety of unfamiliar scenes to depict in words and tinted lithographs. If his illustrations are less impressive than those in his earlier topographical volumes, it is only because of their smaller scale. Typical is his view of the mountain of Sulí, with its footpath skirting a "frightful gorge" leading to the castle of Alí Pashá. The book elicited from Tennyson a poem entitled "To E.L., on his Travels in Greece." The cordial reception accorded this volume led Lear to publish his *Journals of a Landscape Painter in Southern Calabria and Naples* in 1852. The belated *Journal of a Landscape Painter in Corsica* of 1870, which is illustrated with wood engravings, has less interest.

95 EDWARD LEAR

Nonsense Songs, Stories, Botany, and Alphabets. By Edward Lear. London, Robert John Bush, 1871. [8, 182] p. Illus: 59 wood-engraved vignettes after Lear, 50 lithographic plates (some with lithographic text) by Lear. Printer: Watson & Hazell. Page size: 8⅛×6½ inches. Orig. printed boards. Field, p. 157.

This miscellany includes two of Lear's best poems, "The Owl and the Pussy-cat" and "The Jumblies." There is record of Lear's singing his nonsense songs to children as early as 1860.

96 EDWARD LEAR

More Nonsense, Pictures, Rhymes, Botany, etc. By Edward Lear. London, Robert John Bush, 1872. viii, [4, 280] p. Illus: 1 wood-engraved vignette after Lear and 138 lithographic plates with lithographic text, by Lear. Printer: Watson & Hazell. Page size: 8¼×6½ inches. Orig. printed boards. Field, p. 166–170.

Lear's new limericks, withheld from *Nonsense Songs*, make up a good part of this collection. The vignette at the head of the introduction shows Lear on a railway train confounding a fellow passenger who had declared that *A Book of Nonsense* was by the Earl of Derby and that "there was no such person at all as Edward Lear," by showing the skeptic a hat, a handkerchief, letters, and a stick all bearing his name.

97 EDWARD LEAR

Laughable Lyrics: A fourth book of nonsense poems, songs, botany, music, etc. By Edward Lear . . . London, Robert John Bush, 1877. [8, 118] p. + 4 p. ads. Illus: Wood-engraved t.p. vignette and 7 wood-engraved vignettes after Lear, 36 lithographic plates by Lear, each with lithographic text. This copy lacks the half title and 4 p. text, apparently never bound in. Printer: E. J. Francis and co. Page size: 7⅞×6½ inches. Publisher's green cloth. Field, p. 172–175.

(94) Edward Lear, *Journals of a Landscape Painter in Albania*

This final collection, which Lear was dissuaded from calling "Learical Lyrics and Puffles of Prose" (Noakes, p. 272), added "The Dong with a Luminous Nose," "The Courtship of the Yonghy-Bonghy-Bo," and "The Pobble who has no Toes" to the canon. Henceforth Lear languished in San Remo, at first in the Villa Emily, until his view of the Mediterranean was blocked by a hotel "be-scattered with horrid Germen, Gerwomen, and Gerchildren" (Noakes, p. 281), and then in the Villa Tennyson, where he lamented that "Long ago he was one of the singers, / But now he is one of the dumbs."

98 ALFRED, LORD TENNYSON

Poems by Alfred, Lord Tennyson. Illustrated by Edward Lear. London, Boussod, Valadon & co. . . . 1889. [8], iv, [2], 51, [1] p., printed on rectos only. No. 4 of 100 copies signed by Tennyson. Illus: Photogravure front., 7 photogravure vignettes, and 17 photogravure plates after Lear. Printer: Boussod, Valadon, and co. Page size: 12⅜ × 9⅝ inches. Publisher's three-quarter brown morocco. Field, p. 180.

Lear and Tennyson became friends in 1849. In later life their relations were clouded, since the poet on occasion found Lear's fun exasperating, as when he remarked, after "Northern Farmer, Old Style" had been succeeded by "Northern Farmer, New Style," that if Tennyson wrote any more

he could publish the lot in a "Farmacopoeia" (Noakes, p. 237). Yet Lear's affection for Emily Tennyson never faltered, and the Laureate remained his favorite poet. He set some of Tennyson's poem songs to music, and he worked for many years on a series of "Landscape illustrations of Tennyson," of which those published in this volume are a selection. Franklin Lushington's comment in the preface that they are "not so much illustrations in the ordinary sense" as "Lear's sermons on text taken from Tennyson" (p. iv) explains their remoteness from the poet's text.

≈ Autograph manuscript, dated Villa Tennyson, March 11, 1886. 7 stanzas, entitled: "Incidents in the life of my Uncle Arly." Narrow 8vo.

Lear sent copies of this "obituary," as his biographer calls it, to his closest surviving friends. It was his last notable nonsense poem. The statement that "his shoes were far too tight" has elicited the most diverse interpretations.

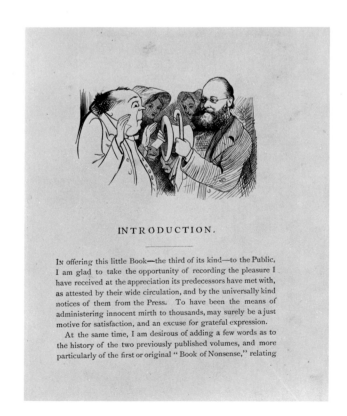

(96) Edward Lear,
More Nonsense,
vignette for Introduction

Printing in Color from Wood or Metal

Printing in color has a long history, but it was only in the nineteenth century that it came into general use, with England showing the way to the rest of the world. Moreover, it was employed not only in expensive books of limited circulation like Savage's *Hints on Decorative Printing* and the volumes of Henry Shaw, but also in books priced cheaply enough to be bought even by the poor, like the part issue of Charles Knight's *Old England* (2 volumes, 1845) and the thousands of "yellow-backs" that crowded the railway stalls from the 1850s on. For decades Victorian color printing, whether from wood and metal or from stone, has taken second place to the black-and-white illustration of the period, but thanks to the labors of Ruari McLean and others its great interest is now widely appreciated.

REFERENCES Abbey, *Life in England*; Burch; Evans; Hardie; Lewis, *George Baxter*; Lewis, *Picture Printing*; McLean, *Victorian Book Design*; Muir, *Illustrated Books*; Sadleir.

William Savage (1770–1843)

99 WILLIAM SAVAGE

Practical Hints on Decorative Printing, with illustrations engraved on wood, and printed in colors at the type press. By William Savage. London, published for the proprietor . . . 1822. Color-printed front., dedication, [6], vi, 118 p., [3] l., [4] p. Illus: Color-printed front., dedication, and 33 color-printed plates, 11 black-and-white plates, 6 plates of color samples, 2 pages of typographical samples. Page size: 14¾ × 10⅝, large-paper copy. Cloth. Abbey, *Life*, 233.

Columbia University Libraries

Savage's magnum opus, which was announced in 1815, appeared in parts between 1818 and 1823. It is both a highly idiosyncratic volume and a notable landmark in the history of color printing from wood, anticipating Baxter by about ten years. Only some of the illustrations after Callcott and others are colored, but the most elaborate of these,

that for Collins's "Ode to Mercy," required twenty-nine blocks and went through fifty-five proofs in its printing. The book is rare, since Savage destroyed the blocks to safeguard the interests of his subscribers. (Burch, pp. 116–121.) See Plate XXIII.

George Baxter (1804–1867)

Baxter was primarily a producer of individual prints, but he also had a part in a number of illustrated books. His first illustrations printed in color from woodblocks to appear in books were frontispiece vignettes for the two volumes of Mudie's *Feathered Tribes of the British Islands* of 1834. In applying for a patent the following year, he claimed that his process produced "coloured impressions of a high degree of perfection, and far superior to those which are colored by hand." As more and more amateurs of art came to share this estimate, Baxter's vogue was established. After a long period of neglect, his prints are once again a popular collecting specialty.

100

The Pictorial Album; or, Cabinet of Paintings, for the year 1837. Containing eleven designs, executed in oil colours, by G. Baxter, from the original pictures, with illustrations in verse and prose. London, Chapman & Hall, [1836]. [4], xvi, 71, [1] p. Illus: Color-printed front., t.p. vignette, and 9 color-printed plates by Baxter after other artists. Printer: Bradbury and Evans. Page size: 9⅝ × 7⅜ inches. Publisher's red morocco.

In the preface Baxter's patent agent, Carpmael, sketches the history of color printing from the fifteenth century, referring ungraciously in conclusion to the "imitative coloured drawings" of *Practical Hints on Decorative Printing*, of which "it is impossible to speak . . . in terms of commendation" (p. xii). With some fanfare he then goes on to describe Baxter's own process of "PICTURE-PRINTING": "The first faint impression, forming a ground, is from a steel plate; and above this ground, which is usually a neutral tint, the positive colours are impressed from as many wood-blocks as there are distinct tints in the picture. Some idea of the difficulty of Picture-Printing may be conceived, when the reader is informed, that, as each tint has to be communicated by a separate impression, some of the subjects required not less than *twenty* blocks; and that even the most simple in point of colour, have required not less than *ten*." (P. xiii.) Baxter chose his eleven subjects with a view to showing that "Picture-Printing" could produce perfect facsimiles of various kinds of paintings, whether they were landscapes, interiors, portraits, or genre pieces. The resulting book is hardly above the *Keepsake* level aesthetically, but as a demonstration of his process it is undeniably impressive. Since the preface is dated November 1, 1836, it was presumably produced for the Christmas trade of that year. The publisher's inlaid morocco binding is in keeping with the richness of Baxter's plates.

101

Gems of the Great Exhibitions. London 1851. New York 1853. [London? 1854?] [Cover title.] 2 p. letterpress text as pastedowns. Illus: 5 color-printed plates. Page size: 12 × 7⅝ inches. Publisher's brown cloth.

This volume contains five "gems" (1 to 4 and 6), though the text describes only four. The one not covered is Kiss's "Amazon on horseback spearing a tiger." (Lewis, *George Baxter*, pp. 362–367.) Both larger and more characteristic than the prints in *The Pictorial Album*, they show that Baxter's appeal was not only in the elaboration and finish of his work, but also in his eye for subjects approved by Victorian taste. Each of the thirteen statues depicted is a "sermon in stone." The Belgian sculptures of plate II, for example, are "The Lion in Love," an exemplification of "the capabilities of attachment to man" of "this noble animal"; "The Unhappy Child," who is distressed because he has broken his toy; and a Persian peasant girl about to dispatch a carrier dove to her lover.

Henry Shaw (1800–1873)

102 HENRY SHAW

Dresses and Decoration of the Middle Ages by Henry Shaw F.S.A. . . . . London, William Pickering, 1843. 2 v.

I: [10, 73] l. II: [3, 56] l. Illus: Added color-printed t.p. and 93 color-printed, hand-colored, or tinted plates, numerous color-printed initials and woodcut vignettes. Printer: C. Whittingham. Page size: 10⅞ × 7¼ inches. Red morocco.

Pierpont Morgan Library

Shaw's career was devoted to rescuing the English past through a long series of imposing books on architecture and art, published chiefly by William Pickering at the Chiswick Press. He used a variety of processes to reproduce his drawings: copper engravings, lithographs, chromolithographs, wood engravings, and woodblocks printed in color. *Dresses and Decorations of the Middle Ages*, which appeared in parts between 1840 and 1843, is one of the finest of his works. Emphasizing its typographical distinction, McLean (*Victorian Book Design*, p. 66) holds that it may be "the most handsome book produced in the whole of the nineteenth century." See Plate XLV. A specimen of Shaw's later work is given below (234).

"Yellow-Backs"

One of the most commercially rewarding of the applications of color printing was the "yellow-back," that is to say a book bound in yellow glazed-paper over boards. Edmund Evans tells in his *Reminiscences* (ed. McLean, pp. 26–28) of introducing the style for inexpensive reprints, usually novels, in 1853. For many years he was the printer to whom most publishers repaired for work of this sort. Among the illustrators called upon for drawings were Crowquill, Cruikshank, Foster, Gilbert, Keene, Phiz, and later Caldecott and Crane.

✑ "Alfred Crowquill" (Alfred H. Forrester, 1804–1872), 72 graphite and watercolor designs for "yellowback" covers:

Cooper, [*The Heathcotes, or*] the *Wept of the wish ton wish*. Routledge. Sheet size: 6¾ × 5½ inches.

Cooper, *Mark's Reef*. Bentley. Sheet size: 6⅞ × 5½ inches.

Cooper, *Ned Myers*. Bentley. Sheet size: 6¾ × 4½ inches.

Cooper, *The Sea Lions*. Routledge. Signed. Sheet size: 6¾ × 5¼ inches.

Despite the fact that his drawings were for novels (32 of them, indeed, for the works of James Fenimore Cooper), Crowquill preferred calligraphic or emblematic to pictorial designs. The publishers

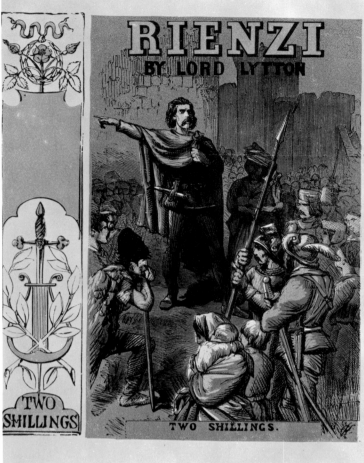

Alfred Crowquill, drawing for "yellow-back" cover

Charles Keene, proof of a "yellow-back" cover

most frequently represented are Bentley, Hodgson, and Routledge.

▸ Seventy-five color-printed proofs for "yellow-back" covers:

Bulwer Lytton, *Rienzi*. 6½ × 5¼ inches. From a drawing by Charles Keene.
Mrs. Marsh, *Angela*, 6¾ × 4⅛ inches.

This collection, which was formed by Michael Sadleir, extends from the 1850s to the 1890s, and includes examples from most firms which dealt extensively in fiction. *Rienzi* and *Angela* date from about 1870.

Benjamin Fawcett (1808–1893) and Alexander Francis Lydon (1836–1917)

103 SHIRLEY HIBBERD

Rustic Adornments for Homes of Taste, and recreations for town folk, in the study and imitation of nature. By Shirley Hibberd. Author of "Brambles and bay leaves," "The town garden," &c., &c. . . . London, Groombridge and sons, 1856. [1], added color-printed t.p., vi, 353, [1] p. + 12 p. ads. Illus: Color-printed front., added color-printed t.p., 5 color-printed plates, 7 wood-engraved plates, and 60 wood-engraved vignettes. Page size: 7⅛ × 4¾ inches. Publisher's green cloth.

Benjamin Fawcett of Driffield in Yorkshire was the leading provincial color printer of the age. The most agreeable of the early books for which he supplied color plates is *Rustic Adornments*. Its author emerges as a sort of urban Humphrey Repton, seeking to extend the amenities of the middle classes rather than those of the aristocracy. Certainly Fawcett's plates of various aquariums, an aviary, and a rockery are persuasive arguments for Hibberd's aim, "the realization, as far as possible, of the much sought *Rus in urbe*" (p. iv).

104   F. O. Morris

A Series of Picturesque Views of Seats of Noblemen and Gentlemen of Great Britain and Ireland. With descriptions and historical letterpress. Edited by the Rev. F. O. Morris, B.A. . . . London, William Mackenzie, [1864?–1880]. 6 v. I: Added color-printed t.p., iv, 90 [1] p. II: Added color-printed t.p., iv, 80 p. III: Added color-printed t.p., iv, 80 p. IV: Added color-printed t.p., iv, 82 p. V: Added color-printed t.p., iv, 80 p. VI: Added color-printed t.p., iv, 88 p. Illus: Each volume with color-printed front., color-printed added t.p., and 39 plates. Page size: 10⅝ × 8⅜ inches. Publisher's red morocco.

Fawcett's most interesting works were the result of his collaboration over many years with the water-color painter Alexander Francis Lydon. The *Seats of Noblemen and Gentlemen* is the most ambitious of these joint ventures. The book's publishing history is complicated. It is described as having been issued in parts between about 1864 and 1880, but selections from it like *The Ancestral Homes of Britain* of 1868 also appeared during this period. Since over 10,000 copies were published, it remains one of the few major examples of nineteenth-century color printing still reasonably available. The spirit in which Fawcett and Lydon worked was not in the least antiquarian. Indeed, the accompanying commentary by Fawcett's habitual collaborator, the Reverend F. O. Morris, records many recent events in the careers of the gentry living in these stately homes. In every scene the lawns are clipped, the hedges trimmed, and the buildings in sparkling repair. There are virtually no people, but one can easily imagine the action of *Daniel Deronda*, or *The Egoist*, or *The Duke's Children* unrolling before such backdrops. It may fairly be said that these volumes accomplish for color printing what Pyne's *Royal Residences* (42) did for aquatint engraving. See Plate LXIII.

105   Frederick Ross

The Ruined Abbeys of Britain. By Frederick Ross, F.R.H.S. Illustrated with coloured plates and wood engravings from drawings by A. F. Lydon. London, William Mackenzie, [1882]. 2 v. I: viii, 148 p. II: [iv], 288 p. Illus: 116 wood-engraved vignettes and 13 wood-engraved initials, color-printed fronts. and 10 color-printed plates after Lydon. Printer: B. Fawcett. Page size: 14⅛ × 10½ inches. Publisher's green cloth.

Despite the claims of *English Lake Scenery* of 1880 and *Scottish Loch Scenery* of 1882 the concluding selection from among the books of Lydon and Fawcett must be their *Ruined Abbeys*. Here they did concern themselves with antiquities. Possibly echoing a passage in the study of Nathaniel Hawthorne which Henry James had written for the English Men of Letters series three years earlier (*Hawthorne*, London, 1879, pp. 43–44), Frederick Ross explains that "when an American visits his ancestral fatherland of England, his supreme desire is to look upon the cathedrals, the ancient castles, and the mutilated remains of the old abbeys, which lie scattered about so profusely over the length and breadth of our island. There are no abbey ruins in his own land." (I, v.) Since the English themselves shared this desire, a pictorial history of the chief abbeys was clearly needed. There are only twelve color plates, but their large scale makes them perhaps the most impressive of any that resulted from the collaboration of Fawcett and Lydon.

William Dickes (1815–1892)

106   Philip Henry Gosse

Actinologia Britannica. **A History of the British Sea-Anemones and Corals.** With coloured figures of the species and principal varieties . . . London, Van Voorst, 1860. xl, 362 p. + 2 p. ads. Illus: Color-printed front. and 10 color-printed plates, 1 uncolored plate, and numerous wood-engraved vignettes. Printer: R. Clay. Page size: 8¼ × 5¼ inches. Publisher's green cloth.

Dickes was a prominent licensee of the Baxter process. His specialty was books of useful knowledge, with particular emphasis on natural history. Among the scientific writers to whom he became illustrator in ordinary was Philip Henry Gosse, the father of Edmund Gosse. The *Sea-Anemones* contains the most successful of his plates for Gosse. Despite the limitations of space within which he was forced to work Dickes manages to invest the naturalist's crowded drawings with something of the mystery and opulence of those in *The Temple of Flora* (39).

107 MRS. ISABELLA BEETON

The Book of Household Management . . . London, S. O. Beeton, 1861. xxxix, 1112 p. Illus: Added color-printed t.p. and 12 color-printed plates, numerous wood-engraved vignettes. Printer: Spottiswoode and co. Page size: 6⅞×4⅜ inches. Publisher's half morocco.

Mrs. Beeton's manual of "modern household cooking" and management, the best-known work for which Dickes supplied colored prints, shows him wandering from his usual line of country. The recipes gave Mrs. Beeton's book its fame, and it is these that Dickes illustrates. "CHRISTMAS PLUM PUDDING (*Very Good.*)" accompanies a recipe that suggests the heroic scale of Victorian cookery. Each of these quart puddings served seven or eight persons, and Mrs. Beeton recommends making five or six of them at a time. It is to be regretted that an illustrator was not employed as well to capture the general spirit of Mrs. Beeton's work. On the one hand, she was a devoted handmaiden: "Men are now so well served out of doors,—at their clubs, well-ordered taverns, and dining houses, that in order to compete with these places, a mistress must be thoroughly acquainted with the theory and practice of cookery, as well as thoroughly conversant with all the other arts of making and keeping a comfortable home" (p. iii). On the other hand, she was a thorough autocrat: "As with the Commander of an Army, or the leader of any enterprise, so is it with the mistress of a house. Her spirit is seen through the whole establishment." (P. 1.) Happy in the role she is playing, Mrs. Beeton finds no inconsistency between these attitudes.

"E.V.B."

108 SARAH AUSTIN

The Story without an End. From the German of Carové. By Sarah Austin. With illustrations printed in colours after drawings by E.V.B. London, Sampson Low, Son, and Marston, 1868. vi, [1], 40 p. Illus: Tinted wood-engraved front., wood-engraved t.p. vignette, and 13 wood-engraved vignettes, 15 color-printed plates. Page size: 9⅞×7⅛ inches. Publisher's green cloth with inlaid central ivory panel.

(108) E.V.B., illustration for Sarah Austin's *The Story without an End*

"E.V.B." was the Honorable Mrs. Robert Boyle, wife of a younger son of the Earl of Cork and Orrery. Though her production was small, she had as unmistakable a style as that of any Victorian illustrator. The world of her imagination, which has obvious links with those of Arthur Hughes and Richard Doyle, is most fully realized in the illustrations of the familiar rhymes, reproduced by the "anastatic" process, that make up *Child's Play* of 1852. Yet *The Story without an End* has a fantastic element not present in the earlier book, and by showing it the color printing of Leighton Brothers, as George Leighton called his firm, can also be represented.

(110) Page of "The Railway ABC"
in *Aunt Louisa's London Picture Book*

J. M. Kronheim (1810–1896)

109

The Nobility of Life, its graces and virtues, portrayed in prose and verse by the best writers. Selected and edited by L. B. C. Valentine. With twenty-four original pictures painted in colors, elaborate borders, headings, and vignettes. London, Frederick Warne and co., 1869. [1], viii, 192 p. + 2 p. ads. Illus: numerous wood-engraved vignettes and borders, 24 color-printed plates. Printer: Dalziel Brothers. Page size: 10¼ × 7⅞ inches. Publisher's red cloth.

Kronheim was another Baxter licensee. He and Edmund Evans each supplied twelve color prints for this ambitious undertaking. The result is an unexpected triumph for Kronheim. If the line of both engravers leaves much to be desired, Kronheim's coloring is rich and even, while Evans's is thin and scratchy. The choice of artists for the color plates included Charles Green, Mahoney, Poynter, and J. D. Watson, but only Poynter had much success in coping with the publisher's formula of illustrating the virtues through anecdotal subjects. Indeed, the best designs in the book are Houghton's six vignette headpieces in black and white.

110

Aunt Louisa's London Picture Book. Comprising A. Apple Pie. The Railway ABC. Nursery Rhymes. With eighteen pages of illustrations, printed in colors by Kronheim. London, Frederick Warne and co., 1886. [5] l. Illus: Color-printed front. and 17 color-printed plates each with 1 l. letterpress text. Page size: 10⅜ × 9 inches. Publisher's green cloth.

This jolly toy book is far more typical of Kronheim's work than the pompous *Nobility of Life,* and despite the relative crudity of its drawings, it is also far more enjoyable. One of the offered subjects is

> A bright new RAILWAY, like the one
> That rushes up and down,
> And carries nearly every day
> Our dear Papa to town.

The twenty-four scenes in "The Railway ABC" (I and J are combined and Z is left unillustrated), with their glimpses of a London line in settled use, afford a pleasant complement to the plates of Bury (45) and Bourne (85 and 86) decades earlier.

George Cruikshank (1792–1878)

Cruikshank began his career as a political caricaturist in the tradition of Gillray and Rowlandson, taking the radical side on issues of the day with the Prince Regent as his particular target. Pierce Egan's *Life in London* brought him to wide public notice as an illustrator, and for the next twenty-five years he poured forth drawings of unprecedented abundance, variety, and excellence. Novels, both classic and contemporary, were his particular specialty, but when the books of others did not present themselves, he offered volumes of his own like *My Sketch Book*, *George Cruikshank's Omnibus*, and *George Cruikshank's Table Book*. By the late 1840s, however, his time of anticlimax had arrived. Other illustrators had come to the fore, and his crusade against drinking and smoking seemed increasingly bizarre.

Thackeray, who remains his best critic, particularly praised the "grotesque beauty" of his earlier work. "There must be no smiling with Cruikshank," he declared. "A man who does not laugh outright is a dullard." The comic marks most of his drawings, even those for *Oliver Twist*, before 1840, the date of Thackeray's essay. Yet an almost equally important element in Cruikshank's makeup was his acute sensitivity to misery, vice, and corruption. He came more and more to emphasize these aspects of life in the haunting scenes of mystery and horror that dominate his illustrations of Ainsworth and W. H. Maxwell. It was only a step to the reforming zeal of his later years.

Until 1968 Cruikshank was not so much neglected as taken for granted. Since then there have been many exhibitions, articles, and books devoted to him, with more still to come. Enthusiasts for his work now confidently describe him as "the greatest of English illustrators" (*Princeton University Library Chronicle*, p. 33). Not everyone will accept this judgment, but no one will deny his inexhaustible fancy, his skill in dramatic composi-

tion, his mastery as an etcher, or the amazing fertility that enabled him to leave behind so vast a body of idiosyncratic and vital work.

REFERENCES Cohn; Harvey; McLean, *Cruikshank*; Miller; Muir, *Victorian Illustrated Books*; *Princeton University Library Chronicle*; Reid; Thackeray, *Westminster Review*; University of Louisville Libraries.

111 PIERCE EGAN

Life in London; or the day and night scenes of Jerry Hawthorne, Esq. and his elegant friend Corinthian Tom, accompanied by Bob Logic, the Oxonian, in their rambles and sprees through the metropolis . . . embellished with thirty-six scenes from real life, designed and etched by I. R. & G. Cruikshank; and enriched also with numerous original designs on wood, by the same artists. London, for Sherwood, Neely, and Jones, 1821. xvi, 376 p. + 8 p., ads. Illus: Colored etched front., 35 colored etched plates, and 17 wood-engraved vignettes by Isaac Robert and George Cruikshank; 3 engraved sheets of music. Printer: Merchant. Page size: 9½×6⅛ inches. Red morocco by Zaehnsdorf. Cohn 262, first issue; Abbey, *Life*, 281; Tooley 196.

Pierpont Morgan Library

Cruikshank shared the illustration of this book with his brother Robert. His work is rough-hewn in comparison with what he did two years later, and Tom, Jerry, and Logic are hardly the most agreeable of companions. Yet their progress through the often raffish and occasionally tawdry demimonde of the metropolis is invariably colorful and entertaining.

Pencil and watercolor drawing, "Tom, Jerry, & Logic masquerading it," related to "Tom and Jerry larking at a masquerade supper at the Opera House," *Life in London*, p. 192. Signed and inscribed by the artist. Sheet size: 7⅜×4⅛ inches.

Pierce Egan, autograph letter signed, dated [London], August 31, 1830, addressed to George Cruikshank. With pen and ink drawing at top of first page. 3 p., 8vo, with address.

Writing with the same mixture of slang, puns, and pompous commonplaces that he had employed in *Life in London*, the impoverished Egan pleads with Cruikshank for "half a dozen designs to illustrate my ideas," dotting his letter with hopeful allusions to old times together.

112   JACOB AND WILHELM GRIMM

German Popular Stories, translated from the Kinder und Haus Märchen, collected by M. M. Grimm, from oral tradition. London, by C. Baldwyn, 1823 [II: London, James Robins & co.; Dublin, Joseph Robins Junr. & co., 1826]. 2 v. I: [2], added etched t.p., xii, 240 p. II: [2], added etched t.p., iv, 256, [2] p. Illus: Etched fronts., titles, and 18 etched plates by George Cruikshank, with an extra set of plates printed in brown inserted in Vol. I. Printer: Richard Taylor. Page size: 7×4 inches. Brown morocco by Riviere. Cohn 369, second issue.

This is Cruikshank's most original work. Thackeray had it particularly in mind when he wrote that it was Cruikshank who "brought English pictorial humour and children acquainted." His delicate and fanciful designs fixed what fairy tale illustration ought to be once and for all in the minds of English readers. The etchings are seen at their best in the *suites* on special paper which were issued with a few copies of volume I. See Plate XXIV.

113   [ADELBERT VON CHAMISSO]

Peter Schlemihl: from the German of Lamotte Fouqué . . . London, G. & W. B. Whittaker, 1824. 12, 165 p., lacking the half title. Illus: Etched front., and 7 plates by George Cruikshank. Page size: 7×4¼ inches. Printer: Cox & Baylis. Contemp. half calf. Cohn 475, third issue.

In the same vein as those for *German Popular Stories*, these etchings illustrate the fantastic yet moral tale of a man who sold his shadow to the devil.

114   [CHARLES DICKENS]

Sketches by "Boz," illustrative of every-day life and every-day people . . . London, John Macrone, 1836. 2 v. I. viii, 348 p. II: [4], 342 p. Illus: Etched fronts., and 14 plates by George Cruikshank. Page size: 7¾× 4⅞ inches. Printer: Whiting. Publisher's green cloth. Cohn 232; Eckel, p. 11.

115   [CHARLES DICKENS]

Sketches by Boz: illustrative of every-day life, and every-day people. **The Second Series.** Complete in one volume. London, John Macrone, 1837. Added etched t.p., viii, 377 p. + 20 p. ads. Illus: Etched front., added etched t.p., and 8 plates by George Cruikshank. Page size: 7¾×4¾ inches. Printer: Thomas Curson Hansard. Publisher's pink cloth. Cohn 233, second issue; Eckel, p. 12.

Sketches by "Boz," as Dickens noted, constituted his "first voyage in company" with Cruikshank. If Cruikshank's etchings lack the dramatic element of those for *Oliver Twist*, they remain his most comprehensive and faithful picture of day-to-day London life.

❧ India-paper proofs of illustrations for *Sketches by Boz*, in an early state before letters. 28 plates, plus two additional plates issued in the second edition of the Second Series. Page size: 11¼×8½ inches. Red morocco by Bedford.

The fine draftsmanship of these small-scale illustrations is best seen in these India-paper impressions.

114A–115A   [CHARLES DICKENS]

Sketches by Boz illustrative of every-day life and every-day people. With forty illustrations . . . New edition, complete. London, Chapman and Hall, 1839. Added etched t.p., viii, 526 p. Illus: Etched front., added etched t.p., and 38 etched plates by George Cruikshank. Page size: 8⅝× 5½ inches. Printer: Whiting. Publisher's purple cloth. Cohn 234; Eckel, p. 13.

For the reissue of the two series of *Sketches by "Boz"* in twenty monthly parts between November, 1837, and June, 1839, Cruikshank redrew his illustrations on a larger scale and added enough new subjects to provide two etchings for each part. This change in size has been deprecated, but it at least brought the illustrations of *Sketches by "Boz"* into line with the format he henceforth to use in his etchings for contemporary novels.

116   [CHARLES DICKENS]

Oliver Twist; or, the parrish boy's progress. By "Boz" . . . London, Richard Bentley, 1838. 3 v. I: [4], 331 p. + 4 p. ads. II: [4], 307 p. III: [2], 316 p. + 2 p. ads. Illus: Etched fronts., and 21 etched plates by George Cruikshank. Page size: 7⅞×4¾ inches. Printer: I, III: Samuel Bentley; II: Whiting. Publisher's brown cloth. Cohn 239, first issue; Eckel, p. 59.

Dickens's fiction was written to be illustrated, and Cruikshank's etchings for this novel are simply incomparable. Oliver makes an appealing focus for the events of the plot, even if he does look like an undersized Lord Byron, while Fagin, Sikes, and their followers are a source initially of macabre comedy and latterly of thrilling terror. See Plate XXV.

117 WILLIAM HARRISON AINSWORTH

Jack Sheppard. A romance . . . with illustrations by George Cruikshank . . . London, Richard Bentley, 1839. 3 v. I: viii, 352 p. + 1 p. ads. II: iv, 292 p. III: vi, [2], 312 p. Illus: Engraved front. by R. J. Lane; 2 fronts., 25 plates, and 2 woodcuts by George Cruikshank. Printer: I, III: Samuel Bentley; II: Schulze & co. Page size: 8×4⅞ inches. Publisher's green cloth. Cohn 12.

Cruikshank's connection with Ainsworth was more enduring than that with Dickens. He illustrated six of Ainsworth's novels as well as contributing to the first six volumes of *Ainsworth's Magazine*. His greatest success was with *Jack Sheppard*, that most notorious of "Newgate Novels," though he did not

Drawing for W. H. Ainsworth's *Guy Fawkes; or The Gunpowder Treason*

(118) W. H. Maxwell, *History of the Irish Rebellion in 1798*

THE MANIAC FATHER AND THE CONVICT BROTHER ARE GONE.——THE POOR GIRL, HOMELESS, FRIENDLESS, DESERTED,
DESTITUTE, AND GIN-MAD, COMMITS SELF-MURDER.

(120)
George Cruiksha
The Drunkard's C.

take the same delight in Ainsworth's crop-haired hero or in Jonathan Wild as he had in Fagin and his gang. This copy is inscribed on the title page of volume 1: "Percival W. Banks, Esquire From his friend the Author."

❧ Two drawings for Ainsworth's *Guy Fawkes; or The Gunpowder Treason,* 3 volumes, 1841:

Pencil and watercolor drawing and sketches, "Guy Fawkes & Catesby landing the powder," I, front. Signed and inscribed by the artist. Sheet size: $8\frac{7}{8} \times 7\frac{3}{8}$ inches.

Pencil and watercolor drawing for "Guy Fawkes and Humphrey Chetham rescuing Father Oldcorne & Viviana Radcliffe from the pursuivant," II, 115. Signed by the artist. Image size: $4\frac{7}{8} \times 3\frac{5}{8}$ inches.

118 W. H. MAXWELL

History of the Irish Rebellion in 1798, with memoirs of the union, and Emmett's insurrection of 1803 . . . London, Baily brothers, 1845. vii, [1], 477, [1] p. + 18 p. ads. Illus: Engraved front. and 5 other ports. by P. Lightfoot, and 21 etched plates by George Cruikshank. Page size: $8\frac{5}{8} \times 5\frac{1}{2}$ inches. Printer: J. & H. Cox brothers. Publisher's green cloth. Cohn 541.

By the time he reached middle age Cruikshank was a thorough partisan of law and order, and he did not spare the reader in his etchings for Maxwell's vivid narrative of this violent insurrection. Indeed, the almost unrelieved succession of scenes of violence which he offers calls to mind Goya's *Disasters of War.*

❧ Pencil and watercolor drawing, "The loyal little drummer boy," *History of the Irish Rebellion,* p. 115. Signed and annotated by the artist. Image size: 4×6 inches; sheet size (with marginal sketches): $7\frac{3}{8} \times 8\frac{7}{8}$ inches.

Pierpont Morgan Library

This belongs to a set of twenty-one pencil and watercolor designs for *The Irish Rebellion.* Cruikshank's etchings, which were made from them, show much elaboration of detail. Blues, greens, and yellows predominate in the artist's color scheme for his drawings. In avoiding red, despite the many opportunities for its use offered by his bloody subject, Cruikshank may have had in mind the susceptibilities of possible purchasers of the set.

The Bottle . . . London, published for the artist by D. Bogue . . . [1847] [cover title]. Illus: 8 tinted glyphograph plates by George Cruikshank. Page size: 11 × 15¼ inches. Printer: Spottiswoode and Shaw. Orig. printed wrappers. Cohn 194.

Pierpont Morgan Library

The Drunkard's Children, a sequel to *The Bottle*. In eight plates . . . London, published for the artist by D. Bogue . . . 1848 [cover title]. Illus: 8 tinted glyphograph plates by George Cruikshank. Page size: 11 × 15⅜ inches. Printer: Spottiswoode and Shaw. Orig. printed wrappers. Cohn 195.

Pierpont Morgan Library

These designs, which form a "progress" like those of Hogarth's rake and idle apprentice, trace the evils of drink through two generations. In the opening scene "the bottle is brought out for the first time" at a happy family gathering. In the last "the maniac father and the convict brother are gone. The poor girl, homeless, friendless, deserted, destitute, and gin-mad, commits self-murder." Cruikshank had each series published "in one large sheet of double imperial, at one shilling" to make them generally accessible, and of *The Bottle* 100,000 copies were sold within a few days of its appearance. The superior tinted issue, described here, cost six shillings.

&❧ Autograph letter signed, dated [London], May 8, 1860, addressed to [John Camden] Hotten. 2 p., 12mo.

The lengths to which Cruikshank allowed his cru-sade against drink to carry him are shown in this reply to a proposal from the publisher Hotten: "The prominent position in which I stand as an advocate of the Temperance cause prevents me from having *my name* mixed up—in any way—with the names of those humbug poisons—Wine, Beer & Spirits—unless it be for the purpose of denouncing them, and therefore, although with much regret, I feel that I must decline illustrating any of my old & esteemed friend Douglas Jerrold's writings, if they are to be published under the title of 'Old Wine in New Bottles.' I fear you will think me a little *too* particular."

&❧ Pencil sketch, "The modern Guy Faux," apparently unpublished [watermarked 1868]. Signed ["D. Dark"] and inscribed by the artist. Sheet size: 9 × 14 inches.

That Cruikshank's instinct as a political cartoonist could still be stirred in later life is shown by this cartoon of the liberal statesman John Bright, an extreme advocate of electoral reform, contemplating the destruction of the House of Lords sometime after the passage of the Reform Bill of 1867. Cruikshank told his correspondent: "*Reverse* it if you like. I think it would be best to do so. Do not let *any one* see this sketch—and I shall want it back when you have done with it. If it cannot be published by itself, some of the 'Punch' books who are opposed to Mr B. might take it, but mind the *name* of C^k must not in any way be put to it."

Apparently unpublished political caricature, c. 1868

William Makepeace Thackeray (1811–1863)

Thackeray began to sketch in early childhood. When he lost his fortune as a young man, he for several years attempted a career as a painter, assuring himself that he could "draw better than anything else." After he became a professional writer, he illustrated most of his own books. It was in this way that his achievement as an illustrator came to surpass that of any other great novelist, with the possible exception of Victor Hugo. A skeptic might accept this judgment, however, and still be mindful of Dr. Johnson's comment about a dog's walking on his hinder legs: "It is not done well; but you are surprised to find it done at all." And indeed, Thackeray's draftsmanship, as it is displayed even in *Vanity Fair* or *The Rose and the Ring*, leaves much to be desired. He himself once described the figures in his illustrations as "Nuremburg dolls." But as his drawings show, this deficiency is to be attributed largely to his own uncertainty with the etching needle on the one hand and to the inability of the wood engravers to deal with his sketches on the other. In compensation his illustrations have the transcending merit of coming directly from the mind that created the work being illustrated. Becky Sharp in *Vanity Fair*, Major Pendennis in *Pendennis*, the Baroness Bernstein in *The Virginians*, and even Bulbo in *The Rose and the Ring* derive their vitality as characters from Thackeray's pictures as well as from his text. Moreover, in such adornments as initial letter vignettes, where the point to be made is as much literary as graphic, he displays a wit and ingenuity that are unsurpassable. Thus Thackeray deserves his place beside Cruikshank, Phiz, Leech, and Doyle, though his accomplishment as an illustrator is of a special kind.

REFERENCES Harvey; Stevens; Szladits and Simmonds; Van Duzer.

"Caracatura" of Henry Esmond in his Virginian retirem

121

Flore et Zéphyr, ballet mythologique . . . par Théophile Wagstaff. London, J. Mitchell; Paris, Rittmer & Goupil, 1836. [8] p. Illus: Colored lithographic cover and 8 colored lithographic illustrations after "Théophile Wagstaff." Printer: Graf & Sorel. Page size: 13¼×9⅝ inches. Orig. wrappers.

Living in Paris during the great days of *La caricature* and *Le charivari*, Thackeray inevitably tried his hand at a series of drawings for lithographs. His dancers perform in "La Sylphide," the ballet that Taglioni made famous. As one would expect, Thackeray is at some pains to emphasize the comic aspects of his potentially glamorous subject.

122 WILLIAM MAKEPEACE THACKERAY

Vanity Fair. A novel without a hero. By William Makepeace Thackeray. With illustrations on wood and steel by the author. London, Bradbury & Evans, 1848. Added etched t.p., xvi, 624 p. Illus: Etched front., added etched t.p., and 38 etched plates by Thackeray, 83 wood-engraved vignettes and 66 wood-engraved initials after Thackeray. Printer: Bradbury & Evans. Page size: 8¾×5½ inches. Publisher's blue cloth.

Modern editions of this classic novel almost invariably omit Thackeray's vignettes and often give only a selection from his etchings. The reader is deprived thereby not only of much amusement but also of important clues to the meaning of the story. In his text, for example, Thackeray leaves unanswered the question of whether or not Becky Sharp brought about the death of Jos Sedley. His etching of "Becky's second appearance in the character of Clytemnestra" more than hints that she did. See Plate LII.

≫ Sheet of 7 pen and ink drawings: 1 landscape and 6 scenes of a boxing match. Inscribed by the artist. Sheet size: 6⅞×9⅝ inches.

Thackeray's record of this boxing match between Bendigo and Buddick of Hookham Snivvy for "£200 a side" includes a sketch of "Peter Crawley, Esqʳᵉ" He is perhaps a descendant of the sporting parson Bute Crawley of *Vanity Fair*, whose tastes he seems to share.

123 WILLIAM MAKEPEACE THACKERAY

The History of Pendennis. His fortunes and misfortunes, his friends and his greatest enemy. By William Makepeace Thackeray. With illustrations on wood and steel by the author. London, Bradbury & Evans, 1849–50. 2 v. I: Added etched t.p., viii, 384 p. II: Added etched t.p., xii, 372 p. Illus: Etched fronts., titles, and 44 etched plates by Thackeray, 53 wood-engraved vignettes and 77 wood-engraved initials after Thackeray. Printer: I: Bradbury & Evans; II: Smith, Elder, and co. Page size: 8¾×5½ inches. Publisher's blue cloth.

Apart from *Vanity Fair* Thackeray illustrated only *Pendennis* among his full-length novels of modern life. He entrusted *The Newcomes* (144) to Doyle and *Philip* to Frederick Walker. As in his earlier novel, text and drawings make a seamless web, and his realizations of Captain Costigan and Major Pendennis in particular are masterpieces of characterization.

≫ Graphite, pen and ink, and watercolor drawing of Captain Costigan. Signed by the artist. Sheet size: 5½×4¼ inches.

A finished drawing for the woodcut of chapter 42 (II, 35).

≫ Pen and ink and watercolor drawing: "Caracatura of Colon! Esmond." Signed and inscribed by the artist on the verso. Sheet size: 6⅞×4¾ inches.

Thackeray here purports to offer a caricature by Hogarth of the hero of *The History of Henry Esmond* as he appeared in his Virginian retirement. Believing that *Esmond* was too grave a book for his style of drawing, he let the first edition appear without illustrations; but he was not averse to amusing his friends with portraits of his somber hero, who on occasion is referred to in the novel as "Don Dismalo." The classic illustrations of *Esmond* are by du Maurier (196).

124 WILLIAM MAKEPEACE THACKERAY

The Rose and the Ring; or, the history of Prince Giglio and Prince Bulbo. A fire-side pantomime for great and small children. By Mr. M. A. Titmarsh . . . London, Smith, Elder, and co., 1855. iv, 128 p. + 16 p. ads. Illus: Wood-engraved front., t.p. vignette, 7 wood-engraved plates, and 47 wood-engraved vignettes after Thackeray. Printer: Bradbury & Evans. Page size: 7× 5⅜ inches. Half red morocco by Zaehnsdorf, orig. wrappers bound in.

This was the last of Thackeray's six Christmas books. In its day it rivalled *A Christmas Carol* in public esteem, but Dickens's narrative power and pathos have outlasted Thackeray's wit and literary sophistication. Nevertheless, this "Fireside Pantomime for Great and Small Children" remains

HIS R. H. THE PRINCE OF CRIM TARTARY.

[*To face p.* 43.

(124) W. M. Thackeray, *The Rose and the Ring*

Drawing in the manuscript of *The Rose and the Ring*

Thackeray's most successful visit to "happy, harmless fable land." In its small way it is as complete and harmonious a marriage of story and illustration as *Vanity Fair* itself.

124A   WILLIAM MAKEPEACE THACKERAY

The Rose and the Ring. [By] William Makepeace Thackeray. Reproduced in facsimile from the author's original illustrated manuscript in The Pierpont Morgan Library. With an introduction by Gordon N. Ray. New York, The Pierpont Morgan Library, 1947. [2], xviii, [90] p. Printer: Spiral Press. Page size: 8⅜ × 11 inches. Publisher's red cloth.

❧ Autograph manuscript of *The Rose and the Ring* with original watercolor drawings. [90] p. Illus: 73 pen and ink vignettes and 9 full-page pen and ink drawings, some colored. Page size: 5½ × 8¼ inches. Red morocco.

Pierpont Morgan Library

The Rose and the Ring had its origin early in 1854 when Thackeray began a tale about some Twelfth Night characters he had drawn for a children's party in Rome. He went on to compose this manuscript for Edith Story, the small daughter of friends, who was convalescing from malarial fever. Later in the year he turned his tale into a Christmas book, revising it substantially and leaving out many of the illustrations. A comparison of manuscript and book shows how much Thackeray's drawings lost in being engraved.

❧ Drawings and engravings in the form of comic playing cards:

Pen and ink drawing of Gibbon, Boswell, and Johnson "from the originals in sticking plaster by Miss Williams." Inscribed by the artist. Sheet size: 2¼ × 3½ inches.

Three engravings with watercolor, 1 with graphite work: Dr. Birch's establishment; Uncle Tom, Simon Legree, and Little Eva; Macbeth, Banquo, and the witches. The last is inscribed by the artist. Sheet size: 2¼ × 3½ inches.

In his later years Thackeray projected a pack of comic playing cards, but though he made many drawings and had some of them engraved, the enterprise was never brought to completion.

Drawing for a pack of comic playing cards

Phiz (Hablot K. Browne) (1815–1882)

Phiz, to call Hablot K. Browne by the name by which he is remembered, has until recently been poorly served by scholars and critics. The one ostensible biography devoted to him is singularly lacking in documentary information, and no one has done for his illustrations what Albert M. Cohn has for Cruikshank's or W. B. Osgood Field for Lear's and Leech's. Yet Phiz was an abundant and delightful artist who served Victorian storytellers well. Altogether at home with the slapdash novel of the 1830s and 1840s, he took endless pains to realize in vivacious and faithful detail the comic and dramatic scenes offered him by Dickens, Lever, and Ainsworth. Even at this period, however, his talent was essentially literary, finding its inspiration in reading and fancy rather than in life. When the Victorian novel took its decisive turn towards realism and psychological truth after the appearance of *Vanity Fair* in 1847–1848, Phiz's puppets came to seem increasingly out of keeping with the texts they were designed to illustrate, and after *A Tale of Two Cities* even Dickens gave him up. He lived for a while by accepting the occasional commissions for book illustration that his former reputation still brought his way, by making copies in watercolor of his etchings for Dickens's novels, and by producing innumerable sketches of lovely ladies and cherubic children. In 1867 he suffered a serious and prolonged illness which aged him prematurely and drastically impaired his ability to draw, and his last fifteen years were a time of neglect and frustration.

REFERENCES Browne; Harvey; Johannsen; Muir, *Victorian Illustrated Books*; Thomson.

125 CHARLES DICKENS

The Posthumous Papers of the Pickwick Club. By Charles Dickens. With forty-three illustrations, by R. Seymour and Phiz. London, Chapman and Hall, 1837. xiv, [2], 609 p. Illus: Etched front., added etched t.p., and 35 etched plates by Phiz; 7 etched plates by Seymour. Printer: Bradbury & Evans. Page size: 8½ × 5½ inches. Publisher's purple cloth.

For publication of *The Pickwick Papers* in book form Phiz redrew his early etchings for the part issue which were too worn for further service, in the process effecting a striking improvement in his realization of the scenes depicted. See Plate XXXVIII.

126 ROBERT SURTEES

Jorrocks's Jaunts and Jollities; or, the hunting, shooting, racing, driving, sailing, eating, eccentric, and extravagant exploits of that renowned sporting citizen, Mr. John Jorrocks . . . with twelve illustrations by Phiz. London, Walter Spiers, 1838. [7], 358, [1] p. Illus: Etched front. and 11 etched plates by Phiz. Printer: W. Spiers. Page size: 8½ × 5⅜ inches. Contemp. half morocco.

A presentation copy to Surtees's sister inscribed: "E. M. Surtees—with the author's respectful Comp^ts Ap^l 7/38." The fame of Henry Alken's illustrations for Surtees's novel (47) has caused Phiz's lively drawings to be forgotten.

☙ Graphite and pen and ink drawing, an unused illustration for "Mr. Jorrocks at Margate." Image size: 4¾ × 4¾ inches.

Mr. Jorrocks, who has lost his trousers while bathing, is pursued through Margate by a mob: "There's old cutty skirt!"—"Who's got your breeches, old cock?" (p. 195).

127 CHARLES LEVER

The Confessions of Harry Lorrequer. With numerous illustrations by Phiz . . . Dublin, William Curry, Jun. and co. . . . 1839. Added etched t.p., xv, 344 p. Illus: Etched front., added etched t.p., and 20 etched plates by Phiz. Printers: John S. Folds. Page size: 8⅞ × 5⅝ inches. Publisher's purple cloth.

☙ Three graphite drawings, 1 with wash: preliminary sketches for "Lorrequer practicing physic," *The Con-*

fessions of Harry Lorrequer, p. 137. Image sizes: 4×4¾, 4½×4½, 3¾×4 inches.

128 CHARLES DICKENS

The Life and Adventures of Martin Chuzzlewit. By Charles Dickens. With illustrations by Phiz. London, Chapman and Hall, 1844. Added etched t.p., xiv, [1], 624 p. Illus: Etched front., added etched t.p., and 38 etched plates by Phiz. Printer: Bradbury & Evans. Page size: 8⅜×5¼ inches. Red morocco by Riviere.

☙ Graphite and watercolor drawing for "Truth Prevails, and Virtue is Triumphant," *The Life and Adventures of Martin Chuzzlewit*, p. 120. Signed by the artist. Sheet size: 5¾×4½ inches.

Phiz's depiction of the two great grotesques of this novel, Mrs. Gamp and Mr. Pecksniff, has fixed them once for all in posterity's mind. This scene shows Pecksniff and his daughters Charity and Mercy ("Not unholy names, I hope?" Pecksniff inquires of Mrs. Todgers) parading their merits before old Martin Chuzzlewit in chapter 10.

129 GEORGE HALSE

Sir Guy de Guy: a stirring romaunt. Showing how a Briton drilled for his Fatherland; won a heiress; got a pedigree; and caught the rheumatism. By Rattlebrain. Illustrated by Phiz. London, Routledge, Warne, and Routledge, 1864. [3], 167 p. Illus: Wood-engraved front., wood-engraved t.p. vignette, 39 wood-engraved vignettes, and 5 wood-engraved plates, all after Phiz. Printer: Edmund Evans. Page size: 7¾×5⅜ inches. Publisher's blue cloth.

☙ Graphite, china white, and pen and ink drawing, perhaps a rejected frontispiece, relating to "Delirium of Hero" in *Sir Guy de Guy*, p. 44. Signed by the artist. Sheet size: 8⅜×7⅛ inches.

130 ANTHONY TROLLOPE

Can You Forgive Her? By Anthony Trollope . . . with illustrations. In two volumes . . . London, Chapman and Hall, 1864–5. 2 v. I: vi, [2], 320 p. + 4 p. ads. II: vi, [2], 320 p. Illus: I: Etched front. and 19 etched plates by Phiz. II: Wood-engraved front. and 19 wood-engraved plates. Printer: William Clowes and sons. Page size: 8¾×5⅝ inches. Publisher's red cloth.

This novel first appeared in twenty as nineteen monthly parts. Phiz was replaced after part 10, which concluded volume I, so abruptly that the cover of part 11 still carries the words "With Illustrations by H. K. Browne." Trollope's discontent is easily comprehended if one compares Phiz's

Drawing for *Martin Chuzzlewit*, "Truth Prevails, and Virtue is Triumphant"

work with that which Millais had done for *Orley Farm* (168) not long before.

☙ Graphite and chalk drawing for "Baker, you must put Dandy on the bar," *Can You Forgive Her?*, I, 168. Signed by the artist, annotated by Trollope on the verso. Sheet size: 5⅛×7¼ inches.

One of Trollope's complaints against Phiz was his inattention to detail. On the back of this drawing he has written: "The off beast should be a mare. The two are Dandy & Flirt. The man is at Dandy's head."

Facing drawings in "Cholera mortality tables"

[Ludwig Dyrsen, **Beobachtungen und Erfahrungen über die epidemische Cholera** . . . Riga, Frantzen, 1831.] [10] p., 83 folding tables. Inscribed by Phiz: "Cholera mortality tables. A delightful new work in 3 vols. from the General circulating library." Page size: $7\frac{1}{2} \times 7$ inches. Contemp. boards.

Phiz has decorated this book with some sixty chalk drawings. A good many are of idealized women, children, and dogs in the rococo style that appealed to his patrons of the 1860s, but most are somber, grim, even sinister sketches which suggest that by this time Phiz, like Webster, was "much possessed by death" and "saw the skull beneath the skin." There are skeletons and death's heads, sometimes by themselves, sometimes confronting his ideal figures. There are graveyard scenes. There are tableaus calling to mind Gavarni's "Les lorettes vieillies" (30 lithographs, 1852–1853): a haggard old woman, for example, assuring a beautiful young girl that "As I am such shall you be." Most moving of all in their implications are the rudimentary drawings of scampering skeletons that

fill several pages. Entitled "The Coming Race," an allusion to Bulwer Lytton's novel of that name published in 1871, they offer a hint of Phiz's bleakness of mind during his later years.

131 CHARLES DICKENS

The Posthumous Papers of the Pickwick Club by Charles Dickens. With fifty-seven illustrations by "Phiz". London, Chapman and Hall, [1871]. xii, 400 p. Illus: wood-engraved front., t.p. vignette, 52 vignettes, and 3 plates, all after Phiz. Printer: Virtue & co. Page size: $9\frac{3}{4} \times 7\frac{3}{8}$ inches. Publisher's green cloth.

The illustrations to this book, the first volume of the Household Edition of Dickens's *Works* published between 1871 and 1879, have found few admirers. If one looks only at the engravings by the Dalziels and others it is hard to blame Chapman and Hall for deserting Phiz in the volumes that followed. Indeed, those illustrated by J. Mahoney (212, 213) were notably successful.

∾ "Scrap album": 33 leaves, on which are mounted 59 graphite and chalk drawings, 22 of which are for the 1871 edition of *The Pickwick Papers*. Album sheet size: 10½ × 8⅞ inches. The sheet size of the drawings for *The Pickwick Papers* varies, but that reproduced is 4½ × 5½ inches. Original brown cloth.

We learn from Edgar Browne (*Phiz and Dickens*, p. 313) that Phiz made these drawings at "the beginning of his convalescence" from the severe illness mentioned above. He had "lost the use of his right thumb, and part use of his right leg, . . . and though he could not close his thumb over his pen-cil, he continued to draw, holding his pencil between his fingers alone." Nonetheless, a comparison of Phiz's drawing of Mr. Weller introducing Sam to his fellow coachmen at a public house with what the engraver made of it (p. 313) may suggest that the wholesale condemnation of his work for the Household Edition has been too severe. Moreover, of these twenty-two drawings only two present scenes that he had dealt with in the 1837 edition of the novel. Thus this album offers a considerable extension of Phiz's visual record of *The Pickwick Papers*.

Drawing for *The Pickwick Papers*, 1871, Mr. Weller introducing Sam to fellow coachmen

John Leech (1817-1864)

Leech was a Victorian gentleman, trained at Charterhouse school, and at home in good society. If success did not come to him at once, his services as an illustrator were in constant demand from 1840 on, and two years later he found his lifetime's occupation by joining the staff of *Punch*. It is a tribute to Leech's amiability that, though his great friend on the magazine was Thackeray, who wrote what remains the most sympathetic and penetrating essay elicited by his work, he was also on good terms with Douglas Jerrold, whose social views he cannot have shared. Indeed, he illustrated much of Jerrold's fiction and none of Thackeray's. His vast production bears testimony to a life devoted primarily to his art, in which he put to good use the materials that came his way in his happy family circle, in London society, and in the sporting pursuits he enjoyed.

Leech was at ease in his world, and human existence as seen in his drawings, though it has its annoyances and setbacks, is on the whole agreeable and amusing. If he took what Walter Bagehot called "the optional view of life," he was thoroughly aware of the selectiveness of his vision. In ironical illustration of the simplicity of his tastes, for example, he once said that, given his bottle of claret and his hunter, he was happy. So he put to one side the misery and poverty he saw around him and contrived to give whatever subjects experience brought him a wry and entertaining turn. The panorama Leech was thus enabled to offer of his fellow creatures jogging comfortably along at home, in social intercourse, and at play is among the most congenial in English illustration.

REFERENCES Field, *Leech*; Muir, *Victorian Illustrated Books*; Rose; Spielmann; Thackeray, *Quarterly Review*.

132 RICHARD BARHAM

The Ingoldsby Legends or mirth and marvels by Thomas Ingoldsby, esquire. London, Richard Bentley, 1840. Etched t.p., v, [2], 338, [2] p. Illus: 6 etched plates by Leech. Printer: Samuel Bentley. Page size: $8 \times 5\frac{1}{4}$ inches. Publisher's brown cloth.

Leech's rendering of the jackdaw of Rheims under the curse of bell, book, and candle confirmed the appearance of a comic artist of the first order. He also contributed etchings to the second and third series of *Ingoldsby Legends* in 1842 and 1847.

133 PERCIVAL LEIGH

Portraits of Children of the Mobility. Drawn from nature by J. Leech. With memoirs and characteristic sketches by the author of "The comic English grammar," etc. London, Richard Bentley, 1841. [3], 47 p. + 1 p. ads. Illus: 8 lithographic plates by Leech. Printer: Samuel Bentley. Page size: $12\frac{1}{4} \times 9\frac{7}{8}$ inches. Publisher's brown cloth.

The 1830s had been the heyday of the lavishly produced gift book heaping obsequious flattery on the nobility. In this collection of scenes from London street life, Leech's mild parody extends to a coat of arms with such bearings as "a shocking bad Hat" and "a Pot of Heavy." But there is no real political animus; his aim is to show the humor and pathos of his small subjects.

134 W. H. MAXWELL

The Fortunes of Hector O'Halloran, and his man Mark Antony O'Toole. By W. H. Maxwell . . . with illustrations by J. Leech. London, Richard Bentley, [April 1842 – May 1843]. 13 parts. [3], 412 p. Illus: Etched front. and 26 etched plates by Leech. Printer: Samuel Bentley. Page size: $9 \times 5\frac{5}{8}$ inches. Orig. printed wrappers.

This story of the adventures of an Irish soldier in the Napoleonic wars brought forth some of Leech's most varied and lively illustrations.

☙ Five graphite and chalk drawings for *Hector O'Halloran*, pages 194, 226, 262, 295, and 359. Sizes vary, but "The House of Call" (p. 226), which is reproduced, measures $4\frac{1}{8} \times 5\frac{3}{8}$ inches.

Drawing for *Hector O'Halloran,* "The House of Call"

135 CHARLES DICKENS

A Christmas Carol. In prose. Being a ghost story of Christmas. By Charles Dickens. With illustrations by John Leech. London, Chapman & Hall, 1843. [5], 166 p. + 2 p. ads. Illus: Colored etched front. and 3 colored etched plates by Leech, 4 wood-engraved vignettes after Leech. Printer: Bradbury and Evans. Page size: 6½ × 4 inches. Publisher's brown cloth.

Leech had unavailingly sought the job of illustrating *The Pickwick Papers* after Robert Seymour's death. Given his chance at last to illustrate Dickens in *A Christmas Carol*, he rose to the opportunity, just as had Phiz with *The Pickwick Papers* (125) and Cruikshank with *Oliver Twist* (116), and the result in each case is the artist's best-known book. To be fully appreciated Leech's etchings should be seen in the first edition, the careful hand-coloring of which he directed himself. See Plate XLVII.

136 GILBERT A'BECKETT

The Comic History of England. By Gilbert A'Beckett. With ten coloured etchings and one hundred and twenty woodcuts by John Leech . . . Published at the Punch Office, 1847–8. 2 v. I: xii, 320 p. II: xii, 304 p. Illus: Colored etched fronts. and 18 colored etched plates by Leech, 35 wood-engraved initials, wood-engraved t.p. vignettes and 164 wood-engraved vignettes after Leech. Printer: Bradbury and Evans. Page size: 8¾ × 5½ inches. Publisher's purple cloth.

The 1840s saw a series of books offering comic versions of serious subjects, a circumstance that led Douglas Jerrold to predict a "Comic Sermon on the Mount." In fact, though there is some labored facetiousness in A'Beckett's text, the element of comedy in the book is provided exclusively by Leech's illustrations.

137 ROBERT SURTEES

Handley Cross; or, Mr. Jorrocks's hunt. By the author of "Mr. Sponge's sporting tour," "Ask Mama," etc. etc. With illustrations by John Leech. London, Bradbury, Evans, & co., 1854. viii, [2], 550 p. Illus: Colored etched front. and 15 colored etched plates by Leech, 20 wood-engraved initials, t.p. vignette and 89 wood-engraved vignettes after Leech. Printer: Bradbury, Evans, and co. Page size: 8¾ × 5½ inches. Publisher's brown cloth.

Mindful of his friend's fondness for hunting, Thackeray sent Surtees to Leech in 1851 for the illustrations to *Mr. Sponge's Sporting Tour*. The book was so well received that Leech was next asked to provide drawings for *Handley Cross*, the best of Surtees's novels, which had been published as an unillustrated "three-decker" in 1843. He also made drawings for *Ask Mama*, *Plain or Ringlets?*, and *Mr. Facey Romford's Hounds*. All five books have become sporting classics. For *Handley Cross* Leech insisted on adding Mr. Jorrocks's name to Surtees's title, seeing at once the comic possibilities of this ardent cockney sportsman. The many etchings and woodcuts Leech devoted to him established Mr. Jorrocks as one of the half dozen most memorable figures in the pantheon of Victorian illustration. See Plate XLVIII.

138

One Hundred and Seventy Designs and Etchings by John Leech . . . London, Richard Bentley, 1865. 2 v. I: [2] l. II: [2] l. Illus: 170 etched plates by Leech. Page size: 17¼ × 11 inches. Publisher's purple cloth.

This imposing memorial to Leech was issued by Bentley in an edition of "not more than forty" copies. It includes most of the illustrations that he did for that publisher, with the substantial exceptions of those for *Hector O'Halloran* and Albert Smith's *Christopher Tadpole*, printed from the original plates on fine paper. Since only the captions of individual plates are given in these volumes, it is useful to know that the original appearance of each etching is recorded in the volume for 1865 of Bentley's *List of the Principal Publications Issued from New Burlington Street* (London, privately printed, 1909).

139

John Leech's Pictures of Life and Character from the collection of "Mr. Punch." London, Bradbury, Agnew, & co., 1887. 3 v. I: [2], 284 p. II: [4], 276 p. III: [2], 267, [1] p. Illus: Each page with multiple wood-engraved vignettes after Leech. Printer: Bradbury, Agnew & co. Page size: 12¼ × 9½ inches. Publisher's red cloth.

Leech was *Punch*'s leading artist from 1842 until his death. In all he made over 3,000 drawings for the magazine. This mass of work is most conveniently studied in his *Pictures of Life and Character*, the five volumes of which were initially published between 1854 and 1859. Reviewing the first of these, Thackeray compared Leech's drawings with the examples of graphic farce and satire that he had seen as a child. "Whilst we live we must laugh," Thackeray remarked, "and have folks to make us laugh. We cannot afford to lose Satyr with his pipe and dances and gambols. But we have washed, combed, clothed, and taught the rogue good manners." If Cruikshank made English comic art fit for English homes, Leech took the further step of making it a school for gentlemanly behavior. And indeed prosperous mid-Victorian life is nowhere more fully and sympathetically depicted than in Leech's *Punch* engravings. Particularly prominent is Mr. Briggs, the artist's middle-class counterpart to Mr. Jorrocks, who is also seen as a rule in some sporting misadventure.

&❧ Twelve graphite sketches, "Railway miseries" in *Punch's almanac*, 1846. Sizes vary, but the first, "Out with the hounds—meeting with something like a check!" which is reproduced, measures $3\frac{5}{8} \times 6$ inches.

After 1841 "Punch's Almanac" occupied the opening twelve pages of the first number of *Punch* each year. Since 1845 had witnessed the "railway mania," that is to say rampant speculation attendant on the great expansion of railway lines, it was fitting that this phenomenon should receive attention in *Punch*. Leech here deals with his topic in the setting he knew best, its relationship to sport.

Drawing for "Railway Miseries," "Out with the hounds—meeting with something like a check!"

Drawing for the title page of *The Loving Ballad of Lord Bateman*

Richard Doyle (1824–1883)

Richard ("Dicky") Doyle was the son of John Doyle, an Irish Catholic whose lithographs over the signature "H.B." provided a running commentary on English political affairs from 1829 to 1851; the brother of James Doyle, who wrote and illustrated Edmund Evans's edition of *A Chronicle of England* (241); and the uncle of Sir Arthur Conan Doyle. His precocity as an artist is attested by the survival of several early illustrated manuscripts, among them *Jack the Giant Killer*. Since his father charged him with keeping a pictorial record of London ceremonies and processions, he developed a special facility in drawing crowds, a gift that was to set the pattern for several of his later books. His first important commission as an illustrator was for W. H. Maxwell's *Hector O'Halloran* (134), where his work appeared beside that of Leech. He joined the staff of *Punch* in 1843 and enjoyed a great success with *Manners and Customs of Ye Englyshe*, but he felt compelled to withdraw in 1850 because he could not condone the magazine's campaign against the so-called Papal Aggression. Henceforth he devoted himself chiefly to books. His illustrations for the work of other writers include Ruskin's *The King of the Golden River*, his friend Thackeray's *Rebecca and Rowena* and *The Newcomes*, and Thomas Hughes's *The Scouring of the White Horse*, but his most characteristic designs bodied forth his own conceptions, notably in *The Foreign Tour of Messrs. Brown, Jones, and Robinson, Birds-eye Views of Modern Society*, and above all *In Fairyland*, where Allingham's text was merely a starting point. Like Phiz he had the misfortune of outliving his favor with the public by many years, but his whimsical fancy and quaint individuality of style have recently brought him new admirers.

REFERENCES   Muir, *Victorian Illustrated Books*; Hambourg; Spielmann.

140   RICHARD DOYLE

Jack the Giant Killer, by Richard Doyle. London, Eyre and Spottiswoode, [1888]. 48 p. Illus: Each page with

George Cruikshank, etching for *The Loving Ballad of Lord Bateman*, 1839

colored wood-engraved border and colored illustrations after Doyle. Page size: $9\frac{3}{4} \times 8$ inches. Publisher's blue cloth.

Though the book was not published until after Doyle's death, it seems appropriate to begin with this color facsimile of an illustrated manuscript of 1842. Doyle's refined and fanciful talent at least assured that Jack's story would receive its least gruesome rendering. The giants are unmistakably Irish.

Pencil drawing: design of a title page for "Certayne passages from ye Ballade of ye Lorde Bateman illustrated." Sheet size: $9\frac{1}{4} \times 10\frac{5}{8}$ inches.

The Loving Ballad of Lord Bateman, a poem which is not necessarily as primitive as it purports to be, was published in 1839 with etchings by Cruikshank

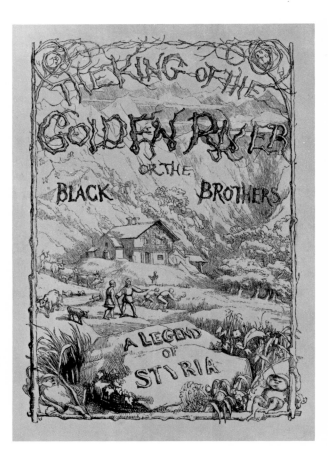

(142) John Ruskin, *The King of the Golden River*, frontispiece and title page

and mock-learned notes by Dickens. In designing the title page for an edition which was never carried to completion, Doyle chose a passage early in the story. Lord Bateman on his travels has been imprisoned by a Turk, who chains him to a tree; but salvation is at hand in the person of Sophia, the Turk's daughter, who is later to liberate and finally to wed him. It will be seen that Doyle's conception of the two lovers is quite different from that of Cruikshank, in whose drawings, moreover, the Turk does not appear at all.

141 PERCIVAL LEIGH

Manners and Customs of Ye Englyshe, drawn from ye quick by Richard Doyle. To which be added some ex-

tracts from Mr. Pips hys diary. Contributed by Percival Leigh. [London], Bradbury & Evans, [1849]. [3], 40 l. Illus: Wood-engraved t.p. and 40 wood-engraved plates after Doyle. Page size: 8¼ × 10⅞ inches. Publisher's half morocco, printed cover.

In this series of drawings the varied scenes of a London season are comprehensively displayed: a wedding breakfast, a musical tea, and a soirée; Greenwich Fair, Lord's cricket ground, and Mme Tussaud's wax works; Hyde Park, Kensington Gardens, and St. James's. Usually Doyle's effects depend on his skilful disposal of groups of figures, but he can also put celebrities like Lord Brougham and Disraeli to good use in arranging his compositions.

142 JOHN RUSKIN

The King of the Golden River; or, the black brothers: a legend of Stiria. Illustrated by Richard Doyle. London, Smith, Elder & co., 1851. Added wood-engraved t.p., [6], 56 p. + 2 p. ads. Illus: Wood-engraved front., added wood-engraved t.p., 16 wood-engraved vignettes, and 4 wood-engraved initials, all after Doyle. Printer: H. Vizetelly. Page size: 7 × 5¼ inches. Publisher's printed boards.

This is a young man's book. Ruskin wrote it when he was twenty-two, and ten years later entrusted its illustration to Doyle, who was then twenty-seven. Well prepared for the assignment by the drawings for similar texts which he had done for his own amusement, the artist made a little masterpiece of Ruskin's fairy tale of good and bad brothers, a bugle-nosed dwarf, and a Treasure Valley "lost by cruelty" and "regained by love."

143 RICHARD DOYLE

The Foreign Tour of Messrs. Brown, Jones, and Robinson, being the history of what they saw, and did, in Belgium, Germany, Switzerland, & Italy. By Richard Doyle. London, Bradbury & Evans, 1854. [1], 80, [1] l., each l. with wood-engraved illustration and letterpress text. Page size: 11½ × 9⅛ inches. Contemp. half morocco.

This is Doyle's most personal book with respect to his life in the world, though *In Fairyland* brings us closer to his imaginative life. The artist Brown, in whom there is a good deal of Doyle himself, records in scores of little scenes the vicissitudes and humors encountered by his companions and himself during a summer's excursion to Germany and northern Italy. There is even a moment of excitement when the three are arrested as spies in Verona, but they are soon extricated from their predicament by the intervention of Brown's near relation, the governor of the city, "Field-Marshal Lieutenant Count Brown, of the Imperial Service."

144 WILLIAM MAKEPEACE THACKERAY

The Newcomes. Memoirs of a most respectable family, edited by Arthur Pendennis, esq. With illustrations on steel and wood by Richard Doyle . . . London, Bradbury & Evans, 1854–55. 2 v. I: viii, 380 p. II: Added etched t.p., viii, 375 p. Illus: Etched fronts., added etched titles, 44 etched plates, 43 wood-engraved vignettes, and 76 wood-engraved initials, all after Doyle. Printer: Bradbury & Evans. Page size: 8¾ × 5⅝ inches. Publisher's green cloth.

(144) William Makepeace Thackeray, *The Newcomes*

Doyle's drawings for this book are much of a piece stylistically with those for *The Foreign Tour of Messrs. Brown, Jones, and Robinson,* and indeed many of Thackeray's chapters are also laid on the Continent. The author was not at first pleased with his artist, but in time he became accustomed to Doyle's way of doing things and gave his friend credit for the immense pains he had taken. The attention of the novel's initial readers no doubt centered on Doyle's etchings, which made Colonel Newcome almost as familiar a personage as Phiz's Mr. Pickwick or Cruikshank's Fagin, but his woodcut vignettes and above all his initial letters, in which his fancy gets full play, also have great charm.

145 RICHARD DOYLE

Birds-eye Views of Modern Society, in sixteen plates taken by Richard Doyle. Reprinted from the Cornhill Magazine. [London, 1864]. Illus: 16 wood-engraved plates after Doyle. Page size: 8⅞ × 13¼ inches. Publisher's printed wrappers.

Doyle's designs first appeared in the *Cornhill Magazine* during 1861 and 1862. There is a startling contrast between these dense, almost claustrophobic, scenes of London life and the open and airy drawings he made for *Manners and Customs of Ye Englyshe*. Examining these designs, which fairly teem with smiling, well-groomed humanity, one wonders if fifteen years of dining out had not in-

duced in Doyle a revulsion comparable to that which led Trollope a decade later to write *The Way We Live Now.*

146 WILLIAM ALLINGHAM

In Fairyland, a series of pictures from the Elf-world by Richard Doyle, With a poem, by William Allingham. London, Longmans, Green, Reader, & Dyer, 1870. [4], 31 p. Illus: Colored wood-engraved front. and 15 colored wood-engraved plates after Doyle. Printer: E. Evans. Page size: 14⅞ × 10⅞ inches. Publisher's green cloth.
Miss Julia P. Wightman

Looking within himself, Doyle found a fantastic, but consistently imagined world in which fairies and elves live in the open air among birds, butterflies, snails, and beetles as large as themselves. If his elves and fairies also like to congregate, their convivialities, unlike those of his massed human beings, are never oppressive. Edmund Evans's fine wood engravings for this volume are the largest that he made during his long career as a color printer. See Plate LXXII.

"Dalziel's Fine Art Books"

Considerations of space have relegated craftsmen to the background in this survey, but the Dalziel Brothers cannot be denied a prominent place in presenting the wonderful efflorescence of books illustrated with wood engravings that were published in the third quarter of the century. George (1815–1902), Edward (1817–1905), John (1822–1869), and Thomas (1823–1906) Dalziel grew up in Bewick's town, Newcastle-on-Tyne. All were artists, but only the youngest brother made painting and drawing his career. The other three earned positions among the leading wood engravers of their time. Beginning in the middle 1850s, when they established arrangements under which Rout-

ledge, Warne, and others published books for them, they were responsible for the appearance of a long series of "Dalziel's Fine Art Books" in which illustrations were the be-all and end-all. In the process they became the leading patrons of book illustrators in general, as well as a sort of special providence to a few of them, notably Houghton, North, Pinwell, and Walker. Their chief books with engravings after several artists appear in this section. Other books with engravings after a single artist appear subsequently under the names of the artists concerned.

REFERENCES *Brothers Dalziel*; Muir, *Victorian Illustrated Books*; Forrest Reid.

Thomas Dalziel, manuscript of Tennyson's "The May Queen"

⊷ Four watercolor, pen and ink, and graphite drawings from "Shreds from Shakespeare Illustrated by Members of the Crayon Club 1854." Image size: 4⅞ × 6⅞ inches.

Thomas Dalziel, "She's gone for ever!" *King Lear*, Act 5, Scene 3.

John Dalziel, "Those high wild hills, and rough uneven ways," *Richard the Second*, Act 2, Scene 3.

George Dalziel, Anne Page. "Wil't please your worship to come in, sir?" Slender. "No I thank you, forsooth, heartily; I am very well." *The Merry Wives of Windsor*, Act 1, Scene 1.

Edward Dalziel, "Where should this music be?" *The Tempest*, Act 1, Scene 2.

The other members of the Crayon Club, who also contributed drawings, were Augustine Aglio, Jr., W. J. Ferguson, Edmund Gill, Mason Jackson, Elisha Noyce, J. Abbott Pasquier, and John Sleigh. A second series of Crayon Club drawings by the same eleven artists was collected the following year, this time with "Proverbs and Sayings" as its theme.

⊷ The May Queen, a poem by Alfred Tennyson. Illustrated by T.B.G.S. Dalziel. 1855. [A calligraphic manuscript, signed on the final l.: "TBGS Dalziel."] 48 l. Illus: 81 pen and ink drawings. Page size: 14⅝ × 10⅜ inches. Contemp. purple morocco.

These delicate and harmonious drawings emphasize the aspects of Tennyson's pathetic poem that once made it a household favorite. Thomas Dalziel may have intended his work as the mid-Victorian equivalent of a medieval illuminated manuscript, but had he produced it a few years later, at the period of the Brothers' great success, they would no doubt have made it into a book. It deserves reproduction today.

147 WILLIAM ALLINGHAM

The Music Master, a love story. And two series of day and night songs. By William Allingham . . . London, G. Routledge . . . 1855. xii, [1], 221, [1] p. + 2 p. ads. Illus: wood-engraved front. and 7 plates after A. Hughes, 1 wood-engraved plate after J. E. Millais, and 1 wood-engraved plate after D. G. Rossetti. Printer: Savill and Edwards. Page size: 6½ × 4¼ inches. Publisher's green cloth.

In his preface Allingham thanks the "excellent painters" who illustrated his poems for having "submitted their genius to the risks of wood engraving" (p. ix). Their satisfaction with what the Dalziels made of their drawings paved the way for Tennyson's *Poems* two years later. Rossetti's "The Maids of Elfen-Mere" has become famous, but Hughes's contributions also make their characteristic appeal.

148 ALFRED, LORD TENNYSON

Poems by Alfred Tennyson, D.C.L., Poet Laureate. London, Edward Moxon, 1857. xiii, [1], 375, [1] p. Illus: 54 wood-engraved vignettes after T. Creswick, J. C. Horsley, W. H. Hunt, D. Maclise, J. E. Millais, W. Mulready, D. G. Rossetti, and C. Stanfield. Printer: Bradbury & Evans. Page size: 8¾ × 6¼ inches. Publisher's blue cloth.

Moxon conceived this book in 1855, paid handsomely for the illustrations (£30 for each drawing to Rossetti, £25 to the other artists), put up with Rossetti's delays, and published an edition of several thousand copies. The Dalziel Brothers engraved nearly half the drawings, however, and despite Rossetti's only half-jesting protest against their work ("O woodman spare that block"), it seems fair to include the volume among their "Fine Art Books." Moxon's impartial division of the illustrations among traditional and Pre-Raphaelite artists did not satisfy the book-buyers of the day. "The greater proportion were in favour of the work done by prominent artists of the old school," Holman Hunt recalled, "and their admirers were scandalised by the incorporation of designs by members of the Pre-Raphaelite Brotherhood; while our fewer appreciators would not buy the book in which the preponderance of work was by artists they did not approve." (*Some Poems by Alfred, Lord Tennyson,* pp. 23–24.) After offering copies at a discount, Moxon at last sold his remaining stock to Routledge. The book's subsequent celebrity has made the original edition valuable, though it is not rare even today. See Plate LVI.

148A ALFRED, LORD TENNYSON

Poems by Alfred Lord Tennyson, D.C.L. Poet Laureate. Illustrated. London, Macmillan and co., 1893. xiii, [1], 374, [2] p. Illus: Engraved front. and 54 wood-engraved vignettes after T. Creswick, J. C. Horsley W. H. Hunt, D. Maclise, J. E. Millais, W. Mulready, D. G. Rossetti, and C. Stanfield. All illustrations are printed on India paper. Printer: R. Clay and sons. Page size: 10¼ × 6⅞, large-paper copy. Publisher's blue cloth.

In this handsome new edition the engravings are printed from the original blocks on transparent India paper.

148B ALFRED, LORD TENNYSON

Some Poems by Alfred Lord Tennyson, with illustrations by W. Holman Hunt, J. E. Millais, and Dante Gabriel Rossetti printed from the original wood blocks cut for the MDCCCLXVI edition with photogravures from some of the original drawings now first reproduced. With a preface by Joseph Pennell treating of the illustrators of the Sixties & an introduction by W. Holman Hunt. London, Freemantle & co., 1901. xxiv, 135, [1] p. Illus: Photogravure front. and 6 photogravure plates, and 30 wood-engraved plates after the above artists. Printer: Riverside Press. Page size: 10⅛ × 7⅝ inches. Publisher's quarter morocco.

Seeking to avoid a book "overloaded with many engravings of little or no value," the publishers reprinted only the poems in the 1857 volume illustrated by Hunt, Millais, and Rossetti in an edition of 150 copies. The plates were again printed from the original blocks on transparent India paper. The novelty of the book lies in its reproductions of six drawings from surviving photographs, three by Hunt and three by Rossetti, opposite the engravings made from them, and in Hunt's introductory recollections of the circumstances which led to the original publication of the Moxon Tennyson.

149 ROBERT ARIS WILLMOTT, EDITOR

The Poets of the Nineteenth Century. Selected and edited by the Rev. Robert Aris Willmott, incumbent of Bearwood. Illustrated with one hundred engravings, drawn by eminent artists, and engraved by the Brothers Dalziel. London, G. Routledge & co., 1857. xv, 398, [2] p. Illus: 100 wood-engraved vignettes after F. M. Brown, E. H. Corbould, T. Dalziel, B. Foster, J. Gilbert, A. Hughes, J. Tenniel, and others. Printer: R. Clay. Page size: 8⅝ × 6⅜ inches. Publisher's red cloth.

This volume is as ambitious in conception as Tennyson's *Poems*, but largely traditional in its illustrators, with Thomas Dalziel, Birkett Foster, and Tenniel in the ascendant. The three Pre-Raphaelite designs (Ford Madox Brown's for "The Prisoner of Chillon" and Millais's for Byron's "The Dream" and Coleridge's "Love") constitute its chief appeal today.

150 ROBERT ARIS WILLMOTT, EDITOR

English Sacred Poetry, of the sixteenth, seventeenth, eighteenth, and nineteenth centuries. Selected and edited by Robert Aris Willmott, M.A., incumbent of Bear Wood. Illustrated by Holman Hunt, J. D. Wat-

(150) *English Sacred Poetry*, illustration by Frederick Sandys for "The Little Mourner"

son, John Gilbert, J. Wolf, etc., engraved by the Brothers Dalziel. London, Routledge, Warne, & Routledge . . . 1862. xix, 387 p. Illus: Wood-engraved front. and 79 wood-engraved vignettes after J. Gilbert, W. H. Hunt, C. Keene, F. Sandys, F. Smallfield, J. D. Watson, F. Walker, and H. Weir. Printer: R. Clay, Son, and Taylor. Page size: 7⅝ × 6⅜ inches. Publisher's blue cloth.

This is a particularly savory potpourri. Keene, Sandys, and Walker are well represented, but the dominating contributions come from J. D. Watson.

151

Dalziel's Illustrated Arabian Nights' Entertainments, the text revised and emendated throughout by H. W. Dulcken, Ph.D. . . . One hundred illustrations by J. E. Millais, R.A., J. D. Watson, A. B. Houghton, John Tenniel, Thomas Dalziel, G. J. Pinwell, engraved by the Brothers Dalziel. London, Ward and Lock, 1865. 2 v. I: [6], 400 p. II: x, [1], [401]–822 p. Illus: Wood-engraved fronts., wood-engraved t.p. vignettes, and 216 wood-engraved vignettes after the above artists; each page has wood-engraved borders and numerous wood-engraved initials. Printer: Camden Press. Page size: 10½ × 7½ inches. Publisher's green cloth.

The *Arabian Nights* is perhaps the Dalziels' most successful collaborative volume. Houghton and Thomas Dalziel, the book's major artists, worked closely together, the Anglo-Indian Houghton sharing his knowledge of India with his English colleague and giving him free access to his collection of Indian materials (*Brothers Dalziel*, p. 222). With remarkable uniformity of style the abundant illustrations show the fantastic adventures related in this familiar text played out before a consistently imagined background inspired by actual Indian life. See Plate LXIV.

152

The Spirit of Praise, a collection of hymns old and new. London, F. Warne and co., n.d. [10], 250, [1] p. Illus: 150 wood-engraved vignettes after A. W. Bayes, J. Burlison, E. Dalziel, T. Dalziel, Paul Gray, A. B. Houghton, P. Hundley, J. W. North, G. J. Pinwell, W. Small, and F. Smallfield, 8 color-printed. Initial letters, ornamental headings, etc., after P. Hundley. Printer: Camden Press. Page size: 9½ × 6⅞ inches. Publisher's red cloth.

Printed throughout in two or more colors, this is the most ornate of the "Dalziel's Fine Art Books." For once, indeed, the illustrations, chiefly by Thomas Dalziel, are subordinated to the decorations. This copy has the Dalziels' embossed bookplate and is inscribed: "To Margaret Dalziel from her Brothers December 1868."

153

A Round of Days described in original poems by some of our most celebrated poets, and in pictures by eminent artists, engraved by the Brothers Dalziel. London, George Routledge and sons, 1866. [6] l., 93, [1] p. + 2 p. ads. Illus: 21 wood-engraved plates and 47 wood-engraved vignettes after A. W. Bayes, Warwick Brookes, W. P. Burton, T. Dalziel, Paul Gray, A. B.

Houghton, T. Morten, J. W. North, G. J. Pinwell, F. Walker, and J. D. Watson. Printer: Camden Press. Page size: 9⅞ × 7¾ inches. Publisher's red morocco.

This and the next three books might well be selected to represent the illustrators of the sixties at their most characteristic. Limited largely to landscapes and scenes of common life, their engravings provide a graphic counterpart to the early novels of George Eliot (*Adam Bede*, *Silas Marner*, and *The Mill on the Floss*) and the later fiction of Mrs. Gaskell (*Sylvia's Lovers*, *Cousin Phillis*, and *Wives and Daughters*). The series had its origin when the Dalziels commissioned Frederick Walker to make thirty drawings on wood for a volume to accompany Birket Foster's *Pictures of English Landscape* (191). Walker never completed the series, but the drawings that he finished formed the nucleus of this book. (*Brothers Dalziel*, p. 196.) Adding engravings after other artists, most notably Houghton, North, and Pinwell, the Dalziels put together *A Round of Days*, described in their preface as "a Collection of Poems and Pictures representing every-day scenes, occurrences, and incidents" which show "the alternate cloud and sunshine of men's actual experience." See Plate LXV.

154 ROBERT BUCHANAN

Wayside Posies: original poems of the country life. Edited by Robert Buchanan. Pictures by G. J. Pinwell, J. W. North, and Frederick Walker. Engraved by the Brothers Dalziel . . . London, George Routledge and sons, 1867. [7, 91] l. + 2 l. ads. Illus: 22 wood-engraved plates and 20 wood-engraved vignettes after the above artists. Printer: Camden Press. Page size: 10⅛ × 8 inches. Publisher's red morocco.

In this sequel to *A Round of Days*, the Dalziels made virtually no changes in format, design, and content. To Walker's five remaining drawings, they added eighteen each by North and Pinwell. Since the three were friends, working in a common idiom, the result is a singularly harmonious and attractive book.

155 JEAN INGELOW

Poems by Jean Ingelow. With illustrations by G. J. Pinwell, E. J. Poynter, J. W. North, E. Dalziel, J. Wolf, T. Dalziel, A. B. Houghton and W. Small. Engraved by the Brothers Dalziel. London, Longmans, Green, Reader, & Dyer, 1867. xiv, [1], 318, [1] p.

Illus: Wood-engraved front. and 97 wood-engraved vignettes after the above artists. Printer: Camden Press. Page size: 8⅞×6⅝ inches. Publisher's blue cloth.

This is not as agreeable a piece of bookmaking as *Wayside Posies*, but the quality of its illustrations remains high, with Thomas Dalziel taking Walker's place alongside Houghton, North, and Pinwell.

156 ROBERT BUCHANAN

North Coast and other poems by Robert Buchanan, with illustrations by J. Wolf, T. Dalziel, A. B. Houghton, G. J. Pinwell, J. B. Zwecker, W. Small, E. Dalziel, engraved by the Brothers Dalziel. London, George Routledge and sons, 1868. xiv, [1], 250 p. + 6 p. ads. Illus: Wood-engraved front. and 52 wood-engraved plates after the above artists. Printer: Camden Press. Page size: 8⅞×6⅜ inches. Publisher's blue cloth.

In this companion volume to Jean Ingelow's *Poems*, Thomas Dalziel has become the dominant illustrator, though there is enough work by Houghton and Pinwell to link the book closely with the three that went before.

157 JOHN BUNYAN

The Pilgrim's Progress from this world to that which is to come, by John Bunyan. With one hundred illustrations by Frederick Barnard and others, engraved by the Dalziel Brothers. London, Strahan and co., 1880. xvi, 277, [1] p. + 2 p. ads. Illus: Wood-engraved front. and numerous plates and vignettes after Barnard and others. Printer: Camden Press. Page size: 10⅞× 8½ inches. Publisher's brown cloth.

The characteristic note of the sixties is altogether missing from this book. The success of the *Graphic* had established new expectations with regard to elaborately presented volumes illustrated with wood engravings. That the Dalziel Brothers could adapt themselves to changing taste is witnessed by this cold but imposing volume.

158

Dalziel's Bible Gallery. Illustrations from the Old Testament. From original drawings by Sir Frederick Leighton, P.R.A., E. J. Poynter, R.A., H. H. Armstead, R.A., F. Madox Brown, S. Solomon, F. Sandys, E. G. Dalziel, W. Small, A. B. Houghton, G. F. Watts, R.A., E. Armitage, R.A., F. R. Pickersgill, R.A., E. Burne Jones, T. Dalziel, E. J. Brewntnall, Fs. [sic] Walker, R.H.A., A. Murch, and Holman Hunt. Engraved by the Brothers Dalziel. London, Camden Press, [1880].

(154) *Wayside Posies*, illustration by J. W. North for "Glen-Oona"

[5, 62] l. Illus: 62 wood-engraved plates after the above artists. All text and plates are India-paper proofs. Sheet size: 22⅜×15⅜ inches. Publisher's portfolio.

Moved by the excellence of Millais's drawings for *The Parables* (170), the Dalziel Brothers as early as 1862 thought of embarking on an illustrated Bible. They approached the leading artists of the period, and many of them responded with enthusiasm, writing to reserve the scenes that appealed to them most. Frederick Leighton, for example, undertook to provide twelve drawings of "broad, simple, and very pictorial subjects," including the "Four Riders" of the Apocalypse (*Brothers Dalziel*, pp. 238, 244). The scheme proved unrealizable, but it left a noble residue in the engravings of this book, the artistic level of which is surely higher than that in any other of the Dalziels' collaborative volumes. The book is best seen in the India-paper proof copies for presentation, issued in portfolios. This copy is inscribed: "Professor E. J. Poynter RA with regards and many thanks from Dalziel Brothers Octr 1880." In 1894 these drawings were reprinted by the S.P.C.K. with twenty-eight additional engravings in a volume called *Art Pictures from the Old Testament*. See Plate LXXVII. The *Bible Gallery* was the first of several sumptuous folios which the Dalziels themselves issued from "their Camden Press," perhaps aware that their heyday was over and seeking to preserve the high points of their achievement in permanent form. Other volumes in the series are Birket Foster's *Pictures of English Land-scape* (191A), *English Rustic Pictures*, and *Twenty India Proofs . . . to the Parables* (170A).

159

English Rustic Pictures drawn by Frederick Walker . . . and G. J. Pinwell . . . and engraved by the Brothers Dalziel. India proofs. London, George Routledge and sons, [1882]. [4, 31] l. + 1 l. ads. Illus: 15 wood-engraved plates after Walker and 15 wood-engraved plates after Pinwell, printed as India-paper proofs. No. 210 of 300 copies. Printer: Camden Press. Page size: 15¼ × 11 inches. Publisher's vellum.

This book was conceived by the Dalziels as a "Companion Volume" to their large-paper edition of Birkett Foster's *Pictures of English Landscape* (191A). Though the engravings are entirely drawn from *A Round of Days* and *Wayside Posies*, they are to be seen here in their most attractive setting.

Bookplate of the Dalziel Brothers

Books in Which Magazine Wood Engravings Are Republished

Our interest in this survey is in books, and as far as the wood engravings of the third quarter of the century are concerned, these are well exampled in "Dalziel's Fine Art Books." Yet magazines played so significant a part in the English illustration of the period that it would be misleading to omit them altogether. Their existence was a crucial element in the economic structure that made illustration attractive to artists and engravers alike, and their editors sometimes displayed not only enterprise but also a high degree of artistic taste. Luckily the vogue attained by wood engraving led the proprietors of several of these magazines to gather their best cuts for republication in book form. The resulting volumes, though sometimes awkward to handle, have the merit of being carefully printed on good paper.

REFERENCES Forrest Reid; White.

160

The Cornhill Gallery, containing one hundred engravings from drawings on wood, (being designs for the illustrations of "The Cornhill Magazine"). By Frederick Leighton, A.R.A., John Everett Millais, R.A., George du Maurier, J. Noel Paton, R.A.S., Frederick Sandys, George A. Sala, W. M. Thackeray, Frederick Walker, engraved by the Brothers Dalziel, W. J. Linton, and Joseph Swain. London, Smith, Elder & co., 1864. [4] p. Illus: 100 plates after the above artists. Printer: Camden Press. Page size: 12½×9⅞. Publisher's half red morocco.

When that prince of publishers, George Smith, launched this new kind of book with a selection of engravings from his *Cornhill Magazine,* he did it in style. For the magazine itself, with a circulation of over 100,000 copies, illustrations had to be printed from electrotype casts. Here the original woodblocks were impressed on special paper in a spacious format and with no distracting text. As Smith claimed, the result was "an elegant Portfolio," and if a guinea was hardly a "nominal price" in 1864, Millais's illustrations for *Framley*

Parsonage (167) and *The Small House at Allington* (169), Leighton's for *Romola* (206), and Walker's for *Philip* and several shorter stories at least gave the purchaser full measure.

161

Idyllic Pictures drawn by Barnes, Miss Ellen Edwards, Paul Gray, Houghton, R. P. Leitch, Pinwell, Sandys, Small, G. Thomas, etc. etc. London, Cassell, Petter, and Galpin, 1867. 203 l. + 4 p. ads. Illus: Wood-engraved front. and 49 wood-engraved plates after the above and other artists. Page size: 8⅝×6⅜ inches. Publisher's green cloth.

This collection is made up of engravings which first appeared in *The Quiver.* Names of artists are not given, but Forrest Reid provides them in *Illustrators of the Sixties* (pp. 14, 17).

162

Touches of Nature by eminent artists and authors. London, Alexander Strahan, 1867. [4], 98 l. Illus: Wood-engraved t.p. vignette and 98 plates after du Maurier, Houghton, Hunt, Keene, Lawless, Millais, Morten, Pinwell, Sandys, Small, Tenniel, Walker, Watson, and others. Printer: Camden Press. Page size: 12¼×9⅝ inches. Publisher's blue cloth.

With one exception all the engravings in this imposing volume are drawn from the magazines published by Strahan: *The Argosy, The Sunday Magazine,* and, most notably, *Good Words.* They are seen to good advantage in their new surroundings.

163 WALTER THORNBURY

Historical and Legendary Ballads & Songs. By Walter Thornbury. Illustrated by J. Whistler, F. Walker, John Tenniel, J. D. Watson, W. Small, F. Sandys, G. J. Pinwell, T. Morten, M. J. Lawless, and many others. London, Chatto and Windus, 1876. xxiii, [1], 280, [2] p. + 2 p. ads. Illus: 81 wood-engraved vignettes by the above and other artists. Printer: Camden Press. Page size: 9⅝×7¼ inches. Publisher's red cloth.

This agreeable volume provides the most convenient way of sampling the wood engravings published in *Once a Week*, though the reader must put up with the twaddling verses composed by Thornbury to replace the texts which the designs were originally intended to illustrate. Thus George Meredith's "The Old Chartist," which elicited one of Sandys's best drawings, is replaced by Thornbury's "The Miller's Meadow" (p. 214). Despite Sandys's contributions and those of Whistler, the book really belongs to M. J. Lawless. Millais is altogether omitted, perhaps because some of his work for *Once a Week* had already appeared in *Millais' Illustrations* (171). See Plate LXXIV.

☛ Wood-engraved proof touched with graphite and china white, "The Dead Bride," engraved by Swain after Lawless for *Historical and Legendary Ballads*, p. 41. Annotated by the artist. Image size: 7⅛ × 8¼ inches.

The changes requested by Lawless were not made.

164

The Graphic Portfolio, a selection from the admired engravings which have appeared in The Graphic and a description of the art of wood-engraving with numerous illustrations. London, The Graphic Office, 1876. [10] p., 50 l. Illus: 50 wood-engraved plates after numerous artists. Printer: Edmund Evans. Page size: 18 × 14¾ inches. Orig. printed boards.

Soon after *The Graphic* began to appear at the end of 1869, it attained the same sort of prestige that accrued to *Once a Week*, *The Cornhill Magazine*, and *Good Words* in the early 1860s. Though many Sixties illustrators are represented in the fifty plates of this volume, its format, which is only slightly larger than *The Graphic* itself, causes their contributions to seem radically different from their earlier work. The sensation of the first number was an example of the new "social realism," Luke Fildes's "Houseless and Hungry" (the design that led Dickens to choose him as illustrator for *The Mystery of Edwin Drood*), but *The Graphic* soon became a haven for notable illustrators of varied styles. Unwieldy though its volumes may be, a file of this magazine is essential to any collection concerned with English illustration in the last three decades of the century.

(164) *The Graphic Portfolio*

Wood-engraved proof of "The Dead Bride" after M. J. Lawless

"Buy from us with @ golden curl"

GOBLIN MARKET
and other poems
by Christina Rossetti

"Golden head by golden head"

London and Cambridge
Macmillan and Co. 1862

(165) Christina Rossetti, *Goblin Market*

Dante Gabriel Rossetti (1828–1882)

Rossetti made his powerful impression as a book artist through ten drawings and a few binding designs. Each of his ostensible illustrations is virtually an independent work of art, and thus a worthy complement to his paintings, while most of his designs for book covers are marked by a simplicity and elegance that set them apart from the elaborately ornate work of mid-Victorian craftsmen.

REFERENCES   Fredeman; Life; Forrest Reid.

☙ Wood-engraved proof, "The Maids of Elfen-Mere" in William Allingham, *The Music Master*, 1855, p. 202. Image size: 5 × 3 inches.

Burne-Jones described this engraving for *The Music Master* (147) as "the most beautiful drawing for an illustration I have ever seen" (*Oxford and Cambridge Magazine*, 1856, p. 60).

[148C ALFRED, LORD TENNYSON]
Poems by Alfred Tennyson, D.C.L., Poet Laureate. Illustrated by T. Creswick, J. E. Millais, W. Mulready, D. Maclise, Clarkson Stanfield, J. C. Horsley, &c. London, Edward Moxon and co., 1860. xiii, [2], 375, [1] p. Illus: 54 wood-engraved vignettes after T. Creswick, J. C. Horsley, W. H. Hunt, D. Maclise, J. E. Millais, W. Mulready, D. G. Rossetti, and C. Stanfield. Printer: Bradbury and Evans. Page size: 8½ × 5⅞ inches. Green morocco by Hayday.

This copy of a reissue of Tennyson's *Poems* (148) has one remarkable feature. Late in 1859 W. A. Turner desired to make his son a Christmas present of the Moxon Tennyson with Rossetti's signature under each of his five illustrations. He bought this copy, the imprint of which had the following year's date as was customary with gift books issued for the holiday trade, and sent it to the artist. In returning the book with the requested inscriptions, Rossetti wrote: "The glazed paper of the *Tennyson* will not take ink, so I was obliged to write in pencil as the only resource."

165 CHRISTINA ROSSETTI
Goblin Market and other poems. By Christina Rossetti. With two designs by D. G. Rossetti. Cambridge,

Macmillan and co. . . . 1862. Added wood-engraved t.p., vii, 192 p. + 16 p. ads. Illus: Wood-engraved front. and added wood-engraved t.p. after D. G. Rossetti. Printer: Bradbury and Evans. Page size: 6⅝ × 4¼ inches. Publisher's blue cloth.

Rossetti launched this book for his sister, as he did *The Prince's Progress*, by designing the binding and providing a frontispiece and title page vignette. Since there are no further illustrations in either book, the contrast between the opulence of their openings and the austerity of what follows is striking.

Wood-engraved proof of "The Maids of Elfen-Mere" in William Allingham's *The Music Master*

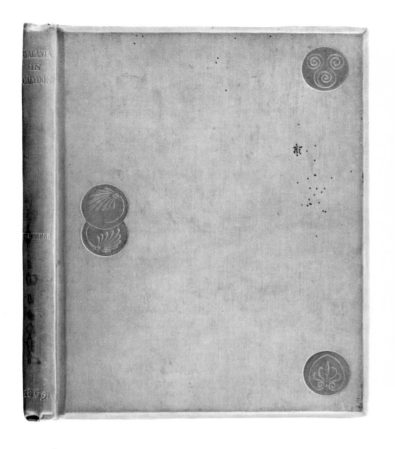

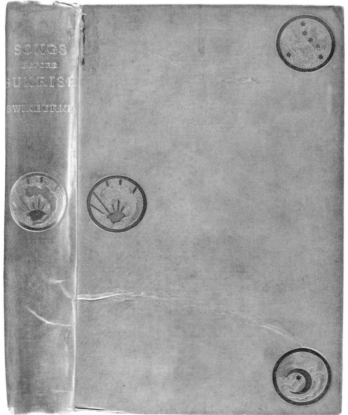

Four bindings designed by Rossetti

The Prince's Progress and other poems by Christina Rossetti. With two designs by D. G. Rossetti. London, Macmillan and co., 1866. Added wood-engraved t.p., viii, 216 p. Illus: Wood-engraved front. and added wood-engraved t.p. after D. G. Rossetti. Printer: R. Clay. Page size 6¾×4¼ inches. Publisher's green cloth.

❧ Four bindings designed by Rossetti:

(A) A. C. Swinburne, *Atalanta in Calydon*, 1865. 9×7 inches.

This gold on cream binding is thirty years ahead of its time, approaching the irreducible minimum of Beardsley's design for Dowson's *Verses* of 1896.

(B) D. G. Rossetti, *Poems*, 1870. 7¾×5⅜ inches.

In this and the following volume Rossetti's designs were used both for the ordinary issues, bound respectively in blue and green cloth, and for fine-paper issues of twenty-five copies each, bound in cream cloth.

(C) A. C. Swinburne, *Songs before Sunrise*, 1870. 9¼×6¼ inches.

(D) Thomas Gordon Hake, *Parables and Tales*, 1872. 7½×6⅛ inches.

There is a legend that this binding, which Rossetti designed for his friend and patron Dr. Hake, was deemed unsatisfactory and withdrawn after a few copies had been issued, but in fact the decorated cover seems to be commoner than the plain cloth binding in which the book also appears. Nonetheless, it is certainly the least characteristic of Rossetti's cover designs.

Sir John Everett Millais (1829–1896)

Of the painters included in this survey Millais is one of the half dozen greatest. As an illustrator in the narrow sense of an artist who interprets the words of a writer he is perhaps the best of all. His instinct for the most effective and dramatic way of representing an offered human situation was unfailing, and his draftsmanship was superb. Anthony Trollope, the author who benefitted most from Millais's services, paid him this tribute: "In every figure that he drew it was his object to promote the views of the writer whose work he had undertaken to illustrate, and he never spared himself any pains in studying that work, so as to enable himself to do so. I have carried on some of those characters from book to book, and have had my own early ideas impressed indelibly on my memory by the excellence of his delineations." (*Autobiography*, chapter 9.)

Millais's early illustrations are exampled in the Dalziels' collaborative volumes, *The Music Master* (147), Tennyson's *Poems* (148), and *The Poets of the Nineteenth Century* (149). He came into his own, however, in the sixties. The varied and imaginative drawings which he made for the first nine volumes of *Once a Week* (1859–1864) would themselves have sufficed to confirm his reputation, but they were accompanied by eighty-seven drawings for Trollope's novels; by twenty drawings for *The Parables*, his masterpiece among masterpieces; and by much other fine work for books and magazines alike. He did little illustrating in his later years.

REFERENCES Fredeman; Life; Lutyens; Forrest Reid.

❧ Watercolor and china white drawing touched with varnish, "A Squire with his two sons." Signed by the artist and dated 1844. Sheet size: 7¾×6 inches.

This is a characteristic example of Millais's apprentice work at the Royal Academy Schools, where his precocity aroused general admiration.

"HE IS OF THAT SORT THAT THEY MAKE THE ANGELS OF," SAID THE VERGER.

(169) Anthony Trollope, *The Small House at Allington*

167 ANTHONY TROLLOPE

Framley Parsonage. By Anthony Trollope . . . with six illustrations by J. E. Millais, R.A. . . . London, Smith, Elder and co., 1861. 3 v. I: [4], 333, [1] p. II: [3], 318, [1] p. III: [3], 330, [1] p. + 16 p. ads. Illus: Wood-engraved fronts. and 3 plates after Millais. Printer: Smith, Elder and co. Page size: 7⅝ × 4⅞ inches. Publisher's purple cloth.

The six drawings that Millais made for *Framley Parsonage* established the gracious and urbane conception of English upper-class life within which he was to work in his much fuller illustration of Trollope's later stories.

168 ANTHONY TROLLOPE

Orley Farm. By Anthony Trollope . . . with illustrations by J. E. Millais . . . London, Chapman and Hall, 1862. 2 v. I: viii, 320 p. II: viii, 320 p. Illus: Wood-engraved fronts. and 37 wood-engraved plates after J. E. Millais. Printer: William Clowes and sons. Page size: 8⅝ × 5⅜ inches. Publisher's purple cloth.

Writing of *Orley Farm* a contemporary critic remarked: "The real interest of the story is concentred upon well-to-do, decorous, and deservedly prosperous people, who solve, with a good deal of contentment and self-satisfaction, the difficult problem of making the most of both this world and the next." Millais's main effort is to do justice to the characters of Trollope's wonderfully rich and varied novel and to the situations in which they find themselves, yet the comfort, even elegance, of Victorian existence on the right side of the social line is nowhere more attractively presented than in his forty drawings for this novel. Trollope thought that Millais's illustrations were the best he had seen "in any novel in any language" (*Autobiography*, chapter 9). See Plate LX.

169 ANTHONY TROLLOPE

The Small House at Allington. By Anthony Trollope. With eighteen illustrations by J. E. Millais, R.A. . . . London, Smith, Elder and co., 1864. 2 v. I: [4], 312 p. II: [4], 316 p. Illus: Wood-engraved fronts. and 16 wood-engraved plates after Millais. Printer: Smith, Elder and co. Page size: 8⅝ × 5⅝ inches. Publisher's green cloth.

It was George Smith's pleasant custom to begin each installment of the novels he published in the *Cornhill Magazine* with an illustrated initial letter. The twenty which Millais drew for this story (between September, 1862, and April, 1864) are in fact small vignettes which supplement the interpretation he provided in his eighteen full-page drawings. These initial letters do not appear in the book issue.

170

The Parables of Our Lord and Saviour Jesus Christ: with pictures by John Everett Millais. Engraved by the Brothers Dalziel. London, Routledge, Warne, and Routledge, 1864. [6], 48 [1] l. + 2 p. ads. Printed on rectos only. Illus: 20 wood-engraved plates after Millais. Printer: Dalziel Brothers. Page size: 9⅞ × 7⅞ inches. Publisher's brown morocco.

The Small House at Allington in the *Cornhill Magazine*

Attracted by the proposed subject matter and by the prospect of illustrating a book entirely by himself, Millais agreed in 1857 to provide the Dalziel Brothers with thirty drawings for the Parables. He treated each illustration as "a separate *picture*," making many sketches before settling upon his final conception. Twelve engravings from his drawings appeared in *Good Words* between January and December, 1863, with elaborate interpretations by Thomas Guthrie, D.D. After he completed twenty designs, it became apparent that no more would be forthcoming, and the Dalziels contented themselves with turning these into a book. They meticulously followed Millais's instructions in his letters and in the touched proofs that he returned to them, and they stood by the resulting engravings as examples of the best work they could do. The publishers in their turn produced a handsome volume, at least as judged by contemporary taste, particularly in the copies bound in morocco for presentation. This copy is inscribed: "Geo Bentley Esqr with compliments of the Brothers Dalziel Jany 1864." See Plate LXI.

170A

Twenty India Paper Proofs of the Drawings of Sir John Everett Millais, Bart., P.R.A., to the Parables of Our Lord engraved on wood by the Brothers Dalziel. With which is given a collection of twenty autograph letters (in facsimile) from Millais to the Dalziels during the progress of the work. The number of copies of this book possible is under fifty, and they are issued privately from the Camden Press by Charles Dalziel. [6] l. Illus: 20 wood-engraved plates on India paper after Millais each with 1 l. letterpress text, 21 facsimile letters, 1 plate facsimile drawings after Millais on India paper. Page size: 14½ × 11¾ inches. Publisher's brown morocco.

In 1864 the Dalziel Brothers had fifty sets of the engravings for *The Parables* specially printed on India paper. After Millais's death they made these the basis of a privately printed folio volume, including as well facsimiles of the letters Millais had written to them while he was working on his drawings. This copy belonged to Sir Walter Miéville, one of the original subscribers, and later to Thomas Balston.

170B

Illustrations to "The Parables of Our Lord" by Sir John Everett Millais, Bart., P.R.A. n.p., 1921 [cover title]. [2] l. Illus: 20 plates after Millais. Page size: 11¼ × 8¾ inches. Orig. brown wrappers.

A note on the cover reads: "Thirty copies have been printed from the original wood blocks for private distribution."

171

Millais' Illustrations, a collection of drawings on wood by John Everett Millais, R.A. London, Alexander Strahan, 1866. [4] p. Illus: Added wood-engraved t.p. and 80 wood-engraved plates after Millais. Printer: Bradbury, Evans and co. Page size: 12¼ × 9⅝ inches. Publisher's brown cloth.

Drawn both from books and magazines, this volume offers good impressions without accompanying text on a page of generous size. *Once a Week* is represented by twenty-four engravings, making this the best available sampling of his work for that magazine, *Good Words* by sixteen, *Orley Farm* by sixteen, and Tennyson's *Poems* (148) by thirteen.

❧ Wood-engraved proofs of Millais's engravings for *Once a Week*: "La Fille Bien Gardée" and Harriet Martineau's *The Anglers of the Dove* (pp. 20 and 74 of *Millais' Illustrations*); "Maid Avoraine" (*Once a Week*, VII, 98), "Endymion" (*Once a Week*, VIII, 42), and "Death Dealing Arrows" (*Once a Week*, New Series, I, 79). Sizes vary, but "Death Dealing Arrows," which is reproduced, measures 5½ × 3½ inches.

172

Twenty-nine Illustrations by John Everett Millais, R.A. designed for "The Cornhill magazine." With extracts descriptive of each picture. London, Smith, Elder & co. 1867. [2] l. + 4 p. ads. Illus: 29 wood-engraved plates after Millais. Page size: 12¾ × 9¾ inches. Publisher's purple cloth.

In this selection by Smith, Elder from the pages of the *Cornhill Magazine* all the engravings for *Framley Parsonage* and *The Small House at Allington* are reprinted as well as those for four poems and a story. These fine impressions on India paper show Millais's work to its best advantage.

173 ANTHONY TROLLOPE

Phineas Finn, the Irish member. By Anthony Trollope. With twenty illustrations by J. E. Millais, R.A. . . . London, Virtue & co., 1869. 2 v. I: vi, [1], 320 p. II: vi, [1], 328 p. Illus: Wood-engraved fronts. and 18 wood-engraved plates after Millais. Printer: Virtue & co. Page size: 8⅝ × 5⅝ inches. Publisher's green cloth.

It is fitting that Millais should have illustrated one of Trollope's Parliamentary Novels as well as three of his Barsetshire Novels, but his twenty drawings for *Phineas Finn*, though as gentlemanly as ever, seem a shade perfunctory in comparison with his earlier work.

❧ John Austen Fitzgerald, pen and ink sketch of Millais, drawn on blotting paper. Image size: 4¼ × 2¾ inches.

This hasty portrait, jotted down in the mid-1860s, was preserved in the Smallfield album.

Wood-engraved proof of "Death Dealing Arrows"

Wood-engraved proof of "The Old Chartist"

Frederick Sandys (1832–1904)

Like Rossetti, Sandys made a great impression as an illustrator through a very small *oeuvre*. Indeed the twenty-five engravings from his drawings are perhaps an even greater achievement than the ten from Rossetti's. Modelling himself on Dürer, he worked with an acute sense of what his engravers could and could not do, and he kept them up to the mark. In 1861, for example, he would not allow "The Sailor's Bride" as cut by Hooper to appear in *Once a Week*, though it is an engraving that most artists would be proud to acknowledge. Nearly all of Sandys's work was published in *Once a Week* and other magazines. It is most conveniently sampled in the nine engravings reprinted in Thornbury's *Historical and Legendary Ballads and Songs* (163). Sandys is also represented by two engravings in *English Sacred Poetry* (150). Unfortunately the quality of the illustrations in Mrs. Sandys's portfolio, *Reproductions of Woodcuts by F. Sandys, 1860–1866*, is inferior.

REFERENCES Brighton Museum; Fredeman; Forrest Reid.

❧ Wood-engraved proof, "The Sailor's Bride," 1861. Image size: $3\frac{3}{8} \times 5$ inches.

❧ Wood-engraved proof, "The Old Chartist," *Once a Week*, VI (1862), 183. Image size: $4\frac{1}{8} \times 5$ inches.

This remains Sandys's best-known illustration, though he himself preferred "Amor Mundi."

❧ Frederick Sandys, 5 autograph letters to Joseph Swain, 9 pages, n.d. [1862].

These letters from Sandys to his engraver testify to the artist's close supervision of Swain's work, to his satisfaction with the way it was executed, and to Rossetti's involvement in passing on the engraving of "The Old Chartist" and other designs.

❧ Wood-engraved proof, "If," *The Argosy*, March, 1866, p. 336. Image size: $6\frac{1}{4} \times 4\frac{1}{2}$ inches.

❧ Wood-engraved proof, "Danae in the Brazen Chamber," 1867. Image size: $7 \times 4\frac{1}{2}$ inches.

When Sandys refused to cover the genitals of Danae's lover, the editor of *Once a Week* decided against using this engraving (Forrest Reid, p. 63). It was not published until 1888. Sandys averred that his drawing had been "perfectly cut by Swain, from my point of view the best piece of wood-cutting of our times."

(174) Tennyson, *Enoch Arden*, p. 62

Arthur Hughes (1832–1915)

In contrast to Rossetti, Hughes was a prolific and persistent book illustrator whose career extended through nearly sixty years. His drawings for Allingham's *Music Master* (147) date from 1855, but most of his best work came after his day as a Pre-Raphaelite painter was effectively over. In *Enoch Arden* and *Tom Brown's School Days* he presents the recognizable Victorian world, albeit from a highly personal perspective. It was only when he turned to the books of George MacDonald and Christina Rossetti, where children and the fancies of childhood were the offered subject, that he formed the unique style which has assured him of a succession of ardent admirers. In these books even his sometimes uncertain draftsmanship contributes to one's pervading sense of strangeness.

REFERENCES Fredeman; Muir, *Victorian Illustrated Books*; Forrest Reid.

174 ALFRED, LORD TENNYSON

Enoch Arden. By Alfred Tennyson. Illustrated by Arthur Hughes. London, Edward Moxon, 1866. [4], 81, [2] p. + 16 p. ads. Illus: Engraved front.; 21 wood-engraved vignettes and 4 wood-engraved plates after Hughes. Printer: Bradbury, Evans and co. Page size: 8⅝ × 6½ inches. Publisher's green cloth.

These familiar illustrations have not lost their charm, though Tennyson's poem lacks the element of fancifulness that usually elicited Hughes's best work. Rockwell Kent may have profited from the land- and seascapes in the volume.

175 GEORGE MACDONALD

Dealings with the Fairies . . . by George MacDonald, author of "David Elginbrod," "Alec Forbes of Howglen," etc. London, Alexander Strahan, 1867. [8], 308 p. + 4 p. ads. Illus: Wood-engraved front. and 11 wood-engraved plates after Hughes. Printer: J. and W.

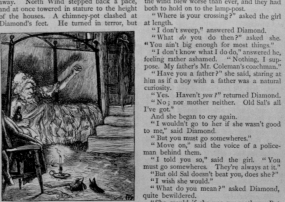

George MacDonald, *At the Back of the North Wind*, in *Good Words for the Young*, April, 1869

Rider. Page size: 5¼ × 4⅛ inches. Publisher's green cloth.

This book began Hughes's long collaboration with George MacDonald, and later his son Greville, which ended only with the latter's *Jack and Jill: A Fairy Story* in 1913.

Good Words for the Young, 1869, edited by Norman Macleod [Volume I] . . . and illustrated by Arthur Hughes, J. Pettie, F. A. Fraser, J. B. Zwecker, J. Mahoney, W. S. Gilbert, W. J. Wigand, A. Houghton, Edward Dalziel, C. [sic] J. Pinwell, and others. London, Strahan & co., [1868–]1869. [1], 859, [1], v–vi p. Illus: Numerous plates and vignettes. Printer: R. Clay, Sons, and Taylor. Page size: 9⅛ × 6¼ inches. Publisher's blue cloth.

An exception to the rule excluding periodicals must be made in the case of *Good Words for the Young*. During the five years of its existence Hughes contributed 231 drawings to this magazine, including those for MacDonald's *At the Back of the North Wind* (1868–1870), *Ranald Bannerman's Boyhood* (1870), and *The Princess and the Goblin* (1871). The double-column page, with its clusters of engravings, is particularly suited to displaying Hughes's work.

176 THOMAS HUGHES

Tom Brown's School Days, by an Old Boy. New edition with illustrations by Arthur Hughes and Sydney Prior Hall. London, Macmillan & co., 1869. xxii, [1], 376 p. Illus: Engraved front.; 8 wood-engraved initials, 6 wood-engraved vignettes, and 1 wood-engraved plate after Hall; 9 wood-engraved initials, 12 wood-engraved vignettes, and 22 wood-engraved plates after Hughes. Printer: R. Clay, Sons, and Taylor. Page size: 7¾×5⅝ inches. Blue morocco, original blue cloth cover and spine bound in.

This is still Hughes's best book for those who prefer the sturdy to the eerie. See Plate LXX.

177 GEORGE MACDONALD

At the Back of the North Wind by George MacDonald, LL.D., author of "The princess and the goblin," "Ranald Bannerman's boyhood," "Dealings with the fairies," etc. With illustrations by Arthur Hughes. London, Strahan & co., 1871. viii, 378 p. Illus: 76 wood-engraved vignettes after Hughes. Printer: Charles Dickens and Evans. Page size: 6¾×4⅝ inches. Publisher's green cloth.

Hughes's masterpiece in the style he made his own. See Plate LXXI.

178 GEORGE MACDONALD

The Princess and the Goblin by George MacDonald, author of "Ranald Bannerman," "At the back of the north wind," etc. etc. London, Strahan & co., 1872. vi, 313 p. + 32 p. ads. Illus: 30 wood-engraved vignettes after Hughes. Printer: Virtue and co. Page size: 6⅝×4⅜ inches. Publisher's blue cloth.

The goblins have a winning oddity, and the book contains Hughes's most memorable vignette.

179 CHRISTINA ROSSETTI

Sing-Song. A nursery rhyme book. By Christina Rossetti. With one hundred and twenty illustrations by Arthur Hughes. Engraved by the Brothers Dalziel. London, George Routledge and sons, 1872. x, [1], 130 p. + 2 p. ads. Illus: Wood-engraved front., wood-engraved t.p. vignette, and 121 wood-engraved vignettes after Hughes. Printer: Camden Press. Page size: 7⅛×5½ inches. Publisher's green cloth.

Hughes maintained so high a level of quality in his illustrations that it is impossible to omit this and the two following entries.

180 THOMAS GORDON HAKE

Parables and Tales. By Thomas Gordon Hake, author of "Madeline," etc. With illustrations by Arthur Hughes. London, Chapman and Hall, 1872. [7], 98 p. + 6 p. ads. Illus: Wood-engraved front. and 8 wood-engraved vignettes after Hughes. Printer: Camden Press. Page size: 7⅛×4⅞ inches. Publisher's blue cloth.

181 CHRISTINA ROSSETTI

Speaking Likenesses. By Christina Rossetti with pictures thereof by Arthur Hughes. London, Macmillan and co., 1874. viii, 96 p. Illus: Wood-engraved front., wood-engraved t.p. vignette, 5 wood-engraved vignettes and 6 wood-engraved plates after Hughes. Printer: R. Clay. Page size: 7⅛×4¾ inches. Publisher's blue cloth.

(178) George MacDonald,
The Princess and the Goblin, p. 110

Wood-engraved proof of "The Traveller" after Ford Madox Brown

Other Illustrators in the Pre-Raphaelite Ambiance

After the appearance of Tennyson's *Poems* in 1857 painters in the Pre-Raphaelite circle were readily persuaded to provide drawings for wood engravings. Their designs typically appeared, however, in periodicals or in volumes where they shared the task of illustration with other artists. Hence the need for this catchall section in which such occasional illustrators are represented chiefly in the form of engraver's proofs.

REFERENCES Christian; Fredeman; Life; Forrest Reid; White.

Ford Madox Brown (1821–1893)

Brown made only nine drawings for wood engravings. The two which follow, along with "The Prisoner of Chillon" in *The Poets of the Nineteenth Century* (149), are perhaps his best.

❧ Wood-engraved proof, "Elijah and the Widow's Son," *Dalziel's Bible Gallery* (158). Image size: $9 \times 5\frac{7}{8}$ inches.

Reid surmises that Brown's three drawings for this book may date from the early 1860s.

✍ Wood-engraved proof, "The Traveller," *Once a Week*, III (1869), 145. Image size: $4\frac{5}{8} \times 7\frac{1}{4}$ inches.

✍ Manuscript answers to a questionnaire submitted by a "Committee of Ladies," October 2, 1866:

Who is your
FAVOURITE

King	Pul King of Assyria
Queen	Jezebel
Hero	Goliah of Gath
Poet	Swinburn [sic]
Artist	(Afraid to say)
Author	Anon.
Virtue	Discretion
Colour	Magenta
Air	"Blow, blow thou winter wind"
Dish	Thunder & Lightning, a Cornish dish prepared with pitchards, mutton, treacle & garlic
Flower	Ornithogalum spicatum monspelliensium
Costume	Bathing dress
Name	Peter
Occupation	Selling pictures
Amusement	Flirting
Motto	"All Serene"
Dislike	Onions
Locality	Ratcliffe Highway
Ambition	To be mistaken for a swell

F. Madox Brown
Fitzroy Sqʳ

Another category has been added, presumably by Brown though not in his hand, "To be avoided," with a corresponding entry: "One of a Committee of Ladies."

Edward Burne-Jones (1833–1898)

Burne-Jones's major work as an illustrator came much later in his career (258), but examples of his naïve and charming early designs must not be omitted.

182

The Fairy Family: a series of ballads & metrical tales including the fairy mythology of Europe . . . London, Longman, Brown, Green, Longmans, & Roberts, 1857. Added etched t.p., xv, 283, [1] p. + 4 p. ads. Illus: Etched front., added etched t.p., and 1 wood-engraved vignette, all after Burne-Jones. Printer: Spottiswoode & co. Page size: $7\frac{5}{8} \times 5$ inches. Publisher's green cloth.

The publisher used only three of the drawings which Burne-Jones made for this anthology. They are all reproduced by John Christian in his 1973 article for *The Burlington Magazine*.

✍ Wood-engraved print of "King Sigurd, the Crusader," *Good Words*, III (1862), 248. Image size: $5\frac{7}{8} \times 4\frac{3}{8}$ inches.

Wood-engraved proof of "King Sigurd, The Crusader" after Edward Burne-Jones

✍ Wood-engraved print of "The Summer Snow," *Good Words*, IV (1863), 380. Image size: $5\frac{5}{8} \times 4\frac{1}{8}$ inches.

These are two among many prints after the drawings of Pre-Raphaelite artists in an album kept by relatives of R. Anning Bell.

William Holman Hunt (1827–1910)

The best of Hunt's few and scattered illustrations are to be found in Tennyson's *Poems* (148). Like Rossetti, he was initially displeased with the Dalziels' engravings of his drawings, finding "a certain wirelike character in all the lines" which was "eminently disenchanting" (*Some Poems by Alfred Lord Tennyson*, London, 1901, p. xxiii), but with the passage of time he came to entertain a better opinion of their work. He also contributed to *English Sacred Poetry* (150) and *Dalziel's Bible Gallery* (158).

✍ Wood-engraved proof of "Eliezer and Rebekah at the Well," *Dalziel's Bible Gallery* (158). Image size: $7 \times 5\frac{5}{8}$ inches.

M. J. Lawless (1837–1864)

Lawless devoted much of his short career to illustrations for *Once a Week* and other periodicals. His only substantial memorial in book form is Thornbury's *Historical and Legendary Ballads and Songs* (163), though he is also represented in *Passages from Modern English Poets* (218). His contemporaries thought his carefully meditated and meticulously executed drawings equal to those of Frederick Sandys.

&◦ Two pages devoted to Lawless in the Smallfield album:

Two carte de visite photographs of Lawless.

Pen and wash drawing of a peasant couple embracing, signed "M. J. Lawless. 1862." Image size: $4\frac{1}{2} \times 2\frac{3}{4}$ inches.

Pencil drawing of a medieval religious procession, signed "M.J.L. 1863." Image size: $3\frac{1}{4} \times 3\frac{1}{2}$ inches.

Photograph, $6\frac{1}{2} \times 10\frac{1}{4}$ inches, with an accompanying slip which reads: "A sick call to my friend Fred Smallfield with his best regards M. J. Lawless 1863."

"The Sick Call," exhibited at the Royal Academy in 1863, was the one important painting which Lawless lived to complete.

Drawing by M. J. Lawless

Wood-engraved proof from "Illustrations of Jewish Customs" after Simeon Solomon

E. J. Poynter (1836–1919)

Apart from his drawings for *Once a Week* and other magazines, Poynter is represented in Jean Ingelow's *Poems* (155) and *The Nobility of Life* (109), but his best work was for *Dalziel's Bible Gallery* (158).

&◦ Wood-engraved proof of "Moses slaying the Egyptians," *Dalziel's Bible Gallery* (158). Image size: $7 \times 6\frac{1}{8}$ inches.

Simeon Solomon (1840–1905)

George Eliot might have made the story of Solomon's initial success and subsequent disintegration a thread in *Daniel Deronda*, just as she might have used his ten "Illustrations of Jewish Customs" for *The Leisure Hour* in 1866 as a graphic supplement to that unillustrated novel. This series remains his most distinctive work, though six of his drawings appear in *Dalziel's Bible Gallery* (158) and fourteen more in *Art Pictures from the Old Testament* of 1894.

&◦ 4 wood-engraved proofs, "Illustrations of Jewish Customs." Image size: $3\frac{3}{4} \times 5\frac{3}{8}$ inches.

Sir John Gilbert (1817-1897)

Whether or not Gilbert was "the most prolific black and white artist of his time," as Forrest Reid claims (*Illustrators of the Sixties*, p. 20), he was certainly a wonderfully ready and inventive draftsman. In addition to his thousands of drawings for the *Illustrated London News*, he supplied the illustrations for many books. If his nearly 800 drawings for the Dalziels' edition of Shakespeare constitute his most ambitious effort, Longfellow's *Poetical Works* is perhaps his best single volume.

REFERENCES *Brothers Dalziel*; Forrest Reid.

183 HENRY WADSWORTH LONGFELLOW

The Poetical Works of Henry Wadsworth Longfellow. A new edition, illustrated with upwards of one hundred designs, drawn by John Gilbert, engraved by the Brothers Dalziel. London, George Routledge & co., 1856. [7], 400, [2] p. Illus: 102 wood-engraved vignettes after Gilbert. Printer: Richard Clay. Page size: 8⅝ × 6½ inches. Publisher's red morocco.

The Dalziels' rendering of landscapes and inanimate objects in this book puts it among the most accomplished of their "Fine Art" series.

Album containing 46 graphite and pen and ink drawings for the title pages of the semiannual volumes of *The Illustrated London News*, 1854–1880. Image size varies; the drawing reproduced measures 7 × 4 inches. Red morocco.

These bold and striking designs depart sharply from Gilbert's routine use of the figure in his illustrations. He chose his subjects chiefly from among the great events abroad which the *Illustrated London News* made it a matter of particular pride to report: the Crimean War, English "little wars" with the Chinese, the Afghans, and the Zulus; the struggle for Italian independence, the American Civil War, Stanley's discovery of Livingstone on the shores of Lake Tanganyika, the Congress of Vienna, and so on. One regrets that Gilbert never turned his hand to poster art.

Drawing of Garibaldi for the title page to a semiannual volume of *The Illustrated London News*

Sir John Tenniel (1820–1914)

Tenniel is now remembered almost entirely as the illustrator of *Alice in Wonderland* and *Through the Looking Glass*. Yet these volumes were brief interludes, and not very pleasant ones, in Tenniel's long and active career as an artist. He was on the staff of *Punch* for fifty years, during most of this period serving as that magazine's principal political cartoonist, and his drawings for books, though less abundant, were by no means negligible.

REFERENCES *Brothers Dalziel*; Muir, *Victorian Illustrated Books*; Forrest Reid; Sarzano; Spielmann; Williams and Madan.

184 THOMAS MOORE

Lalla Rookh: an oriental romance. By Thomas Moore. With sixty-nine illustrations from original drawings by John Tenniel, engraved on wood by the Brothers Dalziel; and five ornamental pages of Persian design by T. Sulman, jun. Engraved on wood by H. N. Woods. London, Longman, Green, Longman, & Roberts, 1861. xxiv, 381, [1] p. + 2 p. ads. Illus: 69 wood-engraved vignettes after Tenniel, 4 wood-engraved plates and 1 color-printed plate of Persian design after Sulman. Printer: Richard Clay. Page size: 9 × 6½ inches. Publisher's purple cloth.

This was Tenniel's principal achievement as an illustrator before *Alice in Wonderland*. Some of his designs for "The Fire Worshippers" have a grim power, and the book's "Persian" binding and ornamental title page printed in color make it a salient example of high Victorian taste.

☙ Wood-engraved proof of an unpublished illustration for *The Tempest*. Image size: 6⅜ × 4¾ inches.

One of two surviving engravings by the Dalziels for Bradbury and Evans's abortive edition of Shakespeare's works that was to have been illustrated by Tenniel (*Brothers Dalziel*, pp. 127, 130).

185 "LEWIS CARROLL"

Alice's Adventures in Wonderland. By Lewis Carroll. With forty-two illustrations by John Tenniel. New York, D. Appleton and co., 1866. [9], 192 p. Illus: Wood-engraved front. and 41 wood-engraved vignettes after Tenniel. Printer: Richard Clay. Page size: 7½ × 5 inches. Publisher's red cloth. Williams-Madan-Green 32.

The story of the cancellation of the 1865 edition of *Alice in Wonderland* after Tenniel had protested against its "disgraceful printing" is well known. Warren Weaver located only nineteen copies of this edition in his survey of 1971 ("The First Edition of *Alice's Adventures in Wonderland:* A Census," *Papers of the Bibliographical Society of America*, LXV, 1–40), but the justice of Tenniel's complaint has always been readily demonstrable, since Messrs. Macmillan sold 1,952 sets of the 1865 sheets to Messrs. Appleton of New York for the American edition. See Plate LXIX.

185A "LEWIS CARROLL"

Alice's Adventures in Wonderland. By Lewis Carroll. With forty-two illustrations by John Tenniel. London, Macmillan and co., 1866. [9], 192 p. Illus: Wood-engraved front. and 41 wood-engraved vignettes after Tenniel. Printer: Richard Clay. Page size: 7½ × 5 inches. Publisher's red cloth. Williams-Madan-Green 46.

As an example of the printer's craft this edition is greatly to be preferred to its predecessor, though the impressions of the engravings are perceptibly weaker. Carroll received twenty-four copies for presentation on November 9, 1865. This copy is inscribed: "Rev. H. P. Liddon, with the Author's sincere regards—Nov. 1865."

Un Autre Monde. Transformations, visions, incarnations, ascensions, locomotions, explorations, peregrinations, excursions, stations . . . par Grandville. Paris, H. Fournier, 1849. [4], 295, [1] p. Illus: Wood-engraved front., 36 colored wood-engraved plates, and numerous wood-engraved vignettes after Grandville. Page size: 10¼ × 7⅛ inches. Contemp. blue morocco.

That Carroll and Tenniel were indebted to this extraordinary fantasy, now recognized as an im-

portant precursor of surrealism, would seem to be undeniable. In particular the playing card and animal figures of the frontispiece to *Alice in Wonderland* offer examples of Grandville's influence. See Plate LXIX.

186 "LEWIS CARROLL"

Through the Looking-Glass, and what Alice found there. By Lewis Carroll, author of "Alice's adventures in Wonderland." With fifty illustrations by John Tenniel. London, Macmillan and co., 1872. [9], 224 p. Illus: Wood-engraved front. and 49 wood-engraved vignettes, all after Tenniel. Page size: 7⅛ × 4¾ inches. Publisher's red cloth. Williams-Madan-Green 84.

Though Tenniel's illustrations for this book were if anything more successful than those for *Alice*, he had further disputes with Carroll during its preparation, and he afterwards declined to consider a third collaboration.

187 "LEWIS CARROLL"

Alice's Adventures under Ground, being a facsimile of the original ms. book afterwards developed into "Alice's adventures in Wonderland" by Lewis Carroll,

with thirty-seven illustrations by the author . . . London, Macmillan and co., 1886. viii, [6], 95, [2] p. + 2 p. ads. Printer: Richard Clay. Page size: 7¼ × 4⅞ inches. Publisher's red cloth. Williams-Madan-Green 194.

The manuscript book, which was the first form of *Alice in Wonderland*, came into existence as "a Christmas gift to a dear child in memory of a summer's day." In his preface to this reduced copy (facsimile is hardly the right word), Carroll quotes a correspondent's reference to him as "the 'Alice-man,'" one more testimony to the renown that his two books quickly achieved. Though Williams and Madan doubt that Tenniel "derived any ideas directly from this book" (*The Lewis Carroll Handbook*, p. 134), many of his designs follow Carroll's in their main outlines.

187A "LEWIS CARROLL"

Alice's Adventures under Ground. N.p., n.d. [2], 90 p. [A facsimile of the original manuscript privately printed for Eldrige Johnson while the ms. was in his possession.] Illus: Printed in colors and with a photograph of Alice Liddell. Page size: 7¼ × 4½ inches. Publisher's green morocco, in original slipcase.

This elegant facsimile, complete even to its hard-grained morocco binding and the photograph of the original Alice mounted on its final page, reached general circulation through Dr. Rosenbach, who distributed a number of copies after Eldrige Johnson's death.

☙ Graphite drawing for a political cartoon. Signed by the artist. Image size: 4⅛ × 6¼ inches.

Along with much other work, Tenniel provided the drawings for nearly 2,000 of the "big political cuts" in *Punch*.

Sketchbook, 1854–1858

Charles Keene (1823–1891)

If any artist can be called the English Daumier it is Charles Keene. Both were master draftsmen, and each created his own *comédie humaine* through thousands of drawings of the social world around him. Yet Daumier is celebrated today while Keene is remembered chiefly by specialists. This is not only because Daumier was the greater artist, but also because he lives in our visual consciousness through almost 4,000 lithographs from his own hand which have become familiar in many volumes of reproductions. Most of Keene's drawings, in contrast, were engraved on wood by Joseph Swain and others. These engravings have never been catalogued, still less collected and reproduced. Keene's work as a book illustrator is extensive and interesting (see the appendix by W. H. Chesson in Pennell's *Keene*), but far less significant than his contributions to *Punch* and his drawings, which are accordingly emphasized in what follows.

REFERENCES Hudson; Layard; Muir, *Victorian Illustrated Books*; Pennell, *Keene*; Forrest Reid.

❧ Sketchbook, 24 pages on 19 l., graphite, pen and ink, and watercolor drawings dated 1854–1858. Page size: $5\frac{1}{2} \times 9$ inches.

This all-purpose sketchbook contains drawings of models, studies for illustrations, allegorical scenes entitled "Charity" and "Work," and most interesting of all a series of sketches from life. Reproduced is one of the five pages which record Keene's visit to the Kentish hop fields in the late summer of 1856.

≫ "Scraps" (sketchbook of the "Langham Crypt Sketching Club"), 20 pages of graphite drawings (1 with wash) by Ferguson, Keene, Newton, J. A. Pasquier, Sharp, C. Wilday, and another. Page size: 5¼ × 11⅞ inches.

This informal sketchbook is devoted chiefly to scenes and people casually encountered by Keene and his colleagues at the Langham Chambers Life School.

≫ George Meredith, *Evan Harrington*, in *Once a Week*, February 11 – October 13, 1860. Illus: Numerous wood-engraved vignettes after Keene. Page size: 9¼ × 6½ inches. Publisher's three-quarter green morocco.

Except for *Mrs. Caudle's Curtain Lectures*, *Evan Harrington* elicited Keene's best work as an illustrator, but the wood engravings from his drawings in *Once a Week* were not used when *Evan Harrington* appeared as a "three-decker" in 1861.

≫ Pencil drawing on thin paper for transfer of "The Countess de Saldar," *Once a Week*, III (1860), 113. Image size: 5 × 4 inches.

This drawing depicts the Countess de Saldar as she appears at the picnic in chapter 31 of *Evan Harrington*.

188 DOUGLAS JERROLD

Mrs. Caudle's Curtain Lectures. By Douglas Jerrold. Illustrated by Charles Keene. London, Bradbury, Evans, & co., 1866. xx, 190 p. + 10 p. ads. Illus: Color-printed front., wood-engraved t.p. vignette, 37 wood-engraved initials, and 22 wood-engraved vignettes, all after Keene. Printer: Bradbury, Evans, & co. Page size: 8⅛ × 6½ inches. Publisher's purple cloth.

Jerrold tempered his usually acerbic view of Victorian society when he wrote these lively studies of female domination for *Punch*, thus providing Keene with a congenial text twenty years later. The frontispiece is a fine example of Victorian color printing. See Plate LXVIII.

≫ Wood-engraved proofs of the initial letters to chapters 3 and 13 of *Mrs. Caudle's Curtain Lectures*. Image size: 2½ × 2 inches.

≫ Drawings in brown ink:

Pen and ink and graphite drawing of a pair of sportsmen, signed by the artist. Image size: 7 × 4⅜ inches.

Pen and ink drawing of two men at a doorway. Image size: 7 × 4½ inches. On the verso is a cancelled drawing of the same subject, with traces of china white and graphite. Both this and the above drawing were once in the collection of the artist's brother, Henry Keene.

Keene's reputation as an artist rests primarily on his drawings, chiefly for *Punch*, which have survived in considerable numbers. His finished drawings date for the most part from 1872 and after, when a procedure began to be employed that freed artists from working directly on the wood. Their sketches were instead transferred to the engraver's block photographically, thus enabling them to preserve the originals. The bulk of Keene's drawings are in brown ink, more or less diluted, like the two described above.

≫ Drawings in inks of various colors:

Pen and ink drawing touched with china white of two men drinking at a table. Image size: 4¼ × 6⅞ inches.

Pen and ink drawing touched with china white of an old man with umbrella. Image size: 6⅞ × 4⅛ inches. Signed and inscribed by the artist.

Pen and ink drawing touched with china white of a young man and his landlady. Signed and inscribed by the artist. Sheet size: 5⅜ × 8⅜ inches. Both this and the above drawing are inscribed to Frederick Smallfield.

Joseph Pennell (*Keene*, p. 33) has provided a lively account of Keene's technical experimentation in his later drawings. Those described above testify to the effects Keene obtained from the astonishing mixture of homemade inks and homemade pens which he employed. Needless to say, such drawings called for translation rather than reproduction by his engravers.

≫ Proofs of wood engravings:

Wood-engraved proof, "Mokeanna," in *Punch*, 1863. Image size: 4⅜ × 6¾ inches.

Wood-engraved proof, "Smoking strictly prohibited," *London Society*, 1868. Image size: 6⅞ × 4½ inches.

Wood-engraved proof, "The three names," 1869. Image size: 7 × 4½ inches.

"Mokeanna" illustrates a parody of the contemporary "sensation" novel.

≫ Pen and ink sketch for "The three names," sheet size: 6⅞ × 4½ inches.

189

Our People sketched by Charles Keene. From the collection of "Mr. Punch." London, Bradbury, Agnew, & co., 1881. 156 p. Illus: Numerous wood-engraved vignettes after Keene. Printer: Bradbury, Agnew, & co. Page size: 14¼ × 10⅛ inches. Publisher's green cloth.

The wood engravings of this well-produced volume offer the only convenient way of sampling the nearly 3,000 drawings which Keene made for *Punch* in the forty years following 1851. It is posterity's good fortune that Keene disliked politics and confined himself largely to what the *Punch* staff called "socials," that is to say records of the small encounters of day-to-day existence observed in a genial way. High Society he was content to leave to du Maurier. Indeed, the occasional "Swells" who figure in his drawings are rarely viewed with a friendly eye. Instead, he made it his business to depict the English middle classes as they went their accustomed ways at home, at work, and on holiday. If Keene has a special bent it is for showing them in contact with the vast apparatus of human beings who catered to them: house servants and waiters, cab drivers and barbers, shopkeepers and clerks, policemen and farmers—and,

of course, artists! Keene usually allows his underdogs to score in these little episodes, but his rebukes are very mild. That some small personal animus was nonetheless involved is suggested by the fact that the painters of his drawings were often self-portraits. The solidity and precision of Keene's draftsmanship make him the supreme *Punch* artist. In comparison, Leech seems flimsy, Tenniel wooden, and du Maurier conventional.

190

Twenty-one Etchings by Charles S. Keene printed by F. Goulding. Introduction and notes by M. H. Spielmann. London, Astolat Press, 1903. 20, [1] p. Illus: 21 matted etched plates by Keene. Mat size: 15 × 10⅝ inches. Publisher's portfolio. No. 102 of 105 sets.

Keene is known to have made thirty-six etchings, not counting those he contributed to *Punch's Pocket Books*. When Henri Beraldi near the end of Keene's life asked an intermediary to seek information that would allow him to include the artist in *Les graveurs du XIXe siècle*, the answer was a decided negative: "I have only scratched a few studies of sketches . . . —the merest experiments! Titles they have not. To save my life I couldn't tell the dates . . . Try to choke the French biographer off." (Layard, *Keene*, p. 38.) But Keene's disdain did not prevent his fellow etchers from admiring his prints.

⁐ Etched proof of an old man in a top hat standing before a stove, image size: $4\frac{1}{2} \times 3\frac{1}{8}$ inches.

Proofs of Keene's etchings are uncommon, since they have survived only through his occasional gifts to friends. This example is from the Frederick Smallfield Album. The tiny inscription etched on the left of the plate is Keene's reminder to himself about details of the biting.

Wood-engraved proof of
"Smoking Strictly Prohibited"

Wood-engraved proof of "The Three Names"

Drawing in brown ink of "The Three Names"

Birket Foster (1825–1899)

"The most successful and highly paid exponent of English water-colour in the second half of the century" (Reynolds, *English Water-Colour Painting*, p. 45), Foster was also much in demand for illustrations of country scenes in the 1850s and 1860s. The hundreds of small wood engravings that flowed from these commissions induce a sense of surfeit in the viewer, who soon feels the need of some added element to raise them above the commonplace. Edmund Evans hit upon such a feature in 1859 when he made a delightful volume of Goldsmith's *Poems* (238) by printing Foster's drawings in color. The Dalziel Brothers found it again in 1861 when they secured thirty large drawings for their *Pictures of English Landscape*. The resulting book is certainly Foster's best, particularly when it is seen in the sumptuous folio reissue of 1881, though even here one understands why Ruskin, after telling the Dalziels that their engravings were "very charming," regretted at the same time that they did not go beyond charm to educate, as well as meet, the public taste (*Brothers Dalziel*, p. 154).

REFERENCES *Brothers Dalziel*; Evans; Forrest Reid.

191 TOM TAYLOR

Birket Foster's Pictures of English Landscape. (Engraved by the Brothers Dalziel) with pictures in words by Tom Taylor. London, Routledge, Warne, and Routledge, 1863. [6, 30] l., printed on rectos only, + 1 p. ads. Illus: 30 wood-engraved plates after Foster. Printer: Camden Press. Page size: 9¾ × 7½ inches. Blue morocco, publisher's brown morocco cover bound in.

See Plate LIX.

191A TOM TAYLOR

Birket Foster's Pictures of English Landscape, engraved by the Brothers Dalziel, with pictures in words by Tom Taylor. India proofs. London, George Routledge, [1881]. [6, 31] l. + 2 l. ads. Illus: 30 wood-engraved plates after Birket Foster, printed as India-paper proofs. No. 487 of 1,000 copies. Printer: Camden Press. Page size: 15¼ × 11 inches. Publisher's vellum.

192

Beauties of English Landscape Drawn by Birket Foster, engraved by Dalziel Brothers, J. Cooper, E. Evans, H. Harral, and others. London, George Routledge and sons, 1874. xvi, 301, [1] p. Illus: Wood-engraved front. and 260 wood-engraved illustrations after Foster. Printer: Camden Press. Page size: 9⅝ × 7¾ inches. Publisher's blue morocco.

This is Routledge's collection of engravings after Foster which they had previously published in their illustrated gift books. It is a handsome volume in itself, as well as a convenient way of sampling his smaller drawings.

" Behold the wild growth from her nape !"

(194) George du Maurier, *A Legend of Camelot*, part 1

George du Maurier (1834–1896)

Du Maurier continues to be affectionately remembered as an intelligent and attractive man who led an interesting life, as the author of *Trilby*, and as one of *Punch's* shrewdest graphic commentators. If his merit as an artist is to be fully realized, however, attention should be focussed on his relatively unfamiliar work of the 1860s. His draftsmanship was then at its best, and he used it effectively both to embody his own conceptions and to interpret the writings of others. At that period he was second only to Millais as an illustrator of fiction. He did for Mrs. Gaskell what Millais did for Trollope, indeed, and his drawings for the stories of half a dozen other authors are almost equally distinguished.

REFERENCES Forrest Reid; Muir, *Victorian Illustrated Books*; Ormond; Whiteley.

193 MRS. GASKELL

Wives and Daughters. An every-day story. By Mrs. Gaskell. With eighteen illustrations by George du Maurier . . . London, Smith, Elder and co., 1866. 2 v. I: [4], 336 p. II: [4], 332 p. Illus: Wood-engraved fronts. and 16 wood-engraved plates after du Maurier. Printer: Smith, Elder and co. Page size: 8½×5½ inches. Publisher's purple cloth.

Du Maurier's drawings for this novel, the greatness of which has come to be generally recognized only during the last ten or fifteen years, show that he was fully aware of both its strength and its delicacy. Like *Orley Farm* (168), *Wives and Daughters* was a *Cornhill* serial, and the reader is consequently deprived of half of du Maurier's illustrations in the first book edition, where the initial letter vignettes are not reprinted. See Plate LXVI.

194 GEORGE DU MAURIER

A Legend of Camelot, pictures and poems &c. by George du Maurier. London, Bradbury, Agnew, & co., 1898. [5], 95, [1] l., printed on rectos only. Illus: 16 wood-engraved plates and numerous wood-engraved vignettes after du Maurier. Printer: Bradbury, Agnew, & co. Page size: 9½×12 inches. Publisher's blue cloth.

This collection of du Maurier's burlesques and parodies, drawn chiefly from *Punch*, is presented here for its title poem, which appeared in that magazine in 1866. The passage of time has not greatly impaired the fun of this most telling of Pre-Raphaelite parodies. No one has more neatly underlined the characteristic oddity of the movement's images and diction. Du Maurier's drawings speak for themselves. Here are some examples of his verse:

> Her pale feet glimmered, in and out,
> Like tombstones as she went about. . . .
> Quoth Sir Gauwaine: "I know her not!"
> "Who quoth you *did?*" quoth Lancelot. . . .
> The bold Sir Lancelot mused a bit,
> And smole a bitter smile at it. . . .

❧ Wood-engraved proof for *A Legend of Camelot*, part 3, "On which there stood a stately maid." Image size: 5×6⅞ inches.

❧ Wood-engraved proof for *A Legend of Camelot*, part 4, "Two royal heads of hair he saw." Image size: 8⅝ ×4½ inches.

195 DOUGLAS JERROLD

The Story of a Feather. By Douglas Jerrold. Illustrated by G. du Maurier. London, Bradbury, Evans, & co.,

(196) William Makepeace Thackeray,
The History of Henry Esmond

1867. xv, 259 p. + 4 p. ads. Illus: Wood-engraved front., wood-engraved t.p. vignette, 45 wood-engraved initials, 27 wood-engraved vignettes, and 3 wood-engraved plates, all after du Maurier. Printer: Bradbury, Evans, & co. Page size: 8⅛×6½ inches. Publisher's purple cloth.

The fantastic humor of du Maurier's initial letter vignettes is nicely contrasted with the *Beggar's Opera* realism of his larger illustrations.

196 WILLIAM MAKEPEACE THACKERAY

The History of Henry Esmond, Esq., a colonel in the service of Her Majesty, Queen Anne. Written by himself. Edited by W. M. Thackeray . . . with illustrations by George du Maurier. London, Smith, Elder and co., 1868. xv, [1], 452 p. Illus: Wood-engraved front. and 7 wood-engraved plates after du Maurier. Printer: Spottiswoode and co. Page size: 8¼×5¼ inches. Publisher's green cloth.

Thackeray's good luck with his illustrators persisted beyond his death. *Esmond* had appeared without illustrations in 1852; sixteen years later du Maurier made nineteen drawings which do justice to the novel as a stirring tale of adventure on the one hand and as a high drama of domestic life on the other. Du Maurier was admittedly under the spell of Beatrix Esmond, after whom he named his first child, and her career is presented in detail, from the little girl of the frontispiece to the defeated schemer of "The Last of Beatrix."

☙ Four wood-engraved proofs for *Esmond*: "Parting," image size: 5½×4 inches. "The Chevalier de St. George," image size: 3⅞×5½ inches. "Monsieur Baptiste," image size: 4×5⅜ inches. "The Last of Beatrix," image size: 3⅞×5½ inches.

It should be observed that in these proofs the captions of "Parting" and "The Last of Beatrix" are transposed.

197

English Society at Home, from the collection of "Mr. Punch." By George du Maurier. London, Bradbury, Agnew & co., 1880. [8, 42] p. + 1 p. ads. Illus: 63 wood-engraved plates after du Maurier. Page size: 13⅝×9⅞ inches. Publisher's blue cloth.

This representative selection from du Maurier's earlier work for *Punch* is luxuriously presented with fine impressions of the engravings on India paper. It will be noted that, unlike Keene, he depends heavily on the dialogue that accompanied his drawings. Du Maurier's essentially literary approach no doubt explains why Henry James held him to be the best of *Punch*'s artists, a bewildering judgment on other grounds.

198

Society Pictures drawn by George du Maurier, selected from "*Punch*"... London, Bradbury, Agnew, & co., [ca. 1893]. 2 v. I: [4], 256 p. II: [4], 256 p. Illus: Numerous wood-engraved illustrations after du Maurier. Page size: 12¼×9⅞ inches. Publisher's brown cloth.

These volumes, in which the engravings date almost entirely from the 1870s and 1880s, offer a comprehensive survey of du Maurier's later work for *Punch*.

Drawing for *Punch*, "Compensation"

🙠 Pen and ink drawing, "Compensation." Signed by the artist. Image size: $8\frac{3}{8} \times 14\frac{1}{4}$ inches.

According to a note on the back, this drawing appeared in *Punch* under the title COMPENSATION with the following legend: "That's Mrs. Grimshaw who lectures on bimetallism. I've heard how exasperatingly clever she can be." "Yes—but how consolingly ugly!"

🙠 Autograph letter signed, dated New Grove House, Hampstead Heath, 3 Mai [1874], to a French critic. 4 p. 8vo.

Du Maurier writes about his work for *Punch*: "je me sens plus porté à dépeindre le côté gracieux de la vie sociale et domestique en Angleterre que le côté drôle ou bouffon. Je dessine mes figures avec beaucoup de soin et me sers de modèles absolument comme si je faisais de la peinture à l'huile. Je puis ajouté qu'il nous est absolument défendu de toucher à certains sujets—la réligion, et les amours illicites, par example—...la circulation de Punch étant tres grande, surtout dans les familles."

199 GEORGE DU MAURIER

Trilby, a novel, by George du Maurier, author of "Peter Ibbetson" with 121 illustrations by the author. London, Osgood, McIlvaine & co., 1895. x, 447 p. + 5 p. ads. Illus: Wood-engraved front. and 120 wood-engraved vignettes after du Maurier. Printer: R. & R. Clark. Page size: $7\frac{3}{8} \times 5\frac{1}{2}$ inches. Publisher's blue cloth.

These illustrations were designed for the double-column page of *Harper's New Monthly Magazine*, where du Maurier's novel appeared between January and November, 1894. The story was published without illustrations as a belated "three-decker" late in the same year. Du Maurier's drawings were restored in the volume of 1895, but they seem less at home in its octavo format, for which some of them had to be drastically reduced in size. Since Trilby, Svengali, Taffy, the Laird, and Little Billee derive their vitality at least as much from their creator's illustrations as from his text, the *Harper's* version is well worth acquiring. Du Maurier's other romantic autobiographical novels, *Peter Ibbetson* of 1892 and *The Martian* of 1898, are also abundantly illustrated.

Arthur Boyd Houghton (1836–1875)

Despite his short life, Houghton ranks with Millais among illustrators of the sixties for the abundance and excellence of his work. If he imposed himself on a subject, rather than adapting himself to it like Millais, he thereby impressed his personality on his drawings all the more unmistakably. From 1862 on he labored extensively for the magazines, the culmination of this aspect of his career coming with his inspired reporting of life in Paris, London, and the United States for the newly established *Graphic*. Vincent van Gogh, who knew the volumes of the *Graphic* in which his engravings appeared, was struck by Houghton's drawings "of Quakers, and a Morman church, and Indian women, and immigrants." Houghton had "something mysterious like Goya," van Gogh continued, "with a wonderful soberness which reminds me of Meryon." (Quoted by Hogarth, *Artists on Horseback*, p. 50.) The seventy-one engravings which make up the series called "Graphic America" and its continuations (1870–1873) rival Winslow Homer's work for *Harper's Weekly*. They have never been collected in a book, though Sinclair Hamilton has listed and commented upon them and Paul Ho-

28

(200) *Home Thoughts and Home Scenes*

(201) Miguel de Cervantes, *Adventures of Don Quixote de la Mancha*

garth gives a good sampling from them in *Artists on Horseback*. So presented, their mordant observation and superb design might well sustain comparison with Doré's *London* (207).

Houghton was equally active as a book illustrator. He had the principal hand in the Dalziels' *Arabian Nights* (151), and he was the sole illustrator of their *Home Thoughts and Home Scenes* and *Don Quixote*. Finally, he joined his friends Pinwell and Walker in providing the idyllic pictures that make *A Round of Days* (153), *North Coast* (156), and Jean Ingelow's *Poems* (155) a continuing source of peace and refreshment to those who know them.

REFERENCES Hamilton; Hogarth, *Arthur Boyd Houghton*; Hogarth, *Artist as Reporter*; Hogarth, *Artists on Horseback*; Housman, *Houghton*; Muir, *Victorian Illustrated Books*; Forrest Reid; Sullivan, *Print Collector's Quarterly*; University of Nottingham.

200

Home Thoughts and Home Scenes. In original poems by Jean Ingelow, Dora Greenwell, Mrs. Tom Taylor, the Hon. Mrs. Norton, Amelia B. Edwards, Jennett Humphreys, and the author of "John Halifax Gentleman." And pictures by A. B. Houghton, engraved by the Brothers Dalziel. London, Routledge, Warne, and Routledge, 1865. [5, 25] l., printed on rectos only, + 2

p. ads. Illus: 25 wood-engraved plates after Houghton. Printer: Camden Press. Page size: 9⅞ × 7¾ inches. Publisher's brown morocco.

This book provides the chief record of one of Houghton's early specialties, "the children's little world," so treated as to evoke "the tenderest of human sympathies" (advertisement). His plump-cheeked, large-headed infants, who seem all to belong to one large family, go about their active play with total self-confidence, largely unchecked by adults. Houghton's vision of them is anything but sentimental, yet his emphasis on their togetherness grows a little oppressive. This presentation copy in publisher's morocco is inscribed: "Honourable Mrs Norton with compliments of Dalziel Brothers Decʳ 1864."

201 MIGUEL DE CERVANTES

Adventures of Don Quixote de la Mancha. Translated from the Spanish of Miguel de Cervantes Saavedra by Charles Jarvis. With one hundred illustrations by A. B. Houghton, engraved by the Brothers Dalziel. London, Frederick Warne and co., 1866. xii, 710 p. + 2 p. ads. Illus: Wood-engraved front. and 100 vignettes after Houghton. Printer: Camden Press. Page size: 8¾ × 6½ inches. Publisher's purple cloth.

The conjunction of Cervantes and Houghton might have been expected to yield something memorable, but in fact his drawings for *Don Quixote* are disappointing when they are compared with those of the French mid-nineteenth-century illustrators of the book, Tony Johannot, Celestin Nanteuil, and Gustave Doré. Houghton is his shrewd and inventive self, but neither Spain nor the Don really excited him. He seems to have found Sancho Panza more congenial.

202 LAURENCE HOUSMAN

Arthur Boyd Houghton, a Selection from His Work in Black and White, printed for the most part from the original wood-blocks. With an introductory essay by Laurence Housman. London, Kegan, Paul, Trench, Trübner and co., 1896, 189 p. Illus: Gravure front. and 4 gravure plates, 84 wood-engraved plates, all after Houghton. Printer: Ballantine, Hanson & co. Page size: 11¼ × 8¾ inches. Publisher's green cloth.

Though Housman's primary concern, both in his choice of engravings and in his fine introduction, is with *The Arabian Nights*, he prints eight cuts from "Graphic America" from the original blocks.

THE POOR HELPING THE POOR.

William Makepeace Thackeray,
The Adventures of Philip

Frederick Walker (1840–1875)

Though Walker is one of the principal illustrators of the sixties, it is not easy to represent him in an exhibition of books. His drawings for fiction rivalled those of Millais and du Maurier, but virtually none of them were included when the stories appeared in volume form. Another exception to the rule excluding periodicals has accordingly been made in the case of Thackeray's *Philip*, where Walker's best drawings of this kind appear, as published in the *Cornhill Magazine*. One would like to do the same for his illustrations to Anne Thackeray's *The Village on the Cliff* and Mrs. Henry Wood's *Oswald Cray*. As already noted, it was Walker's drawings that gave the Dalziel Brothers the nucleus for *A Round of Days* (153) and *Wayside Posies* (154), the two outstanding albums of Victorian "idyllic pictures."

REFERENCES *Brothers Dalziel*; Forrest Reid.

❧ Thackeray, *The Adventures of Philip, Cornhill Magazine*, January, 1861, to August, 1862.

When Thackeray found himself unable to illustrate this serial to his satisfaction, he turned the task over to Walker. It was the young man's first major commission, and he made the most of it. His drawings rank with Millais's for *Orley Farm* (168) and du Maurier's for *Wives and Daughters* (193), but they were not used when the novel appeared as a "three-decker" in 1862. Since *Philip* is Thackeray's least interesting novel, their merits have hardly been noticed subsequently except by enthusiasts for the illustrations of the sixties.

❧ Wood-engraved proofs for *A Round of Days*, "Broken victuals," p. 3. Image size: $6 \times 4\frac{5}{8}$ inches. "Winter days," p. 43. Image size: $6\frac{1}{2} \times 4\frac{5}{8}$ inches.

❧ Wood-engraved proofs, "The bathers," 4 blocks. Image size of each: $4\frac{7}{8} \times 2\frac{7}{8}$ inches.

These proofs of four parts of a single cut show how the engravers of the sixties confidently shared out their work, knowing that the blocks would fit perfectly when assembled.

❧ Pen and ink drawing, "A gentleman leaning on his cane." Image size: 4×2 inches.

" You need be under no uneafinefs," cried I, " about felling the rims, for they are not worth fixpence, for I perceive they are only copper varnifhed over.—p. 50.

(203) Oliver Goldsmith, *The Vicar of Wakefield*, in *Dalziel's Illustrated Goldsmith*

George John Pinwell (1842–1875)

Pinwell's brilliant career as an illustrator was compressed between his boyhood struggle with ignorance and poverty and his early death. Much of his best work was done for the magazines, but fortunately the Dalziels chose him as sole illustrator of one major book, their selection from Goldsmith's works. His great success in this volume is with *The Vicar of Wakefield*. Though he had little sense of period, he caught the spirit of Goldsmith's story to perfection. Whether he is dealing with his beloved country scenes, the tribulations of the Reverend Dr. Primrose, or little Dick's story of the dwarf, the giant, and the damsel in distress, he is equally at home. His most characteristic drawings, however, were for the Dalziels' four collaborative volumes of idyllic pictures: *A Round of Days* (153),

Jean Ingelow's *Poems* (155), Buchanan's *North Coast* (156), and particularly *Wayside Posies* (154). Here his feeling for landscape and the small concerns of daily living led to the creation of many memorable images.

REFERENCES *Brothers Dalziel*; Hartley; Forrest Reid; Williamson.

203 OLIVER GOLDSMITH

Dalziel's Illustrated Goldsmith: comprising The Vicar of Wakefield, The Traveller, The Deserted village . . . and a sketch of the life of Dr. Oliver Goldsmith, by H. W. Dulken, Ph.D. With one hundred pictures drawn by G. J. Pinwell, engraved by the Brothers Dalziel. London, Ward and Lock, 1865. xx, 378 p. + 2 p. ads. Illus: Wood-engraved front. and 99 vignettes after Pinwell. Printer: Camden Press. Page size: $10\frac{5}{8} \times 7\frac{1}{2}$ inches. Publisher's brown cloth.

Wood-engraved proofs for *Wayside Posies*, "Shadow and substance," p. 8, image size: $6\frac{5}{8} \times 4\frac{7}{8}$ inches. "The swallows," p. 22, image size: $6\frac{1}{2} \times 5$ inches. "The goose," p. 42, image size: $4\frac{5}{8} \times 5$ inches. "The Island bee," p. 47, image size: $6\frac{1}{4} \times 4\frac{7}{8}$ inches.

Proof of "Shadow and Substance"

Other Artists Who Drew for Wood Engravers

The so-called "Sixties" illustrators were so numerous and talented that any selection from their ranks is bound to be radically incomplete. The artists in this section are among the most interesting of those not already noticed.

REFERENCES   Muir, *Victorian Illustrated Books*; Pennell, *Savoy*; Forrest Reid.

(204) Wood engraving after Samuel Palmer for William Adams, *Sacred Allegories*

Samuel Palmer (1805–1881)

204   WILLIAM ADAMS

Sacred Allegories. By the Rev. William Adams . . . New edition, with engravings from original designs by Charles W. Cope, R.A., John C. Horsley, A.R.A., Samuel Palmer, Birket Foster, and George E. Hicks. London, Rivingtons, 1859. vi, [1], 294 p. + 1 p. ads. Illus: 9 wood-engraved vignettes after Cope, 7 after Foster, 4 after Hicks, 7 after Horsley, head- and tailpieces and 1 vignette after T. Macquid, 9 wood-engraved vignettes after Palmer. Printer: R. Clay. Page size: 8⅝ × 6¼ inches. Publisher's blue cloth.

Palmer's most memorable illustrations are his etchings (215, 220, 222) and the plates made from drawings which he did not live to etch (222, 223), but a number of his designs were also engraved on wood. The best of these were for "The Distant Hills," one of the four stories in the Reverend William Adams's *Sacred Allegories*. Adams here relates how two orphaned sisters, Minna and Rhoda, are rescued from the forest by a kind stranger. He leaves them with a warning: they must keep their eyes upon the distant hills and avoid a ruined wall nearby. Minna's happy contemplation is untroubled, but Rhoda to her undoing becomes involved in the swarming life of the wall. Lest the reader miss the allegorical meaning of all this, detailed catechisms follow each section of the narrative. Palmer has no interest in Adams's pious polemics. His drawings are inspired by the text: "I will lift up mine eyes unto the hills, from whence cometh my help." And some of his magic is indeed captured by the wood engravers. Nonetheless, Joseph Pennell's praise of the cuts in *The Savoy* (I, 113) seems excessive: "Three of these must rank with Turner. Palmer has given the effect of the setting sun over great landscape as no one ever did before, and no one has attempted since."

Charles H. Bennett (1829–1867)

205

The Fables of Aesop and others translated into human nature. Designed and drawn on the wood by Charles H. Bennett, author of 'Shadows.' Engraved by Swain. London, W. Kent & co., [1857]. [3], 22 l., printed on rectos only. Illus: Colored wood-engraved front., t.p. vignette, and 22 colored wood-engraved plates after Bennett. Printer: G. Barclay. Page size: 9⅞ × 8 inches. Polished calf by Riviere, original wrappers bound in.

This notable book has only recently begun to attract the attention it deserves. Bennett translated Aesop's fables quite specifically into human nature as it displayed itself in the contemporary London world. His beasts represent with verve and malice many of the types one finds in mid-Victorian fiction, among them the callous footman, the idle officer, the exposed swindler, the ignorant patron of the arts, and the foolish social climber. See Plate LVII.

Frederick, Lord Leighton (1830–1896)

206 George Eliot

Romola by George Eliot with illustrations by Sir Frederick Leighton, P.R.A. In two volumes . . . London, Smith, Elder and co., 1880. 2 v. I: x, [1], 396, [2] p. II: xi, [1], 403, [1] p. Illus: Wood-engraved fronts., 22 wood-engraved plates, 14 wood-engraved initials, and 1 wood-engraved vignette after Leighton. All illustrations are on India paper. Printer: R. Clay, Sons, and Taylor. Page size: 10½ × 7¼ inches. Publisher's brown cloth.

Lord Leighton's work as an illustrator dates from the early 1860s, before he became too grand to accept such commissions, and is confined almost entirely to *Romola*, which appeared in the *Cornhill Magazine* from July, 1862, to August, 1863, and to *Dalziel's Bible Gallery* (158). These drawings, which used to be dismissed as cold and academic, are now justly esteemed for their strikingly dramatic design. It must be regretfully noted, however, that

Frederick J. Shields, touched engraver's proof for *Illustrations for Bunyan's Pilgrim's Progress*

BLESSED IS (S)HE THAT CONSIDERETH YE POOR

Swain's engravings for *Romola* are greatly inferior to the Dalziels' for their *Bible Gallery*. A merit of the 1880 edition of George Eliot's novel is that it reprints Leighton's admirable initial letter vignettes as well as his full-page illustrations.

Gustave Doré (1832–1883)

207 BLANCHARD JERROLD

London. A pilgrimage. By Gustave Doré and Blanchard Jerrold. London, Grant & co., 1872. Added wood-engraved t.p., [6], xii, 191, [1] p. Illus: Numerous wood-engraved plates, vignettes, and initials after Doré. Printer: Grant & co. Page size: 16¾ × 12⅝ inches. Publisher's brown cloth.

The theme of this book had been anticipated by Matthew Arnold three years earlier when he wrote of "London, with its unutterable external hideousness, and with its internal canker of *publicé egestas, privatim opulentia*—to use the words which Sallust puts into Cato's mouth about Rome,—unequalled in the world" (*Culture and Anarchy*, London, 1869, p. 31). Doré's devastating realization of the contrast of wealth and poverty in a modern metropolis makes *London* one of the great illustrated books of the world. The English edition antedates the French by four years, and indeed it is a handsomer book, except for the few copies of the French edition printed on *papier de Chine*. See Plate LXXIII.

John Dawson Watson (1832–1892)

208 JOHN BUNYAN

The Pilgrim's Progress from this world to that which is to come. By John Bunyan. A new edition . . . illustrated with one hundred and ten designs by J. D. Watson, engraved on wood by the Brothers Dalziel. London, George Routledge & sons, 1867. [8], xxii, [1], 407, [1] p. Illus: Wood-engraved front. and 110 wood-engraved vignettes after Watson. Printer: R. Clay. Page size: 8½ × 6¼ inches. Publisher's purple morocco.

For their virtually mandatory edition of *The Pilgrim's Progress*, the Dalziels turned to Watson, a sound and experienced illustrator with a penchant for religious themes. He is also abundantly represented in *English Sacred Poetry* (150).

Frederick J. Shields (1833–1911)

Shields was a painter of repute, marginally associated with the Pre-Raphaelites. He has two distinctive books to his credit: Defoe's *History of the Plague of London* and *Illustrations for Bunyan's Pilgrim's Progress* of 1864. The former, described by Forrest Reid (*Illustrators of the Sixties*, p. 208) as "by far the rarest on our list," is usually found in an undated reprint by Thomas Laurie, which is sometimes mistaken for the first edition.

❧ Wood-engraved proof, touched with china white and yellow gouache, "Blessed is (s)he that considereth ye poor," *Illustrations for Bunyan's Pilgrim's Progress.* Annotated by the artist. Sheet size: 10⅞ × 8⅜ inches. Image size: 4¼ × 6⅛ inches.

Thomas Morten (1836–1866)

209 JONATHAN SWIFT

Gulliver's Travels into several remote regions of the world. By Dean Swift. A new edition . . . illustrated by T. Morten. London, Cassell, Petter, and Galpin, [1865]. [Color-printed front. and ads dated 11/73 indicate a later issue]. [3], xliii, [1], 352 p. + 4 p. ads. Illus: Color-printed front., numerous wood-engraved vignettes and plates after Morten. Printer: Cassell, Petter, and Galpin. Page size: 10¼ × 7¼ inches. Publisher's brown cloth.

Morten's illustrations to *Gulliver's Travels*, his one notable book, do not reach the level of Grandville's, but they are certainly the best for any edition in English before Rex Whistler's. Though Morten was evidently inspired by what Doré had done for Rabelais in 1854 and for Balzac's *Contes drolatiques* in 1855 when he dealt with Gulliver's voyages to Lilliput and to Brobdingnag, his drawings for the voyages to Laputa and to the Houyhnhnms are both inventive and spirited. It is perhaps a commentary on Victorian taboos that he virtually ignores the Yahoos. In later editions of this book the title page reads: "illustrated by the late T. Morten."

❧ Watercolor drawing, "Portrait of a curmudgeon." Signed "T.M." Image size: 3½ × 2⅛ inches.

Sir William Schwenck Gilbert (1836–1911)

210–211 W. S. GILBERT

The "Bab" Ballads. Much sound and little sense. By W. S. Gilbert. With illustrations by the author. London, John Camden Hotten, 1869. ix, [2], 14–222 p. + 4 p. ads. Illus: Wood-engraved front., t.p. vignette, and 111 wood-engraved vignettes after Gilbert. Printer: Judd and Glass. Page size: 7¼ × 5½ inches. Publisher's green cloth.

"He called aloud to me not to disturb his webs."—*Page 215*.

(209) Jonathan Swift, *Gulliver's Travels*, The voyage to Laputa

J. Mahoney, Drawing for *Little Dorrit*

(212) Charles Dickens, *Little Dorrit*

THE PUPIL OF THE MARSHALSEA. (*See page* 369.)

More "Bab" Ballads. Much sound and little sense by W. S. Gilbert with illustrations by the author. London, George Routledge and sons, [1873]. viii, [1], 14–222 p. + 4 p. ads. Illus: Wood-engraved front., t.p., vignette, and 114 wood-engraved vignettes after Gilbert. Printer: Camden Press. Page size: 7 × 5¼ inches. Publisher's green cloth.

A fondness for the ballads themselves, with their many anticipations of the Savoy operas, must be offered as an excuse for the inclusion of these two volumes. Indeed, even Gilbert felt it necessary to enter the plea that his drawings "were not much worse" than his verses, and that "the little pictures would have a right to complain if they were omitted" ("*Bab*" Ballads, p. vi). In judging "Captain Reece" and "The Bumboat Woman's Story," then, the amiable reader will keep *Pinafore* firmly in mind.

John William North (1841–1924)

North survived to a ripe old age, unlike Houghton, Pinwell, and Walker, the three illustrators with whom he had most in common. Nearly all of his work is concentrated in the sixties, however, and more particularly in *Wayside Posies* (154) and Jean Ingelow's *Poems* (155).

J. Mahoney

Mahoney is one of the minor masters of Victorian illustration. An uneducated London waif, he was accepted in the world of illustration for a time because of his gift as a draftsman, but his objectionable habits kept him always on the edge of disaster. The very somberness of his life made logical the Dalziels' choice of Mahoney as their illustrator in the Household Edition for those novels in which the darker side of London life is Dickens's primary concern: *Oliver Twist, Little Dorrit,* and *Our Mutual Friend.* If he hardly rivals Cruikshank in the first (116), he is in far closer harmony with Dickens's text than is Phiz in the second or Marcus Stone in the third.

212 CHARLES DICKENS

Little Dorrit by Charles Dickens [the Household Edition]. With fifty-eight illustrations by J. Mahoney. London, Chapman and Hall, n.d. viii, 423 p. Illus: Wood-engraved front., t.p. vignette, 3 wood-engraved plates, and 53 wood-engraved vignettes after Mahoney. Printer: Virtue and co. Page size: 9¾ × 7⅜ inches. Publisher's green cloth.

Mahoney's success with the sinister Rigaud should not go unnoticed.

❧ 5 pen and ink and graphite drawings, various subjects in *Little Dorrit,* [Household Edition], signed by the artist. Image size: 3⅝ × 5⅜ inches.

In addition to Mahoney's drawing of Arthur Clennam as a prisoner in the Marshalsea (p. 361), there are drawings for the illustrations on pages 25, 105, 257, and 321.

213 CHARLES DICKENS

Our Mutual Friend by Charles Dickens [the Household Edition]. With fifty-eight illustrations by J. Mahoney. London, Chapman and Hall, n.d. viii, 419, [1] p. Illus: Wood-engraved front., t.p. vignette, 3 wood-engraved plates, and 53 wood-engraved vignettes after Mahoney. Printer: Virtue and co. Page size: 9⅝ × 7⅜ inches.

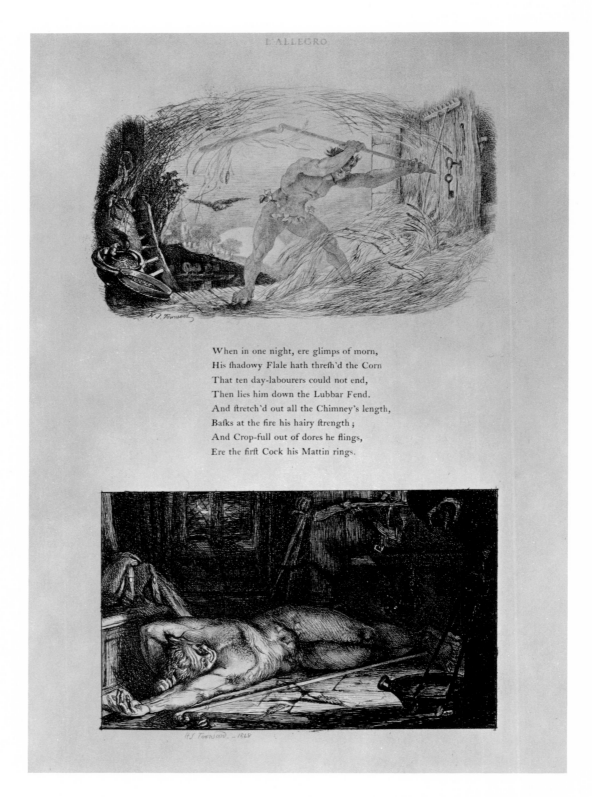

When in one night, ere glimps of morn,
His fhadowy Flale hath threfh'd the Corn
That ten day-labourers could not end,
Then lies him down the Lubbar Fend.
And ftretch'd out all the Chimney's length,
Bafks at the fire his hairy ftrength ;
And Crop-full out of dores he flings,
Ere the firft Cock his Mattin rings.

(217) Etchings by H. J. Townsend in Milton, *L'Allegro*

The Revival of Etching

To use the word "revival" in connection with the books which follow is in a way misleading since etching was extensively used, as we have seen, by such illustrators as Cruikshank, Leech, and Phiz. Yet the emergence of the Etching Club in 1841 inevitably gave new impetus to etching as a consciously artistic medium. Its members saw the volumes produced under the Club's sponsorship as a means of placing their work before the public in a way calculated to bring them both prestige and profit. The publications of the Club did not differ greatly in content from such woodcut volumes of the period as *The Book of British Ballads* (61). Some of the same artists were employed, and there was a like emphasis on genre and landscape subjects. But at least in the large-paper issues, with proof impressions of the etchings on India paper, far more care was exercised than in the usual commercial publication; and the best pages of these books, adorned by artists like Samuel Palmer and Henry James Townsend (1810–1890), can be elegant indeed. Though the Etching Club and its offshoot the Junior Etching Club remained active until 1880, their later volumes are albums of plates rather than proper books.

After 1860 the influence of French etchers, and in particular of Charles Meryon, began to be felt in England through the example of Seymour Haden and Whistler. Whistler contributed two plates to the Junior Etching Club's *Passages from Modern English Poets* in 1862, and Haden published his splendid *Etudes à l'eau-forte* in 1866. Confirmed in its position by the appearance of Philip Gilbert Hamerton's *Etching and Etchers* of 1868 and by the successive volumes of his annual *The Portfolio*, which began to appear in 1870, etching became recognized by amateurs as an important province of art. The etchings of native pioneers like Geddes and Wilkie were collected, and after Keene's death most of his plates were published (190).

Curiously enough, both in France and in England etching was widely regarded until the 1880s as the best defence against photography. In partial explanation of why he did not want Colnaghi to photograph his paintings for a volume of plates, Holman Hunt wrote to W. J. Broderick: "I have moreover a secret intention to etch my pictures if my new picture gains for me the reputation I am working for, and my chance of repayment for this expensive but more truthful and artistic means of representation would I fear be very much interfered with by the previous appearance of these photographs" (manuscript letter, November 2, 1857).

REFERENCES Gray; Hamerton; Harrington; Life; Lister; Sparrow.

214 OLIVER GOLDSMITH

The Deserted Village of Oliver Goldsmith. Illustrated by The Etching Club. London, Longman, Brown, Green, and Longmans, 1842. [1] p., [3], 40 l. Illus: Each text l. with engraved text and etched vignettes, by John Bell, C. W. Cope, T. Creswick, J. C. Horsley, R. Redgrave, C. Stonehouse, F. Tayler, H. J. Townsend, and T. Webster. All plates are India-paper proofs. Printer: Gad & Kenningale. Page size: 10¼ × 7¾ inches. Publisher's green morocco.

Genre, as represented by Charles West Cope (1811–1890), Richard Redgrave (1804–1888), and Thomas Webster (1800–1886), predominates over landscape, as represented by Thomas Creswick (1811–1869), in the Club's first book.

215 WILLIAM SHAKESPEARE

Songs of Shakespeare, illustrated by The Etching Club. London, 1843[–52]. [19] l. Illus: Each l. with engraved text and etched vignettes by Ansdell, Bell, Cope, Creswick, Hook, Horsley, Knight, Palmer, Redgrave, Stone, Stonehouse, Tayler, Townsend, and Webster. All plates are India-paper proofs. Page size: 16½ × 11 inches. [The plates were probably remounted when rebound.] Purple morocco by Zaehnsdorf.

Songs of Shakespeare was published in two installments. A note in the second, which appeared as *Songs and Ballads of Shakespeare* in 1852, states that "the first nine Plates were originally published in the year 1843, and Subscribers to that part may purchase the last nine Plates separately." "The Vine" is the tenth plate in this copy. Hence Palmer's contributions presumably figured in the second installment. However, there is a contradictory advertisement in *L'Allegro* of 1849 which lists "THE SONGS OF SHAKESPEARE, Part I. Seventeen Original Etchings on Steel." In any event, this is the most attractive of the Club's publications, at least in copies like this one made up of "LARGE PAPER PROOFS, HALF-IMPERIAL." The two etchings by Palmer ("The Vine") and the three by Townsend ("Where the Bee Sucks," "Fairies' Song") are notable achievements, and the genre studies by Cope, John Callcot Horsley (1817–1903), Redgrave, and J. Frederick Tayler (1802–1889) gain greatly from their spacious setting. See Plate XLVI.

216 THOMAS GRAY

Elegy Written in a Country Churchyard, by T. Gray. Illustrated by The Etching Club. London, J. Cundall for The Etching Club, 1847. [3], 18 l. Illus: Each text l. with engraved text and etched vignettes by Bell, Cope, Creswick, Horsley, Redgrave, Stonehouse, Tayler, and Townsend. All plates are India-paper proofs. Printer: Gad & Kenningale. Page size: 11 × 8¼ inches. Publisher's brown calf.

Creswick's half-dozen landscapes give this volume its chief appeal, but Townsend is as animated as ever. The etchers treated their text with considerable freedom. For example, Cope turns Gray's "village-Hampden" into a farmer resisting the invasion of his land by the local hunt.

217 JOHN MILTON

L'Allegro by John Milton, illustrated by The Etching Club. London, Joseph Cundall for The Etching Club, 1849. [3, 20] l. Illus: All plates with letterpress text and etched vignettes by Cope, Creswick, Horsley, Redgrave, Stonehouse, Tayler, and Townsend. All l. —including letterpress preliminaries—are India-paper proofs. Page size: 10⅞ × 8¼ inches. Publisher's brown calf.

The larger scale of these etchings makes *L'Allegro*

a more impressive book than *The Deserted Village.* Townsend is represented by five of his strongest designs.

The Germ: thoughts towards nature in poetry, literature, and art. London, Aylott & Jones, 1850. 192 p. Illus: 4 plates by W. Holman Hunt, J. Collinson, F. M. Brown, and W. H. Deverell. Printer: G. F. Tupper. Page size: 8¾ × 5½ inches. Four parts in original wrappers.

As is suggested by the letter from Holman Hunt quoted above, the Pre-Raphaelites approved of etching. Hunt contributed four plates to the productions of the Etching Club, and Millais contributed five. The Brotherhood's most characteristic etchings, however, are the frontispieces to the four issues of their magazine, *The Germ*, published between January and April, 1850: Holman Hunt's "My Beautiful Lady," James Collinson's "The Child Jesus," Ford Madox Brown's "Cordelia," and W. H. Deverell's "Viola and Olivia."

218

Passages from Modern English Poets. Illustrated by The Junior Etching Club. Forty-seven etchings. London, Day & son, [1862]. [4], 45 l. Illus: 45 etched plates by F. Barwell, Viscount Bury, J. Clark, J. R. Clayton, Lord G. F. Fitzgerald, W. Gale, C. Keene, M. J. Lawless, A. J. Lewis, H. S. Marks, J. E. Millais, H. Moore, J. W. Oakes, F. Powell, C. Rossiter, W. Severn, J. Sleigh, F. Smallfield, J. Tenniel, H. C. Whaite, and J. Whistler. Page size: 16⅝ × 11½ inches. Large-paper copy. Publisher's half black morocco.

The distinction of several individual contributions to this volume renders it the most important production by either of the Etching Clubs, though as a book it is far less pleasing than *Songs of Shakespeare*. Keene's "Scene of the Plague in London, 1655," Lawless's "Sisters of Mercy" and "The Bivouac," Millais's "Summer Indolence," and Whistler's "The Angler" and "A River Scene" are its outstanding designs. See Plate LXII. A curiosity of the volume is Frederick Smallfield's etching of a terrified woman reading *The Red Vial* by candlelight. Her book is clearly a new "sensation novel," on the pattern of Miss Braddon's *Lady Audley's Secret* of 1862, but the etching's accompanying poem, called appropriately enough "Supping on Horrors," concerns the Gothic novel and its degenerate successor, the "blood" of earlier decades.

(223) *The Shorter Poems of John Milton*

Sir Francis Seymour Haden (1818–1910)

219 PHILIPPE BURTY

Etudes à l'eau-forte par Francis Seymour Haden. Notice et descriptions par Philippe Burty . . . Paris, 1866. 41, [2] p. Illus: 25 etched plates by Haden, each with printed tissue guard. Page size: 22 × 15¼ inches. Three-quarter red morocco by Hammond.

Since the French critic Philippe Burty was the moving spirit behind this book, it was printed in Paris with a French text. Colnaghi's exhibit of the etchings composing it was held in London during December, 1865, however, and the great majority of the 180 completed copies were sold in England. (Sparrow, pp. 202–203.) Hence this great collection of landscape etchings may fairly be regarded as one of the high points of the English illustrated book. In this example, inscribed "Selected Copy F. Seymour Haden," the artist has used a wide variety of old papers to bring out the special qualities of his several plates. See Plate LXVII.

220 PHILIP GILBERT HAMERTON

Etching & Etchers. By Philip Gilbert Hamerton. London, Macmillan & co., 1868. xxvi, [1], 354, [1] p. Illus: 35 etched and engraved plates by and after Callot, Cope, Daubigny, Hamerton, Haden, Jongkind, Ostade, Palmer, Rembrandt, Tayler, and others. Printer: R. Clay. Page size: 9⅞ × 6¾ inches. Publisher's half blue morocco.

Intact copies of this influential book, which used to be readily available, have virtually disappeared, as the "breakers" have raided it for original etchings by Callot, Daubigny, Haden, Jongkind, Palmer, and Rembrandt.

Andrew Geddes (1783–1844) and Sir David Wilkie (1785–1841)

221 DAVID LAING

Etchings by Sir David Wilkie . . . and by Andrew Geddes, A.R.A. With biographical sketches by David Laing, F.R.S. Edinburgh, 1875. xii, 42, [1] p. Illus: 14 etchings by Wilkie (5 in facsimile), 43 etchings by Geddes (5 in facsimile), and 3 others. Printer: R. & R. Clark. Page size: 13¼×6 inches. Contemp. (publisher's?) half brown morocco.

Each of these Scottish worthies published a selection from his etchings: Wilkie a portfolio of seven in 1824 and Geddes a portfolio of ten in 1826. It was not until 1875, however, that the antiquary David Laing carried out his long-meditated plan of assembling all their etched work in a single volume. He printed nine of Wilkie's fourteen etchings, and thirty-eight of Geddes's forty-three, from the original plates.

Samuel Palmer (1805–1881)

It is only in recent years that the greatness of Palmer's etchings has been fully appreciated. As Raymond Lister points out, these "hymns sung among the hills of Paradise at eventide" recapture much of the "lost vision" that marked the paintings and drawings of Palmer's early Shoreham years (p. 15). Insofar as they appeared in books at all, his thirteen completed etchings, counting the two illustrations to "The Vine" in *Songs of Shakespeare* (215) as one, are scattered through a number of volumes. He survives as an illustrator, therefore, primarily through two posthumous works, *The Eclogues of Virgil* and *The Minor Poems of John Milton* and through his drawings for wood engravings (204).

222 VIRGIL

An English version of **The Eclogues of Virgil** by Samuel Palmer, with illustrations by the author. London, Seeley & co., 1883. xv, 102 p. Illus: 1 etched plate by S. Palmer, 4 etched plates by S. and A. H. Palmer, and 9 facsimile etchings after S. Palmer, each plate with 1 l. text. Printer: Strangeways and sons. Page size: 12⅜×8½ inches. Publisher's green cloth.

Assembled here are one finished etching by Palmer ("Opening the Fold," p. 76), four begun by him and finished by his son A. H. Palmer (pp. 22, 54, 82, 88), and nine facsimiles of his drawings. See Plate LXXIX. A second, small-paper edition of the *Eclogues* appeared in 1884.

223 JOHN MILTON

The Shorter Poems of John Milton with twelve illustrations by Samuel Palmer, painter & etcher. London, Seeley & co., 1889. xx, 124 p. Illus: 12 etched facsimiles. Printer: Strangeways & sons. Page size: 14¾ ×10¼ inches. Publisher's vellum.

This stately volume contains twelve facsimiles of drawings by Palmer. They rank with his best work, and three notable etchings were inspired by them, including "The Early Ploughman," published in Hamerton's *Etching and Etchers*.

Chromolithography

Chromolithography had its start in England with Charles Hullmandel's invention of lithotint. First employed in J. D. Harding's *Sketches at Home and Abroad* of 1836, it soon became a popular medium for topographical albums. "From 1837," writes Martin Hardie (*English Coloured Books*, pp. 245–246), "there is an endless succession of books illustrated in this manner. . . . They assume a stereotyped form; and a glance at the pictorial title-page, the dedication page in lithographic 'copper-plate' writing, and the succession of tinted landscape views, will fix the date of the book as between 1836 to 1845." The principal artists employed for these volumes were Harding himself, Boys, Nash, and Louis Haghe. During the same period the technique of chromolithography proper, that is to say lithography printed in several colors, was also being developed by Owen Jones for the depiction of details in his *Alhambra* and by Hullmandel and Boys for larger views in *Picturesque Architecture in Paris*. By the middle 1840s chromolithography was in general use. The next twenty years were its heyday, as such men as Owen Jones, Henry Noel Humphreys, Henry Shaw, M. Digby Wyatt, J. B. Waring, and the Audsley brothers applied it to a variety of books calling for colored illustrations, and it continued to be widely employed until it was superseded by the three-color process at the end of the century.

REFERENCES Abbey, *Life in England*; Abbey, *Scenery*; Abbey, *Travel*; Burch; Groschwitz; Hardie; Lewis, *George Baxter*; Lewis, *Picture Printing*; McLean, *Victorian Book Design*; Roundell; Tooley; Twyman.

J. D. Harding

224

Harding's Portfolio [of sketches at home and abroad]. London, Charles Tilt, 1837. Illus: Tinted lithographic front., t.p. vignette, and 20 tinted lithographic plates after Harding, touched with color by hand. Printer: Hullmandel. Page size: 19¼ × 10½ inches. Publisher's red half calf.

Harding's folio *Sketches at Home and Abroad* and imperial quarto *Portfolio* were in fact published the same year, though the latter is dated 1837. All copies were "tinted in exact imitation of the original drawings," the tint used being yellow, with highlights left in white. Some copies of the *Portfolio*, as is the case with this one, had substantial additional hand coloring as well. (Twyman, pp. 203–206.) Like its predecessor it contains "sketches at home and abroad," the English views, though only seven in number, being among the most attractive.

Thomas Shotter Boys (1803–1874)

225

Picturesque Architecture in Paris, Ghent, Antwerp, Rouen, etc. Drawn from nature & on stone by Thomas Boys. London, Thomas Boys, 1839. [2] p. Illus: 26 tinted and chromolithographed plates by Boys. Printer: Hullmandel. Page size: 21⅞ × 17½ inches. Three-quarter red morocco by Zaehnsdorf. Abbey, *Travel*, 33, the issue mounted on cards.

Paul Mellon

As early as 1833 Boys had expressed a desire to make "a work on Paris to follow up Girtin's" in showing "Paris as it is." He filled his portfolio with sketches of the city, and after his cousin Thomas Boys became a successful publisher, his dream was realized. Long a close student of the medium, Boys had from his "first insight into the powers of lithography, desired to produce colour." (Roundell, pp. 45–47.) Working with Hullmandel on *Picturesque Architecture* (though Boys dedicated the book to Hullmandel, there was later a controversy over the contribution of each party), he encompassed this ambition as well. "The whole of the Drawings comprising this volume," it is asserted in the Descriptive Notice, "are produced entirely by means of Lithography: they are printed with oil-colours, and come from the press precisely as they now appear. It was expressly stipulated by the Publisher that not a touch should be added afterwards, and this injunction has been strictly adhered to. They are Pictures drawn on Stone and re-produced by printing with Colours: every touch is the work of the Artist, and every impression the product of the press. This is the first, and, as yet, the only attempt to imitate pictorial effects of Landscape Architecture in Chroma-lithography; and in its application to this class of subjects, it has been carried so far beyond what was required in copying polychrome architecture, hieroglyphics, arabesques, &c., that it has become almost a new art." *Picturesque Architecture* is both a major work of graphic art, which triumphantly sustains comparison with Girtin's *Views of Paris* (37), and a landmark in the history of color printing. It may be preferred, indeed, even to Boys's other masterpiece, *Original Views of London as It Is* (87). See Plate XL.

Owen Jones (1809–1874)

Jones was a Welsh architect who launched his career as an artist with *Details and Ornaments from the Alhambra*, a vast folio published in twelve parts at his own expense between 1836 and 1845. As an early monument of chromolithography its place is secure, but its reproductions of "hieroglyphics, arabesques, etc.," as Boys described them, do not make the *Alhambra* a book of vivid appeal except perhaps to fellow architects. In the course of its publication, however, Jones designed and in some cases printed a number of more accessible volumes like *Ancient Spanish Ballads* which were decorated or "illuminated" with chromolithographs, and during the following decade he was responsible for a further series of illuminated giftbooks, many of them in embossed leather bindings. It would seem that these productions did not find a ready market, since their sale at reduced prices in 1854 is recorded by Ruari McLean. Then came the culminating work of Jones's career, *The Grammar of Ornament* of 1856. In his later years he turned from this magnificent compilation and interpretation of the designs of others to original designs of his own.

The "Victoria Psalter" is the most imposing of his last books, *Paradise and the Peri* perhaps the most attractive.

226 JOHN GIBSON LOCKHART

Ancient Spanish Ballads; historical and romantic. Translated, with notes, by J. G. Lockhart, esq. A new edition, revised. With numerous illustrations from drawings by William Allan, R.A., David Roberts, R.A., William Simpson, Henry Warren, C. E. Aubrey, and William Harvey. The borders and ornamental vignettes by Owen Jones, architect. London, John Murray, 1841. Added chromolithographed t.p., [16, 100] l. + 4 l. ads. Illus: Added chromolithographed t.p. and 3 chromolithographed plates, 6 tinted wood-engraved plates, numerous wood-engraved vignettes, each page with color-printed typographic, wood-engraved, or chromolithographed border. Printer: Vizetelly & co. Page size: 9¾ × 7⅞ inches. Publisher's brown cloth.

This luxurious giftbook is less significant for its illustrations, wood engravings by William Harvey and others, which are inferior to those in *The Book of British Ballads* (61), than for its illuminations in the Moorish style: four ornamental volume or section titles chromolithographed in three colors, and many page borders in two or one.

227

The Song of Songs. [Illuminated by Owen Jones]. [London], Longman & co., 1849. [16] l. Illus: Chromolithographed text with chromolithographed borders, initials, etc. Page size: 7¾ × 5¼ inches. Publisher's embossed brown calf.

The Song of Songs is a characteristic example of the increasingly elaborate giftbooks which Jones produced in the late 1840s and the early 1850s.

228 OWEN JONES

The Grammar of Ornament by Owen Jones. Illustrated by examples from various styles of ornament. One hundred folio plates, drawn on stone by F. Bedford, and printed in colours by Day and son. London, Day and son, 1856. [1], 6, [2], 4, 6, 4, 2, 4, 4, 4, 2, 8, 2, 3, 2, 2, 7, 5, 15, [1], 4, 14, 4 p. Illus: Added chromolithographed t.p. and 100 chromolithographed plates, numerous wood-engraved vignettes. Page size: 21¾ × 14½ inches. Publisher's three-quarter brown morocco.

In this work Jones surveys and illustrates ornament from savage tribes and the ancient world through the Middle Ages and the Renaissance.

On the hundred folio plates chromolithographed by Francis Bedford from his drawings several thousand individual examples are compactly but harmoniously arranged. Moreover, Jones's rationale of ornamental art, stated in his preface and in thirty-seven propositions concerning "the arrangement of form and colour in architecture and the decorative arts," gives him a perspective from which to interpret this immense mass of data. "The future progress of Ornamental Art," he claims, "may be best secured by engrafting on the experience of the past the knowledge we may obtain by a return to Nature for fresh inspiration." Only through this process will the student "find an ever-gushing fountain in place of a half-filled, stagnant reservoir." (Pp. 1–2.) Jones's remarkable synthesis is not only a notable illustrated book, but a great book *tout court*. See Plate LV.

229 THOMAS MOORE

Paradise and the Peri. [By] Thos. Moore. [Illuminators Owen Jones and Henry Warren, on stone by Albert Warren]. [London], Day and son, [1862]. [27] l. Illus: Versos of chromolithographed text with borders, initials, etc., rectos with chromolithographed vignettes, borders, etc. Page size: 12½ × 6½ inches. Publisher's brown calf.

In this poem Tom Moore, like a sort of boudoir Milton, tells a story from Persian myth. A fallen angel ranges the countries of the East in an ultimately successful search for a gift that will open the gates of heaven to her. The ornate decorations and formalized pictures sort well with Moore's style and subject. As in the designs of Edmund Dulac, who must have known these illustrations, any touch of realism would be out of place.

230

The Psalms of David, illuminated by Owen Jones. [London, 1862]. [3] l., 100 p. Illus: Each page with letterpress text, chromolithographed borders, initials, vignettes, etc. Page size: 16½ × 12 inches. Publisher's embossed brown calf.

The Queen accepted the dedication of this lavish volume, which Jones seems to have regarded as his masterpiece. It accordingly became known as the "Victoria Psalter," and indeed is so identified on its embossed leather binding. The illuminations, though restricted in color to blue, red, and

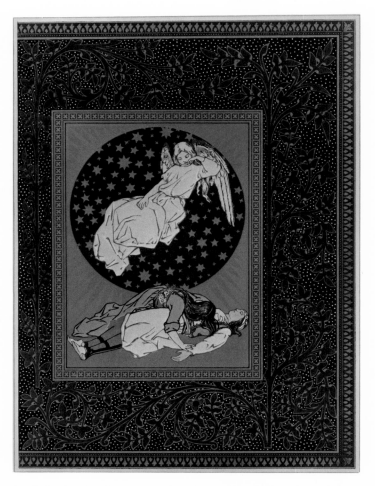

(229) **Design by Owen Jones for Thomas Moore,** *Paradise and the Peri*

gold, are so rich as to be overpowering. Perhaps the dedication pages, where the cream background provides welcome relief to the eye, offer the volume's most agreeable opening.

Henry Noel Humphreys (1810–1879)

Humphreys, who was born and educated in Birmingham, spent some years of his youth in Italy, where he immersed himself in the study of early manuscripts. On his return to England he made it the object of his life to apply "the Art of Illumination" to book decoration. In 1849, indeed, he embodied his ideas on this subject in a handsome volume called *The Art of Illumination and Missal Painting: A Guide to Modern Illuminators.* Not content merely to imitate his medieval predecessors, he created fresh designs in their spirit, thus producing some of the most attractive of chromolithographic books. Though his career as an illuminator extended from *The Illuminated Books of the Middle Ages* of 1844 to *The Penitential Psalms* of 1861, he can best be represented by three early volumes which are also remarkable for their bindings of black plaster composition over *papier maché*, still further examples of his search for new creations reviving old traditions. It should be noted that the use of chromolithography enabled Longmans to sell these books in substantial editions at moderate prices. Of *The Black Prince* 1,000 copies were offered at a guinea apiece.

231

Parables of Our Lord. London, Longman & co., 1847. [32], ii p. Illus: Chromolithographed t.p. and 31 chromolithographed pages, with text, borders, initials, vignettes, etc. Page size: 6¼ × 4½ inches. Publisher's *papier-maché* boards.

The sixteen openings of the *Parables*, counting the first and last page as one, alternate between many colors and gold and black. In both sequences the borders are adorned with flowers, leaves, and fruit, but the gold and black openings also have miniatures of New Testament episodes. Humphreys explains the symbolism of his borders in a concluding printed sheet. Of "The Pharisee and the Publican" he writes: "The 'modest daisy' is universally regarded as an image of humility, and the 'flaunting tulip,' of pride and arrogance; they have therefore suggested the ornaments of these pages. In page 24, in illustration of the text 'Every one that exalteth himself shall be abased,' &c. &c., the tulip is seen withered and fallen, while the daisy is expanded and raised above it." See Plate LI.

232

The Miracles of Our Lord. London, Longman & co., 1848. [1], 31, iv p. Illus: Chromolithographed t.p. and 31 chromolithographed pages with text, borders, initials, vignettes, etc. Page size: 6½ × 4½ inches. Publisher's *papier-maché* boards.

This companion volume to the *Parables* also alternates openings in many colors with openings in gold and black and has borders of imaginary foliage, but Humphreys's unifying theme is now the Apostles and their symbols. The miracle of "water turned into wine," for example, is shown in "an illuminated miniature of original design," accompanied by portraits of St. Paul after Schongauer and St. Matthew after Dürer. The former

bears "the Gospels, and the sword with which he suffered decapitation," the latter holds "the Gospels and a lance—the instrument of his martyrdom." In his accompanying "Remarks of an Illuminator" Humphreys asserts the importance of "the meaning, spirit, and symbolism of Christian art," defending it from the charge of "Romanism" by an apt quotation from Dr. Arnold.

233

A Record of the Black Prince. Being a selection of such passages in his life as have been most quaintly and strikingly narrated by chroniclers of the period, embellished with highly wrought miniatures and borderings selected from various illuminated MSS . . . by Henry Noel Humphreys. London, Longman, Brown, Green, and Longmans, 1849. [6], xciv, [1], ii p. Illus: 6 chromolithographed vignettes, 4 with chromolithographed borders, 2 wood-engraved borders, repeated (once in red), numerous wood-engraved initials. Printer: Vizetelly Brothers and co. Page size: 7⅜ × 5 inches. Publisher's pierced *papier-maché* boards over red paper.

In this book Humphreys turned to secular history, selecting quaint and striking passages from early chroniclers which he illustrated with borders and miniatures freely copied from manuscripts of the period.

Henry Shaw (1800–1873)

234 HENRY SHAW

The Decorative Arts Ecclesiastical and Civil of the Middle Ages. By Henry Shaw, F.S.A. London, William Pickering, 1851. 32, [3, 86] p. Illus: Numerous wood-engraved, chromolithographed, and etched plates, some colored, numerous wood-engraved vignettes and initials. Page size: 10¾ × 7 inches. Publisher's (?) red morocco.

An example of Shaw's early productions, *Dresses and Decorations of the Middle Ages*, is described above (102). *Decorative Arts of the Middle Ages* may stand as an example of his later work, in which considerable use is made of chromolithography. Finding these "somewhat repellent books, . . . typographically of small account," Geoffrey Keynes (*Pickering*, p. 37) omitted them from his bibliography of William Pickering fifty-one years ago. Ironically enough, Shaw's books are now among the most sought after of those published by the Chiswick Press, and only marginally for Pickering's contribution.

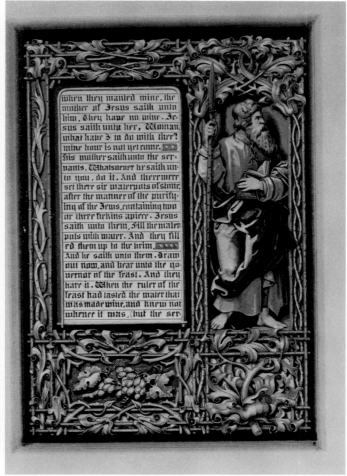

(232) Designs by Henry Noel Humphreys for *The Miracles of Our Lord*

235 M. DIGBY WYATT

The Industrial Arts of the Nineteenth Century. A series of illustrations of the choicest specimens produced by every nation at the Great Exhibition of works of industry, 1851 . . . by M. Digby Wyatt, architect. London, Day and son, 1851[–53]. 2 v. I: viii p., 72 l. II: xii p., 73–158 l. Illus: Chromolithographed fronts., 2 chromolithographed titles in v. II, and 158 chromolithographed plates, each with 1 l. letterpress text. Page size: 19⅝ × 13 inches. Contemporary red morocco by Webb & Hunt.

Wyatt relates in his postscript (II, ix–xii) that, though this book was conceived only in April, 1851, it proved possible to issue its forty parts between October 1 of that year and March 7, 1853. Twenty artists, including the young Millais, made the 160 drawings, which were then chromolithographed, chiefly by Francis Bedford. The average number of printings required for a subject was seven, the maximum fourteen. When it is remembered that the stone had to be wiped clean after each printing of 1,300 copies of every plate, the overwhelming amount of expert work required will be appreciated. Wyatt intended his book to be "a faithful record of the characteristics of those productions displayed at the Great Exhibition of 1851, which best illustrate the advanced condition of the Industrial Arts of the Nineteenth Century" (I, iii). In his mind the word "advanced" tended to be synonymous with "elaborated," and the richness of the objects depicted is sometimes almost suffocating. The pretensions of "The Crystal Fountain," a Birmingham creation located in the transept of the Palace of Glass, are relatively modest. Wyatt's claim that *The Industrial Arts of the XIXth Century* was "the most important application of chromo-lithography . . . which has yet appeared" must certainly be affirmed. See Plate LIII.

236 J. B. WARING

Art Treasures of the United Kingdom from the Art Treasures Exhibition, Manchester. Edited by J. B. Waring, chromolithographed by F. Bedford. The drawings on wood by R. Dudley. With essays by Owen Jones, Digby Wyatt, A. W. Franks, J. B. Waring, J. C. Robinson, & G. Scharf, Jun. London, Day and son, 1858. [17], 42, [1], 31, [1], 32, [1], 17–80, [2], 27 p. Illus: 100 chromolithographed plates, mostly after Bedford, 78 wood-engraved vignettes after Dudley. Page size: 15 × 11 inches. Publisher's brown calf.

If Wyatt's record of the Great Exhibition celebrated contemporary design, Waring's record of the Manchester Exhibition of 1857 celebrated the heritage from the past on which contemporary design was based. He hoped that his text and plates would be enjoyed by amateurs of the "Ornamental Arts" and put to use by practitioners of the "Industrial Arts." Some of his plates, such as

the reproduction of an embroidered Indian book cover in the section on "Textile Art," are miracles of fidelity. The publisher's binding of inlaid calf is a pastiche by Leighton Son and Hodge after a Renaissance binding by Le Gascon in the Exhibition. Waring was also responsible for a larger book of the same kind, *Masterpieces of Industrial Art and Sculpture at the International Exhibition*, published in three volumes in 1862.

W. and G. Audsley

237

The Sermon on the Mount. Illuminated by W. & G. Audsley, architects, Liverpool. Illustrated by Charles Rolt, chromolithographed by W. R. Tymms. [London], Day & son, 1861. Illus: Chromolithographed front. (tipped in) and 26 l. with chromolithographed text and borders. Page size: 21⅞ × 17¼ inches. Publisher's brown morocco.

In this work the Audsley brothers, who were Liverpool architects, offered a volume hardly less ambitious than those of Wyatt and Waring, but intended to have an aesthetic rather than a practical appeal. Their varied and exuberant decorations, printed in the brightest colors available, were drawn chiefly from medieval manuscripts. The publisher's gold-embossed morocco binding is in keeping with the magnificence of the text. The Audsleys' other notable illuminated book is *The Prisoner of Chillon* of 1865.

Edmund Evans (1826–1905)

Evans might well have appeared in the earlier section on color printing from wood or metal, but it seems more appropriate to place him just before Walter Crane, Randolph Caldecott, and Kate Greenaway, since it is for their nursery giftbooks that he is best remembered. After a seven-year apprenticeship with the engraver Ebenezer Landells, Evans struck out for himself in 1847. His first ventures in color printing came in 1852, and, as already noted, he was the chief supplier of yellow-back covers beginning in 1853. His most interesting books between that time and 1860 contain color-printed illustrations after Birket Foster, who had been his fellow apprentice under Landells. James Doyle's *Chronicle of England*—"the most carefully executed book he had ever printed," so Evans told Martin Hardie (p. 270)—and Richard Doyle's *In Fairyland* (146) were the high points of his next decade. Meanwhile, he had begun in 1865 to collaborate with the firm of Routledge and Warne on an extensive series of toy books, paperbound pamphlets with six pages of text and six pages of colored illustrations which sold initially for sixpence and later for a shilling. This enterprise, which revolutionized the field of children's books, led directly to Evans's memorable association with Crane, Caldecott, and Kate Greenaway. Among his later volumes were an edition of Lewis Carroll's *The Nursery 'Alice'* with twenty colored enlargements from Tenniel's illustrations of 1890, Crane's *A Floral Fantasy in an Old English Garden* of 1899, and W. Graham Robertson's *Old English Songs and Dances* (284).

REFERENCES Burch; Evans; Hardie; Lewis, *Picture Printing*; McLean, *Victorian Book Design*; Muir, *Victorian Illustrated Books*.

Birket Foster (1825–1899)

238   OLIVER GOLDSMITH

The Poems of Oliver Goldsmith. Edited by Robert Arris Willmott . . . with illustrations by Birket Foster and H. N. Humphreys. Printed in colours from wood blocks. London, George Routledge and co., 1859. [2], xvi, 159, [1] p. Illus: 40 color-printed wood-engraved vignettes after Foster, numerous wood-engraved head- and tailpieces (some tinted) after Humphreys. Printer: E. Evans. Page size: 8⅝×6½ inches. Publisher's brown morocco.

This is one of Evans's most charming books. The nine or ten colors in which Foster's forty illustrations are printed give them a freshness and salience rarely achieved by that artist's work in black and white. Evans told Martin Hardie (p. 268) how he faithfully followed proofs of the engravings colored by Foster himself, using colors bought from the artist's supplier and seeking "to reproduce as accurately as possible the texture of the original." Noel Humphreys's tinted decorations are also attractive, and each page is surrounded by a gold border. See Plate LVIII.

238A   OLIVER GOLDSMITH

The Poems of Oliver Goldsmith. Edited by Robert Arris Willmott . . . a new edition, with illustrations by Birket Foster and H. N. Humphreys. Printed in colours by Edmund Evans. London, Routledge, Warne, and Routledge, 1860. xxi, [1], 161, [1] p. Illus: Color-printed wood-engraved front. and 51 color-printed wood-engraved vignettes after Foster, numerous wood-engraved head- and tailpieces (some tinted) after Humphreys. Printer: E. Evans. Page size: 8¾×6¼ inches. Publisher's purple cloth.

Proud of his handiwork, which was an immediate success, Evans made substantial improvements in the second edition of Goldsmith's *Poems*. A frontispiece appears for the first time, and eleven cuts in the text were added, chiefly to the second half of the book which had been virtually without illustration. Moreover, both the coloring and the arrangement on the page of the original illustrations were altered for the better.

239   THOMAS MILLER

Common Wayside Flowers. By Thomas Miller. Illustrated by Birket Foster. London, Routledge, Warne, and Routledge, 1860. [1], vi, 184, [1] p. Illus: Added color-printed wood-engraved t.p., 1 color-printed wood-engraved plate, and 22 color-printed wood-engraved vignettes after Foster. Printer: E. Evans. Page size: 8⅝×6¾ inches. Publisher's brown cloth.

Thanks to Evans's brilliant coloring, the detailed engravings of flowers in this book are among Foster's best illustrations. Further colored flower engravings serve as onlays for the book's striking binding, one of the most ornate even of the mid-Victorian period.

Birket Foster and others

240

A Book of Favorite Modern Ballads. Illustrated with fifty engravings, from drawings by the first artists. London, W. Kent & co., 1860. xiii, [2], 167, [1] p. Illus: Tinted wood-engraved front. and added t.p., 48 tinted wood-engraved vignettes after C. W. Cope, E. H. Corbould, G. Dodgson, E. Duncan, B. Foster, D. H. Fristen, W. J. Grant, W. Harvey, G. E. Hicks, J. C. Horsley, S. Palmer, G. H. Thomas, P. Skelton, A. Solomon, E. Weedon, and H. Weir; ornamental designs after A. H. Warren. Printer: E. Evans. Page size: 9⅛×6¾ inches. Publisher's (?) three-quarter red morocco.

This attractive giftbook differs somewhat in style from Evans's other volumes of the period. The fifty wood engravings are printed in black and white on a grey background, and the elaborate decorations are in gold. Foster predominates, but a number of other artists are represented, including Samuel Palmer.

241 JAMES DOYLE

A Chronicle of England, B.C. 55 – A.D. 1485. Written and illustrated by James E. Doyle. The designs engraved and printed in colours by Edmund Evans. London, Longman, Green, Longman, Roberts, & Green, 1864. [1], viii, 462 p. Illus: 81 color-printed wood-engraved vignettes after Doyle. Printer: E. Evans. Page size: 10¼×7¾ inches. Publisher's (?) red morocco.

Doyle's illustrations for this medieval chronicle are as modest and unassuming as his text. Indeed, he disclaimed any purpose beyond showing clearly and truthfully the action depicted. When he compliments Evans on the "creditable manner" in which his drawings have been reproduced (p. iv), he underlines the sole reason for his book's continuing appeal. These bright and fresh engravings, printed in as many as ten colors, are dropped into the text about once every six pages, and the going is heavy in between. In "Death of the Kingmaker" (p. 422) Doyle has characteristically been at more pains to get the costumes of Warwick and his assailants right than to give animation to his scene.

(241) James Doyle,
A Chronicle of England

Walter Crane (1845–1916)

A Liverpool boy with a gift for drawing, Crane was apprenticed between 1859 and 1862 to W. J. Linton, the wood engraver. His chief duty was to copy drawings on the wood, both his own and those of other artists. This practical introduction to the craft of illustration stood him in good stead throughout his career. His association with Edmund Evans began with designs for yellow-back covers. Their subsequent collaboration on toy books raised these already familiar amenities of the nursery to a new level of attractiveness and in the process made Crane's reputation. The remainder of his long life was full and active. He became a painter, a designer of everything from wallpaper to ceramic tiles, a socialist of the William Morris persuasion, and a writer on decorative art. His production of illustrated books did not falter, but the volumes from his hand became increasingly stylized and pretentious. Crane may have seen his later books as a progression towards a decorative ideal, but most amateurs prefer his more spontaneous earlier work. Still, the extent to which some of his books of the late 1880s and 1890s embody Art Nouveau motifs has given them a considerable vogue in recent years, particularly among continental European collectors.

REFERENCES Engen; Evans; Hardie; Massé; Mc-Lean, *Victorian Book Design*; Muir, *Victorian Illustrated Books*.

242 NATHANIEL HAWTHORNE

Transformation: or, the romance of Monte Beni. By Nathaniel Hawthorne, author of "The Scarlet Letter," "Our old home," etc. Illustrated edition. London, Smith, Elder and co., 1865. [1], xi, 400 p. + 4 p. ads. Illus: Wood-engraved front., added wood-engraved t.p., and 3 plates after Crane. Printer: Smith, Elder and co. Page size: 7½ × 4⅞ inches. Publisher's red cloth.

Crane's most interesting illustrations before his toy books are for a reprint of *Transformation*, the English title of Hawthorne's *The Marble Faun*. The experience of making engravings after Sixties illustrators during his three years' apprenticeship with Linton has left its mark on these designs, where Crane focusses quite as directly on interpreting the characters and incidents of the story

(242) Nathaniel Hawthorne, *Transformation*

A FROLIC OF THE CARNIVAL   p. 389.

(243) *Sing a Song of Sixpence*

his desire to encourage "good art in the nursery," but far more by his feeling that "in a sober and matter-of-fact age they afford perhaps the only outlet for unrestricted flights of fancy open to the modern illustrator" (*Of the Decorative Illustration of Books*, pp. 156–158). His drawings are bolder and less crowded than those in *Transformation*, yet he still takes a healthy interest in the situations and people he is depicting. For some, Crane's early toy books represent the classic phase of his career as an illustrator. He does not neglect design (indeed his application of what he has learned from Japanese prints can be fascinating), but decoration has by no means become an end in itself.

244

The Baby's Opera, a book of old rhymes with new dresses by Walter Crane, the music by the earliest masters. Engraved, & printed in colours by Edmund Evans. London, Frederick Warne and co., [1877]. 56 p. Illus: Numerous vignettes, borders, and plates after Crane. Printer: E. Evans. Page size: 7 × 7 ¼ inches. Publisher's decorated boards.

With this little book of English nursery rhymes, Crane began a final series of toy books, priced at five shillings. Its companion "triplets," as he came to call them, are *The Baby's Bouquet* of 1879 and *Baby's Own Aesop* of 1886. Though not as bold and striking as his earlier efforts in this line, they are more delicate, restrained, and harmonious.

245   MRS. MOLESWORTH

A Christmas Child, a sketch of a Boy-life by Mrs. Molesworth, author of 'Carrots,' 'Cuckoo clock,' etc. Illustrated by Walter Crane . . . London, Macmillan and co., 1880. viii, [1], 223 p. + 24 p. ads. Illus: Wood-engraved front., wood-engraved t.p. vignette, and 6 wood-engraved plates after Crane. Printer: R. & R. Clark. Page size: 6⅝ × 4½ inches. Publisher's red cloth.

This book for older children, like the many others by Mrs. Molesworth which Crane illustrated between 1878 and 1890, is concerned after its fashion with the real Victorian world. Though Crane always leaned towards the fanciful, he was able to deal effectively with this sort of material as well, just as Arthur Hughes did in *Tom Brown's School Days* (176).

as does Millais in his illustrations of Trollope. In the best of the series, "A Frolic of the Carnival," Kenyon is shown at bottom right, a lonely figure amid the prevailing saturnalia, while above are other major figures of the novel, each presented with studied care. At this crucial moment of Hawthorne's tale, Hilda has aimed a rosebud at Kenyon, whom she will later marry. "It hit the mark; he turned his sad eyes upwards, and there was Hilda, in whose gentle presence his own secret sorrow and the obtrusive uproar of the carnival alike died away from his perception" (p. 389).

243

Sing a Song of Sixpence. London, George Routledge & sons, n.d. [cover-title]. 6 l. Illus: Color-printed wrappers and 8 color-printed plates after Crane. Page size: 9¾ × 7¼ inches. Publisher's decorated wrappers.

In a list that he believes to be complete Percy Muir (*Victorian Illustrated Books*, pp. 176–177) lists forty toy books by Crane, thirty-two in a sixpenny series between 1865 and about 1876, and eight in a shilling series, about 1875. This is one of the earliest. Crane was attracted to toy books in part by

Household Stories from the collection of the Bros: Grimm: translated from the German by Lucy Crane; and done into pictures by Walter Crane. London, Macmillan & co., 1882. [1], x, 269, [1] p. Illus: Wood-engraved front., wood-engraved t.p., 10 wood-engraved plates, numerous wood-engraved head- and tailpieces, numerous wood-engraved initials, all after Crane. Printer: R. & R. Clark. Page size: 9⅝ × 6¼ inches. Large paper. Publisher's blue cloth.

Until the luxurious *First of May, a Fairy Masque* of 1881, Crane had applied himself to inexpensive books sold in large numbers. Henceforth he turned more and more to elaborately produced books for well-to-do buyers, thus anticipating his fellow socialist William Morris in his venture with the Kelmscott Press. The 250 copies of this handsome volume sold out on publication. It is perhaps the best of Crane's more ambitious works. The book is a triumph in his characteristic mode of decoration, yet its designs, even the headpieces and initial letters, remain true illustrations. See Plate LXXVIII.

247 WALTER CRANE

Flora's Feast, a masque of flowers penned and pictured by Walter Crane. London, Cassell & co., 1889. 40 p. + 9 p. ads. Illus: Each page with color-printed wood-engraved illustration and lettered text after Crane. Page size: 9⅞ × 7⅜ inches. Publisher's decorated boards.

    Pierpont Morgan Library

Because of books like *Flora's Feast* with its ornate patterns of flowers and ideal figures, Crane has sometimes been hailed as an early master of Art Nouveau. John Russell Taylor contends, however, that "from first to last Crane was an Arts and Craftsman, and though his books have their sober charms they are nearly all fatally lacking in the grace, elegance or imaginative life of real art nouveau" (*The Art Nouveau Book in England*, p. 67).

☞ Sketchbook: 37 graphite drawings dated 1883–1886. "Acanthus" is dated 1884. Page size: 8⅝ × 6½ inches. Linen boards.

    Pierpont Morgan Library

If any proof is required of the closeness with which Crane studied nature in designing his floral patterns it is provided by his study of acanthus in this sketchbook.

(247) Walter Crane, *Flora's Feast*

248 NATHANIEL HAWTHORNE

A Wonder Book for Girls & Boys, by Nathaniel Hawthorne. With 60 designs by Walter Crane. London, Osgood, McIlvaine & co., 1892. x, 210 p. Illus: Color-printed front., 18 color-printed plates, numerous wood-engraved head- and tailpieces (some color-printed), numerous wood-engraved initials, all after Crane. Printer: Riverside Press. Page size: 9 × 6¼ inches. Publisher's decorated white cloth.

The drawings for this volume were done in Florida for initial publication by Houghton Mifflin of Boston. Though Crane's settings are avowedly Mediterranean, their warm colors must surely reflect the sunny locale in which they were drawn. Blake's influence is as evident as it had been in *Flora's*

Feast, even if it takes a different form. The English edition of the *Wonder Book* may properly be regarded as a companion volume in color to *Household Stories*.

249 WALTER CRANE

Of the Decorative Illustration of Books Old and New, by Walter Crane. London, George Bell and sons, 1896. [1], xii, 335, [1] p. Illus: Numerous wood-engraved, halftone, and facsimile illustrations. No. 68 of 130 copies on Japan vellum. Printer: Chiswick Press. Page size: 9 × 6 ⅛ inches. Red morocco by De Sauty.

This book is the most interesting of Crane's writings on decorative art. In the first three chapters, taken from lectures delivered in 1889, he offers a historical survey of "decorative treatment" as opposed to "pictorial statement" (p. v) in the illustration of books. His test for decoration—does it treat the page as "a space to be made beautiful in design?" (p. 6)—leads him to some strange preferences, notably for Stothard over Hogarth (p. 136) and Turner (p. 146). Among the abundant illustrations to this part of the book are six wood engravings by Edward Calvert printed from the original blocks (pp. 141, 143). Chapter 4, written six or seven years later, offers a valuable pioneering survey of recent English illustration and its influence in Europe. Here Crane admits that he may have been too sweeping in his earlier advocacy of "ornament" over "graphic power." "I should say at once that sincere graphic or naturalistic drawing, with individual character and style, is always preferable to merely lifeless, purely imitative, and tame repetition in so-called decorative work" (p. 208). A final chapter sums up his general principles of book design.

Randolph Caldecott (1846–1886)

Caldecott had no formal training as an artist. He grew up in the midlands countryside and was employed for a time as a bank clerk in Manchester before his illustrations for Washington Irving's *Old Christmas*, published for the holiday season of 1875, led Edmund Evans to choose him as Crane's successor when that artist was forced by the pressure of other work to give up drawing toy books. After Caldecott had illustrated two a year from 1878 to 1885, he also was famous. Many commissions in black and white also came his way before his early death. Caldecott once declared that he practiced "the art of leaving out as a science," explaining that "the fewer the lines, the less error committed" (quoted by Martin Hardie, *English Coloured Books*, p. 279). Because of his mastery of the economical use of line, particularly for humorous scenes, his illustrations depend far less on color for their effect than do those of Crane and Kate Greenaway.

REFERENCES Blackburn; Evans; Hardie; Muir, *Victorian Illustrated Books*; Smith.

250

A set of 16 toy books illustrated by R. Caldecott, [1878–1885]:

The house that Jack built.

The diverting history of John Gilpin.

The mad dog.

The babes in the wood.

An elegy on the glory of her sex, Mrs. Mary Blaize.

The queen of hearts.

The farmer boy.

The great Panjandrum himself.

Sing a song for sixpence.

The three jovial huntsmen.

The milkmaid.

Hay diddle diddle and baby bunting.

A frog he would a-wooing go.

The fox jumps over the parson's gate.

Come lasses and lads.

Ride a cock horse to Banbury & A farmer went trotting upon his grey mare.

Each volume measures 9 by 8 inches and has original wrappers.

Caldecott's toy books, though still priced at a shilling, are more elaborate than those in Crane's series. Able to count from the first on a sale of 10,000 copies, Evans eliminated blank pages by supplying nine colored illustrations, many black and white drawings, and more text. Eventually he printed editions of 100,000. The reasons for Caldecott's success are apparent in the initial volumes of the series. The animals in *The House That Jack Built* of 1878 could not be improved. And the delicious humor of *John Gilpin* of the same year is perfectly conveyed through the artist's rendering of the staid dignity of this elderly linen draper during his quiet preparations for a day of pleasure, the grim tenacity with which he adheres to his runaway horse, the enthusiastic interest that the whole countryside takes in his wild ride, and the good humor he displays during moments of relief from adversity. In the scene illustrated in Plate LXXV, Gilpin is sweeping by the inn at Edmonton where his family waits impatiently for the wedding anniversary celebration to begin:

"Stop, stop, John Gilpin!—Here's the house!"
   They all at once did cry;
"The dinner waits, and we are tired;"
   Said Gilpin—"So am I!"

251

More "Graphic" Pictures by Randolph Caldecott. London, George Routledge & sons, 1887. 71 p. Illus: Color-printed wood-engraved front., t.p. vignette, and 32 color-printed wood-engraved plates after Caldecott. Printer: "The Graphic." Page size: 10½ × 14½ inches. Publisher's decorated boards.

The contents of this album, as of the others drawn from Caldecott's contributions to the *Graphic*, are extremely varied, but mildly comic episodes of private life predominate. Most are contemporary, but occasionally Caldecott returns to an earlier setting such as he had used in *Old Christmas*. His other *Graphic* albums are: *"Graphic" Pictures*, 1883; *Last "Graphic" Pictures*, 1887; and *Gleanings from the "Graphic,"* 1889.

252   WASHINGTON IRVING

Old Christmas: from the sketch book of Washington Irving. Illustrated by R. Caldecott. London, Macmillan & co., 1892. xiv, [2], 165, [1] p. Illus: Tinted wood-engraved front., tinted wood-engraved t.p., 7 tinted wood-engraved plates, and numerous wood-engraved vignettes, all after Caldecott. No. 47 of 250 large-paper copies. Printer: R. & R. Clark. Page size: 10⅛ × 7 inches. Publisher's red cloth.

Caldecott's illustrations to his first notable book are seen to their best advantage in the large-paper copies of this sumptuous reissue. Though Irving's text dates from the early part of the century, one has no sense of watching a costume party. The observation is as sharp, and the rendering as spare and precise, as in Caldecott's sketches of the passing scene.

Four graphite sketches for an unidentified boys' story. The size of that reproduced is 5 × 3¼ inches.

Two pen and ink sketches of a contested election, "The Enlightened borough." Size: 4½ × 7 inches.

The pencil sketches would appear to date from early in Caldecott's career as an illustrator, the pen sketches from his later years. In comparing Caldecott with Phil May, Martin Hardie wrote (p. 279): "nobody knows the true inwardness of his work . . . till he has seen his carefully finished pencil sketches." See above, page xxxii.

Kate Greenaway (1846–1901)

Among collectors the popularity of this third "academician of the nursery" now surpasses that of either Crane or Caldecott. Such a tide of taste has its baffling aspects. No doubt Kate Greenaway's vision of child life was original and consistent, but surely it was also placid and narrow. Her comely children, whose regular features rarely betray any emotion and the immaculate grooming of whose vaguely eighteenth-century costumes is hardly ever disturbed, inhabit an idyllic countryside where life is as sedate as it is uneventful. Each book after *Under the Window* offers essentially "the mixture as before." Even the vogue of Kate Greenaway's drawings seems excessive. A single design is no doubt a precious example of decorative art, but a wall lined with her drawings could border on the monotonous.

REFERENCES Evans; Hardie; Muir, *Victorian Illustrated Books*; Smith; Spielmann and Layard.

253 KATE GREENAWAY

Under the Window. Pictures and rhymes for children by Kate Greenaway. Engraved & printed by Edmund Evans. London, George Routledge & sons, [1878]. 64 p. Illus: Numerous color-printed wood-engraved vignettes after Greenaway. Printer: E. Evans. Page size: 9¼ × 7¼ inches. Publisher's decorated boards. Spielmann and Layard, p. 285.

In his *Reminiscences* (pp. 59–63) Evans tells how Kate Greenaway's sketches and the verses written for them were offered to him, how he took great pains to ensure that his engravings should reproduce her designs exactly, how his edition of 20,000 copies at six shillings each sold out at once, how Ruskin took her up, and how imitators of her work appeared everywhere. Certainly Evans spared no pains to make *Under the Window* attractive, from the graceful pictorial cover to the miniature cuts in the table of contents to the larger illustrations of the poems themselves. A child's world could hardly be more agreeable than it is in this book, though it might be more exciting. See Plate LXXVI.

254

Mother Goose or the old nursery rhymes, illustrated by Kate Greenaway. London, Frederick Warne and co., [1881]. 52, [1] p. Illus: Numerous color-printed wood-engraved vignettes after Greenaway. Printer: E. Evans. Page size: 6¼ × 4¼ inches. Publisher's decorated boards. Spielmann and Layard, p. 286.

The static quality of Kate Greenaway's art is nowhere better exampled than in this pretty book. Indeed, she contrives to bypass nearly all the action in these violent poems. Little Miss Muffet is oblivious of the spider, which in any event is not very frightening, and Humpty Dumpty is shown before his fall.

255 JANE AND ANN TAYLOR

Little Ann and Other Poems by Jane and Ann Taylor, illustrated by Kate Greenaway, printed in colours by Edmund Evans. London, Routledge & sons, [1882]. 64 p. Illus: Numerous color-printed wood-engraved vignettes after Greenaway. Page size: 9 × 6 inches. Printer: E. Evans. Publisher's decorated boards. Spielmann and Layard, p. 289.

In this volume Kate Greenaway is oddly coupled with a pair of highly moral writers who preach the gospel of things as they are. Yet the bad children reproved in their hectoring verses hardly differ in appearance and manner from the good children described in her own gentle and happy poems. There is a certain "dirty Jim," for example, concerning whom the Miss Taylors conclude:

> The idle and bad
> Like this little lad,
>   May love dirty ways to be sure;
> But good boys are seen
> To be decent and clean,
>   Although they are never so poor.

ON THE WALL TOP.

DANCING and prancing to town we go,
On the top of the wall of the town we go.
Shall we talk to the stars, or talk to the moon.
Or run along home to our dinner so soon?

Though Jim is hardly as *soigné* as the usual Green-away child, his disorderliness is indicated chiefly by his uncombed hair. It must have been this book, or one very like it, that led Belloc to introduce a note of realism into nursery poetry with *The Bad Child's Book of Beasts* and *More Beasts (for Worse Children)* (327).

256

Marigold Garden. Pictures and rhymes by Kate Greenaway. Printed in colours by Edmund Evans. London, George Routledge and sons, [1885]. 60 p. Illus: Numerous color-printed wood-engraved vignettes after Greenaway. Printer: Edmund Evans. Page size: 10½ × 8¾ inches. Publisher's decorated boards. Spielmann and Layard, p. 287.

The children that people *Marigold Gardens* have not changed, but the larger size of the book led the artist to a variety of decorative arrangements that she had not tried before. Its spacious pages particularly suit the horizontal panels that she favored.

← A.l.s., dated January 20, 1891, to an unidentified correspondent. 3 p., 12mo.

In this gracious answer to an inquiry about her work as an illustrator, Kate Greenaway writes: "I do not know why I cared most to draw children in old-fashioned dresses, except that old-fashioned things were always very pleasing to me I know nothing that caused me to do them." Noting that her early drawings for "christmas cards and children's magazines" were "of much the same sort" as those for her books, she goes on to list her publications. She concludes with an account of her training: "I first studied drawing at a class connected with the Kensington Art Schools. Others at those Schools and later for a short time at Heatherlys and evening classes at the Slade."

William Morris (1834–1896) and the Kelmscott Press

An early publication of Morris's Kelmscott Press was *The Nature of Gothic* from Ruskin's *Stones of Venice* (31). Ruskin had called this chapter "precisely and accurately the most important in the whole book," and Morris described it in the preface to his edition as "one of the very few necessary and inevitable utterances of the century," pointing out "a new road on which the world should travel." The key section of "The Nature of Gothic" is Ruskin's contrast between a nineteenth-century English room and a Gothic cathedral. The precision and finish of the factory-made objects in the one were for him signs of the "degeneration of the operative into a machine," while the quaintness and variety of the sculpture that adorned the other offered proof of the "liberty of every workman who struck the stone."

In the middle 1880s, the period in which the Arts and Crafts movement had its start, Morris set forth his version of the Ruskinian lesson of "Useful Work *versus* Useless Toil" in such essays as that on "The Decorative Arts." Scorning the manufacturers of cheap, mass-produced goods, he called instead for "handicraftsmen," cooperating on equal terms with artists, who would have "the pleasure of working soundly and without haste in making goods that we could be proud of." Through their labors art would at last become the possession of society at large and no longer have to live a "poor thin life among a few exceptional men."

Through the next two decades Morris's doctrine gave inspiration to many creators of illustrated books, whether or not they regarded themselves as belonging to the Arts and Crafts movement. Its most obvious fruition is to be found in the private presses among such men as Morris himself, Charles Ricketts, and Lucien Pissarro, but it was also a prominent element in the background of William Strang, William Nicholson, Laurence Housman, Edward Gordon Craig, and other artist-craftsmen. All this made for an extraordinary harvest of fine illustrated books, even if Morris's dream of art as the possession of society at large remained as far as ever from realization.

It was Morris's admiration of fifteenth-century printing which dictated the program of the Kelmscott Press from its first conception in 1888. He took the same care with all aspects of production as had the bookmakers of that time. His types were imitated from theirs, his printing by hand press followed their example. The resulting books are notably opulent, but illustrations make a relatively minor contribution to their richness. Some Kelmscott volumes are entirely typographical; many others are ornamented, sometimes extravagantly, by Morris, who described himself as "a decorator by profession." Only a few are illustrated, and usually even in these the effect of the illustrations depends to a surprising extent on their surrounding decorations. It will suffice, then, to represent the Press by three books.

REFERENCES Franklin; Morris; Ransom; Sparling.

Charles March Gere (1869–1957)

257 WILLIAM MORRIS

News from Nowhere: or, an epoch of rest, being some chapters from a utopian romance, by William Morris. [London, Kelmscott press, 1892]. [4], 305, [1] p. Illus: Wood-engraved front. after C. M. Gere, wood-engraved borders and initials after Morris. Page size: 8¼ × 5½ inches, on vellum. Limited to 300 copies on paper and 10 on vellum. Publisher's limp vellum. Sparling 12.

This copy is one of ten on vellum, Morris's substitute for the large-paper editions offered by other publishers of the 1890s. His choice finds its justification in such openings as that at the beginning of the text, which has far less clarity and force in paper copies. The dwelling depicted in the illustration, which typically is the only one in the book, is Morris's Manor House at Kelmscott. Indeed, C. M. Gere's woodcut was reprinted in the fourth number of *The Quest* in 1894 under this title. Gere also provided the woodcuts for the Ashendene Press's edition of Dante's *Opere* in 1909.

Sir Edward Burne-Jones

258 GEOFFREY CHAUCER

The Works of Geoffrey Chaucer [edited by F. S. Ellis]. [London, Kelmscott press, 1896]. ii, 554 p. Illus: Wood-engraved front. and 87 wood-engraved vignettes after Burne-Jones, borders and initials after Morris. Page size: 16½ × 11 inches, on vellum. Limited to 425 copies on paper and 13 on vellum. Half niger morocco by Douglas Cockerell, 1899. Sparling 40.

Pierpont Morgan Library

The Chaucer is not only the most important of the Kelmscott Press's productions; it is also one of the great books of the world. Its splendor, particularly in vellum copies like the one described, can hardly be matched among the books of the time. Yet it should not be heresy to suggest that its illustrations are less valuable in themselves than for the contribution they make to the book as a whole. They are gratifyingly abundant; indeed this is one of the few editions of Chaucer in which the minor poems and even the prose are as well illustrated as *The Canterbury Tales* and *Troilus and Cressida*. Thanks to R. Catterson-Smith's bold redrawing in ink of Burne-Jones's pencil designs and the fine wood engravings which W. H. Hooper made from Catterson-Smith's work, they have something of the strength and stylistic consistency of the best fifteenth-century illustrations. But Burne-Jones's succession of small groups of statuesque figures, posed sometimes in a room or a garden, sometimes in the foreground of a landscape with hills, a lake, or a castle in the distance, hardly does justice to Chaucer's varied and lively depiction of the human comedy. The artist's design for "The Prioress's Tale," which catches the tenderness and pathos of that little story, is a welcome exception to this generalization. See Plate XC.

A. J. Gaskin

259 EDMUND SPENSER

The Shepheardes Calender: conteyning twelve aeglogues proportionable to the twelve monethes. [London, Kelmscott press, 1896]. [1], 98 p. Illus: Wood-en-

(259) Design by A. J. Gaskin for Edmund Spenser, *The Shepheardes Calendar*

graved front. and 11 wood-engraved plates after A. J. Gaskin, wood-engraved initials after Morris. Page size: 9 × 6¼ inches. Limited to 225 copies on paper and 6 on vellum. Blue morocco by Minnie Louise MacLean. Sparling 44.

Gaskin's twelve designs are perhaps the most successful of Kelmscott Press illustrations. No doubt recognizing that they could stand without support, Morris did not provide his usual decorative borders. The artist's depiction of his idealized shepherds and Botticelli shepherdesses is as close to Spenser's text as it is remote from actual rustic life. Accompanied by their docile and well-groomed sheep, they live a tranquil existence, visited by an occasional cupid or fawn, in uncluttered fields and groves.

Charles Ricketts (1866–1931) and the Vale Press

The history of Ricketts's reputation is a signal instance of time's revenges. Though his faith in his accomplishments as a book artist never wavered, he was bitterly disappointed at his failure to receive adequate recognition from his contemporaries, and by 1915 he could write that his "book-illustration work has been swamped for ever by the success of Beardsley" (*Self-Portrait*, p. 227). If there was a time in which he was treated as a follower of William Morris, worth a few paragraphs in a summary of the private press movement, this period of neglect has long since come to an end. Critics now take it for granted that he is a major figure. John Russell Taylor, who describes Ricketts as "the hero of the art nouveau book—even, in certain respects, of art nouveau in general," goes on to contend that "the best of his work . . . marks one of the high points, perhaps the high point, of British book design" (*The Art Nouveau Book in England*, pp. 71, 92).

Ricketts met Charles Haslewood Shannon (1863–1937), who was to be his lifetime companion, in 1882. Both were then apprentices to a wood engraver. They were living at the Vale, a house in Chelsea where Whistler had once resided, when they put together the first number of their "occasional publication," *The Dial*, seven years later. It is clear from the concluding "Apology" that this miscellany of text and drawings was intended as a manifesto. Believing that "the artist's conscientiousness cannot be controlled by the paying public," they hoped to overcome the "intelligent ostracism" they had thus far encountered and gain sympathy for their aims. Though four further numbers of *The Dial* had appeared by 1897, it fell far short of achieving their purpose, but it did make them many new friends, among whom was Oscar Wilde.

Wilde put Ricketts in the way of work as a binding designer. He also entrusted to him the illustration of *A House of Pomegranates*, an interesting mis-

fire, and of *The Sphinx*. Thus encouraged, Ricketts devoted much of his time to book design, producing *Daphnis and Chloe* and *Hero and Leander*, the two books in the making of which he and Shannon were collaborators, apart from *A House of Pomegranates*, before the founding of the Vale Press in 1896. Like Morris at the Kelmscott Press, Ricketts created his own types, but though he closely supervised all aspects of the Vale Press operation, he had no printing works of his own. In eight years he issued forty-six titles, all of them books that were "no longer trade commodities, but things made to abide their proper season with us, and to show what value we moderns set upon our accumulated inheritance of poetry and prose" (*Defence*, p. 32). In this way the Vale Press earned £36,000 (*Self-Portrait*, p. 106) without infringement by "the paying public" on his "artistic conscientiousness." Yet by 1904 Ricketts was ready to consign his types to the Thames and concentrate on painting, scene-designing, and the remarkable collection of art objects to which he and Shannon devoted much of their attention.

Vale Press books are typically slighter and less elaborate than those of the Kelmscott Press. In writing of Morris, Ricketts said that "certain books like the Chaucer should be perused at a lectern," and he may also have had Kelmscott productions in mind when he wrote of decoration: "let it accompany the text, and not gobble it up" (*Revival of Printing*, pp. 11, 36). His own books are easier to handle, more varied in content and appearance, and pleasanter to read. Their greatest appeal, however, comes from the abundant decorations and illustrations which Ricketts himself designed and for the most part cut on wood. Engraving was necessarily his constant occupation during his Vale Press years. The initials for Keats's *Poems* took "four tiresome days" each and an illustration for *The Parables* three (*Self-Portrait*, p. 74). But he found the labor well warranted for through it he

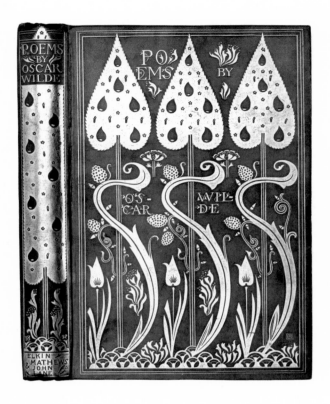

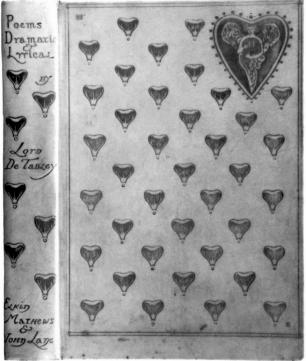

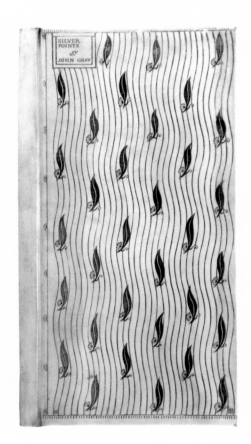

Bindings designed by Charles Ricketts

was able to demonstrate to a generation accustomed to the mechanical reproduction of drawings how a craftsman could secure "the sweetness of effect produced by engraving alone, . . . refining upon his design" in a way that "an interpreter however skilfull cannot be relied upon [to achieve], and that cannot exist at all in process work, however perfected" (*Defence*, p. 33).

REFERENCES Franklin; Gray; John Lewis; Moore, *Ricketts*; Ricketts, *Defence*; Ricketts, *Oscar Wilde*; Ricketts, *Self-Portrait*; J. R. Taylor.

❧ Four bindings designed for books published by Elkin Mathews and John Lane:

Wilde, *Poems*, 1892, one of 200 signed copies. Size: 7⅝ × 5 inches.

Symonds, *In the Key of Blue and Other Prose Essays*, 1893, one of 50 large-paper copies bound in vellum. Size: 8 × 5½ inches.

Lord de Tabley, *Poems Dramatic and Lyrical*, 1893, one of 100 copies on Japanese vellum bound in vellum. Size: 7¾ × 5 inches.

John Gray, *Silverpoints*, 1893, one of 25 copies bound in vellum. Size 8½ × 4 inches.

In his *Recollections of Oscar Wilde* (p. 36) Ricketts tells how his friend "secured work for me as a designer of books and bindings from his successive publishers." His bindings for Osgood and McIlvaine, among them one for the first edition of *Tess of the D'Urbervilles* of 1891, are relatively simple, but those for Mathews and Lane vie with each other in opulence, particularly when seen in the gold-stamped vellum of the limited issues.

260 LONGUS

Daphnis and Chloe, a most sweet and pleasant pastoral romance for young ladies, done into English by Geo. Thornley, Gent. [London, The Vale, 1893]. 106, [1] p. Illus: 36 wood-engraved vignettes and numerous wood-engraved initials, all by C. Ricketts and C. Shannon. Printer: Ballantyne press. Page size: 11⅛ × 8⅝ inches. Limited to 210 copies. Publisher's green cloth.

Working under the inspiration of "the sunny pages of the Venetian printers" (*Defence*, p. 19), Ricketts and Shannon shared the illustration of *Daphnis and Chloe*, but "Ricketts drew all the designs on the block . . . to attain unity of effect" (Moore, p. 10). The lighthearted spirit in which they worked is suggested by Ricketts's whimsical summary of the

tale: "Two foundlings brought up by shepherds fall in love, but like the Young Lady of Slough, they found they didn't know how. They are, of course, identified by their respective parents after countless fairy-tale adventures and interpolated legends. The story is curiously silly, corrupt, fresh, and exquisite." (*Self-Portrait*, pp. 324–325.) The graceful yet sensual woodcuts of the book are halfway between the *Hypnerotomachia* and Rex Whistler. In the most ambitious of them all, incidentally, one finds the principals of the Vale circle assembled at the wedding feast of Daphnis and Chloe. C. J. Holmes (*Self and Partners*, New York, 1936, p. 169) gives the key. He is the tall figure seated at the bottom left of the table, and across from him are Ricketts (with head upraised), Shannon, T. Sturge Moore, Lucien Pissarro, and Reginald Savage, with a certain Mr. Riley standing in the background. See Plate LXXXVII.

261 CHRISTOPHER MARLOWE and GEORGE CHAPMAN

[**Hero and Leander.** By Christopher Marlowe and George Chapman. London, The Vale, 1894]. [2], 112, [1] p. Illus: 7 wood-engraved vignettes, 1 wood-engraved border, and numerous wood-engraved initials, all by Ricketts and Shannon. Printer: The Ballantyne press. Page size: 7¾ × 5⅛ inches. Limited to 200 copies. Publisher's vellum.

Hero and Leander was another book of Renaissance Italian inspiration, issued "in commemoration of the edition of 'Hero and Leander' by Musaeus, published in Venice by Aldus" in 1494 (Prospectus). The simple plot line of this tragic poem did not call for illustrations as exuberant and varied as those for *Daphnis and Chloe*. Hence Ricketts and Shannon contented themselves with seven small woodcuts.

262 OSCAR WILDE

[**The Sphinx** by Oscar Wilde. With decorations by Charles Ricketts. London, Elkin Mathews and John Lane, 1894]. [18] l. Illus: 9 wood-engraved plates, 1 wood-engraved vignette, and 1 wood-engraved initial, all by Ricketts. Printer: Ballantyne press. Page size: 8½ × 6¾ inches. Limited to 200 copies. Publisher's vellum.

Ricketts thought that *The Sphinx* was his "best work as an illustrator," but Wilde disagreed: "No, my dear Ricketts your drawings are not your best.

You have seen them through your intellect, not your temperament." The book was delayed for a year because of the expected publication in 1893 of *Salomé* with Beardsley's illustrations (315), though in the event this book was also delayed until 1894, and when *The Sphinx* finally appeared in an edition of two hundred copies, press hostility to Wilde ensured its failure. Ricketts concludes this tale of woe by noting that "the book is very rare, a considerable portion having perished in a fire at the Ballantyne Press, where the unsold copies had been stored." (*Recollections of Oscar Wilde*, p. 38.)

Both Ricketts and Wilde were right. *The Sphinx* is his best book, and he did see his drawings through his intellect. No illustrated book was ever more thoroughly planned. To compensate for the brevity of Wilde's poem and the length of its lines (*In Memoriam* quatrains printed as couplets), Ricketts spread Wilde's text over many pages, and by printing it in capital letters "made an effort away from the Renaissance towards a book marked by surviving classical traits." "In the pictures," he continues in his *Defence of the Revival of Printing* (p. 25), "I have striven to combine, consciously or unconsciously, those affinities in line work broadcast in all epochs. My attempt there as elsewhere was to evolve what one might imagine as possible in one charmed moment or place, just as some great Italian masters painted as they thought in the antique manner."

The result is a perfect whole, as harmonious as it is dazzling. The haunting designs gold-stamped on the vellum covers propose the subject. The poet's mood is established by the figure of Melancholia gazing at the Sphinx in the pictorial title. The adventures of this hybrid creature through the "weary centuries" are obliquely presented in the designs that follow. And the poet's final turning back from "the foul dreams of sensual life" that she has imposed upon him to the creed of the crucifixion is displayed in the conclusion. Ricketts's subsequent books were to have the advantage of Vale types and illustrations that he himself cut on the block, but this remains his most original and consistent work. See Plate LXXXVIII.

&❦ Pen and ink drawing, touched with pink gouache, for the frontispiece of *The Sphinx*. Image size: 7⅛ × 8½ inches. Signed by the artist.
Mrs. Donald F. Hyde

263 WILLIAM BLAKE

Poetical Sketches. [London, The Vale press, 1899]. xciii, [2] p. Illus: 1 wood-engraved plate, 3 wood-engraved borders, and 3 wood-engraved initials, all by Ricketts. Printer: Ballantyne press. Page size: 7¾ × 5 inches. Limited to 210 copies on paper and 8 on vellum. Publisher's blue boards.

This volume stands out primarily because of its splendid opening pages. Otherwise it is a run-of-the-mill Vale Press book, handsomely printed and agreeably decorated, but no more.

264

De Cupidinis et Psyches Amoribus fabula anilis. [London, Vale press, 1901]. xxx, [1] p. Illus: 5 wood-engraved vignettes, 1 wood-engraved border, and 1 wood-engraved initial, all by Ricketts. Printer: Ballantyne press. Page size: 11¾ × 7¾ inches. Limited to 310 copies on paper. Publisher's blue boards.

Ricketts's Latin *Cupid and Psyche* appeared four years after his English version, but the first three of its four designs date from the earlier period (*Self-Portrait*), p. 52). The powerful emotion informing "Eros Leaving Psyche" has made it one of his best-known woodcuts.

(264) *De Cupidinis et Psyches Amoribus*

The Parables from the Gospels. With ten original woodcuts designed and engraved on the wood by Charles Ricketts. [London, Vale press, 1903]. lxxv, [1] p. Illus: 10 wood-engraved plates by Ricketts. Printer: Ballantyne press. Page size: 8½ × 5¾ inches, on vellum. Limited to 300 copies on paper and 10 on vellum. Publisher's limp vellum.

As early as 1937 Basil Gray contended that "The Vale Press books are the most perfect examples of the English illustrated book." He based this judgment not on *Daphnis and Chloe* and *Hero and Leander*, the figures in which he found emaciated and exhausted, but on the principal illustrated books of the last years of the Press, the woodcuts in which "reach the highest possible pitch of feeling without ever upsetting the proportions or conventions of the printed page." (*The English Print*, pp. 148–149.) With regard to *The Parables* at least Ricketts would have agreed with him. While he was engraving his drawings for this volume, he noted that they were "the high water-mark in my work, as far as design goes" (*Self-Portrait*, p. 69). Ricketts, who possessed albums and portfolios of engravings after the Pre-Raphaelites, Houghton, and Keene, had delighted in Millais's designs for *The Parables of Our Lord* (170) from his earliest years. His own woodcuts were if possible even more carefully studied than those of Millais. Indeed, he made oil paintings from some of his designs. Ricketts was fond of the parable as a literary form, and in later life he retold the story of the wise and foolish virgins in a sense directly opposite to that of the Bible (*Beyond the Threshold*, London, 1929, pp. 42–43), but in this volume he was content to give the parables their New Testament meaning. His picture of the rich man whose soul God seizes, just as he resolves to take his ease, eat, drink, and be merry for many years, is alive with contending passions: that of God's faithful emissary wrenching the soul away, that of the rich man grasping it for dear life as his deluding possessions fall to the floor around him. See Plate LXXXIX.

Lucien Pissarro (1863–1944) and the Eragny Press

Lucien Pissarro was the son of Camille Pissarro. By the time he settled in London in 1890, he was already an accomplished illustrator and engraver. Encouraged by Ricketts, of whose circle at the Vale he was a member, Pissarro published *The Queen of the Fishes* in 1896. This and fifteen succeeding volumes of the Eragny Press, named after the village in Normandy where his father lived, were printed in Vale type and distributed by the firm of Hacon and Ricketts. The remaining sixteen volumes were printed in Pissarro's own Brook type and sold by himself. Pissarro hoped that his books would eventually support him in his career as a painter, but they never did. Printed on a small handpress and limited to 226 copies or less, they were for the most part of very restricted scope. Only a few years before the Press's termination in 1914 did two French societies of bibliophiles give him the opportunity of showing what he could do with larger resources. Nevertheless, the wood engravings that he and his wife, Esther, made from his own drawings, those of his father, and those of friends like Sturge Moore give Eragny Press volumes a unique cachet, particularly when they are printed in color.

REFERENCES Franklin; Moore, *Eragny Press*; Pissarro.

266 JULES LAFORGUE

Moralités légendaires. [London, Eragny press, 1897–1898]. 2 v. I: cxi, [2] p. II: cxxvi, [3] p. Illus: Wood-engraved fronts., 4 wood-engraved borders, and numerous wood-engraved initials, all after L. Pissarro. Printer: Eragny press. Page size: $8\frac{5}{8} \times 5\frac{3}{8}$ inches. Limited to 220 copies. Publisher's half grey boards.

This is the most considerable of the Eragny books printed in Vale type. Like many of Pissarro's other volumes, it is French in everything except origin and typography. Camille Pissarro singled out his son's engraving of Salomé, who seems more Norman peasant girl than eastern princess, for special praise.

267 GERARD DE NERVAL

Histoire de la reine du matin & de Soliman, prince des génies. London, Eragny press for Les Cent Bibliophiles, 1909. 159, [1] p. Illus: Color-printed wood-engraved t.p. with wood-engraved vignette, 15 color-printed wood-engraved vignettes, 12 color-printed wood-engraved initials, 1 color-printed wood-engraved border, wood-engraved head- and tailpieces (1 color-printed), all after L. Pissarro. Printer: Eragny press. Page size: $8\frac{1}{2} \times 5\frac{1}{4}$ inches. No. 9 of 130 copies. Grey morocco with green and red onlays by Aumaitre/ Stroobants, with slipcase.

Through the intervention of Roger Marx, the society of "Les cent bibliophiles" commissioned this volume from Pissarro. For once he had a free hand with expenses, and the resulting book is a happy marriage of English and French taste, particularly when seen in a copy like this one, for which the original supple leather covers have been replaced by a mosaic morocco binding by Stroobants, yet preserved by being mounted on the sides of an accompanying *étui*. At this period English private-press books were sometimes austere to the point of meagreness, French books for bibliophiles often opulent to the point of grossness. Pissarro's decorations for this extract from Nerval's *Voyage en orient* achieve a selective richness. The book opens with a burst of color and gold leaf, there are monochrome woodcuts dotting the text, and every chapter has a pictorial initial letter printed in color and gold. It is a pity that the book's extreme rarity (most of the 130 copies printed must still be in France) has prevented collectors from becoming acquainted with it.

(266) Jules Laforgue, *Moralités légendaires*, "Salomé"

268 JUDITH GAUTIER

Album de poëmes tirés du livre de jade . . . London, Eragny press, 1911. 27 p. Illus: Color-printed t.p., 8 color-printed wood-engraved vignettes, numerous color-printed wood-engraved tailpieces and decorations, all after L. Pissarro; color-printed typographic initials. Printer: Eragny press. Page size: $7\frac{1}{2} \times 5\frac{1}{8}$ inches, on Japan vellum. No. 116 of 125 copies. Publisher's grey stitched calf.

cynocéphales, des chimères monstrueuses en-
fantées par le génie d'Adoniram.

«Spectacle sublime! s'écrie la reine de Saba.
Ô grandeur! ô puissance du génie de ce mortel,
qui soumet les éléments et dompte la nature!

Il n'est pas encore vainqueur, repartit Soliman avec amertume; Adonaï seul est tout-puis-
sant!»

VI. L'APPARITION.

OUT à coup Adoniram s'aperçoit que le fleuve de fonte déborde; la source béante vomit des torrents; le sable trop chargé s'écroule: il jette les yeux sur la mer d'airain; le moule regorge; une fissure se dégage au sommet; la lave ruisselle de tous côtés. Il exhale un cri si terrible, que l'air en est rempli et que les échos le répètent sur les montagnes. Pensant que la terre trop chauffée se vitrifie, Adoniram saisit un tuyau flexible aboutissant à un réservoir d'eau, et, d'une main précipitée, dirige cette colonne d'eau sur la base des contre-forts ébranlés du moule de la vasque.

70

Mais la fonte, ayant pris l'essor, dévale jusque là: les deux liquides se combattent; une masse de métal enveloppe l'eau, l'emprisonne, l'étreint. Pour se dégager, l'eau consumée se vaporise et fait éclater ses entraves. Une détonation retentit; la fonte rejaillit dans les airs en gerbes éclatan-

tes à vingt coudées de hauteur; on croit voir s'ouvrir le cratère d'un volcan furieux. Ce fracas est suivi de pleurs, de hurlements affreux; car cette pluie d'étoiles sème en tous lieux la mort: chaque goutte de fonte est un dard ardent qui pénètre dans les corps et qui tue. La place est jonchée de mourants, et au silence a succédé un

71

(267) Gerard de Nerval, *Histoire de la reine du matin*

This elegant little book, perhaps the handsomest of any issued by the Eragny Press, was Lucien Pissarro's effort to incorporate the leading features of *Histoire de la reine du matin* in a book that could be acquired by English collectors. The gold and color lavished on its twenty-seven pages cause no sense of surfeit. In binding, paper, and design it offers elements of the oriental book appropriate to the laconic yet evocative poems translated from the Chinese which make up its contents.

269 EMILE MOSELLY

La charrue d'érable. [London, Eragny press for] Le Livre Contemporaine, 1912. 105, [3] p. Illus: Color-printed wood-engraved t.p., 12 color-printed wood-engraved head- and tailpieces, 12 initials, and 12 plates, all after C. Pissarro. Printer: Eragny press. Page size: 8⅜ × 5¾ inches. No. 67 of 116 copies. Publisher's limp green calf, gilt tooled white calf doublures.

Pissarro undertook *La charrue d'érable* for the Parisian society of bibliophiles "Le livre contemporain." It is his monument to his father. The stories of Norman life that make up Moselly's text were written around Camille Pissarro's twelve drawings, which also provide the book's full-page plates. Lucien Pissarro and his wife cut these on wood and added many other colored illustrations and decorations adapted for the most part from Camille Pissarro's slighter sketches. Gold leaf was employed only on the endpapers. *La charrue d'érable* is a splendid impressionist book which the French themselves have rarely matched. See Plate c.

Joseph Crawhall (1821–1896)

Crawhall was a prosperous Newcastle business-man, who concerned himself particularly with the manufacture of rope. His antiquarian tastes led him to collect chapbooks and broadsides, and in 1859 he produced *The Compleatest Angling Book*, a miscellany of old texts illustrated with decorations chosen from the ephemeral publications in his collection. In the early 1880s his work attracted the attention of the London publisher Andrew Tuer, another chapbook enthusiast. Thus began a series of books by Crawhall published by the firm of Field and Tuer at the Leadenhall Press. "I find matter & blocks—," Crawhall noted in 1883, "Field and Tuer do *all* the rest—profits equally divided" (Felver, p. 53). These volumes are collections of old texts, typically from chapbooks and broadsides, printed in old type on rag paper and bound in boards. The illustrations are free copies of decorations from these sources or original designs in the same manner, drawn and engraved by Crawhall, and colored by hand. They are quite unlike any other books of the time.

Though misguided reviewers on occasion dismissed Crawhall's work as uncouth and primitive, this was a radical misconception. No doubt his broad northern humor sometimes required tempering by polite metropolitan taste, but his fondness for the popular materials he had assembled did not impair the shrewd perspective from which he viewed them. Crawhall was a man of knowledge and good sense, a friend of Charles Keene who supplied the artist with many legends and sketches for his *Punch* drawings. He played with his texts and illustrations in a sophisticated way, and took pleasure in the entertaining juxtapositions that they yielded. Moreover, he had a keen and original sense of design. Returning to the bold, simple style of eighteenth-century popular engraving through his heavy black lines and solid blocks of color, he offered a viable alternative to the detail of most late Victorian illustration, and thus prepared the way for the posters of the 1890s and the work of William Nicholson, Gordon Craig, and Lovat Fraser.

REFERENCES   Felver; Macfall, *Fraser*.

270   ISAAK WALTON

Izaak Walton: His Wallet Booke. London, Field & Tuer, 1885. 112, [7] p. + 1 p. ads. Illus: Numerous colored woodcut vignettes, initials, and plates by Crawhall. Printer: The Leadenhall press. Page size: $7\frac{5}{8} \times 4\frac{7}{8}$ inches. Publisher's blue boards.

Though *Chapbook Chaplets* of 1885 is Crawhall's most ambitious work, *Isaak Walton: His Wallet Booke* is just as representative and contains his most amusing single design. This volume is described as a collection of "songs and poesies" from *The Compleat Angler*, "New set forth and Adorn'd with SCULPTURES." It is remarkable for its whimsical and sometimes witty choice of decorations, which may or may not have a discernible connection with the text. With regard to those associated with the apostrophe to music on page 91, for example, the rudimentary horn may pass and caterwauling is no doubt an antimusical symbol. But what are we to make of the two "Assyrian looking human-visaged bulls . . . yoked to the plow" that Crawhall has copied from an illustration to Blake's *Jerusalem* (4) as printed in William Gilchrist's *Life of Blake* (2 volumes, London, 1863, I, 194), particularly when we learn (Felver, p. 66) that the countenances of the two bulls closely resemble Crawhall's own? See Plate LXXX.

William Strang (1859–1921)

Strang was a painter-etcher of distinction who between 1892 and 1902 devoted much of his energy to book illustration. He had come to London from Scotland in 1875 and, trained by Alphonse Legros, he was soon well launched on an *oeuvre* as an etcher which was to total more than seven hundred pieces. Except for his portraits, his work is still not sufficiently appreciated. Most of Strang's illustrations are etchings, published in editions small enough to ensure satisfactory impressions from the plates. In his rugged and somber designs he concerns himself chiefly with people, their trials, their defeats, and their occasional victories. When there was an element of horror present, his needle had a sharper bite. (A favorite story was W. W. Jacobs's "The Monkey's Paw.") Among major books not described below he had considerable success with *The Rime of the Ancient Mariner* of 1896 and *A Series of Thirty Etchings . . . Illustrating Subjects from 'Don Quixote'* of 1902, much less with *Paradise Lost* of 1896, where he did not even try to render Milton's grander flights.

REFERENCES Binyon; Newbolt; Sketchley.

271 WILLIAM STRANG

The Earth Fiend. A ballad made & etched by William Strang. London, Elkin Mathews and John Lane,1892. 21 p. Illus: Etched t.p. and 9 etched plates by Strang. Page size: 15⅜ × 11⅛ inches. Publisher's brown linen.

Strang's skillful ballad tells in broad Scots of a young man who labors in vain to make something of his farm until he learns from a witch that a fiend is thwarting him at every turn. Wrestled to submission by the farmer, the fiend offers to work for him rather than against him. Years pass. The farmer is prosperous and happy. The fiend has become a trusted favorite, even with the children. But there is still something uncanny about him, and one day he seeks out his sleeping master and breaks his neck. Strang's grim yet homely etchings are well suited to this harsh story, with its arbitrary turns of fortune, and he is particularly good

Proof of a rejected etching for *The Pilgrim's Progress,* "*Christian* loses his burden"

with his odd monster: bald, elderly, and gawky, yet the embodiment of primordial terror. See Plate LXXXII. Strang's illustrations to his other Scots ballad, *Death and the Ploughman's Wife* of 1894, which relates how a child is saved from Death by its mother's kindness to a beggar, are equally vigorous.

272 RUDOLF ERIC RASPE

The Surprising Adventures of Baron Munchausen, illustrated by William Strang and J. B. Clark, with an introduction by Thomas Secombe. London, Lawrence and Bullen, 1895. li, 299, [1] p. Illus: Numerous plates, vignettes, head- and tailpieces, all from process blocks after Strang and Clark. Printer: Ballantyne, Hanson & co. Page size: 8⅜ × 5⅜ inches. Publisher's white cloth.

That etching had a limiting as well as a concentrating effect on Strang's gifts as an illustrator is shown by the twenty-five designs which he made for this book. Leaving the fantastic episodes to his collaborator and fellow-etcher Joseph Benwell Clark, Strang devoted himself to the Baron's more mundane adventures. It is a pity that he never attempted *Candide*.

273 JOHN BUNYAN

The Pilgrim's Progress from this world to that which is to come . . . by John Bunyan. Illustrated by W. Strang. London, John C. Nimmo, 1895. [2], xii, 379 p. Illus: Photogravure front., added etched t.p., and 12 etched plates by Strang. Printer: Ballantyne, Hanson & co. Page size: 9⅛ × 6½ inches. Publisher's green cloth.

This is Strang's best book of the ordinary, commercial kind. The grave simplicity and earnestness of his etchings are wholly in keeping with Bunyan's text.

&• *The Pilgrim's Progress* . . . [proofs of a rejected etched t.p. and 12 etchings in early states, each signed by Strang]. Page size: 12⅛ × 8¾ inches. Three-quarter black morocco.

The etchings for the title page and for "*Christian loses his burden*" were not used in the book. This is understandable, since his second plate in each case was much superior. The other etchings are progress proofs differing in small particulars from the final states.

274

A Series of Thirty Etchings by William Strang, Illustrating Subjects from the Writings of Rudyard Kipling. London, Macmillan and co., 1901. [1] l. Illus: Etched front. and 29 etched plates by Strang. Page size: 17 × 13½ inches. Publisher's boards.

These are the most powerful contemporary illustrations for Kipling's short stories. Indeed, Strang is so faithful to the strain of cruelty and violence that dominates tales like "The Mark of the Beast" and "The Man Who Would be King" that his book becomes almost a chamber of horrors. His boldest effort is with "A Matter of Fact." Aboard a tramp steamer a few days out of Cape Town, three newspapermen share a strange experience. As stated in the Englishman's parody of the leading sentence in the American's report, they see "a great sea-serpent, blind, white, and smelling of musk, stricken to death by a submarine volcano, and assisted by his loving wife to die in midocean" (*Many Inventions*, London, 1893, p. 170). They seem at first to have the scoop of the century, but after they reach England, even the American comes to comprehend that no one will ever believe this "matter of fact." Strang somehow contrives to make the sighting of the sea serpents not merely plausible but awesome, even though he gives the stricken male Kipling's profile.

(274) *Thirty Etchings . . . Illustrating . . . the Writings of Rudyard Kipling*

PAGE AND MONARCH FORTH THEY WENT.
FORTH THEY WENT TOGETHER: THROUGH THE
RUDE WINDS LOUD LAMENT AND THE BITTER WEATHER.

"SIRE THE NIGHT IS DARKER NOW. AND THE WIND
BLOWS STRONGER: FAILS MY HEART. I KNOW
NOT HOW. I CAN GO NO LONGER". "MARK MY
FOOTSTEPS. MY GOOD PAGE: TREAD THOU
IN THEM BOLDLY. THOU SHALT FIND THE
WINTER WIND FREEZE THY BLOOD LESS COLDLY"

Arthur J. Gaskin (1863–1926) and the Birmingham School

Gaskin, Charles March Gere (1869–1957), and Bernard Sleigh (1872–1954) were the leading illustrators among the group of painters who worked as teachers or students at the Birmingham School of Art. Edward R. Taylor, Headmaster of the School and a disciple of William Morris, urged his associates to study crafts as well as painting. The three artists named became accomplished wood engravers, and Gaskin was also a prominent designer of jewelry and enamel. Gaskin's allegiance to "Gothic ideals" (Sketchley, p. 10) recommended him to Morris, for whom he illustrated *The Shepheardes Calendar* (259), but did not bring him much popularity. Despite their austerity, his

few books are all of real interest. In addition to those shown, he illustrated Hans Andersen's *Stories and Fairy Tales* of 1893.

REFERENCES Fine Art Society; Sketchley.

275

A Book of Pictured Carols. Designed [by members of the Birmingham Art School] under the direction of Arthur J. Gaskin. London, George Allen, 1893. 74, [2] p. Illus: 12 woodcut plates, including 1 after Gaskin. Printer: Chiswick press. Page size: $8\frac{5}{8} \times 6\frac{7}{8}$ inches. Publisher's half grey boards.

Gaskin's one illustration to this volume was for "Good King Wenceslas," with which he was later to deal more fully. Gere and Sleigh are also represented.

276 S. Baring Gould

A Book of Fairy Tales, retold by S. Baring Gould with pictures by A. J. Gaskin. London, Methuen and co., 1894. ix, 243, [1] p. + 32 p. ads. Illus: T.p. vignette, numerous plates and vignettes from process blocks after Gaskin. Printer: T. and A. Constable. Page size: $7\frac{1}{2} \times 5$ inches. Publisher's black cloth.

This book, like Andersen's *Stories and Fairy Tales*, shows the lighter side of Gaskin's talent. His style is still "Gothic," but the pleasures and fun of life as well as its hardships and pathos are here part of his vision. His characteristic moderation is everywhere in evidence. The giant killed by Jack (p. 10) is not so very large, nor is Hop-o'-my-Thumb (p. 111) so very small.

277

Good King Wenceslas, a carol written by Dr. Neale and pictured by Arthur J. Gaskin with an introduction by William Morris. Birmingham, Cornish Brothers, 1895. [12] l., printed on one side only. Illus: 6 pages, each with woodcut text and illustration after Gaskin. Printer: Guild of Handicraft. Page size: $11 \times 8\frac{3}{4}$ inches. Publisher's half holland.

In his brief preface Morris praises Gaskin's choice of this familiar medieval carol for illustration. The designs are noteworthy, he continues, "both as achievements in themselves and as giving hopes of a turn towards the ornamental side of illustration." This admonitory tale of a good rich man who brings cheer to his humble neighbor is indeed well served by Gaskin's grave yet sympathetic woodcuts.

Laurence Housman (1865–1959)

Laurence Housman, the younger brother of A. E. Housman, wrote some eighty books during his long life. Yet he began his career as an artist, and until failing eyesight made it impossible for him to persist in what he described as his "very detailed style of drawing" (*Unexpected Years*, p. 158) after the turn of the century, he was probably better known for his designs than his writings. Housman saw himself as a successor to the illustrators of the sixties, particularly Rossetti and Houghton. Indeed, his book on the latter (202) is a passionate defence of their work. At the same time he was very much an artist of the nineties. As in the cases of Beardsley, Crane, Nicholson, and Ricketts, his reputation has profited greatly from the revival of Art Nouveau. The bindings which he designed are notable examples of this style, and so are his illustrations and decorations. John Russell Taylor has demonstrated how his work as a book artist was influential beyond that of either Morris or Ricketts in bringing Art Nouveau ideas to bear on commercial publications. The world of Housman's illustrations is strange and highly personal, as remote from actual life as it is consistent and persuasive within itself. The dozen or so books which he illustrated in the 1890s remain a very substantial achievement.

REFERENCES Guthrie; Housman, *Unexpected Years*; Sketchley; J. R. Taylor.

278 GEORGE MEREDITH

Jump to Glory Jane. By George Meredith. Edited and arranged by Harry Quilter. With forty-four designs invented, drawn, and written by Laurence Housman. London, Swan, Sonnenschein & co., 1892. 28, 36 p. Illus: Front., 7 plates, pages 1–36 with calligraphic text and decorations, all from process blocks after Housman. Page size: 7⅜×5 inches. Publisher's boards.

Having failed to secure Linley Sambourne or Bernard Partridge to illustrate the book publication of Meredith's new poem, Harry Quilter, the editor of the *Universal Review* in which it had first appeared, gave the commission to Housman to carry out as he pleased. So we have Jane, a homespun religious enthusiast, bounding through thirty-six pages of calligraphic text and Art Nouveau decoration. As Taylor points out (p. 105), though Housman had Shaker friends, the figures in the eight accompanying illustrations are unmistakably inspired by Houghton's "Shaker Evening at Home" in Houghton's "Graphic America" (202). Housman had not quite found his personal style in *Jump to Glory Jane*, though his people already have a characteristic wispiness.

279 CHRISTINA ROSSETTI

Goblin Market by Christina Rossetti, illustrated by Laurence Housman. London, Macmillan & co., 1893. [3] l., 63, [1] p. Illus: 12 plates and numerous decorations, all from process blocks after Housman. Printer: R. & R. Clark. Page size: 10⅜×6¾ inches. Publisher's green cloth.

This book is a delight to behold. Its slim and elegant format (in the small-paper issue), its highly ornamental binding, its pictorial title page adumbrating the story to follow, its alternation of full-page illustrations, which at once engage the reader in the affairs of the "goblin merchant men," with decorations that might almost be Art Nouveau adaptations of Stothard's designs for Rogers's *The Pleasures of Memory* (54)—all these things combine to make a harmonious and original whole. The goblins themselves, furry earth animals in broad hats and long cloaks, are intent on their business of growing and gathering fruit. If they tempt the unfortunate sisters, it is not out of malice, but because creatures of their sort must behave that way. Christina Rossetti, however, was displeased. She said to a friend: "I don't think my Goblins were quite so ugly!" (*Unexpected Years*, p. 118.) See Plate LXXXVI.

MERCURY GOD OF MERCHANDISE
LOOK ON WITH FAVOURABLE EYES

THE FIELD OF CLOVER

BY LAURENCE
HOUSMAN
LONDON: KEGAN PAUL
TRENCH TRÜBNER & Co
1898

ENGRAVED BY
CLEMENCE HOUSMAN

BE KINDLY TO THE WEARY DROVER
& PIPE THE SHEEP INTO THE CLOVER

(282) *The Field of Clover*

280 JANE BARLOW

The End of Elfintown by Jane Barlow, illustrated by Laurence Housman. London, Macmillan and co., 1894. [4], 77, [1] p. Illus: T.p., 8 plates, and numerous decorations, all from process blocks after Housman. Printer: R. & R. Clark. Page size: 6⅞×4¾ inches. Publisher's brown cloth.

In this book Housman has moved to another part of the enchanted forest. It is less effective than *Goblin Market*, in part because Jane Barlow's poem is conventional and diffuse in comparison with Christina Rossetti's, and in part because Housman's elves, with their angular forms and manes of hair, seem mere despondent humans. One longs for the eupeptic little people of Doyle's fairyland (146). That Rossetti was in the ascendant when Housman conceived these illustrations is suggested by the resemblance between his drawing of King Oberon directing the elves in the construction of his palace and Rossetti's first design for "The Palace of Art" in Tennyson's *Poems* (148).

281 LAURENCE HOUSMAN

All-Fellows, seven legends of lower redemption, with insets in verse by Laurence Housman. London, Kegan, Paul, Trench, Trübner & co., 1896. viii, [2], 137, [1] p. + 6 p. ads. Illus: Photogravure front. and 7 halftone plates after Housman. Printer: Ballantyne, Hanson & co. Page size: 7½×5¾ inches. Publisher's green linen.

Housman the author asked his readers to follow him through many experiments, of which this was one of the less successful. As in several of his other early books, however, Housman the illustrator was fortunately also at hand. The designs are the best things about this book of legends.

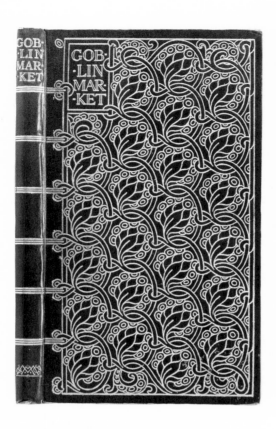

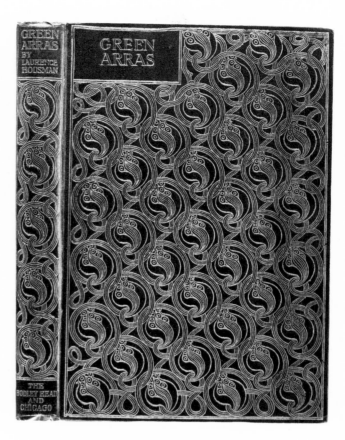

A Farm in Fairyland

Four bindings by Laurence Housman

The Field of Clover

The Field of Clover by Laurence Housman. London, Kegan, Paul, Trench, Trübner & co., 1898. [vi], 148, [1] p. Illus: Front., t.p., and 10 plates after Housman. Printer: John Wilson and son. Page size: 8¾×5½ inches, large paper. Publisher's green cloth.

This book has a source of appeal lacking even in *Goblin Market*. Dedicated "to my dear wood-engraver," it has twelve drawings cut by Housman's sister Clemence (1861–1955), who was one of the leading engravers of her time. She was capable of following her brother's line as faithfully and sympathetically as Ricketts rendered his own conceptions in *The Parables* (265), and at least in large-paper copies like the one described, *The Field of Clover* is almost as attractive as that masterly book.

283 PERCY BYSSHE SHELLEY

The Sensitive Plant. By Percy Bysshe Shelley. Illustrated by Laurence Housman. London, The Aldine house, 1898. 60, [1] p. Illus: Photogravure front. and 11 photogravure plates after Housman. Printer: Ballantyne, Hanson & co. Page size: 8×6 inches. Publisher's blue cloth.

Shelley's lush poem tells of a plant that has its being in a paradisical garden tended by a lovely lady. The lady dies, the garden decays, and winter leaves the plant a "leafless wreck." From the poet's allusion to "the Sensitive Plant, or that / Which within its being like a spirit sat," Housman evolves a little drama, in which the plant becomes one of his attenuated young men, threatened by Pan, but protected by that "charming sentimentalist" the lady of the garden. When she dies, the young man falls before Pan amid the garden's general ruin. To Shelley's belief that "For love, and beauty, and delight, / There is no death nor change," Housman has opposed the conviction that civilization and Nature are always at war, with Nature assured of the final victory.

&❧ Four bindings designed by Laurence Housman:

Christina Rossetti, *Goblin Market*, 1893. Size: 7¼×4 inches.

Laurence Housman, *A Farm in Fairyland*, 1894. Size: 7¾×5¼ inches.

Laurence Housman, *Green Arras*, 1896. Size: 7¾×5¼ inches.

Laurence Housman, *The Field of Clover*, 1898. Size: 9×5½ inches.

Where Beardsley on occasion reduced his cover designs to a few lines, usually on vellum, Housman filled the space available with patterns of repeated dots and reversed curves, usually on green cloth. He thought the cover for *Green Arras* "an extra good one . . . : it was, at all events, very rich and elaborate," though he had to admit that it displeased his austere brother (*Unexpected Years*, p. 162). Occasionally he employed bold pictorial designs. Both styles were widely imitated by contemporary bookmakers.

W. Graham Robertson (1868–1948)

Robertson was a singularly intelligent and engaging man who for a brief span in his long life made book illustration a principal occupation. He is perhaps remembered best today as a collector of William Blake. Reading Gilchrist's biography as a boy, he fell under Blake's spell and began to assemble what was to become the largest and most important collection of Blake's drawings in private hands. This phase of his activity is recorded in Kerrison Preston's volume *The Blake Collection of W. Graham Robertson*. But Robertson was also a painter, a professional man of the theatre, and an author. His whimsical autobiography, *Time Was*, is devoted almost entirely to the first forty years of his life, when he was very much a part of the artistic, theatrical, and literary world of London and Paris. The years during which he applied himself primarily to book illustration came at the

The date of this sketchbook is established by a drawing of Sarah Bernhardt's dog, "Osman Bernhardt Feb 29th 88," and elsewhere in its pages one comes upon Robert de Montesquiou. In striking contrast to Robertson's exotic French friend are the sturdily handsome John Drew and the fresh and lovely Ada Rehan, who serve as reminders of the artist's preoccupation at this period of his life with scene and costume designing for such plays as Tennyson's *The Foresters*.

Drawing of Robert de Montesquiou

Drawing for the book of Genesis

end of this period, from *Old English Songs and Dances* of 1902 to *Gold, Frankincense, and Myrrh* of 1907. Further books followed, but more and more infrequently, as other work claimed his attention. Nonetheless, his gracious and highly personal contribution to book illustration deserves more consideration than it has yet received.

REFERENCES Preston; Robertson.

&▻ Eight pen and ink, watercolor, and graphite drawings for the book of Genesis (late 1880s):

3. "And man became a living soul." Size: $7\frac{1}{2} \times 3\frac{3}{8}$ inches.
7. "And they heard the voice of the Lord God walking in the garden in the cool of the day." Size: $4\frac{3}{4} \times 4\frac{3}{4}$ inches.

In the first flush of his admiration for Blake Robertson made these drawings illustrative of the creation and of the story of Adam and Eve. He seems never again to have essayed so ambitious a subject.

&▻ Pen and ink, watercolor, and graphite sketchbook, 31 l., 1888. Size: $9\frac{1}{4} \times 13\frac{1}{4}$ inches.

W. Graham Robertson 175

284

Old English Songs and Dances. Decorated by W. Graham Robertson. London, Longmans, Green, and co., 1902. [31] l. Illus: Numerous process and screen color-printed vignettes and plates by Robertson. Printer: Edmund Evans. Page size: 15¼ × 11 inches. Publisher's boards.

Except for its traditional text, this handsome folio is altogether Robertson's creation. Edmund Evans had merely to "engrave and print" the manuscript with which the artist provided him. Thus came into being one of the most delightful of English illustrated books, as harmonious in its proportions as it is delicate in its coloring. In its unpretentious way, indeed, it may be seen as a successor to the illuminated books of Robertson's beloved master, Blake. Robertson's vision of an idealized past is his own. The title page vignette of a lady at the spinet, looking out from her panelled room on the sunny English countryside, is representative of the many decorative illustrations that follow. In their uncluttered simplicity his designs owe something to the example of William Nicholson, yet no one could confound the work of the two artists. The sequel to this volume, *French Songs of Old Canada* of 1904, is almost equally attractive.

❧ Incomplete manuscript in pen and ink, graphite, and watercolor of *Old English Songs and Dances* (52 of 62 leaves). Page size: 15¼ × 11 inches.

A comparison of manuscript and book reveals that Edmund Evans's color printing had not fallen off in quality since the great days of his collaboration with Crane, Caldecott, and Kate Greenaway.

285   W. GRAHAM ROBERTSON

A Masque of May Morning by W. Graham Robertson with twelve designs in colour by the author. London, John Lane, 1904. 61, [1] p. + 2 p. ads. Illus: Process, stencil, and three-color front. and 11 plates by Robertson. Printer: Ballantyne, Hanson & co. Page size: 10½ × 8⅜ inches. Publisher's green cloth.

Robertson provided both words and drawings for this volume, but unlike *Old English Songs and Dances*, its text is printed and its illustrations are reproduced by the three-color process. The form of a masque for children was well suited to Robertson's delicate talent. The fragile conception of flowers personified by little girls is gracefully realized in "First Born of the Spring" (p. 14), a snowdrop brought prematurely to life by the winter sun, and similar designs.

286   W. GRAHAM ROBERTSON

A Year of Songs for a Baby in a Garden. By W. Graham Robertson. Illustrated by the author. London, John Lane, 1906. 111 p. Illus: T.p. and 20 vignettes from process blocks after Robertson. Printer: Wm. Clowes & sons. Page size: 8¼ × 6¾ inches. Publisher's green cloth.

The forty songs in this book, distributed ten to a season, record the fancies with which Robertson amused and instructed his little friend during their year together. In black and white the artist's designs, such as that for "The Moon among the Willows" (p. 41) or "Bed Time" (p. 89), are more apt to call Arthur Hughes to mind than Blake.

❧ Graphite self-portrait in old age. Image size: 4¼ × 3¼ inches.

Self-portrait

Edward Gordon Craig (1872–1966)

Craig's accomplishments as a writer and stage reformer have obscured his work as a book artist. A skilled engraver, he published between 1898 and 1902 not only his magazine *The Page* but several original and delightful books illustrated with his own woodcuts. His grandest achievement, of course, was the Cranach Press *Hamlet* of 1929, which lies beyond our geographical and chronological limits.

REFERENCES Craig, *Nothing or the Bookplate*; Craig, *Woodcuts and Some Words*; MacFall, *Print Collector's Quarterly*.

287 EDITH AND GORDON CRAIG

Gordon Craig's Book of Penny Toys. Hackbridge, At The Sign of the Rose, 1899. [44] l., printed on one side only. Illus: 20 colored woodcut plates and numerous colored woodcut vignettes by Craig. Page size: 12¾ × 10 inches. Limited to 550 copies. Publisher's grey boards.

This is a children's book with a difference. Its reason for being is twenty full-page "portraits" of old penny toys, accompanied by whimsical verses by Craig's sister Edith and others. In his prefatory "Words" he addresses himself to adults as well as children, expressing a collector's delight in his toys and enlarging on their merits. Indeed, he is an ardent proselytizer. "The games to be played with these toys are without an end. Five shillings will buy sixty toys at least. Sixty toys flashing brilliantly on a white cloth after tea, with a couple of excitable children opposite you, and you may taste the dearest joy of life." It is now hard to believe that the 550 copies of this book failed for the most part to sell at 10/6 apiece. In *Woodcuts and Some Words* (pp. 121–122) Craig relates that he finally burned 250 of them. "It pleased me to think I burned them," he continues, "for, if I hadn't, I should have had to colour them all by hand. Two hundred I did colour with the aid of one or two of my friends." The copy described is accompanied by a presentation note from the artist to Haldane MacFall and has the bookplates (designed by Craig) of both men. See Plate XCIV.

288

Henry Irving. Ellen Terry. etc. by Gordon Craig. **A Book of Portraits.** [Chicago, H. S. Stone & co., 1899]. Illus: Mounted title and 18 mounted color-printed halftone plates after Craig. Page size: 12⅛ × 9 inches. Publisher's tan cloth.

This slim volume is made up of impressions of Ellen Terry, Craig's mother, and Sir Henry Irving, of whose theatrical company he had been a member.

289

Bookplates from The Sign of the Rose. Hackbridge, 1900 [cover title]. Illus: 45 wood-engraved plates, 23 colored, by Craig. Page size: 9⅞ × 7⅜ inches. Publisher's grey wrappers.

Later in his life Craig recalled how the £2 a week which he earned by making bookplates at the turn of the century enabled him to "stop doing bad stage work for a large weekly salary and turn to the study of the stage." Between 1895 and 1912 he designed and engraved 122 bookplates and printers' marks. (*Nothing or the Bookplate*, pp. v, 6, 15.) Forty-five bookplates, twenty-three of them in color, appeared in this first collection, and twenty more in a second collection of 1902. Meanwhile, Craig had also carried the gospel of the bookplate to a larger audience in a fourteen-penny pamphlet of 1900 called *Bookplates Designed and Cut in Wood*, where he explained: "A Bookplate is to the Book what a Collar is to the Dog, though I fear there is no Battersea for Books. On the Dog Collar we engrave 'I am Smith's Dog.'—Alter the word 'Dog' to 'Book', and add a simple adornment in the shape of a flower, a map, a butterfly or a crest, and lo! the Bookplate."

Dido & Aeneas, an opera by Henry Purcell. Performed by members of the Purcell Operatic Society, Hampstead Conservatoire, on May 17th, 18th, & 19th, 1900. This programme designed and engraved by Edward Gordon Craig. Hackbridge, The Sign of the Rose, 1900. [Collation uncertain, this copy incomplete]. Page size: 10 × 6¼ inches. Publisher's brown wrappers.

Craig could make even a theatre program a work of art. The woodcuts for *Dido and Aeneas,* taken from designs of dresses and masks for the production of the opera which he directed in May of 1900, are among his most striking compositions. According to MacFall (p. 424), to whom Craig gave this copy, it is the "first and extremely rare programme," containing "several wonderful woodcuts" that appeared only in this edition. A "book of the play" was published in March, 1901.

THE SORCERESS.

(290) *Dido and Aeneas*

Sir William Nicholson (1872–1949)

Though Nicholson was a distinguished painter, who ended his career with a knighthood and a high position in the English art establishment, he made his reputation in the 1890s as a graphic designer regarded by some as a troublesome rebel. Beginning in 1893 he and his brother-in-law James Pryde (1866–1941), signing themselves J. and W. Beggarstaff, made a series of posters so simply yet so boldly designed as to change the whole direction of poster-art in England. Nicholson next turned to wood engraving, a craft in which he was self-taught, carrying into this new form the search for spare salience that had marked his posters. Through Whistler's intervention, Heinemann in 1897 commissioned him to make *An Alphabet* at £5 a letter. Meanwhile, W. E. Henley had been publishing Nicholson's woodcut portraits in the *New Review,* and that of Queen Victoria soon became the public's favorite likeness during her jubilee year. Before he turned to other work in 1900, his designs had provided the contents of seven volumes.

Nicholson's woodcuts were reproduced by lithography except for a few portfolios printed directly from the original blocks and hand colored, which were sold at eighty or more times the price of the ordinary editions (£20 to five shillings for *An Alphabet*). Each has a heavy border—Nicholson was known as "the man who puts a thick black line round everything"—and within this border is a striking design, usually a single figure, made up of contrasting masses of black and one or more colors. The decorative appeal of these woodcuts was immediate and lasting. Many years later Walter de la Mare told Nicholson that during his frequent illnesses he had himself shifted to a bedroom where six designs from *Characters of Romance* hung on the walls. "You know what queer prejudices may spring up in illness," de la Mare continued, "and how weary one may get of even the familiar and delighted in. Well, I have surveyed these six pictures in those circumstances—the other six are not framed—thousands of times, and never once without interest and delight." (Quoted by Steen, p. 69.)

It should be added that Nicholson was as attentive to the content as to the design of his prints. Except for *The Square Book of Animals* of 1899 and *Characters of Romance* of 1900, his subject was almost invariably one which he understood thoroughly, English life of his own day. The figures whom he chose for his portraits have for the most part turned out to be men and women in whom posterity continues to take a keen interest, and Nicholson's shrewd characterizations often suggest the reasons for their staying power. His other books, *An Alphabet*, *An Almanac*, and *London Types*, "number the orders of men" in late Victorian England. It is not surprising, then, that two writers as alert to the passing scene as Henley and Kipling should have found it congenial to comment on Nicholson's revealing pictures in pungent verses.

After 1900 Nicholson made only occasional contributions to the book arts—a cover or jacket design, a poster, or a frontispiece such as his striking portrait of Hardy—until the 1920s. Then he illustrated three children's books, Margery Williams's *The Velveteen Rabbit* of 1922 and his own *Clever Bill* of 1926 and *The Pirate Twins* of 1928. In these volumes he no longer worked in the tradition of the chapbook print but rather in that of the colored lithograph as practiced by Bonnard and Vuillard.

REFERENCES Browse; Hillier; Steen.

291 WILLIAM NICHOLSON

An Alphabet by William Nicholson. London, William Heinemann, 1898 [1897]. Illus: Lithographed t.p. and 26 color-printed lithographs after Nicholson. Page size: 12 × 9¾ inches. Publisher's boards.

Each of Nicholson's subjects is carefully chosen. The cover figure is an old-time vendor of prints, "penny plain and tuppence colored," no doubt

(291) *An Alphabet*

the artist's acknowledgment of the popular tradition in which he is working. "A was an artist" shows Nicholson himself. "B for Beggar" has Pryde playing that role, of course with a staff. *An Alphabet* was published in October of 1897.

292 RUDYARD KIPLING

An Almanac of Twelve Sports by William Nicholson, words by Rudyard Kipling. London, William Heinemann, 1898 [1897]. [14] l. + 1 p. ads. Illus: 12 color-printed lithographs after Nicholson. Page size: 12¼ × 9⅞ inches. Publisher's boards.

Taken together, Nicholson's images and Kipling's verses place each of these seasonal sports in the structure of English society. The burly cricketer is a strong imperialist:

> Thank God who made the British Isles
> And taught me how to play,
> I do not worship crocodiles
> Or bow the knee to clay.

August.

(292) *An Almanac of Twelve Sports*

Henley's sonnets are vignettes of city life suggested by Nicholson's woodcuts, the poet in effect supplying the detail that the artist has left out. 'Liza, the flower girl of "Hammersmith," might be a first sketch for Eliza Doolittle in Shaw's *Pygmalion* of 1912.

294

Twelve Portraits by William Nicholson [cover title]. [London, W. Heinemann, 1900]. Illus: 12 color-printed lithographs after Nicholson. Page size: $21\frac{1}{2} \times 14\frac{3}{4}$ inches. Publisher's green cloth portfolio.

This portfolio and *Twelve Portraits: Second Series* of the same year are the summit of Nicholson's graphic achievement. One notes particularly the economy of means by which he achieves his bold yet subtle effects. Except for a few touches, "Whistler" might be an abstract print of the 1970s, yet the elegance and malicious intelligence of its subject are strikingly conveyed. So it is with Sarah Bernhardt's grace and stage presence, with Kipling's pugnacious alertness, and in the *Second Series* with Mark Twain's cocky ebullience. But Nicholson's greatest triumph came in his woodcut of Victoria. She is a plump old lady out walking with her dog, and yet she is every inch a Queen. See Plate xcv.

And the coach driver is a young man on the town. A proof of this design which belonged to Nicholson (Steen, p. 69) shows that Kipling's verses once possessed an additional couplet:

> Youth on the box and liquor in the boot,
> My Lord drives out with My Lord's prostitute.

An Almanac was published in December of 1897.

293 W. E. HENLEY

London Types by William Nicholson. Quatorzaines by W. E. Henley. London, William Heinemann, 1898 [1897]. [9] l. + 1 p. ads. Illus: 12 color-printed lithographs after Nicholson. Page size: $13\frac{1}{4} \times 11$ inches. Publisher's boards.

295 WILLIAM NICHOLSON

Clever Bill by William Nicholson [cover title]. London, William Heinemann [1926]. [1], 23 l. Illus: 24 illustrations by the three-color process after Nicholson. Page size: $6\frac{3}{8} \times 9\frac{5}{8}$ inches. Publisher's boards.

Nicholson's drawings for *Clever Bill* were made for his children and grandchildren. Their softer colors and free admission of detail mark them off from his woodcuts of the 1890s, to which at the same time they are recognizably akin. The toy soldier, Bill Davis, left behind when little Mary packs hurriedly for a visit to her aunt, shows his "cleverness" by following her to Dover.

✎ Poster for *Clever Bill*, inscribed to Thomas Balston. Size: 21×16 inches.

Hugh Thomson (1860–1920)

Days with Sir Roger de Coverley, published in 1886 with Thomson's drawings, can be identified as the starting point for hundreds of volumes illustrated with pen drawings for the giftbook trade which appeared over the next two decades. Thomson's model was Randolph Caldecott's *Old Christmas* (252), but since Caldecott illustrated only one other book in this manner and Thomson illustrated scores, the latter is properly regarded as the *chef d'école*. His most notable book is *Cranford* of 1891, which attained such popularity that the sequence of twenty-four volumes to which it belonged came to be called by Macmillan the "Cranford Series." Also noteworthy are his designs for four of Jane Austen's novels for another series, Macmillan's "Illustrated Standard Novels." As a draftsman Thomson was inferior to Caldecott (in the earlier part of his career, indeed, he tended to avoid the difficulties posed by full-page drawings), but he had a nice feeling for the blander aspects of the English classics, and a sensitive and sympathetic reading of his chosen text invariably lies behind his illustrations.

REFERENCES Balston, *Book Collector's Quarterly*; Balston, *New Paths*; Muir, *Victorian Illustrated Books*; Sketchley.

296 JOSEPH ADDISON

Days with Sir Roger de Coverley, reprint from The Spectator. London, Macmillan & co., 1886. x, [1], 82 [1] p. Illus: Front., numerous head- and tailpieces, and vignettes from process blocks after Thomson. Printer: R. Clay and sons. Page size: 8⅛×6⅜ inches. Publisher's blue cloth.

Though one doubts if life in rural England was ever so sedate and orderly, or its people so quaint and amusing, as they seem in Thomson's designs for his selections from *The Spectator*, this book at least opened the way to a never-never land which readers were delighted to explore with him. His illustrations, which had appeared in the pages of *The English Illustrated Magazine* (in the initial in-stallment as wood engravings), are somewhat out of proportion in the smaller format of this book.

297 MRS. GASKELL

Cranford by Mrs. Gaskell, with a preface by Anne Thackeray Ritchie, and illustrations by Hugh Thomson. London, Macmillan and co., 1891. xxx, 297, [3] p. Illus: Front., numerous head- and tailpieces, and vignettes from process blocks after Thomson. Printer: R. & R. Clark. Page size: 10⅛×6⅞ inches. Large paper. Publisher's red cloth.

We see Thomson at his best in this small masterpiece, though even *Cranford* is hardly so slight and nostalgic a book as his illustrations would suggest. He seems of set purpose to have made his designs a marginal commentary on his text. In the first chapter, for example, when Miss Betsy Barker's Alderney cow falls into a limepit, he does not show the beast in her subsequent costume of grey flannel waistcoat and drawers, but only the villagers regarding her in this state (p. 9); and he bypasses altogether the impassioned confrontation between Miss Jenkyns and Captain Brown over the relative merits of *Rasselas* and *The Pickwick Papers*. Yet by and large Thomson is faithful to the spirit of the book. His single figures are particularly good: Captain Brown, Miss Jenkyns, and above all Mrs. Gaskell's own favorite, Miss Matty, whether she is shown at a moment of human fellow-feeling (as in "God forbid that I should grieve any young hearts" of p. 73) or at a moment of unwitting comedy (as when she receives morning visitors "with bland satisfaction" in two caps, one on top of the other, on p. 111). Particularly in the large-paper issue, to which the copy described belongs, *Cranford* is a gracious and charming book. See Plate LXXXI.

298 JANE AUSTEN

Emma by Jane Austen, illustrated by Hugh Thomson with an introduction by Austin Dobson. London, Macmillan and co., 1896. xviii, 436, [1] p. Illus: Front. and 39 plates from process blocks after Thomson. Printer: R. & R. Clark. Page size: $7 \times 4\frac{3}{4}$ inches. Publisher's red cloth.

The conception of Jane Austen's work that lies behind Thomson's illustrations is summed up in the title of a later succession of volumes, "The Series of English Idylls," in which her novels are illustrated in color by his disciple C. E. Brock. Thomson emphasizes, not the profound and unsparing study of human relationships which has led one critic to refer to Jane Austen's "regulated hatred," but the Cranfordian elements in her work. If Emma herself is simply one more pretty young woman and Mr. Knightley is presented chiefly in terms of his "tall, firm, upright figure," Thomson is adroit in showing the surface peculiarities of the novel's shallower personages, as in his picture (p. 148) of Miss Bates being "very chatty and good-humoured" with Mr. Woodhouse. In contrast to his earlier practice, Thomson relied entirely on full-page illustrations for this book.

Robert Anning Bell (1863–1933) and the Endymion Series

Bell came out of the Arts and Crafts movement, but he was content to draw in line for process reproduction. Though there is a suggestion of Ricketts about some of his work, of *Daphnis and Chloe* (260) in his designs for Keats's poems and of *De Cupidinis et Psyches Amoribus* (264) in his designs for Shelley's, he was an accomplished book artist who knew how to impress his personal style on each of the major books he illustrated. Apart from *The Tempest* of 1901, his best work was done for the Endymion Series, which may stand as representative of the many series of books illustrated with pen drawings which flourished in the later eighteen nineties and early nineteen hundreds. Balston's judgment that the Endymion Series is "altogether too sumptuously illustrated" (*New Paths*, p. 180) seems excessively austere. The designs that fill the pages of these volumes are varied, yet harmonious, and if Bell and Heath Robinson stand out among their illustrators, each book has its particular attractions. The series was offered in two forms: the ordinary issue in pictorial cloth bindings at 6/ or 7/6 and a limited edition of 125 copies on Japanese vellum in undecorated bindings (it was evidently expected that these volumes would be rebound in leather) at a guinea. English commercial bookmaking of the period is here seen at its best.

REFERENCES Balston, *New Paths*; Sketchley; J. R. Taylor.

299 JOHN KEATS

Poems by John Keats. Illustrations by Robert Anning Bell and introduction by Walter Raleigh. London, George Bell and sons, 1897. xxiii, [1], 337, [2] p. Illus: Front. and numerous plates, vignettes, and head- and tailpieces from process blocks after Bell. Printer: Chiswick press. Page size: $7\frac{7}{8} \times 5\frac{1}{4}$ inches. Publisher's tan cloth.

The numerous illustrations to this volume alternate between the decorative and the interpretative. Those for "Endymion" fall into the former category, those for more challenging poems like "Lamia," "La Belle Dame Sans Merci," and "Isabella" into the latter. The drawing of Isabella's brothers watching her love passages with their clerk Lorenzo at first seems out of balance, but how better to fix attention on the furtive malice of their spying than by leaving blank the center of the design? See Plate XCI. Indeed, all four of the

(304) Illustration by W. Heath Robinson for *The Poems of Edgar Allan Poe*

full-page illustrations for this poem are notable for their psychological penetration.

300

English Lyrics from Spenser to Milton. Illustrations by Robert Anning Bell and introduction by John Dennis. London, George Bell and sons, 1898. xv, 222, [1] p. Illus: Front. and numerous plates, vignettes, and head- and tailpieces from process blocks after Bell. Printer: Chiswick press. Page size: 8 × 5¼ inches. Publisher's green cloth.

Bell's illustrations to this much slighter book are predominantly decorative. He shows some of his young men and women in homely old English costumes, as if they were Kate Greenaway children grown up. The charming awkwardness of these figures lends a welcome touch of humor to his designs.

301 PERCY BYSSHE SHELLEY

Poems by Percy Bysshe Shelley. Introduction by Walter Raleigh, illustrations by Robert Anning Bell. London, George Bell and sons, 1902. xxii, [2], 333, [2] p. Illus: Front. and numerous plates, vignettes, and head- and tailpieces from process blocks after Bell. Printer: Chiswick press. Page size: 7⅞ × 5¼ inches. Publisher's tan cloth.

In a preliminary note (p. xxiii) Bell admits the futility of trying to "illustrate" Shelley. Instead he offers "an embroidery of fair designs suggested by a reading of the poems." The principal appeal of the volume lies in its many fine double-page drawings.

Byam Shaw (1872-1919)

302 ROBERT BROWNING

Poems by Robert Browning, with introduction by Richard Garnett, L.L.D. and illustrations by Byam Shaw. London, George Bell and sons, 1897. xix, 377, [1] p. Illus: Front. and numerous plates, vignettes, and head- and tailpieces from process blocks after Shaw. Printer: Chiswick press. Page size: 8½ × 5¼ inches. No. 69 of 125 copies on Japan vellum. Publisher's linen.

Shaw's illustrations, though thoroughly professional, are apt to be eccentric rather than original. It is startling to see some of Browning's mid-Victorians in Edwardian costume, and when he comes to "How It Strikes a Contemporary," he shows a scene that did *not* take place, the Corregidor eating "his supper in a room / Blazing with lights, four Titians on the wall, / And twenty naked girls to change his plate."

A. Garth Jones

303 JOHN MILTON

The Minor Poems of John Milton, illustrated and decorated by A. Garth Jones. London, George Bell and sons, 1898. xiv, 206, [1] p. Illus: Front. and numerous plates, vignettes, and head- and tailpieces from process blocks after Jones. Printer: Chiswick press. Page size: 8 × 5¼ inches. Publisher's blue cloth.

Jones aimed at showing the "severer" and more "intellectual" side of the poet in these bold drawings (p. vii). He hardly rivals Edmund J. Sullivan, but if his designs for "L'Allegro" are sometimes heavy-handed, he succeeds better with "Il Penseroso" and particularly "Samson Agonistes."

W. Heath Robinson (1872-1944)

304 EDGAR ALLAN POE

The Poems of Edgar Allan Poe, illustrated and decorated by W. Heath Robinson, with an introduction by H. Noel Williams. London, George Bell & sons, 1900. xxv, [3], 225, [1] p. Illus: Front. and numerous plates, vignettes, and head- and tailpieces from process blocks after Robinson. Printer: Chiswick press. Page size: 8 × 5¼ inches. Publisher's grey cloth.

Robinson was an illustrator of great and varied abilities, whose later work in color, such as *Bill the Minder* of 1912 and *A Midsummer Night's Dream* of 1914, has received the prolonged attention it deserves in John Lewis's *Heath Robinson: Artist and Comic Genius.* Yet it does Robinson no disservice to represent him by his powerful black and white designs for Poe's *Poems.* These scenes of mystery and imagination are presented in a series of dark panoramas, culminating in "The Night's Plutonian Shore" for "The Raven."

Eleanor Fortescue-Brickdale (1871-1945)

305 ALFRED, LORD TENNYSON

Poems by Alfred Lord Tennyson, with illustrations by Eleanor F. Brickdale. London, George Bell, 1905. x, 402, [1] p. Illus: Front. and numerous plates, vignettes, and head- and tailpieces from process blocks after Brickdale. Printer: Chiswick press. Page size: 8 × 5¼ inches. Publisher's tan cloth.

The artist must have been consciously archaizing in these designs, many of which seem to derive from the Pre-Raphaelite illustrations in the Moxon Tennyson (148) or the drawings of M. J. Lawless. But the borders remind the reader that Art Nouveau has intervened.

Phil May (1864-1903)

Born into a middle-class family, May at an early age was forced out of school and into the streets by his father's failure. He tried many employments, most of them connected with the stage, before he began to draw for his livelihood. After some years as staff artist for the *St. Stephen's Review* in London and the Sydney *Bulletin* in Australia, where he passed three years, *The Parson and the Painter* brought him general recognition in 1891. Much of his best work is to be found in the sixteen volumes of *Phil May's Annual* which appeared between 1892 and 1904, but his designs for the *Graphic, Punch,* the *Sketch,* and other periodicals are also noteworthy. His best single volume is *Phil May's Gutter-Snipes,* published by Andrew Tuer at the Leadenhall Press.

A keen observer of many kinds of life, May never lacked material, but it was above all the precision and economy of his line that made him stand out among the pen draftsmen of his time. His drawings, which appear to come directly out of his sketchbook, were in fact evolved in a very different way. "My ordinary method," he once said, "is to draw my sketch very carefully, putting in all the details, light and shade, and so on. When that is quite finished, I knock away the scaffolding, so to speak, and in my final sketch I put in nothing but what I regard as the essential lines of the picture." His "leaving out" technique underlines May's kinship with Whistler, who wrote of him in the catalogue of the May exhibition of 1895: "There is a brightness and daintiness in what he does, combined with knowledge. These, together with the fact that in his drawings the wit is the artist's, make a vast difference between him and his contemporaries." (*Phil May Folio*, pp. xii–xiii.) His captions, indeed, are as witty as du Maurier's, and much more succinct. Since May was only marginally an illustrator, three books will suffice to represent this notable master of black and white.

REFERENCES Sketchley; Thorpe, *English Illustration*.

306 THE REV. JOSEPH SLAPKINS [WILLIAM ALISON]

The Parson and the Painter: their wanderings and excursions among men and women . . . illustrated by Charlie Summers. London, John Haddon and co., [1891]. viii, 78 p. Illus: numerous halftone illustrations by Phil May. Page size: 14¼ × 9¾ inches. Publisher's black cloth.

This meandering chronicle, which first appeared in the *St. Stephen's Review*, sold thirty thousand copies when republished in book form at a shilling. An end-of-the-century variation on such works as Pierce Egan's *Life in London* (111), it tells of the adventures of the naïve country parson Slapkins and his artist nephew as they wander about England and France. So abundant are May's drawings that the narrative becomes virtually a comic strip. In a typical chapter (pp. 34–35) the pair visit *The Financial Times*, where their request to be told how to turn £300 into £3,000 meets with short shrift.

Pen and ink drawing, "The Punch." Image size: 7½ × 5½ inches. Signed by the artist.

This drawing of a novice's misadventure with a punching bag seems to be related to an illustration on page 7 of *The Parson and the Painter*.

307

Phil May's Gutter Snipes. 50 original sketches in pen & ink. London, The Leadenhall press, [1896]. Illus: 50 plates from process blocks after May + 4 p. ads. Page size: 10¾ × 8½ inches. Publisher's decorated wrappers.

May was at his best with street children, concerning whom he was anything but sentimental. Having been one himself, he knew the compensations as well as the hardships of their lives. He wrote in his prefatory letter to Andrew Tuer: "Children of the gutter roam about free and are often hungry, but what would one give for such appetites?"

308

The Phil May Folio. n.p., [1904?]. Illus: numerous halftone and process illustrations after May. Printer: Alexander Moring. Page size: 16¾ × 10¾ inches. Publisher's half linen.

This volume, which was published not long after May's death, contains the artist's own selections from his *Annuals* presented "in a more sumptuous, artistic and lasting form." His extraordinary range is well displayed: portraits of celebrities and cockneys, of artists and children; scenes in the streets, in bars, at the theatre, in the country, and at the seaside; records of his travels in Australia, France, and the United States. His rapid sketch of Gladstone from *Phil May's Annual* for 1893 catches the harried and frenetic aspect of the "Grand Old Man" as does no other likeness. It remains May's best-known drawing.

Celebrities & Personages

GLADSTONE

(308) *The Phil May Folio*

Edmund J. Sullivan (1869–1933)

Himself the son of an artist, Sullivan began his career in 1890 with three years of portrait drawing for the *Daily Graphic*. He then moved on to more general illustration for the *Pall Mall Budget* and other magazines. Long after he made his mark as a book illustrator in 1896 he continued to draw for periodicals, and in later years he made many designs for advertisements, sturdily maintaining the dignity of this employment. As his friend and fellow-artist A. S. Hartrick remarked: "He could do anything with a pen, . . . and do it with distinction" (quoted by Thorpe, *Sullivan*, p. 14). He was also an accomplished painter, etcher, and lithographer, though he once said of the last medium: "You can't touch grease and not be defiled" (sketchbook for Carlyle's *French Revolution*, p. 6).

Sullivan was a man of keen intellect and broad cultivation, who particularly in his younger years had literary ambitions. These led to nothing very tangible, yet his mastery of words gave him an insight into the texts with which he dealt that few artists could match. His credo as an illustrator, as expressed in his sketchbook for Carlyle's *French Revolution* (p. 6), emphasizes his faith in line as the expression of intelligence: "The Art of Michelangelo and of Dürer is a rock against which the froth and foam of ridicule beat in vain. . . . Both convey ideas by means of form, and if the ideas are fundamental, and the form poetic, they make an amalgam. Impressionism is apt to be merely a report, and not a full expression of a mind. Art can express a mind as well as a vision, and is not limited to Monet's twelve views of a haystack."

Sullivan's first book illustrations were for the familiar and harmless English classics then dear to the editors of popular series. *Lavengro*, *Tom Brown's School Days*, *The Compleat Angler*, and *The Rivals* and *The School for Scandal* all date from 1896. Having made his reputation, he was in a position for two decades to choose the titles that he wished to illustrate, though he continued to accept commissions for established series. In addition to the books represented below, he illustrated *The Pilgrim's Progress* in 1901, H. G. Wells's *A Modern Utopia* in 1905, Shakespeare's *Works* in 1911, *The Rubaiyat of Omar Khayyam* (a favorite project dating from 1900) in 1913, and George Outram's *Legal and Other Lyrics* in 1916. Then changing taste seems to have made his work unmarketable just when he was moving from the detailed precision characteristic of his earlier style, in which he relied chiefly on the pen, to the impressionistic freedom of his later style, in which he relied at least in part on the brush. *Maud* of 1922 contains his only published work in this mode; his drawings for *Don Quixote*, *King Lear*, *Dr. Jekyll and Mr. Hyde*, and *Weir of Hermiston* never reached book form.

To form a true estimate of Sullivan's quality as an artist, his sketchbooks should be studied as well as his finished drawings. When he set out to illustrate a book, he would first read and analyze it with great thoroughness. Then he would dash down a series of preliminary sketches in a burst of energy, often making a hundred or more in a week or two. Developing these into final designs, on the other hand, was a long and deliberate process. "A true sketch," he once wrote, "is always the result of happy work—the work before the 'artist's sorrow' begins. It is a happy thought, an epigram; may even be a brilliant untruth; and should have the exhilarating effect of a glass of champagne." (Quoted by Thorpe, *Sullivan*, p. 17.) Inevitably, Sullivan's preliminary sketches lost something of their verve and brilliance in his final renderings. To reflect on this point is to find some consolation for his failure to turn his sketches for *Don Quixote* and *King Lear* into finished drawings.

No doubt the element in his work which kept Sullivan from attaining the wide and persistent vogue of Arthur Rackham was precisely what earned him the devotion of his smaller group of admirers, the peculiar cast of his mind and imagination. By conventional standards his life was a success; by his own it was a disappointment. His bitterness led, not to cynicism, but to profound self-examination. There is a drawing of 1923 called "Self-Revelation" which shows the artist, brush in hand with sheets of blank paper on the desk before him, staring into a mirror held by a beautiful woman. He is surrounded by faces, all his own, mocking or crying, staring or sneering, this one with a mask, that one with a gag. Sullivan seems to be saying to himself what Thackeray makes Esmond avow in his novel: "I look into my heart and think I am as good as my Lord Mayor, and know I am as bad as Tyburn Jack" (prologue to *The History of Henry Esmond*). Hence his choice of sad, tragic, or sinister subjects for many of his most characteristic and powerful designs. He elected to illustrate *Sartor Resartus*, *Sintram and His Companions*, *The French Revolution*, *The Rubaiyat*, *Maud*, *Don Quixote*, *King Lear*, and *Dr. Jekyll and Mr. Hyde* because they appealed to something deep in his nature, not because the public was clamoring for them. Of another volume, *The Kaiser's Garland* of 1915, one has to grant that its ferocity must have seemed excessive even when it first appeared.

Sullivan's career as an illustrator was one of the most substantial and distinguished in the annals of English art. He was influential through his teaching at Goldsmith's College of Art, his knowledgeable and authoritative books on *Line* of 1921 and *The Art of Illustration* of 1922, and above all through the example of his own work. No doubt he was a belated Victorian, living beyond his due time, who continued to believe in the free yet faithful interpretation of his chosen author, in telling a story and rendering character, and in seeking to arouse in the reader the emotional response that he himself had felt to the text before him. But even for those whose view of illustration is poles apart from Sullivan's, he is saved by his draftsmanship and sense of design. James Thorpe called him "the greatest illustrator in line that this country has produced," and Percy Muir, though he could not quite endorse this claim, puts him with Bewick, Cruikshank, Keene, and Beardsley (*Victorian Book Illustrators*, pp. 201–202).

REFERENCES   John Lewis; Muir, *Victorian Illustrated Books*; Sketchley; Sullivan, *Art of Illustration*; Thorpe, *Sullivan*; Thorpe, *English Illustration*.

309   GEORGE BORROW

Lavengro, the scholar, the gypsy, the priest. By George Borrow. Illustrated by E. J. Sullivan. With an introduction by Augustine Birrell, Q.C., M.P. London, Macmillan and co., 1896. xliii, 588, [1] p. + 6 p. ads. Illus: Front. and numerous plates and vignettes from process blocks after Sullivan. Printer: R. & R. Clark. Page size: 7½ × 5 inches. Publisher's red cloth.

The first book which Sullivan illustrated was Borrow's meandering story of the gypsy Lavengro. Full of colorful characters and exciting episodes, it gave the artist ample scope for certain aspects of his talent. In 1914 Sullivan illustrated the novel again, with considerably less success, this time with twelve plates in color.

❧ Pen and ink and graphite sketch for "It happened that the blow which I struck the Tinker beneath the ear was a right-handed blow" (p. 485). Size: 9¾ × 6¾ inches.

This is a preliminary drawing for a more elaborate rendering of the fight between Lavengro and the Flaming Tinman in chapter 85.

310   THOMAS CARLYLE

Sartor Resartus, the life & opinions of Herr Teufelsdröckh by Thomas Carlyle. Illustrated by Edmund J. Sullivan. London, George Bell and sons, 1898. xxiii, 351, [1] p. Illus: Front. and numerous plates, vignettes, head- and tailpieces, from process blocks, all after Sullivan. Printer: Chiswick press. Page size: 7⅞ × 5¼ inches. No. 147 of 150 copies on Japan vellum. Publisher's white linen.

This first illustrated edition of Carlyle's masterpiece, published sixty-four years after its appearance in *Fraser's Magazine*, came about through Sullivan's initiative. In his sketchbook (p. 32) he set down a "Paradox—[I] illustrate this book by choice—being by force of circumstances an illustrator." Tired of the undemanding volumes that had come his way, he was delighted to grapple with a classic about which he had been "cogitating" for several years (p. 71). One question troubled him. If he treated *Sartor Resartus* in a highly personal way, could he carry the public with him? Should there be "Notes on illustrations in an appendix, for those who love explanations?" (P. 31.) In the end he gave every design a title and provided an explanation of his methods in his introduction.

Drawing for *Sartor Resartus*, "Organic Filaments"

The seventy-eight illustrations (seventy-nine in the large-paper issue) which thus came into being are notably original both in style and in content. In style they are a celebration of the power of blackness. Perhaps Sullivan's mastery of drawing for process reproduction is best demonstrated in his white-line designs on backgrounds of glistening black, as in Carlyle's chapters on the world without clothes and "organic filaments," but all of his drawings are strong and sure. With regard to their meaning, Sullivan set his audience some puzzles. The intent of his abundant portraits is clear, but most of his other conceptions, as he noted in his introduction (p. x), adhere "only to the general spirit of the book, and the fancies stirred by it." It is the open-endedness of his designs, indeed, that

makes *Sartor Resartus* Sullivan's most rewarding book, for though they satisfy the eye at first glance, they yield their full significance only after prolonged speculation. See Plate XCII.

&☞ Pen and ink and graphite sketchbook for *Sartor Resartus*. Size: $12\frac{1}{8} \times 8$ inches.

The first ninety-five pages of this sketchbook are devoted to drawings and notes for *Sartor Resartus*. The far-ranging topics of pages 62–63 are characteristic of Sullivan's approach to his task. His jottings on "Truth and the Prince of Lies" suggest what lay behind this particular design, which is reproduced as Plate XCII. The skeleton warrior is "an armed lie frightened at its own reflection" and "dropping his crooked sword, (like a tongue)." "The Truth advances," Sullivan adds concerning the woman holding the mirror, but she is "une femme incomprise."

&☞ Four finished drawings for *Sartor Resartus*:

"Church-Clothes" (p. 248), pen, ink, and graphite. Size: $4\frac{1}{2} \times 3$ inches.
"The Critical Pen" (p. 261), pen and ink. Size: $2\frac{1}{4} \times 5\frac{1}{2}$ inches.
"Organic Filaments" (p. 283), pen and ink, graphite, and China white. Size: $6\frac{1}{2} \times 3\frac{3}{4}$ inches.
"Organic Filaments" (p. 285), pen and ink, graphite, and China white. Size: $7\frac{1}{4} \times 5\frac{1}{8}$ inches.

In his sketchbook (p. 89) Sullivan notes the recurring motifs of his illustrations: spider's webs, pens, books, wings, skulls, stars, portraits, and characters. How he put these to work is shown in the drawing reproduced for "Organic Filaments," which he describes as a "spider's web across the universe netting stars in its mesh—a beautiful woman at the centre" (p. 60).

311 ALFRED, LORD TENNYSON

A Dream of Fair Women & other poems by Alfred Lord Tennyson. Selected and illustrated by Edmund J. Sullivan, with a postscript by the artist. London, Grant Richards, 1900. xviii, 196, [1] p. Illus: 40 plates from process blocks after Sullivan, each with printed tissue. Printer: R. & R. Clark. Page size: 9×7 inches. Publisher's white linen.

Like *Sartor Resartus* this book was a "labour of love" for Sullivan. He admits in his preface that, in his selection of poems to be illustrated, "regard has been taken rather to their pictorial suggestiveness than to purely poetical qualities" (p. x). Hence no doubt the preponderance of "fair women," in the depiction of whom he was in any event an acknowledged master. The strongest drawings in the book are those which he devotes to occasional manifestations of Tennyson's grim or sardonic strain, such as "St. Simeon Stylites," "The Vision of Sin," and "The Palace of Art," though mention should be made of the lively quartet for "The Goose." Sullivan also speaks of endeavoring "to render concrete the pictures that Tennyson inspires in the fancy" (p. ix). If the illustrations of this book are not quite on a level with his best work, it may be because they are too precise, too free from ambiguity.

⚓ Sketchbook for *A Dream of Fair Women and Other Poems*, pen and ink and graphite. Size: 9×7 inches.

Sullivan made most of his sixty-five preliminary sketches for Tennyson's poems between June 13 and 15, 1899. Some are mere hints to himself for future development. Others, like that for "St. Simeon Stylites" (p. 84), approach finished drawings.

⚓ Ten finished pen drawings for *A Dream of Fair Women and Other Poems*:

Pen and ink and graphite drawing for "A Vision of Sin": "Unto me my maudlin gall / And my mockeries of the world" (p. 109). Size: 6¼×6 inches.

Pen and ink drawing for "The Palace of Art": "Yet not the less held she her solemn mirth / And intellectual throne" (p. 183). Size: 6¼×4¼ inches.

Pen and ink and graphite drawing for "The Goose": "the grave churchwarden doff'd, / The parson smirk'd and nodded" (p. 193). Size: 7⅜×6⅜ inches.

312 F. H. K. DE LA MOTTE FOUQUÉ

Sintram & His Companions by La Motte Fouqué. Translated by A. C. Farquharson, with a frontispiece by Albrecht Dürer, & twenty illustrations by Edmund Sullivan. London, Methuen & co., [1908]. viii, 193, [3] p. Illus: photogravure front. after Dürer and 20 plates from process blocks after Sullivan. Printer: Arden press. Page size: 8¾×5⅝ inches. Publisher's brown cloth.

Early in the nineteenth century a friend sent Fouqué Dürer's celebrated engraving "The Knight, Death, and the Devil" together with a request that he "write a romance . . . in interpretation of these enigmatical figures" (p. vi). The story which Fouqué thereupon devised tells how the wrathful

Biorn pledges the soul of his son, Sintram, to Death and the Devil if he fails to keep a murderous vow. When the intervention of his wife causes Biorn to lose his "ghastly wager," Sintram is saddled with the sinister pair as his intermittent "companions." For many years his life is blighted by the temptations and perils into which the Devil, or "Master Dwarf," leads him, but by withstanding them he becomes the seasoned and indomitable knight whom Dürer depicts.

Though *Sintram* is full of striking incidents, and indeed has a coherent symbolic pattern, Sullivan would hardly have chosen it for illustration if he had not wished to accept the same challenge as an artist that Fouqué accepted as a writer. Offering Dürer's "The Knight, Death, and the Devil" as his frontispiece, Sullivan followed it with twenty drawings in the same style, including one (p. 178) which is directly comparable to Dürer's engraving. Even for a master of line like Sullivan, this was a bold undertaking, yet the resulting designs are a triumphant success. Death and the Master Dwarf play their parts well, but the artist's most notable achievement lies in his depiction of how Sintram, who begins life as wild as Biorn, becomes step by step the self-disciplined hero of Dürer's design. In the illustration at page 135 Sintram is consoled by the pilgrim Wiegand, whose penance for a deed of violence has made him act the part of Death's double, while Sintram's faithful dog, Stovmaerke, lies quietly at his feet. See Plate XCIII.

⚓ Seventeen finished pen and ink and graphite drawings, signed, for *Sintram and His Companions*: Size: 10×7 inches.

" 'Look in, my young knight,' he said, very gravely" (p. 98).

" 'Wait a moment,' he said, 'while I sing this child a slumber-song' " (p. 135).

"How this same Wiegand had fallen asleep like a tired child" (p. 139).

"Once more he began his impious praises of Gabriella's beauty" (p. 178).

The originals of Sullivan's designs are more impressive than the illustrations in the book, which are reduced to 5⅞ by 4 inches. The illustration at page 178 is a simplified version of "The Knight, Death, and the Devil." It comes from chapter 27 in which Fouqué completes his task of interpreting Dürer's figures. The Master Dwarf is engaged in

Albrecht Dürer, engraving of "The Knight, Death, and the D[

Drawing for *Sintram and His Companions*

tempting Sintram for the last time, while Death, who will be the Knight's savior as he has been his tormentor, watches at one side. In this eerie company Stovmaerke, a sort of touchstone for good and evil, cringes beneath Sintram's steed.

∾ Albrecht Dürer, engraving of "The Knight, Death, and the Devil."
The Metropolitan Museum of Art

∾ Sketchbook for *The French Revolution*. Size: 9×7 inches.

Between November 4 and December 8, 1908, Sullivan filled the first 101 pages of this sketchbook with pencil drawings and notes for his edition of Carlyle's *French Revolution*, which appeared in 1910. Taking his task seriously, he was annoyed

when acquaintances remarked about the project: "Ah yes—you will have a fine chance for costume" (p. 28). His greatest problem, as he saw it, was to tell the truth without losing his audience. "I regard it as the illustrator's business," he wrote (p. 3), "to evoke by the terms of his art the emotion he has experienced in reading his author by running a parallel or commentary on the work, a pictorial parallel or commentary or summing up. The pages of the story of the Revolution are smeared and soaked with blood. Who shall complain if my drawings are the same. I have taxed my art to be terrible." The images of starvation and corruption, violence and horror which Sullivan evoked did indeed alienate some readers, who were otherwise impressed by the force and

Drawing for *The French Revolution*

several figures which Sullivan emphasizes: the oblivious unconcern of Louis XVI and Marie Antoinette contrasted with the patient fortitude of Mirabeau.

• Forty-eight pen and brush sketches for *Don Quixote*:
Don Quixote. Size: 6⅜×5 inches.
Sancho Panza. Size: 8¼×6¼ inches.
"The Knighting of Don Quixote." Size: 8⅜×6½ inches.
"Sancho Panza and the Duennas." Size: 8×7 inches.

These sketches date from December of 1921 and January of 1922. Of all Sullivan's unrealized projects for illustrations, it is *Don Quixote* that one would most like to have seen completed. As with Cervantes, his persistent idealism went hand in hand with a clear awareness of hard realities, and he understood Sancho Panza as thoroughly as he did the Don.

313 ALFRED, LORD TENNYSON

Maud, a monodrama by Alfred Lord Tennyson with illustrations by Edmund J. Sullivan. London, Macmillan and co., 1922. [2], x, 102, [1] p. Illus: Color-printed front. and 7 color-printed plates, 12 plates, 26 headpieces, all from process blocks after Sullivan. Printer: R. & R. Clark. Page size: 10⅜×7¼ inches. Large paper. Limited to 520 copies. Publisher's half holland.

For what was to be his last illustrated book, Sullivan turned to his favorite poem by his favorite poet. He set out to capture Tennyson's "exaltation" by paralleling in his drawings the "lyrical outbursts" of Tennyson's protagonist, feeling that only in this way could he avoid costume melodrama. (*Art of Illustration*, p. 158.) In part 1 Sullivan follows the various phases of the young man's love to their culmination in "Come into the garden, Maud." Despite his mood of doubt and defiance, life remains tolerable to him because of Maud. Part 2 on the other hand, after he kills Maud's brother, is given over to images of madness and terror. The dawning of hope in part 3 is suggested by scenes significantly devoid of human figures. Particularly in Sullivan's full-page drawings, brush predominates over pen, a concession to impressionism into which he was drawn by his emphasis on the lyrical aspects of the poem. Macmillan spared no pains to make *Maud* attractive. There are forty-six illustrations, twenty full-page,

vigor of his designs, but his portraits of heroic figures like Danton and Mirabeau were generally admired.

• Finished pen and graphite drawing, signed, for "The Titan Mirabeau." Size: 13½×9 inches.

In Sullivan's sketchbook there are two preliminary sketches for this drawing. The royal family dominates the first which shows "Marie Antoinette with her children—à la Mme. Le Brun—but the children crawling about, adventuring on the two thrones, upsetting the balance." Here Mirabeau—"sweating, nude?"—is hardly more than a beast of burden. In the bolder and simpler second design, on the other hand, attention is concentrated on him, a "*grim* titan, bearing his awkward complacent heavy and difficult burden. The strong man, staggering under his load." (Pp. 36–37.) In the finished drawing it is the relationship of the

Drawings of Sancho Panza and Don Quixote

and eight of these have touches of color. A large-paper issue of 520 copies signed by Sullivan was provided. The edition as a whole must have been a substantial one, for *Maud* is still a relatively common book. But there were no successors.

• Three preliminary brush and pen drawings for "Come into the garden, Maud." Sizes: $7 \times 5\frac{3}{4}$, $9\frac{1}{2} \times 8$, and 7×6 inches.

• Finished brush, pen and graphite drawing for "Come into the garden, Maud." Size: $12\frac{1}{2} \times 9$ inches.

> And the soul of the rose went into my blood,
>   And the music clash'd in the hall;
> And long by the garden lake I stood,
>   For I heard the rivulet fall
> From the lake to the meadow and on to the wood,
>   Our wood that is dearer than all.   (p. 70)

At this climactic moment Sullivan shows both the young man's longing passion and his dark destiny. The first is suggested by his stance as he waits with outstretched arms for Maud's coming, the second by the looming mass of the Hall, symbol of all the forces working against him, as dawn breaks. The reflections of light on water, so miraculously realized in the finished drawing, were a key element in Sullivan's design from his first sketch.

• Sketchbook for *King Lear*, pen and brush and graphite. Size: 9×7 inches. "King Lear" (p. 43).

These thirty-four pages of pen and brush sketches were executed between December 19, 1926, and January 3, 1927. Sullivan planned a book with fifty illustrations, but he seems to have received no encouragement from publishers. In these preliminary sketches each of the principal characters is masterfully presented, but it is Lear himself who haunts the artist. See above, p. xxxi.

• Twenty-two preliminary pen and brush and graphite sketches for *Dr. Jekyll and Mr. Hyde*, taken from a sketchbook. Size: 9×7 inches.

Two pages of sketches for chapter 1, "Story of the Door."

Drawing of "Come into the garden, Maud"

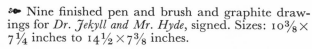

Nine finished pen and brush and graphite drawings for *Dr. Jekyll and Mr. Hyde*, signed. Sizes: 10⅜ × 7¼ inches to 14½ × 7⅜ inches.

"Story of the Door" (chapter 1). Size: 10⅜ × 7⅜ inches.

Of Sullivan's drawings for Robert Louis Stevenson's stories, which date from 1927, those for *Weir of Hermiston* and *Dr. Jekyll and Mr. Hyde* are the most striking. Hyde in particular fascinated him. In his sketches he tries again and again to capture in line what Stevenson could not describe in words. The lawyer Enfield says of Hyde: "There is something wrong with his appearance; something displeasing, something downright detestable. I never saw a man I so disliked, and yet I scarce know why. He must be deformed somewhere; he gives a strong feeling of deformity, although I couldn't specify the point. He's an extraordinary-looking man, and yet I can really name nothing out of the way." (Chapter 1.) Had Sullivan completed and published his illustrations for Stevenson's story, this would have been the first in the series.

Preliminary sketches for
Dr. Jekyll and Mr. Hyde,
"Story of the Door"

Aubrey Beardsley (1872–1898)

Beardsley stands out among end-of-the-century British illustrators, just as Blake stands out among those of the beginning of the century, though for very different reasons. The body of work he accomplished between 1892 and 1896, his years of full activity, is one of the notable achievements of all book illustration. Moreover, it had the widest possible influence. The 1890s, in Max Beerbohm's words, were "the Beardsley period." His designs were a potent force in establishing the vogue of Art Nouveau, not only in England but everywhere, and left their mark, as Lord Clark has shown, on the work of several leaders of the modern movement in painting.

Yet many people who admired Beardsley's masterly draftsmanship have deplored what he used it to represent. That great bookman A. W. Pollard, for example, could not praise his superb use of line for process blocks without adding the words: "degenerate and despicable as was almost every figure he drew" (introduction to Sketchley, p. xviii). In a period like our own, when people are more apt to find Beardsley's vision fascinating than repellent, it is at least possible to judge his artistic accomplishment without excuses. Certainly his reputation has never stood higher than it does today.

It should also be kept in mind that Beardsley was only twenty-five when he died. At the end of his life he told his sister Mabel: "The more society relaxes the less charm and point there is in Bohemianism" (*Letters*, p. 424). His impulse to be "an everlasting annoyance" to British philistinism (p. 129) was fading as he reached maturity. As he himself noted, he had a "genius for work" (p. 168), and had he lived another ten years, his career might have taken a quite different turn, with his books of the nineties coming to seem merely an interesting initial phase.

Not that there is any thinness in what Beardsley did leave behind. He was fortunate in his publishers—Dent, Mathews and Lane, even Leonard Smithers—and nearly all of his drawings found their way to publication, often in the most sumptuous manner. In addition to the books described below, there are many other volumes with his designs, several of them very substantial. It should also be noted that, if in comparison with Charles Ricketts he remains primarily an illustrator rather than a comprehensive book artist, he nevertheless took a close interest in all aspects of the books on which he worked, as is shown in his correspondence with Smithers about *Volpone* (*Letters*, pp. 396–428).

REFERENCES Anon., *Times Literary Supplement*; Beardsley; Gallatin, *Beardsley*; John Lewis; Reade; Reade and Dickinson; J. R. Taylor.

314 SIR THOMAS MALORY

The Birth, Life, and Acts of King Arthur . . . the text as written by Sir Thomas Malory . . . with an introduction by Professor Rhys and embellished with many original drawings by Aubrey Beardsley. [London, J. Dent, 1893]. 3 v. I: xc, 290 p. II: [5], 292–664 p. III: [5], 666–990, [1] p. Illus: Gravure fronts., numerous plates, vignettes, borders, etc., from process blocks after Beardsley. Printer: Turnbull & Spears. Page size: 9⅞×7¾ inches. No. 294 of 300 copies. Publisher's vellum.

Seeking to emulate the books of the Kelmscott Press, John Dent in 1892 offered Beardsley £200 for twenty full-page illustrations, about one hundred smaller designs in the text, and nearly three hundred fifty initial letters for *Le Morte Darthur*. In accepting this formidable commission, the artist anticipated, correctly as it turned out, "a year's hard work." His chief model when he began his task was his friend and patron Burne-Jones, but as he progressed, his designs became almost a parody of the Gothic style. Learning that William Morris had "sworn a terrible oath against me for daring to bring out a book in his manner," Beardsley maintained that, "while *his* work is a mere imitation of the old stuff, mine is fresh and original." He did not falter in this conviction. At the end of his life he was preparing to join with Smithers in a new magazine to be called the *Peacock* which would "attack untiringly and unflinchingly the Burne-Jones and Morris medieval business, and set up a wholesome seventeenth and eighteenth century standard of what picture making should be." (*Letters*, pp. 34, 37, 44, 413.) "How Sir Belvidere cast the sword Excalibur into the water" (III, 967), the next to the last of his full-page plates, marks the distance Beardsley had travelled from his first inspiration. *Le Morte Darthur* appeared initially in twelve parts. The edition consisted of eighteen hundred copies, three hundred of which constituted a "superior issue" on Dutch handmade paper. A few of the latter, like the copy described, were bound in vellum with cover designs by Beardsley. See Plate LXXXIII.

☙ Pen and ink and graphite drawing, a chapter-heading for *Le Morte Darthur*, 1, 231. Image size: 4⅛ × 3½ inches.

315 OSCAR WILDE

Salomé, a tragedy in one act: translated from the French of Oscar Wilde: pictured by Aubrey Beardsley. London, Elkin Mathews & John Lane, 1894. [9], 66, [2] p. + 16 p. ads. Illus: Front., 9 plates, 2 borders, and 1 vignette, all from process blocks after Beardsley. Printer: T. & A. Constable. Page size: 8½ × 6¾ inches. Limited to 100 large-paper copies on Japan vellum. Publisher's green silk.

If *Le Morte Darthur* made Beardsley known, his designs for the first edition in English of Wilde's *Salomé* made him notorious, and it remains the book of which most people think when his name is mentioned. Though he was at work on it by June of 1893, the book's appearance was delayed, in part because of his publisher's fear lest the illustrations be found indecent. Beardsley wrote to a friend late in that year: "I have withdrawn three of the illustrations and supplied their places with three new ones (simply beautiful and quite irrelevant)" (*Letters*, p. 58). When *Salomé* was published, the critics made their expected protest, though Wilde was their primary target, and relations between writer and artist became strained. But even if Beardsley offers amiable caricatures of Wilde in "Enter Herodias" and two other designs, it is mistaken to think that he was contemptuous of the text he was illustrating. It moved his imagination as did few other subjects. This is one of one hun-

Drawing for *Le Morte Darthur*

dred copies on Japanese vellum. When the book was about to appear, Beardsley told a friend to "order a large-paper one or none at all. The difference in the printing of the plates will I think be very great." (*Letters*, p. 55.) See Plate LXXXIV.

315A OSCAR WILDE

Salomé, a tragedy in one act: translated from the French of Oscar Wilde, with sixteen drawings by Aubrey Beardsley. London, John Lane, 1907. xviii, [5], 65, [1] p. + 2 p. ads. Illus: Front., 13 plates and 2 borders, all from process blocks after Beardsley. Printer: Wm. Clowes & sons. Page size: 8⅜ × 6¾ inches. Publisher's green cloth.

This handsome edition, the binding design for which is also by Beardsley, contains several new or unexpurgated plates.

316 ALEXANDER POPE

The Rape of the Lock, an heroi-comical poem in five cantos, written by Alexander Pope. Embroidered with nine drawings by Aubrey Beardsley . . . London,

Four bindings designed by Beardsley

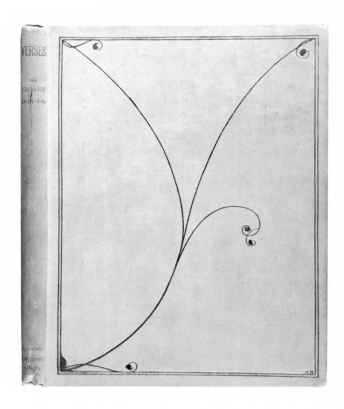

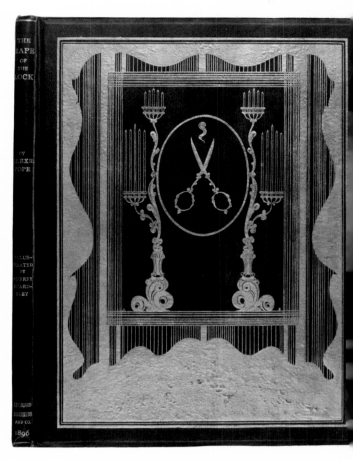

Leonard Smithers, 1896. xiii, 47, [1] p. Illus: Front., 6 plates, and 2 vignettes, all from process blocks after Beardsley. Printer: Chiswick press. Page size: 10×7¾ inches. No. 23 of 25 copies on Japan vellum. Publisher's vellum.

The Rape of the Lock and *Lysistrata*, respectively the least and the most outrageous of Beardsley's major books, are the masterpieces of his later style, though if he had completed his illustrations to *Volpone*, that volume might well have proved superior to either. *The Rape of the Lock* shows what he meant by meeting "wholesome eighteenth century standards," particularly as displayed in the work of Watteau. The statement on the title page that Pope's poem is "embroidered with nine drawings" has sometimes been taken to mean that Beardsley's designs have only a tenuous relation to the text. It is hard to see why. Each of the principal illustrations depicts a significant episode in Pope's fragile story. In that shown (p. 20) the Baron is about to snip a lock of Belinda's hair, a decisive moment described in whimsical detail, though it is true that there is no warrant in the poem for the dwarfish page at the center of the design who invites the reader's complicity in the escapade. The copy described is one of twenty-five on Japanese vellum, a paper that does notable justice to Beardsley's illustrations. The gold of his superb binding design, on the other hand, has more salience against the blue cloth of the ordinary edition than against the vellum of this special edition. There was a charming "bijou edition" of *The Rape of the Lock* in 1897, for which, so Beardsley wrote, his "pictures" were "reduced to well-nigh postage stamps" (*Letters*, p. 297). See Plate LXXXV.

317

The Savoy, an illustrated quarterly. No. 1 [–8]. 1896. 3 v. Inserted proofs. Page size: 10×7⅜ inches. Vellum by Riviere, original blue cloth covers bound in.

Beardsley was closely associated with two periodicals, *The Yellow Book* and *The Savoy*. Though the former is better known, the latter yielded a far richer harvest of drawings. Indeed, in the last of its eight numbers, the fourteen designs that make up the "Art Contents" are all from his hand. The remarkable copy described may well have been made up for Smithers himself. Among the added materials it contains are the poster and prospectus

for the magazine and proofs of the suppressed designs for the covers of the prospectus and of number one. The vellum bindings are stamped in gold with the designs of the cloth cases of the ordinary edition. The set belonging to Beardsley's close friend Herbert C. J. Pollitt had the same vellum binding (Reade and Dickinson, entry 539), but lacked the special contents of this copy.

318 ARISTOPHANES

The Lysistrata of Aristophanes, now first wholly translated into English, and illustrated with eight full-page drawings by Aubrey Beardsley. [Translated by Samuel Smith.] London, 1896. 61 p. Illus: Front. and 7 plates from process blocks after Beardsley. Page size: 11⅜×9 inches. Blue boards, orig. front wrapper bound in.

Shortly after Beardsley made his eight drawings for *Lysistrata* in the summer of 1896, Smithers published them surreptitiously in an edition stated to be of one hundred copies. They continued their under-the-counter existence until 1966, when Brian Reade reproduced them from the original drawings in his *Aubrey Beardsley*. Once they achieved general circulation, there was no denying the graphic directness with which they realize Aristophanes's sexual satire, and Beardsley's judgment at the time he made them, that they were "in a way the best things I have ever done," has been borne out. Though Smithers seems to have been moved solely by greed, it is fortunate that he did not heed Beardsley's famous appeal a few days before his death "to destroy *all* copies of *Lysistrata* and bad drawings." (*Letters*, pp. 150, 439.)

⁂ Four bindings designed by Beardsley:

Dowson, *Verses*, 1896. Size: 7¾×5¾ inches.
Pope, *The Rape of the Lock*, 1896. Size: 10¾×7½ inches.
The Savoy, 3 volumes, 1896. Size: 10¼×7½ inches.
Jonson, *Volpone*, 1898. Size: 11½×8¾ inches.

Beardsley called his cover design for *Volpone*, one of the two large drawings he completed for that book, "*simply ravishing*" and "gorgeous" (*Letters*, pp. 420–421). These adjectives can also be applied to his designs for the bindings of *The Rape of the Lock* and *The Savoy*, whether stamped on vellum or on cloth. The utter simplicity of his design for Dowson's *Verses*, on the other hand, is equally successful.

Sir Max Beerbohm (1872–1956)

Only in *Rossetti and His Circle* can Beerbohm really be called an illustrator, yet it is impossible to omit him from this survey. In ten albums beginning with *A Book of Caricatures* of 1896 and ending with *Heroes and Heroines of Bittersweet* of 1931, he carried caricature to the highest point it has reached in England, at least since the time of Hogarth and Gillray. To his art he brought a wide acquaintance with men and books, a sense of character worthy of a great novelist, and the wittiest of personal styles. In his essay of 1901 on "The Spirit of Caricature" he tells how he works, studying his subject at length under varying circumstances and filtering his recollections through "the unconscious process of exaggeration." Thus "melted down, as in a crucible," the subject will emerge "with not a particle of himself lost, yet with not a particle of himself as it was before. . . . And he will stand there wholly transformed, the joy of his creator, the joy of those who are privy to the art of caricature." "The most perfect caricature," Beerbohm concludes, "is that which, on a small surface, with the simplest means, most accurately exaggerates, to the highest point, the peculiarities of a human being, at his most characteristic moment, in the most beautiful manner." (Beerbohm, pp. 214–216.) Beerbohm's insistence on beauty is significant, for the decorative qualities of his designs often give as much aesthetic satisfaction as one gets from those of Beardsley or Nicholson.

REFERENCES Beerbohm; Gallatin, *Beerbohm*; Jackson.

ᔕ➡ One hundred and ten pen drawings by Alfred Bryan, varying in size from 6¼ × 9¾ inches to 3 × 4½ inches, chiefly of political figures:

"Waiting for the Verdict" [Gladstone]. Size: 8½ × 4 inches.
[Sir William Vernon Harcourt]. Size: 7⅜ × 3 inches.
[Harcourt and Gladstone]. Size: 7⅜ × 3 inches.
"Discussing the Speech" [Gladstone and Harcourt]. Size: 5¾ × 3½ inches.

Nearly always in his early work and often in his later, Beerbohm was content to draw single figures. At the beginning of his career he found his particular inspiration for this sort of subject in the caricature-portraits of Carlo Pelegrini and Alfred Bryan. The latter, usually called "A.B.," was the most prolific of all English black-and-white artists. Beerbohm's devotion to him is set forth in an essay entitled "A.B." where he maintains that "there is more talent in his little finger than in half the emblazoned hierarchy of 'pen-and-ink draughtsmen,' on whose potterings and peddlings we all lavish so much admiration" (*More*, London, 1899, p. 162).

The political drawings described are typical of A.B.'s vast production. Gladstone was his favorite subject, but Sir William Vernon Harcourt (1827–1904), another prominent liberal statesman, yielded his most memorable likenesses. As it happens, A.B.'s renderings of Harcourt may be tested from a description set down by a master hand. He is the "great personage" to whom the Assistant Commissioner reports in *The Secret Agent*. "Vast in bulk and stature," Conrad writes, "with a long white face, which, broadened at the base by a big double chin, appeared egg-shaped in the fringe of thin greyish whisker, the great personage seemed an expanding man. Unfortunate from a tailoring point of view, the crossfolds in the middle of a buttoned black coat added to the impression, as if the fastenings of the garment were tried to the utmost. From the head, set upward on a thick neck, the eyes, with puffy lower lids, stared with a haughty droop on each side of a hooked aggressive nose, nobly salient in the vast pale circumference of the face. A shiny silk hat and a pair of worn gloves lying ready on the end of a long table looked expanded too, enormous." (*The Secret Agent*, London, 1907, p. 191.)

Alfred Bryan, drawing of Sir William Vernon Harcourt

319

Caricatures of Twenty-five Gentlemen by Max Beerbohm. With an introduction by L. Raven-Hill. London, Leonard Smithers, 1896. [6, 25] l. Illus: 25 half-tone plates after Beerbohm. Printer: P. Naumann. Page size: 9¾ × 7¼ inches. Publisher's blue cloth.

This was Beerbohm's first book of caricatures. The sketches in it are halfway between the brilliant likenesses of A.B., which hardly exaggerate at all, and the complex and nuanced caricatures of Beerbohm's later albums. L. Raven-Hill, himself a renowned black-and-white artist, said of Beerbohm at this point in his development: "If Max sees a little man with nothing particularly strange about him except a big moustache, he goes for that big moustache, it becomes bigger and bigger, until it overwhelms everything else. Everything else dwindles beside it, getting smaller and smaller in the right proportion." (Preface, p. vii.) A.B.'s version of Harcourt parallels nearly every detail in Conrad's description; Beerbohm captures Conrad's metaphor of the "expanding man."

❧ Pen and ink self-caricature. Size: 6¼ × 4⅜ inches. Signed and dated February, 1903, by the artist.

(319) *Caricatures of Twenty-five Gentlemen,* Sir William Vernon Harcourt

320

The Poet's Corner by Max Beerbohm. London, William Heinemann, 1904. [2] l. Illus: 20 plates by the three-color process after Beerbohm. Printer: Hazell, Watson, & Viney. Page size: 14½ × 10⅝ inches. Publisher's decorated boards.

Though he had not yet withdrawn to Italy, Beerbohm even in 1904 was largely preoccupied with the past. He managed to see each of his chosen poets from Homer to Kipling in an unaccustomed light. The future Mrs. Humphry Ward inquires of her sardonic uncle, Matthew Arnold: "Why, Uncle Matthew, oh why, will not you be always wholly serious?" The florid Browning and the pallid band of those who study his work ("There's a Me Society down at Cambridge," J. K. Stephen made the poet say) seem to be creatures from different planets. The probable reception in actual life of Coleridge's *Table Talk* is suggested. This last is a design of real power, but even more striking is the famous "Mr. Tennyson, reading 'In Memoriam' to his sovereign." See Plate xcvii.

◆ Pen and ink and watercolor drawing of "Mr. Tennyson reading 'In Memoriam' to his Sovereign" from *The Poet's Corner*. Signed and inscribed by the artist. Image size: 17¾ × 12⅝ inches.
Robert H. Taylor Collection

321

Rossetti and His Circle by Max Beerbohm. London, William Heinemann, 1922. ix l. Illus: 22 mounted plates by the three-color process, each with printed tissue, after Beerbohm. Printer: R. Clay. Page size: 10 × 7½ inches. Publisher's blue cloth.

Beerbohm described these watercolor drawings as "more substantial" and "riper" than his designs for *The Poet's Corner*. Certainly they had behind them the full weight of his prolonged study of that part of the English past which he found most congenial. Choosing Byron, Disraeli, and Rossetti as "the three most interesting men that England had in the nineteenth century," Beerbohm went on to write that the last "mightn't have seemed so very remarkable after all . . . in the Quattrocento and by the Arno. But in London, in the great days of a deep, smug, thick, rich, drab, industrial complacency, Rossetti shone for the men and women who knew him, with the ambiguous light of a red torch somewhere in a dense fog. And so he still shines for me." (Note, p. vi.) Bypassing the major episodes of the Pre-Raphaelite story, Beerbohm depicts for the most part casual encounters of disparate figures: Rossetti and Jowett, Whistler and Carlyle, Holman Hunt and Ford Madox Brown, even the young Millais and the old Millais. But somehow these confrontations between different ways of life set going in the viewer's mind reverberations profounder than would have been produced by high dramatic moments. Only in these drawings among his published work did Beerbohm face the perennial problem of the professional illustrator: making recurring figures recognizably the same from drawing to drawing. His success with Rossetti himself was complete, the most memorable of his portraits with regard to design coming in his drawing of Swinburne reading "Anactoria" to the Rossetti brothers.

Other Pen Draftsmen

The establishment of the process block as the usual method of reproducing an artist's designs effected sweeping changes in book illustration in the late 1880s and 1890s. Though artist-craftsmen like Ricketts, Pissarro, Strang, and Nicholson pursued their individual ways, most books came to be illustrated with pen drawings reproduced by photozincography. The ease and cheapness of this method brought about a large increase in the number of illustrated books and the ranks of the pen draftsmen who contributed to them, the "process servers" as Thomas Balston called them, expanded apace. The most obvious manifestation of these changed conditions was the popularity of illustrated books in series, not only the series for which Hugh Thomson drew, but many others. In his authoritative survey for the *Book Collector's Quarterly* Balston lists the most interesting of these, which comprehend in all 102 titles. Much of the good work of the period, however, was done for books not part of such series, and it is so abundant that any selection must be arbitrary to a degree.

Beardsley, Sullivan, and Thomson stand out, but to the illustrators represented below a dozen more of comparable interest could readily be added.

REFERENCES Balston, *Book Collector's Quarterly*; Balston, *New Paths*; Pennell, *Pen Drawing*; Peppin; Sketchley; Thorpe, *English Illustration*.

Sir J. Barnard Partridge (1861–1945)

322 AUSTIN DOBSON

Proverbs in Porcelain to which is added "Au revoir," a dramatic vignette by Austin Dobson . . . [with twenty-five illustrations by Bernard Partridge]. London, Kegan, Paul, Trench, Trübner, & co., ltd. 1893. 110, [5] p. Illus: Front., added t.p., 23 plates from process blocks after Partridge. The front. and 10 plates are India-paper proofs. Printer: Ballantyne press. Page size: $9\frac{3}{4} \times 7$ inches. No. 92 of 250 copies on large paper. Publisher's grey cloth.

Partridge is chiefly remembered as a *Punch* artist, but he was also an accomplished book illustrator. He illustrated many of "F. Anstey's" lively stories in a casual but vigorous fashion. Far more pains went into his designs for *Proverbs in Porcelain*, which is an elegant book, particularly in the large-paper issue.

Sidney H. Sime (1867–1941)

323 LORD DUNSANY

The Sword of Welleran and other stories by Lord Dunsany . . . with illustrations by S. H. Sime. London, George Allen & sons, 1908. xi, 242, [2] p. Illus: Halftone front. and 9 halftone plates after Sime. Printer: Ballantyne, Hanson & co. Page size: $7\frac{5}{8} \times 6\frac{1}{8}$ inches. Publisher's green cloth.

Sime was a fine draftsman with remarkable gifts of humor and weird invention who drew extensively for the magazines during the 1890s. Of all English black-and-white artists more or less in the Beardsley tradition, he was the most original. If his designs were collected and republished, they might well turn out to be more impressive than those of Edmund Dulac or Kay Nielsen, despite the advantage those artists gained from working in color. His book illustrations were chiefly for the fantasies of Dunsany, in whom he found a kindred spirit. The design reproduced depicts King Nehemoth of Babbulkund, the City of Marvel, "troubled in the nights by unkingly dreams of doom" (p. 66).

(323) Lord Dunsany, *The Sword of Welleran*, illustration by Sidney H. Sime

Edmund H. New (1871–1931)

324 IZAAK WALTON

The Compleat Angler by Izaak Walton and Charles Cotton. Edited with an introduction by Richard Le Gallienne. Illustrated by Edmund H. New. London, John Lane, 1897. lxxxiv, [4], 427, [1], [14] p. Illus: 2 photogravure plates, 51 plates, numerous vignettes, initials, head- and tailpieces from process blocks, all after New. Printer: Ballantyne press. Page size: $9\frac{1}{2} \times 6\frac{3}{4}$ inches. Publisher's linen.

How much more bad to beat a beast
With prickles on its skin.

19

(327) Hilaire Belloc, *More Beasts (for Worse Children)*, illustration by Lord Basil Blackwood

Topographical and architectural drawings, so significant in the illustrated books of the beginning of the century, were not especially favored in the 1890s. New stands out among the artists who did devote themselves to this kind of illustration. A member of the Birmingham School, he worked with the same sobriety and restraint that characterize A. J. Gaskin and C. M. Gere, but he did not allow his concern for accuracy to impair the aesthetic appeal of his designs.

William T. Horton (1864–1919)

325

A Book of Images drawn by W. T. Horton & introduced by W. B. Yeats. London, The Unicorn press,

1898. 16 p. + 2 p. ads. Illus: 23 plates from process blocks after Horton (numbered 17–61). Printer: Morrison and Gibb. Page size: 8½ × 6¾ inches. Publisher's yellow cloth.

For Yeats, secure in his conviction that "all Art that is not mere story-telling, or mere portraiture, is symbolic," Horton's pen drawings for *The Savoy* (317) and *A Book of Images* made him a black-and-white artist in a class with Beardsley and Ricketts (pp. 10–11). As a disciple of "The Brotherhood of the New Life," Horton's "waking dreams" concerned both the errors of the world and the blessedness of assured faith. It must be admitted, however, that the sinister or epicene figures of "Mammon" and "Temptation" are more memorable than the ideal figures of "Ascending into Heaven" or "Rosa Mystica," just as Horton's uncluttered embodiment of "the crooked way" in "The Path to the Moon" is more successful than his use of it as an element in celebrations of militant faith like "St. George" in this book or "Strait is the Gate" in *The Savoy*, II (April, 1896), 77.

Jessie M. King (1876–1949)

326 WILLIAM MORRIS

The Defence of Guenevere and other poems by William Morris. Illustrated by Jessie M. King. London, John Lane, 1904. 310 p. Illus: Front., numerous plates, vignettes, and head- and tailpieces from process blocks, all after King. Page size: 7⅜×5 inches. Publisher's red cloth.

    University of Pennsylvania Library

Jessie M. King evolved a highly individual Art Nouveau style which derived, not from Beardsley, but from Botticelli interpreted in the light of the training she had received at the Glasgow School of Art. During the first two decades of the twentieth century she made designs for many volumes. In *The Defence of Guenevere*, her most characteristic book, she was responsible for decorations and binding as well as illustrations. See Plate XCVIII.

Lord Basil Blackwood

327 HILAIRE BELLOC

More Beasts (for Worse Children). Verses by H.B., pic-tures by B.T.B. London, Edward Arnold, [1897]. 48 p. Illus: T.p. and 44 vignettes from process blocks after Blackwood. Page size: 8½×11 inches. Publisher's white boards.

Belloc's children's books, which extend from *The Bad Child's Book of Beasts* of 1896 to *New Cautionary Tales* of 1930, are among the most sophisticated examples of the genre. He is as didactic as the Miss Taylors in *Little Ann and Other Poems* (225), but he works from a sounder understanding of child nature. *The Bad Child's Book of Beasts* begins:

> I call you bad, my little child,
>   Upon the title page,
> Because a manner rude and wild
>   Is common at your age.
>
> The moral of this priceless work
>   (If rightly understood)
> Will make you—from a little Turk—
>   Unnaturally good.

Despite the whimsical promise of praise from impressed parents he holds out to boys and girls who master his lore about the Llama or the Python, his real aim in *More Beasts* is to amuse the child *moyen sensuel* with unnatural natural history. Blackwood, who illustrated Belloc's first six children's books, knew how to give the poet's beasts a preternatural awareness that makes them seem both shrewder and more congenial than their human associates. Witness the sardonic smile of the porcupine (p. 19) who has just triumphed over a tormenting boy.

Arthur Rackham (1867–1939)

Born into a prosperous middle-class family, Rackham at an early age manifested a gift for drawing which was encouraged both at home and in school. From 1885 to 1892 he combined work in an insurance office with attendance at the Lambeth School of Art. Then he joined the *Westminster Budget* as a staff artist, a post he held for four years. By the end of the century he was devoting most of his time to book illustration, though he still drew for the magazines. Among his early successes were R. H. Barham's *Ingoldsby Legends* of 1898, *Tales from Shakespeare* by Charles and Mary Lamb in 1899, and *Fairy Tales of the Brothers Grimm* in 1900, all of which were reissued a decade or so later with additional illustrations. *Rip Van Winkle* of 1905 was a turning point in his career because of its fifty-one color plates. Known previously as a black-and-white artist, Rackham with this book achieved preeminence as an illustrator working in the three-color process. *Peter Pan in Kensington*

Gardens, his acknowledged masterpiece, was published in 1906. His attempt the following year to rival Tenniel's illustrations to *Alice in Wonderland* (185) was less successful, and he did not proceed to *Through the Looking Glass*, but his designs for *A Midsummer Night's Dream* of 1908 became the standard by which subsequent illustrations of Shakespeare's play have been judged. Henceforth a book or two with his illustrations appeared almost every year until his death, even though the war and its aftermath drastically reduced the market for lavish color-plate books. Among his later volumes, *Comus* of 1921, *The Tempest* of 1926, Andersen's *Fairy Tales* of 1932, and Kenneth Graham's *The Wind in the Willows* of 1940 are outstanding.

It was Rackham's custom to immerse himself in his chosen texts with the aim of seeking out the subjects most congenial to him, which he would then illustrate in full detail. For each of his major books his designs are abundant and carefully finished. On a number of occasions, indeed, he returned to favorite titles to make still further drawings for later editions. Since he usually applied himself to relatively short texts, it may be claimed that not even Gustave Doré surpassed him in the comprehensiveness with which he illustrated the books he selected.

Rackham's art was profoundly eclectic. Derek Hudson (pp. 40, 44, 46) places him in the Pre-Raphaelite tradition, but observes that he also learned from Cruikshank, Caldecott, Richard Doyle, and Houghton, from "the whole German school from Dürer to Menzel and Hans Thoma," from Japanese prints, and among the work of his own time from Beardsley, Art Nouveau in general, and Edmund J. Sullivan. Yet out of these elements he compounded an art of his own, and the finished drawings of his maturity could not be mistaken for those of any other illustrator.

The limits of Rackham's effective range are obvious. His illustrations for heroic legends like *Siegfried and the Twilight of the Gods* of 1911, for books wholly in phase with the real world like *The Compleat Angler* of 1931, or even for stories of horror like *Poe's Tales* of 1935 are relatively conventional, however decorative their design and harmonious their coloring. He was most at home with the fantastic and the poetic, with things "that never were, on sea or land," and his best illustra-

tions are for fairy tales, and more particularly for gentle or grotesque fairy tales. Within these bounds he was a superlative illustrator. Beginning as a fine pen draftsman, he became a master of the craft of adding delicate color to his drawings in just the way that would elicit the best results from the three-color process. He was thus enabled to achieve a lifetime career in illustration that few English artists have matched.

It should be noted finally that Rackham was particularly remarkable for his insight into the minds and feelings of children, and that he actively championed their right of access to the best in art and literature. Believing in "the greatest stimulating and educative power of imaginative, fantastic, and playful pictures and writings for children in their most impressionable years" (quoted by Hudson, p. 80), he vigorously opposed those educational theorists who said, with Mr. Gradgrind at the beginning of Dickens's *Hard Times*: "Now what I want is, Facts. . . . Facts alone are wanted in life." He was one of the best friends that children have ever had.

REFERENCES Baughman; Hudson, *Rackham*; Latimore and Haskell; Sketchley; J. R. Taylor.

328 WASHINGTON IRVING

Rip Van Winkle by Washington Irving. With drawings by Arthur Rackham, A.R.W.S. London, William Heinemann, 1905. viii, 57, [3] p. Illus: Front. and 50 tipped plates by the three-color process, with printed tissues, and wood-engraved decorations, all after Rackham. Printer: Ballantyne, Hanson & co. Page size: 11 × 8¾ inches. No. 101 of 250 copies, this copy with a signed watercolor drawing on the limitation page. Publisher's vellum. Hudson, p. 167.
Columbia University Libraries

Rackham's *Rip Van Winkle* is among the most thoroughly illustrated of English books. Since the text is brief, his fifty illustrations, which are grouped at the end, come at the rate of one to every two or three sentences. If his conception of life in the "Kaatskills" is closer to the "Old England" of Randolph Caldecott than to the rural New York of Irving's narrative, he nonetheless contrives to present Rip's story in the most ingenious and engaging detail.

This book was published in a *de luxe* signed edition of 250 copies as well as a trade edition, and there was a concurrent sale of the watercolor orig-

Drawing for *Rip Van Winkle*, frontispiece

inals of Rackham's illustrations at the Leicester Galleries. Most of his ensuing books, at least through 1919, were presented in the same way. With additional revenue accruing from American and French editions, Rackham became that rare phenomenon an affluent illustrator, admired and envied by his less fortunate colleagues.

☞ Pen and ink and watercolor drawing of the frontispiece for *Rip Van Winkle*, 1905. Image size: 10¾ × 7¼ inches. Signed and dated by the artist.
Columbia University Libraries

For this frontispiece of Rip Van Winkle's awakening from his twenty-year sleep, as for the rest of his illustrations, Rackham made a meticulous pen drawing, which he then tinted delicately with watercolor.

329 JAMES M. BARRIE

Peter Pan in Kensington Gardens by J. M. Barrie . . . with drawings by Arthur Rackham, A.R.W.S. London, Hodder & Stoughton, 1906. xii, 125, [1] p. Illus: Front. and 49 tipped plates by the three-color process, with printed tissues, and wood-engraved decorations, all after Rackham. Printer: T. and A. Constable. Page size: 10¾ × 9 inches. No. 290 of 500 copies, this copy with a signed watercolor drawing on the limitation page. Publisher's vellum. Hudson, p. 168.
Miss Julia P. Wightman

The text of this book is derived, not from Barrie's famous play, but from the chapters about Peter Pan in *The Little White Bird* of 1902. "I think I like best of all," Barrie wrote of Rackham's designs, "the Serpentine with the fairies, and the

Peter in his night-gown sitting in the tree. Next I would [sic] the flying Peters, the fairies going to the ball (as in the 'tiff' & the fairy on cobweb)— the fairies sewing the leaves with their sense of fun (the gayest thing this) and your treatment of snow." (Hudson, *Rackham*, p. 66.) Barrie centers his praise on Rackham's rendering of the fairy world and the story of Peter and Wendy, but the book has much more to offer. The glimpses he provides of stylized London reality effectively set off the fairy life that exists in unsuspected conjunction with it, and he captures the loveliness of the Gardens themselves with masterly skill. See Plate XCIX.

330 WILLIAM SHAKESPEARE

A Midsummer-Night's Dream. By William Shakespeare. With illustrations by Arthur Rackham, R.W.S. London, William Heinemann, 1908. [6], 134, [2] p. Illus: Front. and 39 tipped plates by the three-color process, with printed tissues, and wood-engraved decorations, all after Rackham. Printer: Ballantyne & co. Page size: 11⅝ × 9½ inches. No. 153 of 1,000 copies. Publisher's vellum. Hudson. p. 168.
Columbia University Libraries

Rackham's designs for *A Midsummer Night's Dream* have the same variety of interest as those for *Peter Pan*. The detailed comprehensiveness of his approach does not impair the verve with which he realizes the fairy kingdom, the forest background, and the humors of Bottom and his companions. Subsequent illustrators and stage designers dealing with the play have found it difficult to put Rackham's images out of their minds.

Other Illustrators Who Drew for the Three-Color Process

The halftone process, invented by Meissenbach in 1882, made possible the reproduction in black and white of paintings and drawings as well as photographs from life. It gradually replaced reproductive wood engraving during the 1880s and 1890s, and from it was developed the three-color process,

which came into general use during the early years of this century. The most opulent employment of the three-color process was for *de luxe*, signed editions of children's books for the Christmas trade. These were printed on special paper, with their numerous colored plates on brown mounts protected by tissues, and often bound in vellum. These anticipations of the modern coffee-table book seem to have been placed in glass cases immediately on acquisition. At any rate, surviving copies are usually in fine condition. Even trade editions, which typically sold for fifteen shillings as compared with the two guineas demanded for *de luxe* editions, were hardly nursery books. John Betjeman's memories of "Finger-marked pages of Rackham's Hans Andersen," for example, relate to the drawing room, when it was "Time for the children to come down to tea."

Arthur Rackham was the undisputed master of this sort of book, though he had significant rivals in Edmund Dulac, Kay Nielsen, and Sir William Russell Flint (1880–1944). Among pen draftsmen both Edmund J. Sullivan and Hugh Thomson essayed color, but they were far less successful than in black and white. W. Heath Robinson, on the other hand, was equally at home in both mediums. The work of Beatrix Potter stands somewhat apart from the mainstream of three-color process illustration. It is narrower in range and slighter, but more delicate and personal.

Martin Hardie, a knowledgeable observer of the emergence of the three-color process, believed that it had one irredeemable fault. "It can be understood," he wrote (*English Coloured Books*, p. 294), "that a collector may treasure an aquatint, a chromo-lithograph, a coloured wood-engraving —but a process plate, never." For many years, indeed, collectors avoided books illustrated with process plates, being unable to reconcile themselves to the mechanical nature of their production. This is no longer true. Lavish giftbooks with colored plates are now very much in vogue, whether their illustrations are by Rackham and his followers, or by such American counterparts as Howard Pyle, N. C. Wyeth, and Maxfield Parrish. Ambitious monographs have been devoted to the principal artists who worked in the field, and an enterprising publisher has even found it worth his while to issue a series of mass-market paperbacks which thus far includes selections from Dulac, Nielsen, and Rackham, as well as an omnibus volume called *The Fantastic Kingdom*.

REFERENCES Hardie; Balston, *Book Collector's Quarterly*; Linder; Nicholson; Peppin.

Beatrix Potter (1866–1943)

331 BEATRIX POTTER

The Tale of Peter Rabbit. By Beatrix Potter. Copyright. [London, privately printed, 1901.] [42] l. Illus: Front. printed by the three-color process, 41 plates from process blocks after Potter. Printer: Strangeways. Page size: 5¼×4 inches. Publisher's printed boards. First issue.
Miss Julia P. Wightman

331A BEATRIX POTTER

The Tale of Peter Rabbit, by Beatrix Potter. London, Frederick Warne and co., [1902]. 97, [1] p., printed on one side only. Illus: Front., 27 plates, and t.p. vignette by the three-color process, all after Potter. Printer: E. Evans. Page size: 5⅜×4⅛ inches. Publisher's grey boards.
Miss Julia P. Wightman

The charm of *The Tale of Peter Rabbit*, as Beatrix Potter herself noted, derives in part from the fact that it "was written to a child" in the form of a letter, "not made to order" (Linder, p. 110). Some years later she borrowed this letter to a lame boy to use as the basis for an expanded version of Peter Rabbit's story with forty-two black-and-white illustrations, of which she had 250 copies privately printed in 1901. The following year it was published with illustrations in the three-color process printed by Edmund Evans. Its success was immense. So familiar did her animal characters become among children that Miss Potter was told how "a small boy in church once inquired audibly whether the apostle was Peter Rabbit" (Linder, p. 92). Her next book, *The Tailor of Gloucester* of 1902, also was first printed privately, but thereafter she had a large and eager audience for everything she wrote. See Plate XCVI.

Edmund Dulac (1882–1953)

332

The Sleeping Beauty and Other Fairy Tales from the old French, retold by Sir Arthur Quiller-Couch, illustrated by Edmund Dulac. London, Hodder & Stoughton, [1910]. [10] l., 128, [4] p. Illus: Front. and 29 tipped plates by the three-color process, numerous process vignettes and head- and tailpieces, all after Dulac. No. 987 of 1,000 copies. Page size: 12⅛×9¾ inches. Publisher's brown calf.
Columbia University Libraries

After the appearance in 1907 of *Stories from the Arabian Nights* with fifty plates from his hand,

(332) *The Sleeping Beauty*, illustration by Edmund Dulac

Dulac became Rackham's chief rival in providing colored illustrations for reproduction by the three-color process for the giftbook trade. His best work, however, is to be found in *The Sleeping Beauty and Other Fairy Tales*. His designs for the title story and "Cinderella" have ornate eighteenth-century settings in which some indebtedness to the engravings for *Le cabinet des fées* can be discerned. No less ornate and rather more attractive are the eastern scenes conceived by Dulac for "Bluebeard" and "Beauty and the Beast," in which he repeated his success with *The Arabian Nights* on a larger scale. In the illustration at page 88 the father of "Beauty" is at cross purposes with "the Beast" whom his daughter will eventually restore to his true form.

Kay Nielsen (1886–1957)

333

East of the Sun and West of the Moon, old tales from the north. Illustrated by Kay Nielsen. [London], Hodder & Stoughton, [1914]. [10], 9–206 [1] p. Illus: Tipped front. and 24 tipped plates by the three-color process; t.p. vignette, numerous head- and tail-pieces and vignettes from process blocks, all after Nielsen. Printer: Henry Stone & son. Page size: 11 ⅛ × 9¾ inches. Publisher's blue cloth.
Columbia University Libraries

As is noted in the preface to *East of the Sun and West of the Moon*, these folktales from the works of Asbjörnsen and Moe are by no means for the nursery. The Danish artist Nielsen, being thoroughly at home with the narrative tradition that they represent, was well equipped to present their strangeness and cruelty, as well as their humor and heroism. Though his drawings are highly decorative, they are nonetheless true illustrations. The contrast between Nielsen's bizarre style, filled with echoes of nineties illustrators—for example, Horton's *Book of Images* (325)—and his primitive subject matter greatly enhances the piquancy of the book. It would be hard to find an Art Nouveau troll (p. 176) elsewhere.

The Plates

Tho: Moor L.ᵈ Chancelour.

19   *Imitations of Holbein*, 2 volumes, 1792–1800

J. Farington R.A. del.   Pub. June 1 1793. by J.& J. Boydell, Shakspeare   BLENHEIM.   Gallery Pall Mall & N.° 90, Cheapside.   J. C. Stadler sculp.

36   William Combe, *An History of the River Thames*, 2 volumes, 1794–1796

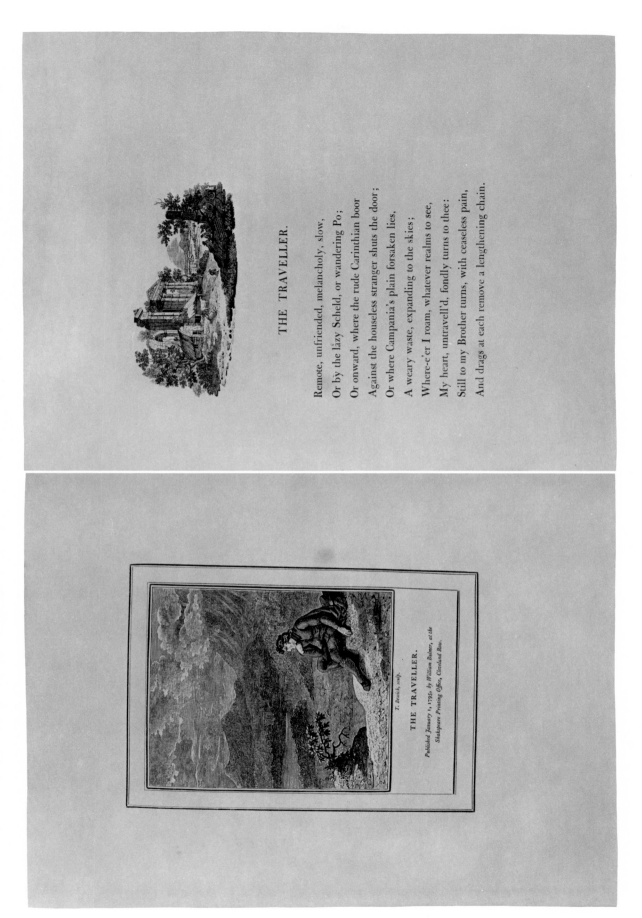

THE TRAVELLER.

Remote, unfriended, melancholy, slow,
Or by the lazy Scheld, or wandering Po;
Or onward, where the rude Carinthian boor
Against the houseless stranger shuts the door;
Or where Campania's plain forsaken lies,
A weary waste, expanding to the skies;
Where-e'er I roam, whatever realms to see,
My heart, untravell'd, fondly turns to thee:
Still to my Brother turns, with ceaseless pain,
And drags at each remove a lengthening chain.

T. Bewick, sculp.

THE TRAVELLER.

Published January 1, 1795, by William Bulmer, at the
Shakspeare Printing Office, Cleveland Row.

50   *Poems by Goldsmith and Parnell, 1795*

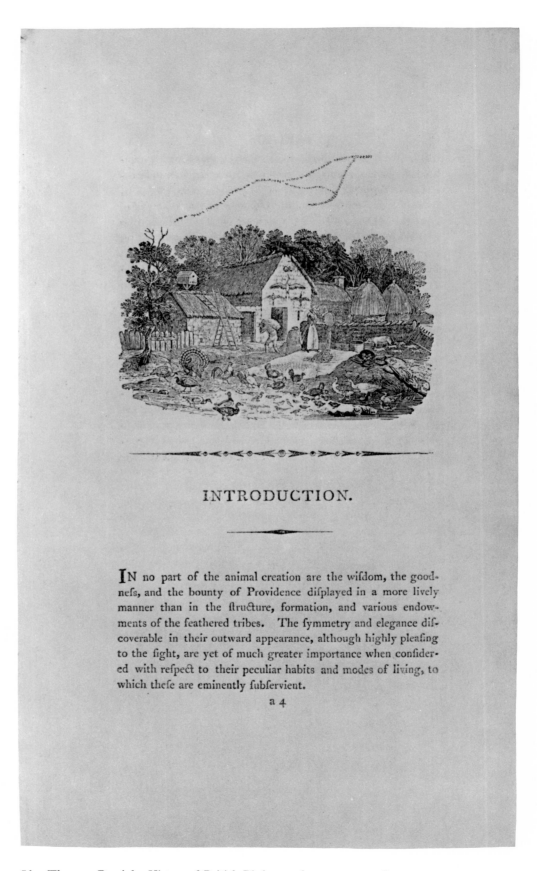

INTRODUCTION.

IN no part of the animal creation are the wifdom, the good-
nefs, and the bounty of Providence difplayed in a more lively
manner than in the ftructure, formation, and various endow-
ments of the feathered tribes. The fymmetry and elegance dif-
coverable in their outward appearance, although highly pleafing
to the fight, are yet of much greater importance when confider-
ed with refpect to their peculiar habits and modes of living, to
which thefe are eminently fubfervient.

a 4

51   Thomas Bewick, *History of British Birds*, 2 volumes, 1797–1804

NIGHT
THE
THIRD,
NARCISSA.

3   Edward Young, *Night Thoughts*, 1797

4 William Blake, *Jerusalem*, 1804–1820

8   *The Book of Job*, 1825

The Flower by Reinagle. Moon-light by Pether. Dunkarton sculp.t

The Night-Blowing Cereus.

London, Published May 10, 1800, by D.r Thornton.

39 Robert James Thornton, *The Temple of Flora*, 1797–1807

37 *Picturesque Views in Paris*, 1803

Drawn by J.M.W.Turner. R.A.

Engraved on Steel by Chas Turner.

SHIELDS on the RIVER TYNE.

RIVERS OF ENGLAND PLATE I.

London. Published June 1 1823 by W.B.Cooke 9 Soho Square

12   *River Scenery* 1807

WATER AT WENTWORTH, YORKSHIRE.

38 *Observations on . . . Landscape Gardening*, 1803

THE SOURCE of the ARVEIRON in the VALLEY of CHAMOUNI SAVOY.

10 *Liber Studiorum*, 1807–1819

COMO.

I LOVE to sail along the LARIAN Lake
Under the shore—though not to visit PLINY,
To catch him musing in his plane-tree walk,
Or angling from his window: * and, in truth,
Could I recall the ages past, and play
The fool with Time, I should perhaps reserve
My leisure for CATULLUS on *his* Lake,

* Epist. I. 3. ix. 7.

13   Samuel Rogers, *Italy*, 1830

14 *Picturesque Views in England and Wales*, 2 volumes, 1832–1838

DRAWING from LIFE at the ROYAL ACADEMY, SOMERSET HOUSE.

London Pub.t Jan.y 1 1808. at R. Ackermann's Repository of Arts, 101 Strand.

22. The Microcosm of London, 3 volumes, 1808–9.

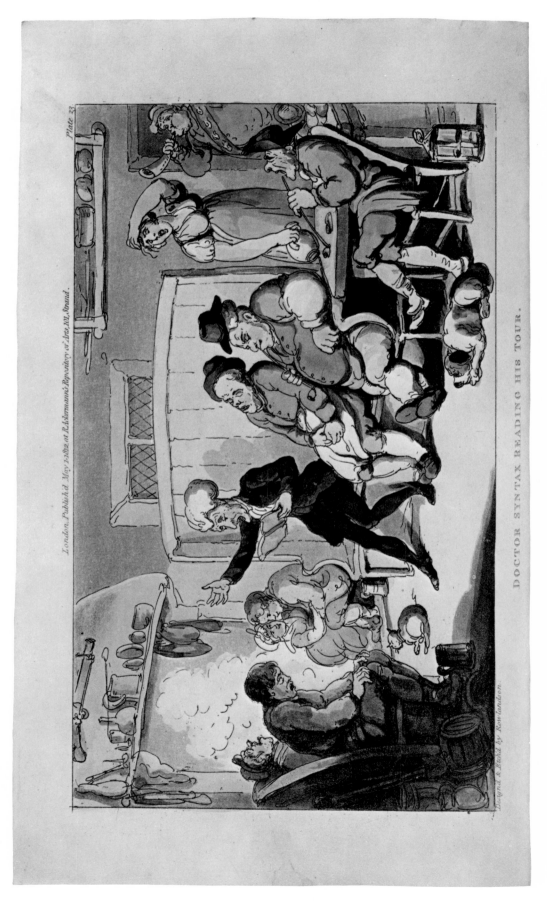

34 William Combe, *The Tour of Doctor Syntax, in Search of the Picturesque*, 1812

Such mortal Sport the Chase attends:
As Break-Neck will the Huntsman Ends

35   William Combe, *The English Dance of Death*, 2 volumes, 1815–1816

The Junction of the Dart with the Sea?

Drawn & Engraved by Will. Daniell.

Published by W. Daniell, Rashell Place, Fitzroy Square, London, May 20, 1825.

41 Richard Ayton, *A Voyage Round Great Britain*, 8 volumes, 1814–1825

40   William Combe, *A History of the University of Oxford*, 2 volumes, 1814

42 W. H. Pyne, *The History of the Royal Residences*, 3 volumes, 1819

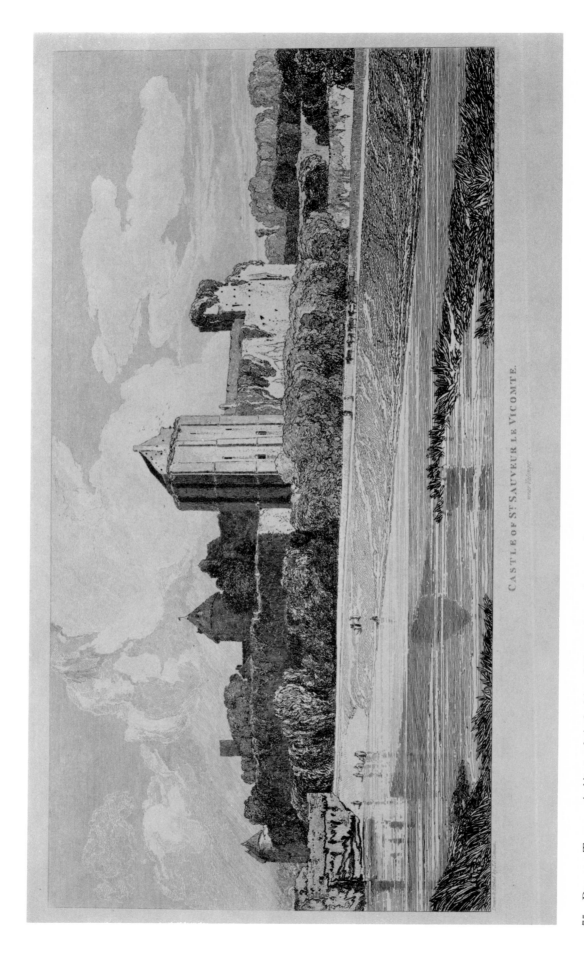

CASTLE OF ST SAUVEUR LE VICOMTE.

near Valognes

75 Dawson Turner, *Architectural Antiquities of Normandy*, 2 volumes, 1822

99 *Practical Hints on Decorative Printing*, 1822

112   Jacob and Wilhelm Grimm, *German Popular Stories*,
2 volumes, 1823–1826

The Last Chance

116   Charles Dickens, *Oliver Twist*, 3 volumes, 1838

44 Richard Westmacott, *The English Spy*, 2 volumes, 1825–1826

69   John Milton, *Paradise Lost*, 2 volumes, 1825–1827

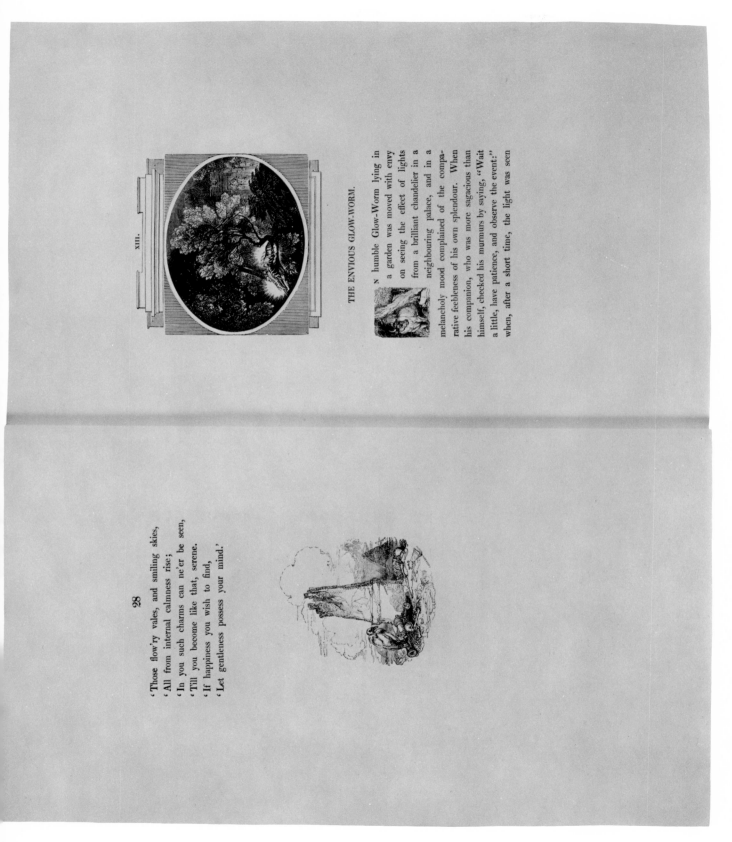

XIII.

THE ENVIOUS GLOW-WORM.

A humble Glow-Worm lying in a garden was moved with envy on seeing the effect of lights from a brilliant chandelier in a neighbouring palace, and in a melancholy mood complained of the comparative feebleness of his own splendour. When his companion, who was more sagacious than himself, checked his murmurs by saying, "Wait a little, have patience, and observe the event:" when, after a short time, the light was seen

28

'Those flow'ry vales, and smiling skies,
'All from internal calmness rise;
'In you such charms can ne'er be seen,
'Till you become like that, serene.
'If happiness you wish to find,
'Let gentleness possess your mind.'

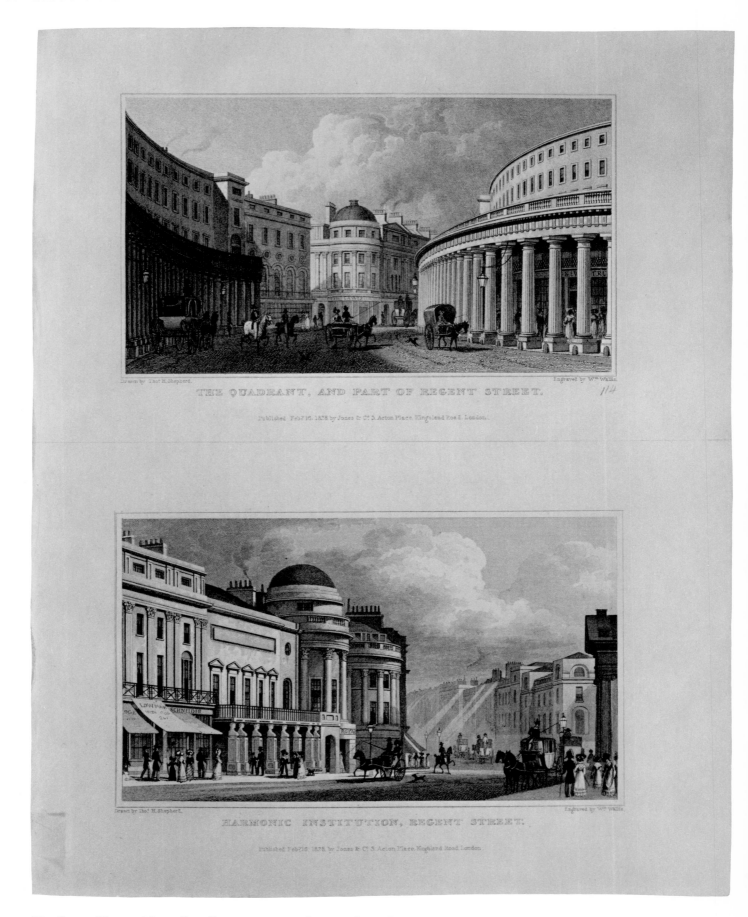

Drawn by Thos H. Shepherd.   Engraved by Wm Walks.

THE QUADRANT, AND PART OF REGENT STREET.

Published Feby 16, 1828 by Jones & Co 3 Acton Place, Kingsland Road, London.

Drawn by Thos H. Shepherd.   Engraved by Wm Walks.

HARMONIC INSTITUTION, REGENT STREET.

Published Feby 16, 1828, by Jones & Co 3 Acton Place, Kingsland Road, London.

23 James Elmes, *Metropolitan Improvements*, 2 volumes, 1829–1831

90 *Illustrations of the Family of Psittacidae, or Parrots, 1832*

91 *Views in Rome and Its Environs*, 1841

There was an old Derry down Derry,
Who loved to see little folks merry:
    So he made them a Book,
    And with laughter they shook,
At the fun of that Derry down Derry!

Published Feb. 10. 1846, by Thos. Mc Lean, 26, Haymarket.

92 *A Book of Nonsense*, 2 volumes, 1846

Viaduct across the Sankey Valley

Painted by John Constable, R.A.

A SUMMERLAND.

London Pub.d by M.r Constable, 35 Charlotte S.t Fitzroy Square, 1831.

Engraved by David Lucas.

71   *Various Subjects of Landscape, Characteristic of English Scenery*, 1833

83   *Facsimiles of Sketches Made in Flanders and Germany*, 1833

77 Augustus Welby Pugin, *Contrasts*, 1836

85　John Britton, *Drawings of the London and Birmingham Railway*, 1839

225 *Picturesque Architecture in Paris*, 1839

87   Charles Ollier, *Original Views of London as It Is*, 1842

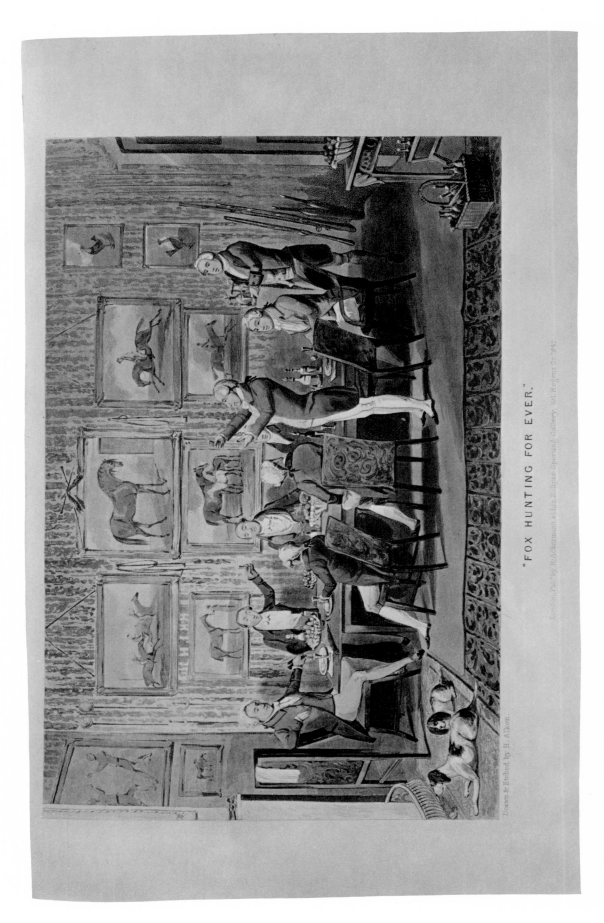

46 C. J. Apperley, *The Life of a Sportsman*, 1842

ROBIN GOODFELLOW

FROM Oberon in fairye land,
The king of ghosts and shadowes there,
Mad Robin I, at his command,
Am sent to viewe the night-sports here.
What revell rout
Is kept about,
In every corner where I go,
I will o'ersee, and merry bee,
And make good sport, with ho, ho, ho!

More swift than lightening can I flye
About this aery welkin soone,
And, in a minutes space, descrye
Each thing that's done belowe the moone,
There's not a hag
Or ghost shall wag,
Or cry, ware Goblins! where I go;
But Robin I their feates will spy,
And send them home, with ho, ho, ho!

Dadd, del   Green, sc.

61   *The Book of British Ballads*, 2 volumes, 1842–1844

88 George Croly, *The Holy Land*, 20 parts, 1842–1845

CONSTANCIA DUCHESS OF LANCASTER, WIFE OF JOHN OF GAUNT.

MONG the most beautiful specimens of illuminated manuscripts preserved in the British Museum, is the one from which the present plate is taken, and which is considered so precious that the leaves have been separately mounted and covered with glass to save them from the common accidents to which such articles are exposed. It was purchased recently of Mr. Newton Scott, one of the attachés to the embassy at Madrid, who bought it there. It is a richly illuminated genealogy relating to the regal house of Portugal, and appears to have been executed about the time of the Emperor Maximilian, for a member of the royal family of that country, who, there is reason for believing, was the Infante Fernando, born in 1507, who died in 1534. It is certainly the work of Flemish artists.

The figure given on our plate is intended to represent Constancia, the

102   Henry Shaw, *Dresses and Decorations of the Middle Ages*, 2 volumes, 1843

THE VINE.

SONG IN ANTONY AND CLEOPATRA — ACT 2. SCENE 7.

SAMUEL PALMER

COME, THOU MONARCH OF THE VINE,
PLUMPY BACCHUS, WITH PINK EYNE;
IN THY VATS OUR CARES BE DROWN'D;
WITH THY GRAPES OUR HAIRS BE CROWN'D;
CUP US, TILL THE WORLD GO ROUND;
CUP US, TILL THE WORLD GO ROUND!

SAMUEL PALMER

215 *Songs of Shakespeare*, 1843–1852

135   Charles Dickens, *A Christmas Carol*, 1843

137 Robert Surtees, *Handley Cross*, 1854

I therefore read them a portion of the service with a loud, unaffected voice, and found my audience perfectly merry upon the occasion.— Page 238.

CHAPTER XXVI.

A REFORMATION IN THE GAOL. TO MAKE LAWS COMPLETE THEY SHOULD REWARD AS WELL AS PUNISH.

THE next morning early I was awakened by my family, whom I found in tears at my bed-side. The gloomy strength of every thing about us, it seems, had daunted them. I gently rebuked their sorrow, assuring them I had never slept with greater tranquillity, and next inquired after my eldest daughter, who was not

2 G

62   Oliver Goldsmith, *The Vicar of Wakefield*, 1843

Sweet vale of Avoca! how calm could I rest,
In thy bosom of shade, with the friends I love best,
Where the storms that we feel in this cold world
should cease,
And our hearts, like thy waters, be mingled in peace.

29 Thomas Moore, *Irish Melodies*, 1846

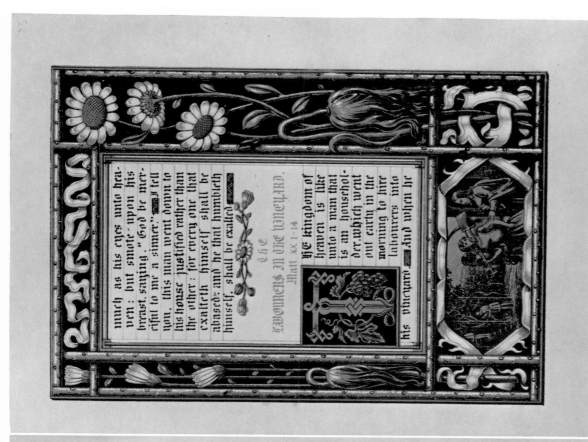

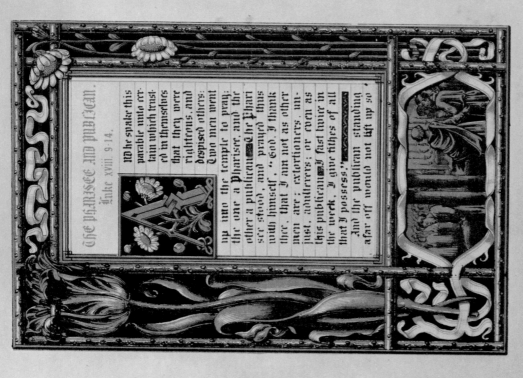

231 *Parables of Our Lord*, 1847

122   William Makepeace Thackeray, *Vanity Fair*, 1848

235   M. Digby Wyatt, *The Industrial Arts of the Nineteenth Century*, 2 volumes, 1851–1853

CHARGE OF THE LIGHT CAVALRY BRIGADE.
25TH OCT 1854.
UNDER MAJOR GENERAL THE EARL OF CARDIGAN.

89   *The Seat of War in the East*, 2 volumes, 1855–1856

GRAMMAR OF ORNAMENT

PLATE XLI

MORESQUE Nº 3

228   Owen Jones, *The Grammar of Ornament*, 1856

THE LADY OF SHALOTT.

PART I.

I.

On either side the river lie
Long fields of barley and of rye,
That clothe the wold and meet the sky;
And thro' the field the road runs by
        To many-tower'd Camelot;

148   Alfred Tennyson, *Poems*, 1857

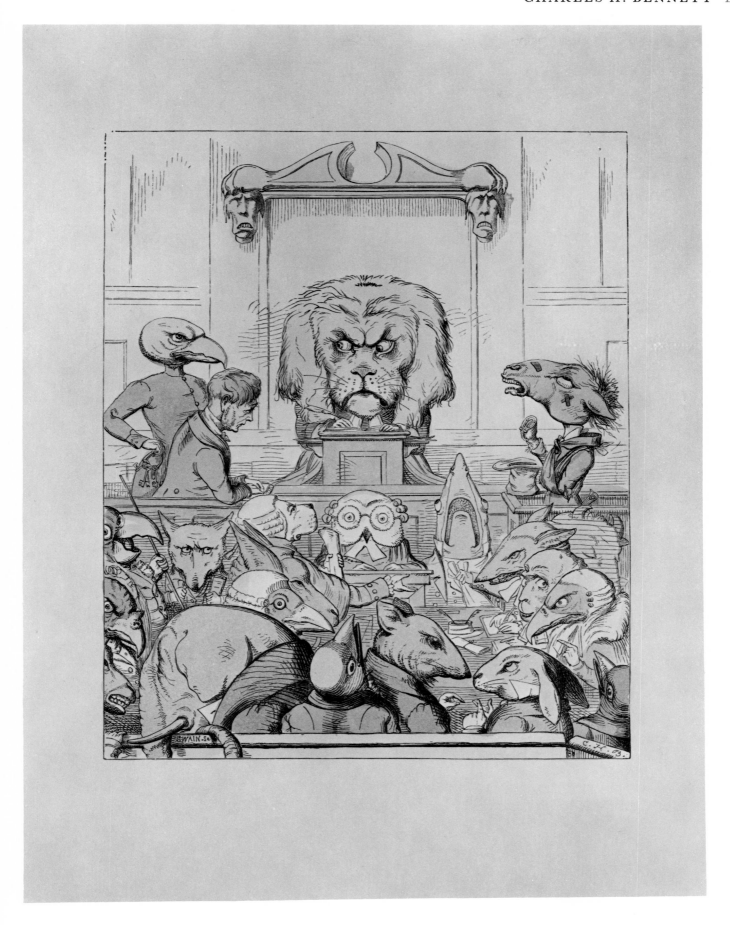

205   *The Fables of Aesop*, 1857

THE TRAVELLER.

Yet still, even here, content can spread a charm,
Redress the clime, and all its rage disarm.
Though poor the peasant's hut, his feasts though small,
He sees his little lot the lot of all;
Sees no contiguous palace rear its head,
To shame the meanness of his humble shed—
No costly lord the sumptuous banquet deal,
To make him loathe his vegetable meal—
But calm, and bred in ignorance and toil,
Each wish contracting, fits him to the soil.
Cheerful at morn, he wakes from short repose,
Breasts the keen air, and carols as he goes;

THE TRAVELLER.

With patient angle trolls the finny deep;
Or drives his venturous ploughshare to the steep;
Or seeks the den where snow-tracks mark the way,
And drags the struggling savage into day.
At night returning, every labour sped,
He sits him down the monarch of a shed;
Smiles by his cheerful fire, and round surveys
His children's looks, that brighten at the blaze—
While his lov'd partner, boastful of her hoard,
Displays her cleanly platter on the board:
And haply too some pilgrim, thither led,
With many a tale repays the nightly bed.

Thus every good his native wilds impart
Imprints the patriot passion on his heart;
And even those ills, that round his mansion rise,
Enhance the bliss his scanty fund supplies:

191   Tom Taylor, *Pictures of English Landscape*, 1863

"There was sorrow in her heart, and deep thought in her mind."

168   Anthony Trollope, *Orley Farm*, 2 volumes, 1862

The Prodigal Son.

170 *The Parables of Our Lord,* 1864

218   *Passages from Modern English Poets*, 1862

WINDSOR CASTLE.

104 F. O. Morris, *Picturesque Views of Seats of Noblemen and Gentlemen*, 6 volumes, 1864?–1880

ALADDIN, IN DESPAIR, CONTEMPLATES SUICIDE.

'He constantly carries it carefully wrapped up in his bosom,' replied the princess: 'I am sure of this, because he once took it out in my presence, showing it as a sort of trophy.'

"'Do not be offended, my princess,' resumed Aladdin, 'at the questions I put to you; they are of the highest importance to us both. But to come at once to the point, that

151 *Dalziel's Arabian Nights*, 2 volumes, 1865

39

153   *A Round of Days,* 1866

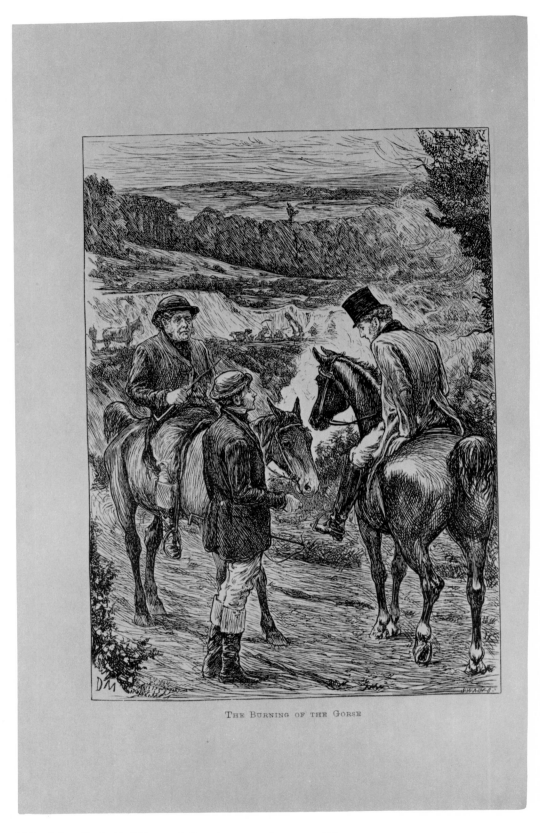

The Burning of the Gorse

193   Mrs. Gaskell, *Wives and Daughters*, 2 volumes, 1866

219 Philippe Burty, *Etudes à l'eau-forte*, 1866

Mr Caudle, having come home a little late, declares that
henceforth "He will have a Key"

188 Douglas Jerrold, *Mrs. Caudle's Curtain Lectures*, 1866

185 Lewis Carroll, *Alice's Adventures in Wonderland*, 1866

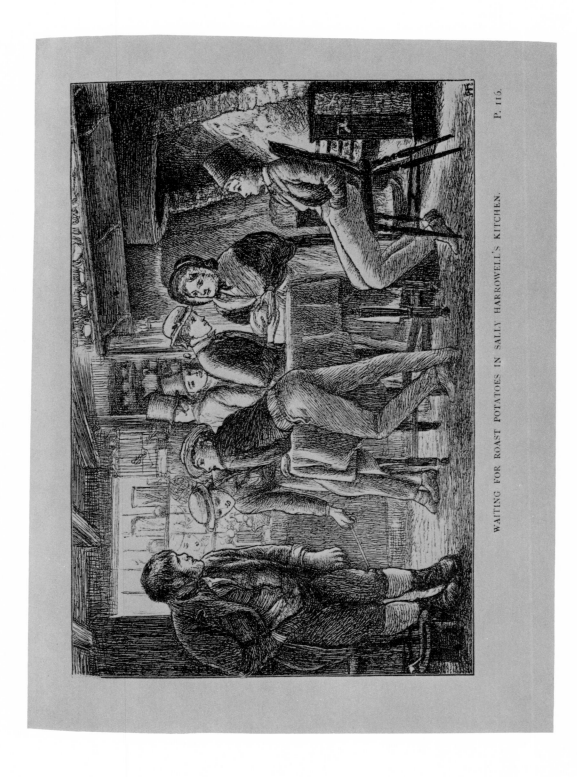

176 Thomas Hughes, *Tom Brown's School Days*, 1869

The voice laughed.

"The law would have some trouble to catch me!" it said.

"But if it's not right, you know," said Diamond, "that's no matter.   You shouldn't do it."

"I am so tall I am above *that* law," said the voice.

"You must have a tall house, then," said Diamond.

"Yes; a tall house: the clouds are inside it."

"Dear me!" said Diamond, and thought a minute.   "I think, then, you can hardly expect me to keep a window in my bed

177   George MacDonald, *At the Back of the North Wind,* 1871

Triumphal March of the Elf-King.

This important personage, nearly related to the Goblin family, is conspicuous for the length of his hair, which on state occasions it requires four pages to support. Fairies in waiting strew flowers in his path, and in his train are many of the most distinguished Trolls, Kobolds, Nixies, Pixies, Wood-sprites, birds, butterflies, and other inhabitants of the kingdom.

146 William Allingham, *In Fairyland*, 1870

207 Blanchard Jerrold, *London*, 1872

163 Walter Thornbury, *Historical and Legendary Ballads and Songs*, 1876

250   William Cowper, *The Diverting History of John Gilpin*, 1878

SCHOOL is over,
  Oh, what fun !
Lessons finished,—
  Play begun.
Who'll run fastest,
  You or I ?
Who'll laugh loudest?—
  Let us try.

K.G.

25

253 Kate Greenaway, *Under the Window,* 1878

158   *Dalziel's Bible Gallery*, 1880

246 Jacob and Wilhelm Grimm, *Household Stories*, 1882

And folded flocks were loose to browse anew
O'er mountain thyme or trefoil wet with dew.

222 The Eclogues of Virgil, 1883

USIC! miraculous rhe-
toric! that speakest
sense
Without a tongue, excel-
ling eloquence;
With what ease might
thy errors be excus'd,
Wert thou as truly lov'd as thou'rt abus'd!
But though dull souls neglect, and some
reprove thee,
I cannot hate thee, 'cause the angels love
thee.

270 *Izaak Walton: His Wallet Booke,* 1885

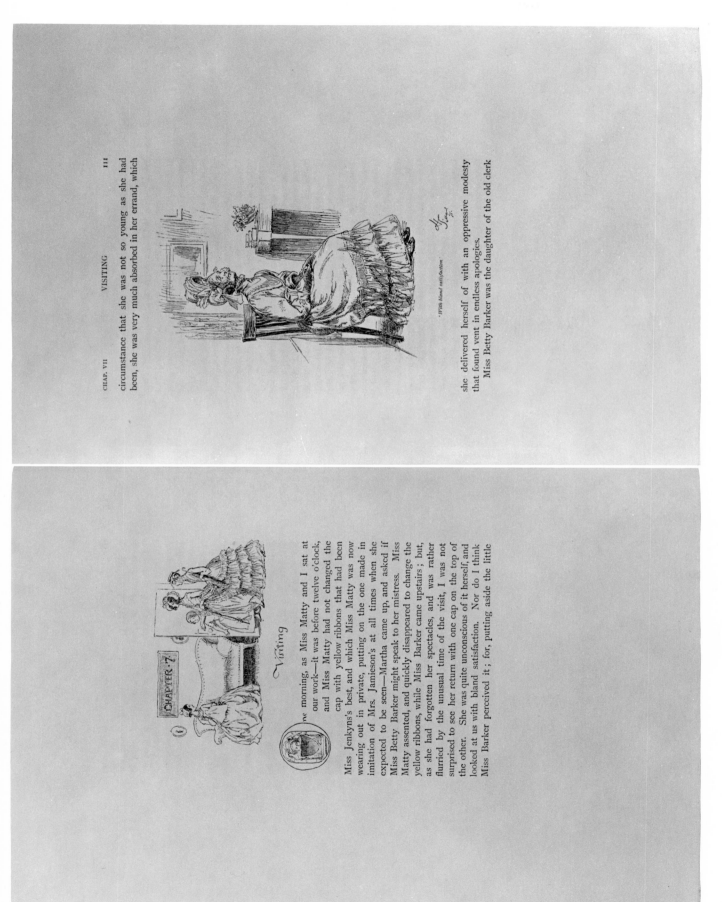

CHAP. VII VISITING 111

circumstance that she was not so young as she had been, she was very much absorbed in her errand, which

"With bland satisfaction."

she delivered herself of with an oppressive modesty that found vent in endless apologies.

Miss Betty Barker was the daughter of the old clerk

CHAPTER 7

Visiting

One morning, as Miss Matty and I sat at our work—it was before twelve o'clock, and Miss Matty had not changed the cap with yellow ribbons that had been Miss Jenkyns's best, and which Miss Matty was now wearing out in private, putting on the one made in imitation of Mrs. Jamieson's at all times when she expected to be seen—Martha came up, and asked if Miss Betty Barker might speak to her mistress. Miss Matty assented, and quickly disappeared to change the yellow ribbons, while Miss Barker came upstairs; but, as she had forgotten her spectacles, and was rather flurried by the unusual time of the visit, I was not surprised to see her return with one cap on the top of the other. She was quite unconscious of it herself, and looked at us with bland satisfaction. Nor do I think Miss Barker perceived it; for, putting aside the little

297 Mrs. Gaskell, *Cranford*, 1891

271 William Strang *The Earth Fiend* 1892

314   Thomas Malory, *Le Morte Darthur*, 3 volumes, 1893

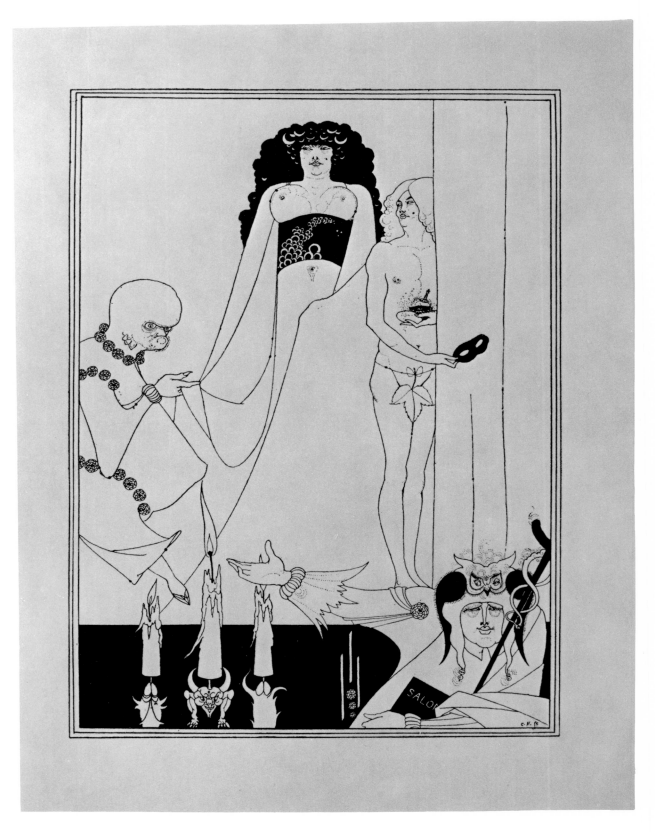

315   Oscar Wilde, *Salomé*, 1894

316   Alexander Pope, *The Rape of the Lock*, 1896

279 Christina Rossetti, *Goblin Market*, 1893

AND CHLOE AFTER THEIR INVENTION THROUGH THE CARE OF THE NYMPHS

MARRIED A WIFE, MY DEAR SONS, when I was yet very young, and, after a while, as I conjectured I should, it was my happinesse to be a Father. For first I had a son born, the second a daughter, and then Astylus the third. I thought there was enow of the

breed

97

OF THE GREAT REJOICINGS AND MERRIMENT AT THE RUSTIC WEDDING-FEAST OF DAPHNIS

habit and, placing him near his own Father, they heard him speak to this purpose;

96

I

260 Longus, *Daphnis and Chloe*, 1893

262   Oscar Wilde, *The Sphinx*, 1894

265   *The Parables,* 1903

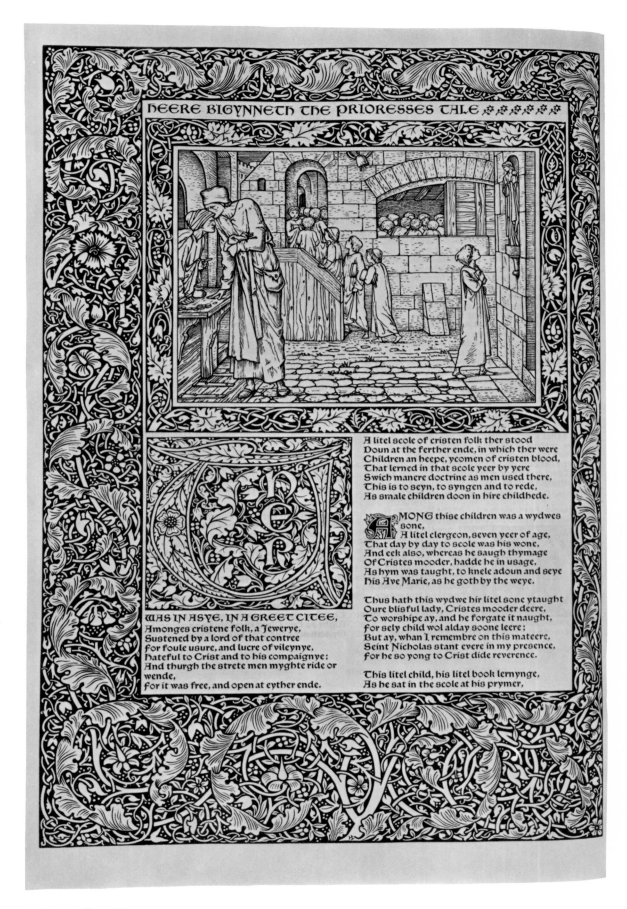

258   Geoffrey Chaucer, *Works*, 1896

LORENZO AND ISABELLA

M

299   *Poems by John Keats,* 1897

TRUTH AND THE PRINCE OF LIES

310   Carlyle, *Sartor Resartus*, 1898

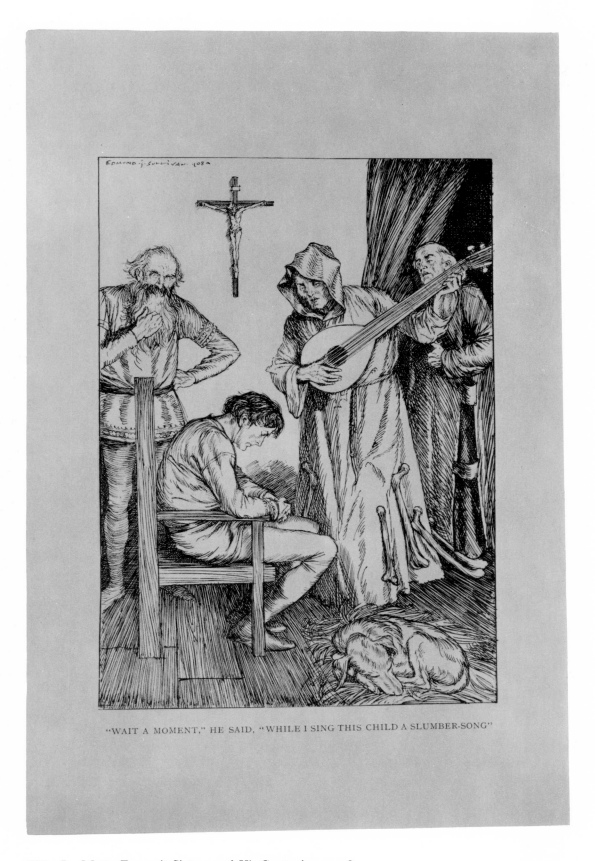

"WAIT A MOMENT," HE SAID, "WHILE I SING THIS CHILD A SLUMBER-SONG"

312   La Motte Fouqué, *Sintram and His Companions*, 1908

287   *Gordon Craig's Book of Penny Toys*, 1899

H.M. The Queen.

294   *Twelve Portraits*, 1900

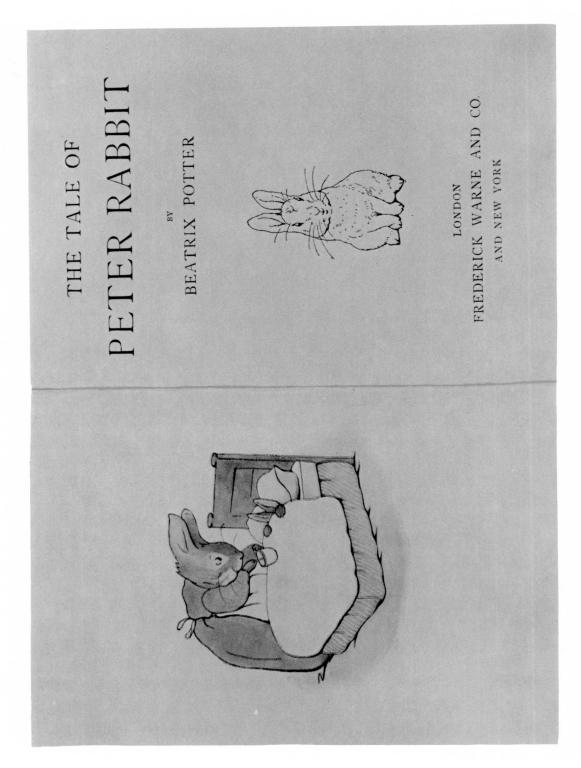

331A   Beatrix Potter, *The Tale of Peter Rabbit*, 1902

MR. TENNYSON, READING "IN MEMORIAM" TO HIS SOVEREIGN.

320 *The Poet's Corner*, 1904

309

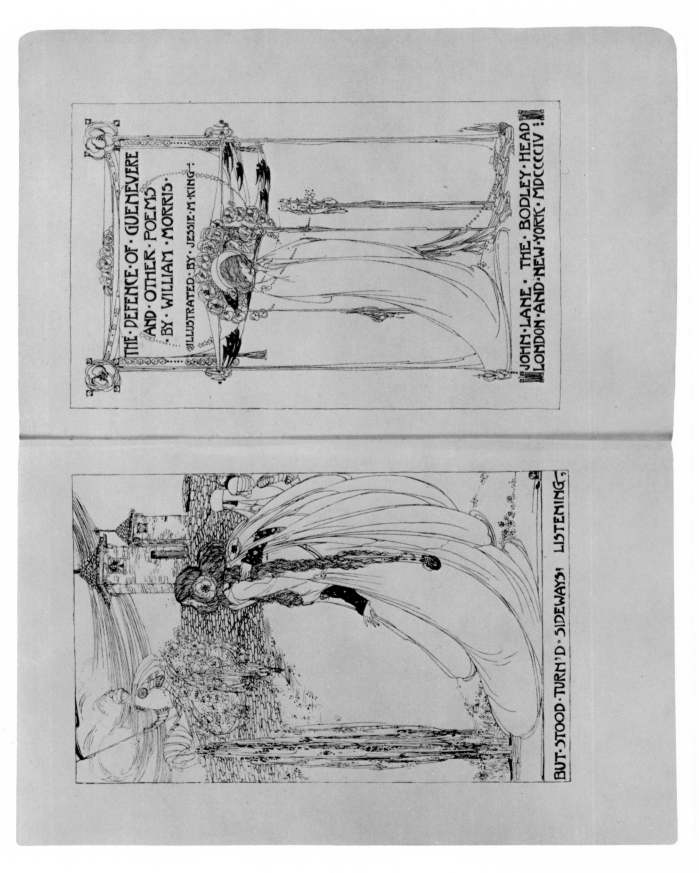

326   William Morris, *The Defence of Guenevere*, 1904

329   J. M. Barrie, *Peter Pan in Kensington Gardens*, 1906

269   Emile Moselly, *La charrue d'érable*, 1912

Appendix

100 Outstanding Illustrated Books Published in England between 1790 and 1914

Roman numerals refer to the section of Plates on pages 213–312.

Arabic numerals refer to entries in the Catalogue.

I FRANCESCO BARTOLOZZI 19 *Imitations of Holbein*, 2 volumes, 1792–1800

II JOSEPH FARINGTON 36 William Combe, *An History of the River Thames*, 2 volumes, 1794–1796

III THOMAS BEWICK 50 *Poems by Goldsmith and Parnell*, 1795

IV THOMAS BEWICK 51 Thomas Bewick, *History of British Birds*, 2 volumes, 1797–1804

V WILLIAM BLAKE 3 Edward Young, *Night Thoughts*, 1797

VI WILLIAM BLAKE 4 William Blake, *Jerusalem*, 1804–1820

VII WILLIAM BLAKE 8 *The Book of Job*, 1825

VIII VICTOR REINAGLE AND OTHERS 39 Robert John Thornton, *The Temple of Flora*, 1797–1807

IX THOMAS GIRTIN 37 *Picturesque Views in Paris*, 1803

X THOMAS GIRTIN AND J. M. W. TURNER 12 *River Scenery*, 1827

XI HUMPHREY REPTON 38 *Observations on . . . Landscape Gardening*, 1803

XII JOHN FLAXMAN 21 Homer, *The Iliad*, 1805

XIII J. M. W. TURNER 10 *Liber Studiorum*, 1807–1819

XIV J. M. W. TURNER AND WILLIAM STOTHARD 13 Samuel Rogers, *Italy*, 1830

XV J. M. W. TURNER 14 *Picturesque Views in England and Wales*, 2 volumes, 1832–1838

XVI THOMAS ROWLANDSON AND AUGUSTUS PUGIN 33 *The Microcosm of London*, 3 volumes, 1808–1810

XVII THOMAS ROWLANDSON 34 William Combe, *The Tour of Doctor Syntax, in Search of the Picturesque*, 1812

XVIII THOMAS ROWLANDSON 35 William Combe, *The English Dance of Death*, 2 volumes, 1815–1816

XIX WILLIAM DANIELL 41 Richard Ayton, *A Voyage Round Great Britain*, 8 volumes, 1814–1825

XX AUGUSTUS PUGIN AND OTHERS 40 William Combe, *A History of the University of Oxford*, 2 volumes, 1814

XXI C. WILD AND OTHERS 42 W. H. Pyne, *The History of the Royal Residences*, 3 volumes, 1819

XXII JOHN SELL COTMAN 75 Dawson Turner, *Architectural Antiquities of Normandy*, 2 volumes, 1822

XXIII WILLIAM SAVAGE 99 William Savage, *Practical Hints on Decorative Printing*, 1822

XXIV GEORGE CRUIKSHANK 112 Jacob and Wilhelm Grimm, *German Popular Stories*, 2 volumes, 1823–1826

XXV GEORGE CRUIKSHANK 116 Charles Dickens, *Oliver Twist*, 3 volumes, 1838

XXVI ROBERT CRUIKSHANK 44 Richard Westmacott, *The English Spy*, 2 volumes, 1825–1826

XXVII JOHN MARTIN 69 John Milton, *Paradise Lost*, 2 volumes, 1825–1827

XXVIII JOHN MARTIN 70 *Illustrations of the Bible*, 10 parts, 1831–1835

XXIX WILLIAM HARVEY 55–56 James Northcote, *Fables, Original and Selected*, 2 volumes, 1828–1833

XXX THOMAS H. SHEPHERD 23 James Elmes, *Metropolitan Improvements*, 2 volumes, 1829–1831

XXXI EDWARD LEAR 90 *Illustrations of the Family of Psittacidae, or Parrots*, 1832

XXXII EDWARD LEAR 91 *Views in Rome and Its Environs*, 1841

Bibliography

References in the text to works consulted are by author's name or cue-title. Full descriptions are given below.

ANON., "A Study in Black and White: The Legend and Letters of Beardsley," *Times Literary Supplement*, January 14, 1972, pp. 25–58

ABBEY, J. R., *Life in England in Aquatint and Lithography, 1770–1860*, London, 1953

ABBEY, J. R., *Scenery of Great Britain and Ireland in Aquatint and Lithography, 1770–1860*, London, 1952

ABBEY, J. R., *Travel in Aquatint and Lithography, 1770–1860*, 2 volumes, London, 1956

ALLDERIDGE, PATRICIA, *The Late Richard Dadd, 1817–1886*, London, 1974

ANTAL, FREDERICK, *Hogarth and His Place in European Art*, London, 1962

ART ANCIEN BULLETIN 25, *A Collection of Books Designed by Charles Ricketts*, Zurich, 1972

BAIN, IAIN, *William Daniell's A Voyage Round Great Britain, 1814–1825*, London, 1966

BALSTON, THOMAS, "English Book Illustrations, 1880–1900," *New Paths in Book Collecting*, ed. John Carter, London, 1934, pp. 163–190

BALSTON, THOMAS, *English Wood Engraving, 1900–1950*, London, 1951

BALSTON, THOMAS, "Illustrated Series of the 'Nineties," *Book-Collector's Quarterly*, No. XI (July, 1933), 33–56; No. XIV (April, 1934), 35–53

BALSTON, THOMAS, "John Boydell, Publisher: 'The Commercial Maecenas,'" *Signature*, New Series, VIII (1949), 3–22

BALSTON, THOMAS, *John Martin, 1789–1854: His Life and Works*, London, 1947

BALSTON, THOMAS, "John Martin, 1789–1854, Illustrator and Pamphleteer," *The Library*, March, 1934, pp. 383–432

BAUDELAIRE, CHARLES, "Quelques caricaturistes étrangers," *Curiosités esthétiques*, in *Oeuvres*, ed. Y. G. Le Dantec, 2 volumes, Paris, 1935, II, 203–213

BAUGHMAN, ROLAND, *The Centenary of Arthur Rackham's Birth*, New York, 1967

BEARDSLEY, AUBREY, *The Letters*, ed. Henry Maas, J. L. Duncan, and W. G. Good, London, 1971

BECK, HILARY, *Victorian Engravings*, London, 1973

BEERBOHM, MAX, "The Spirit of Caricature," *Works*, 10 volumes, London, 1922–1928, X, 205–217

BENTLEY, G. E., JR., *The Early Engravings of Flaxman's Classical Designs: A Bibliographical Study*, New York, 1964

BENTLEY, G. E., JR., and Martin K. Nurmi, *A Blake Bibliography: Annotated Lists of Works, Studies, and Blakeana*, Minneapolis, 1964

BEWICK, THOMAS, *A Memoir*, Newcastle-on-Tyne and London, 1862

BINYON, LAURENCE, "The Etchings and Engravings of William Strang," *Print Collector's Quarterly*, VIII (October, 1921), 349–376

BLACKBURN, HENRY, *Randolph Caldecott: A Personal Memoir of His Early Art Career*, London, 1886

BLAND, DAVID, *A History of Book Illustration*, Cleveland and New York, 1958

BLISS, DOUGLAS PERCY, *A History of Wood-Engraving*, London, 1928

BOSTON MUSEUM OF FINE ARTS and HARVARD COLLEGE LIBRARY, *The Artist and the Book 1860–1960 in Western Europe and the United States*, Boston, 1961

BRAY, MRS., *The Life of Thomas Stothard, R.A.*, London, 1851

BRIGHTON MUSEUM AND ART GALLERY, *Frederick Sandys, 1829–1904* (exhibition catalogue), Brighton, 1974

BRITISH MUSEUM, *English Book Illustration 966–1846* (exhibition catalogue), London, 1965

BROWNE, EDGAR, *Phiz and Dickens*, London, 1913

BROWSE, LILLIAN, *William Nicholson*, London, 1956

BURCH, R. M., *Colour Printing and Colour Printers*, London, 1910

CARTER, JOHN, and PERCY MUIR, editors, *Printing and the Mind of Man*, London, 1967

CAVE, RODERICK, *The Private Press*, London, 1971

CHRISTIAN, JOHN, "Burne Jones's Drawings for 'The Fairy Family,' " *Burlington Magazine*, CXV (February, 1973), 92–100

CLARK, KENNETH, *The Gothic Revival: An Essay in the History of Taste*, London, 1928

COHEN, HENRI, *Guide de l'amateur de livres à gravures du xviiie siècle*, Paris, 1912, sixth edition

COHN, ALBERT M., *George Cruikshank: A Catalogue Raisonné*, London, 1924

COXHEAD, A. C., *Thomas Stothard, R.A.: His Life and Work*, London, 1909

CRAIG, EDWARD GORDON, *Nothing or the Bookplate*, London, 1924

CRAIG, EDWARD GORDON, *Woodcuts and Some Words*, London, 1924

CRANE, WALTER, *An Artist's Reminiscences*, London, 1907

CRANE, WALTER, *Of the Decorative Illustration of Books Old and New*, London, 1896

CURTIS, ATHERTON, *Catalogue de l'oeuvre lithographié et gravé de R. P. Bonington*, Paris, 1939

CURTIS, ATHERTON, *Some Masters of Lithography*, New York, 1897

DALZIEL, GEORGE, *The Brothers Dalziel: A Record of Fifty Years' Work*, London, 1901

DALZIEL, GILBERT, "Wood-Engraving in the 'Sixties' and Some Criticisms of To-day," *Print Collector's Quarterly*, XV (January, 1928), 80–84

DARTON, F. J. HARVEY, *Children's Books in England*, Cambridge, 1932

DE BEAUMONT, ROBIN, "Sixties Illustrators," *Discovering Antiques*, No. 68 (1971), 1617–1621

DOHERTY, TERENCE, *The Anatomical Works of George Stubbs*, Boston, 1975

EASSON, ROGER R., and ROBERT N. ESSICK, *William Blake, Book Illustrator: A Bibliography and Catalogue of the Commercial Engravings*, Normal, Illinois, 1972

ECKEL, JOHN C., *The First Editions of the Writings of Charles Dickens*, New York and London, 1932

ELZEA, ROWLAND, *The Golden Age of American Illustration: 1880–1914* (catalogue of an exhibition at the Delaware Art Museum), Wilmington, Delaware, 1972

ENGEN, RODNEY K., *Walter Crane as a Book Illustrator*, London, 1975

EVANS, EDMUND, *Reminiscences*, ed. Ruari McLean, Oxford, 1967

FELVER, CHARLES S., *Joseph Crawhall, the Newcastle Wood Engraver (1821–1896)*, Newcastle, n.d. [1972?]

FIELD, WILLIAM BRADHURST OSGOOD, *John Leech on My Shelves*, Munich, 1930

FIELD, WILLIAM BRADHURST OSGOOD, *Edward Lear on My Shelves*, Munich, 1933

FILDES, PAUL, "Phototransfer of Drawings on Wood-Block Engraving," *Journal of the Printing Historical Society*, No. 5 (1969), pp. 87–97

FINBERG, ALEXANDER J., *The History of Turner's Liber Studiorum, with a New Catalogue Raisonné*, London, 1924

FINBERG, A. J., *An Introduction to Turner's Southern Coast with a Catalogue of the Engravings*, London, 1929

FINE ART SOCIETY, LONDON, *The Earthly Paradise: F. Cayley Robinson, F. L. Griggs and the Painter-Craftsmen of the Birmingham Group* (exhibition catalogue), London, 1969

FRANKLIN, COLIN, *The Private Presses*, London, 1969

FREDEMAN, WILLIAM E., *Pre-Raphaelitism: A Bibliocritical Study*, Cambridge, Mass., 1965

FRENCH, CECIL, "The Wood-Engravings of Charles Ricketts," *Print Collector's Quarterly*, XIV (July, 1927), 194–217

FURST, HERBERT, "The Modern Woodcut," *Print Collector's Quarterly*, VIII (July–October, 1921), 151–170, 267–298

GALLATIN, A. E., *Aubrey Beardsley: Catalogue of Drawings and Bibliography*, New York, 1945

GALLATIN, A. E., *Sir Max Beerbohm: Bibliographical Notes*, Cambridge, Mass., 1944

GOSLING, NIGEL, *Gustave Doré*, London, 1973

GRAY, BASIL, *The English Print*, London, 1937

GREGO, JOSEPH, *Rowlandson the Caricaturist*, 2 volumes, London, 1880

GRIGSON, GEOFFREY, and HANDASYDE BUCHANAN, *Thornton's Temple of Flora*, London, 1951

GROSCHWITZ, GUSTAVE VON, "The Prints of Thomas Shotter Boys," *Prints*, ed. Carl Zigrosser, New York, 1962, pp. 191–215

GUTHRIE, JAMES, "The Wood Engravings of Clemence Housman," *Print Collector's Quarterly*, XI (April, 1924), 190–204

HAMBOURG, DARIA, *Richard Doyle*, London, 1948

HAMERTON, PHILIP GILBERT, *Etching and Etchers*, London, 1868

HAMILTON, SINCLAIR, "Arthur Boyd Houghton and His American Drawings," *Colophon: New Graphic Series*, II (1939), 79–90

HAMMELMANN, HANNS, "English Eighteenth-Century Book Illustrators," *Book Handbook*, II (September, 1951), 127–135

HAMMELMANN, HANNS, *Book Illustrators in Eighteenth-century England*, ed. T. S. R. Boase, New Haven, 1975

HARDIE, MARTIN, *English Coloured Books*, New York and London, 1906

HARRINGTON, H. NAZEBY, *The Engraved Work of Sir Francis Seymour Haden, P.R.E.*, Liverpool, 1910

HARRISON, MARTIN, and BILL WATERS, *Burne-Jones*, New York, 1973

HARTLEY, HAROLD, "George John Pinwell," *Print Collector's Quarterly*, XI (April, 1924), 162–189

HARVEY, J. R., *Victorian Novelists and Their Illustrators*, London, 1970

HILLIER, BEVIS, *Posters*, London, 1969

HOFER, PHILIP, *Edward Lear*, New York, 1962

HOGARTH, PAUL, *Arthur Boyd Houghton: Introduction and Check-List of the Artist's Work*, London, 1975

HOGARTH, PAUL, *The Artist as Reporter*, London, 1967

HOGARTH, PAUL, *Artists on Horseback: The Old West in Illustrated Journalism, 1857–1900*, New York, 1972

HOLMES, C. J., *Self and Partners (Mostly Self)*, New York, 1936

HOUGHTON LIBRARY, HARVARD UNIVERSITY, *The Turn of a Century, 1885–1910, Art Nouveau–Jugendstil Books* (exhibition catalogue), Cambridge, Mass., 1970

HOUSMAN, LAURENCE, *Arthur Boyd Houghton*, London, 1896

HOUSMAN, LAURENCE, *The Unexpected Years*, London, 1937

HUDSON, DEREK, *Arthur Rackham: His Life and Work*, London, 1974, revised edition

HUDSON, DEREK, *Charles Keene*, London, 1947

HYAMS, EDWARD, *Capability Brown and Humphrey Repton*, London, 1971

JACKSON, HOLBROOK, *The Eighteen Nineties*, London, 1922

JAMES, PHILIP, *English Book Illustration, 1800–1900*, London, 1947

JAMES, PHILIP, *English Book Illustration since 1800* (Council for the Encouragement of Music and the Arts exhibition catalogue), London, 1943

JERROLD, BLANCHARD, *Life of Gustave Doré*, London, 1891

JOHANNSEN, A., *Phiz: Illustrations from the Novels of Charles Dickens*, Chicago, 1956

KEYNES, GEOFFREY, *Blake Studies: Essays on His Life and Works*, Oxford, 1971, second edition

KEYNES, GEOFFREY, *The Illustrations of William Blake for Thornton's Virgil*, London, 1937

KEYNES, GEOFFREY, *William Blake's Engravings*, London, 1950

KEYNES, GEOFFREY, *William Pickering, Publisher*, London, 1969, revised edition

KITSON, SYDNEY D., *The Life of John Sell Cotman*, London, 1937

KLINGENDER, FRANCIS D., *Art and the Industrial Revolution*, ed. and rev. Arthur Elton, London, 1968

KLINGENDER, F. D., ed., *Hogarth and English Caricature*, London and New York, 1944

KONODY, P. G., *The Art of Walter Crane*, London, 1902

LEBLANC, HENRI, *Catalogue de l'oeuvre complet de Gustave Doré*, Paris, 1931

LAMB, LYNTON, *Drawing for Illustration*, London, 1932

LATIMORE, SARAH BRIGGS, and GRACE CLARK HASKELL, *Arthur Rackham: A Bibliography*, Los Angeles, 1936

LAYARD, GEORGE SOMES, *The Life and Letters of Charles Samuel Keene*, London, 1892

LEWIS, C. T. COURTNEY, *George Baxter, the Picture Printer*, London, n.d.

LEWIS, C. T. COURTNEY, *The Story of Picture Printing in England during the Nineteenth Century*, London, n.d.

LEWIS, JOHN, *The Twentieth Century Book*, London, 1967

LIFE, ALLEN ROY, *Art and Poetry: A Study of Two Pre-Raphaelite Artists, William Holman Hunt and John Everett Millais*, doctoral dissertation, University of British Columbia, 1974

LINDER, LESLIE, *A History of the Writings of Beatrix Potter*, London, 1971

LINTON, W. J., *The Masters of Wood-Engraving*, London, 1889

LISTER, RAYMOND, *Samuel Palmer and His Etchings*, London, 1969

LUTYENS, MARY, Introduction to *The Parables of Our Lord and Saviour Jesus Christ*, New York, 1975

MACFALL, HALDANE, *The Book of Lovat Claud Fraser*, London, 1923

MACFALL, HALDANE, "Concerning the Woodcuts of Gordon Craig," *Print Collector's Quarterly*, IX (December, 1922), 406–432

MAN, FELIX H., *Artists' Lithographs: A World History from Senefelder to the Present Day*, New York, 1971

MAN, FELIX H., "Lithography in England (1801–1810)," *Prints*, ed. Carl Zigrosser, New York, 1962, pp. 97–130

MAN, FELIX H., *150 Years of Artists' Lithographs, 1803–1953*, London, 1953

MASSE, G. C. E., *A Bibliography of First Editions of Books Illustrated by Walter Crane*, London, 1923

McLEAN, RUARI, *George Cruikshank: His Life and Work as a Book Illustrator*, London, 1948

McLEAN, RUARI, *Victorian Book Design and Colour Printing*, London, 1972

McLEAN, RUARI, *Victorian Publishers' Book-Bindings in Cloth and Leather*, London, 1974

METZDORF, ROBERT, "Victorian Book Decoration," *Princeton University Library Chronicle*, XXIV (Winter, 1963), 91–100

MEYNELL, FRANCIS, *English Printed Books*, London, 1948

MILLER, J. HILLIS, "The Fiction of Realism: Sketches by Boz, Oliver Twist, and Cruikshank's Illustrations," in *Charles Dickens and George Cruikshank*, Los Angeles, 1971

MOORE, T. STURGE, *A Brief Account of the Origin of the Eragny Press*, London, 1903

MOORE, T. STURGE, *Charles Ricketts, R.A.*, London, 1933

MORRIS, WILLIAM, *A Note on His Aims in Founding the Kelmscott Press*, Hammersmith, 1898

MUIR, PERCY, *English Children's Books, 1600 to 1900*, London, 1954

MUIR, PERCY, *Victorian Illustrated Books*, London, 1971

NEWBOLT, FRANK, *Etchings of William Strang, A.R.A.*, London, n.d.

NICHOLSON, KEITH, *Kay Nielsen*, New York, 1975

NOAKES, VIVIEN, *Edward Lear: The Life of a Wanderer*, Boston, 1968

NOTTINGHAM UNIVERSITY ART GALLERY, *Thomas Shotter Boys (1803–1874)* (exhibition catalogue), Nottingham, 1974

OCHNER, MORDECAI, *Turner and the Poets: Engravings and Watercolours from His Later Period*, London, 1975

ORMOND, LEONÉE, "A Mid-Victorian Parody: George du Maurier's 'A Legend of Camelot,' " *Apollo*, LXXXV (January, 1967), 54–58

ORMOND, RICHARD, and JOHN TURPIN, *Daniel Maclise, 1806–1870* (catalogue of an exhibition at the National Portrait Gallery and the National Gallery of Ireland), London, 1972

PALMER, A. H., *Samuel Palmer: A Memoir*, London, 1882

PARRIS, LESLIE, *Landscape in Britain, c. 1750–1850*, London, 1973

PAULSON, RONALD, *Hogarth's Graphic Works, Revised Edition*, 2 volumes, New Haven and London, 1970

PENNELL, ELIZABETH ROBINS, and JOSEPH PENNELL, *Lithography and Lithographers*, New York, 1915

PENNELL, JOSEPH, "A Golden Decade in English Art," *Savoy*, No. 1 (Jan., 1896), 112–124

PENNELL, JOSEPH, *Pen Drawing and Pen Draughtsmen*, London, 1889

PENNELL, JOSEPH, *The Work of Charles Keene*, New York and London, 1897

PEPPIN, BRIGID, *Fantasy: The Golden Age of Fantastic Illustration*, New York, 1975

PHILADELPHIA MUSEUM OF ART, *Romantic Art in Britain, Paintings and Drawings, 1760–1860* (exhibition catalogue), Philadelphia, 1968

PIPER, JOHN, *British Romantic Artists*, London, 1942

PISSARRO, LUCIEN, *Notes on the Eragny Press, and a Letter to J. B. Manson*, ed. Alan Fern, Cambridge, England, 1957

Pointon, Marcia R., *Milton and English Art*, Manchester, 1970

Popham, A. E., "The Etchings of John Sell Cotman," *Print Collector's Quarterly*, ix (October, 1922), 236–273

Preston, Kerrison, ed., *The Blake Collection of W. Graham Robertson*, London, 1952

Prideaux, S. T., *Aquatint Engraving*, London, 1909

Princeton University Library Chronicle, xxxv (Autumn, Winter, 1973–1974), *George Cruikshank: A Revaluation*, ed. Robert L. Patten

Ransom, Will, *Private Presses and Their Books*, New York, 1929

Rawlinson, W. G., *The Engraved Work of J. M. W. Turner, R.A.*, 2 volumes, London, 1908–1913

Ray, Gordon N., "Contemporary Collectors XXXVII: A 19th-Century Collection," *Book Collector*, xiii (Spring and Summer, 1964), 33–44, 171–184

Reade, Bryan, *Aubrey Beardsley*, New York, 1967

Reade, Bryan, and Frank Dickinson, *Aubrey Beardsley: Exhibition at the Victoria and Albert Museum*, London, 1966

Reid, Forrest, *Illustrators of the Sixties*, London, 1928

Reid, George William, *A Descriptive Catalogue of the Works of George Cruikshank*, 3 volumes, London, 1871

Reitlinger, Henry, *From Hogarth to Keene*, London, 1938

Reynolds, Graham, *An Introduction to English Water-Colour Painting*, London, 1950

Ricketts, Charles, *A Defence of the Revival of Printing*, London, 1899

Ricketts, Charles, *Oscar Wilde: Recollections*, London, 1932

Ricketts, Charles, *Self-Portrait Taken from the Letters and Journals of Charles Ricketts*, ed. T. Sturge Moore and Cecil Lewis, London, 1939

Ricketts, Charles, and Lucien Pissarro, *De la typographie et de l'harmonie de la page imprimée. William Morris et son influence sur les arts et métiers*, London, 1898

Riely, John C., *Samuel Collings' Designs for Rowlandson's "Picturesque Beauties of Boswell,"* privately printed for the Johnsonians, [New Haven], 1975

Rienaecker, Victor, *John Sell Cotman, 1782–1842*, Leigh-on-Sea, 1953

Robertson, W. Graham, *Time Was*, London, 1931

Roscoe, S., *Thomas Bewick: A Bibliography Raisonné*, London, 1953

Rose, June, *The Drawings of John Leech*, London, 1950

Roundell, James, *Thomas Shotter Boys, 1803–1874*, London, 1974

Ruskin, John, *The Elements of Drawing*, London, 1857

Ruskin, John, *Modern Painters*, 5 volumes, London, 1843–1860

Ryskamp, Charles, *William Blake, Engraver: A Descriptive Catalogue of an Exhibition*, with an Introductory Essay by Geoffrey Keynes, Princeton, 1969

SADLEIR, MICHAEL, *XIX Century Fiction: A Bibliographical Record*, 2 volumes, London, 1951

SALAMAN, MALCOLM, *Modern Woodcuts and Lithographs*, London, 1919

SARZANO, FRANCES, *Sir John Tenniel*, London, 1948

SCHWERDT, C. F. G. R., *Hunting, Hawking, Shooting, Illustrated in a Catalogue of Books, Manuscripts, Prints, and Drawings*, 4 volumes, London, 1928–1937

SEZNEC, JEAN, *John Martin en France*, London, 1964

SHIRLEY, ANDREW, *The Published Mezzotints of David Lucas after John Constable, R.A.: A Catalogue and Historical Account*, Oxford, 1930

SITWELL, SACHEVERELL, HANDASYDE BUCHANAN, and J. FISHER, *Fine Bird Books*, London, 1953

SKETCHLEY, R. E. D., *English Book Illustration of To-day*, London, 1903

SLEIGH, BERNARD, *Wood Engraving since Eighteen-ninety*, London, 1932

SMITH, JANET ADAM, *Children's Illustrated Books*, London, 1948

SPARLING, H. HALLIDAY, *The Kelmscott Press and William Morris, Master-craftsman*, London, 1924

SPARROW, WALTER SHAW, *A Book of British Etching from Francis Barlow to Francis Seymour Haden*, London, 1926

SPIELMANN, M. H., *The History of "Punch,"* London, 1895

SPIELMANN, M. H., and G. S. LAYARD, *Kate Greenaway*, London, 1903

STEEN, MARGUERITE, *William Nicholson*, London, 1943

STEVENS, JOAN, "Thackeray's *Vanity Fair*," *Review of English Literature*, VI (1965), 39–55

STONE, REYNOLDS, *Wood Engravings of Thomas Bewick, Selected, with a Biographical Introduction by Reynolds Stone*, London, 1953

SULLIVAN, EDMUND J., "Arthur Boyd Houghton—An Artist's Artist," *Print Collector's Quarterly*, X (February and April, 1923), 94–122, 124–148

SULLIVAN, EDMUND J., *The Art of Illustration*, London, 1921

SYMONS, ARTHUR, "The Lesson of Millais," *Savoy*, No. VI (October, 1896), 57–58

SZLADITS, LOLA L., and HARVEY SIMMONDS, *Pen and Brush: The Author as Artist*, New York, 1969

TAYLOR, BASIL, *The Prints of George Stubbs* (exhibition catalogue), Aldeburgh Festival and Victoria and Albert Museum, 1969

TAYLOR, BASIL, *Stubbs*, London, 1971

TAYLOR, JOHN RUSSELL, *The Art Nouveau Book in Britain*, London, 1966

THACKERAY, WILLIAM MAKEPEACE, "George Cruikshank's Works," *Westminster Review*, June, 1840, pp. 1–60

THACKERAY, WILLIAM MAKEPEACE, "John Leech's Pictures of Life and Character," *Quarterly Review*, December, 1854, pp. 75–86

THOMAS, ALAN G., *Fine Books*, London, 1967

THORPE, JAMES, *E. J. Sullivan*, London, 1948

THORPE, JAMES, *English Illustration: The Nineties*, London, 1935

THORPE, JAMES, *Phil May*, London, 1948

TODD, RUTHVEN, *Tracks in the Snow*, London, 1946

TOOLEY, R. V., *English Books with Coloured Plates, 1790 to 1860*, London, 1954

TURPIN, JOHN, "German Influence on Daniel Maclise," *Apollo*, XCVII (Feb., 1973), 169–175

TWYMAN, MICHAEL, *Lithography, 1800–1850*, London, 1970

UNIVERSITY OF LOUISVILLE LIBRARIES, *The Inimitable George Cruikshank: An Exhibition of Illustrated Books, Prints, Drawings and Manuscripts from the Collection of David Borowitz*, Louisville, 1968

UNIVERSITY OF NOTTINGHAM FINE ARTS DEPARTMENT, *English Influences on Van Gogh* (exhibition catalogue), London, 1974

VAN DEVANTER, WILLIS, "A Checklist of Books Illustrated by Henry Alken," *Homage to a Bookman: Essays on Manuscripts, Books, and Printing Written for Hans P. Kraus*, Berlin, [1967]

VAN DUZER, HENRY SAYRE, *A Thackeray Library*, New York, 1919

VICTORIA AND ALBERT MUSEUM, *"From today painting is dead": The Beginnings of Photography* (exhibition catalogue), London, 1972

VICTORIA AND ALBERT MUSEUM, *George Cruikshank* (exhibition catalogue), London, 1974

VICTORIA AND ALBERT MUSEUM, *Victorian Children's Books* (exhibition catalogue), London, 1973

WAKEMAN, GEOFFREY, *Victorian Book Illustration: The Technical Revolution*, Newton Abbot, Devon, 1973

WALKER ART GALLERY, *William Holman Hunt* (exhibition catalogue), Liverpool, 1969

WARK, ROBERT R., *Rowlandson's Drawings for "The English Dance of Death,"* San Marino, California, 1966

WEEKLY, MONTAGUE, *Thomas Bewick*, London, 1953

WEINTRAUB, STANLEY, *Beardsley: A Biography*, New York, 1967

WEITENKAMPF, FRANK, *The Illustrated Book*, Cambridge, Mass., 1938

WHITE, GLEESON, *English Illustration: The "Sixties:" 1855–1870*, London, 1897

WHITELEY, DEREK PEPYS, *George du Maurier*, London, 1948

WILLIAMS, SIDNEY HERBERT, and FALCONER MADAN, revised by Roger Lancelyn Green, *The Lewis Carroll Handbook*, London, 1962

WILLIAMSON, G. C., *George J. Pinwell and His Works*, London, 1900

WOLF, E. C. J., *Rowlandson and His Illustrations of Eighteenth Century English Literature*, Copenhagen, 1945

WOOD, CHRISTOPHER, *Dictionary of Victorian Painters*, London, 1971

WRIGHT, ANDREW, *Blake's Job: A Commentary*, Oxford, 1972

Index of Artists

All references are to page numbers. Illustrations are designated by boldface type.

Index of Authors and Titles

All references are to page numbers. Illustrations are designated by boldface type.